# PHYSIOLOGICAL ADAPTATIONS IN VERTEBRATES

# LUNG BIOLOGY IN HEALTH AND DISEASE

*Executive Editor*

**Claude Lenfant**
*Director, National Heart, Lung, and Blood Institute*
*National Institutes of Health*
*Bethesda, Maryland*

*Additional Volumes in Preparation*

# PHYSIOLOGICAL ADAPTATIONS IN VERTEBRATES
## RESPIRATION, CIRCULATION, AND METABOLISM

*Edited by*

## Stephen C. Wood

*Lovelace Medical Foundation*
*Albuquerque, New Mexico*

## Roy E. Weber

*University of Aarhus*
*Aarhus, Denmark*

## Alan R. Hargens

*NASA—Ames Research Center*
*Moffett Field, California*

## Ronald W. Millard

*University of Cincinnati*
*College of Medicine*
*Cincinnati, Ohio*

**Marcel Dekker, Inc.**          **New York • Basel • Hong Kong**

Library of Congress Cataloging-in-Publication Data

Physiological adaptations in vertebrates : respiration, circulation,
and metabolism / edited by Stephen C. Wood . . . [et al.].
     p.   cm. -- (Lung biology in health and disease ; 56)
    "This volume originates from a symposium held in Copenhagen in
June of 1989 to commemorate Kjell Johansen, who died March 4, 1987"
-- Pref.
    Includes bibliographical references and index.
    ISBN 0-8247-8558-4 (alk. paper)
    1. Cardiopulmonary system--Adaptation--Congresses.
2. Vertebrates--Physiology--Congresses. 3. Kjell Johansen--
Congresses. I. Wood, Stephen C. II. Johansen, Kjell.
III. Series: Lung biology in health and disease ; v. 56.
    [DNLM: 1. Adaptation, Physiological--congresses. 2. Vertebrates--
physiology--congresses. W1 LU62 v. 56 / QP 82 P578 1989]
QP102.P59   1992
596'.01--dc20
DNLM/DLC
for Library of Congress                                       91-34388
                                                     CIP

This book is printed on acid-free paper.

Marcel Dekker, Inc.
270 Madison Avenue, New York, New York 10016

Current printing (last digit):
10  9  8  7  6  5  4  3  2  1

**Printed in the United States of America**

# INTRODUCTION

Not very long ago, I had occasion to reread two books written by Lazaro Spallanzani. One, *De Fenomeni della Circulazione* (1777), was translated into French by J. Tourdes and first published in Paris in 1800. The other, *Mémoires sur la respiration,* is an 1803 French translation of an unpublished manuscript. Both French texts are preceded by biographies of Spallanzani written, respectively, by J. Tourdes and by J. Sénébier, the translator of the unpublished Italian essay on respiration.

Kjell Johansen knew these two books very well. In fact, we were together in Copenhagen in 1971 when I purchased *Mémoires sur la respiration.* Parenthetically, I should say that Kjell was most envious when, later on, we discovered Christian Bohr's signature on the flyleaf! (The signature was authenticated by Paul Astrup.)

Undoubtedly, Kjell Johansen and Lazaro Spallanzani had much in common. Spallanzani was not only a great scientist, but also a writer and an artist; so was Kjell. Rather than paraphrase those who wrote so eloquently about Spallanzani, let me borrow their words. Tourdes wrote:

> L'art d'expérimenter ne consist pas uniquement à receuillir des faits, à les ordonner, à les classer; il faut auparavant imaginer les procédés qui déterminent le succès

des expériences, et s'assurer du coté par lequel la nature est accéssible. Cet art requiert surtout un grand amour de la verité, l'abandon des opinions les plus favorites, un esprit libre de systêmes et de préjugés, une reason froide et sévère.[1]

J. Sénébier wrote in his biography:

Spallanzani eut toujours le gout des voyages, sa passion pour pénétrer les secrets de la nature, lui faisait étendre le théatre de ses recherches pour multiplier les occasions de découvrir quelque chose de neuf.[2]

These words describe Kjell Johansen just as well!

Kjell knew what August Krogh had professed: "For a large number of problems there will be some animal of choice or a few such animals on which it can be most conveniently studied" (Krogh, 1929). It is of interest that Kjell titled his August Krogh lecture, published in 1987, "The World as a Laboratory."

One could go on endlessly reminiscing about Kjell Johansen. But is it necessary? This volume, *Physiological Adaptations in Vertebrates,* is a voyage through Kjell's scientific life and through the goals that he had for himself and for all who worked with him. The 21 chapters assembled here describe his interests; at one time or another he worked on the topics of all these chapters. In fact, many of the authors, perhaps even all of them, were his students, his colleagues, or both.

The great Greek poet Homer wrote:

Persuasive speech, and more persuasive sighs,
Silence that spoke and eloquence of eyes.

This, too applies to Kjell and easily explains why everywhere in the world he had friends and disciples.

In 1989, Stephen Wood edited a monograph, *Comparative Pulmonary Physiology: Current Concepts,* for the Lung Biology in Health and Disease series. Kjell Johansen was supposed to have been a contributor, but he died before finishing his manuscript. We dedicated the book to him. This new volume reports the proceedings of a symposium that was held in his memory prior to the 1989 Helsinki Congress of the International Union of Physiological Sciences. I am sure Kjell Johansen would have loved to have seen this new volume, and, more

---

[1]The art of experimentation does not consist of merely recounting the facts, putting them in order, and classifying them; it is first necessary to conceive of the processes which will determine the success of the experiments, and to ascertain the direction by means of which nature is accessible. This art requires above all a great love of truth, an abandonment of one's favorite opinions, a spirit free of systems and prejudices, and cold, harsh reason.

[2]Spallanzani always had a penchant for travel; his passion for penetrating the secrets of nature made him expand the theater of his research in order to multiply the opportunities for discovering something new.

important, would want the thoughts and ideas reported here to be an inspiration to young scientists and future students.

Recently, I read a poem by Li Po, the great Chinese poet of the 8th century. It said:

> Among the flowers with a whole pot of wine
> —a solitary drinker with no companion—
> I raise my cup to invite the bright moon:
> It throws my shadow
> and makes us a party of three.

Kjell would like that!

**Claude Lenfant**
Bethesda, Maryland

# PREFACE

This volume originates from a symposium held in Copenhagen in June of 1989, to commemorate Kjell Johansen, who died March 4, 1987. The topics of the symposium and the title of this volume, *Physiological Adaptations in Vertebrates: Respiration, Circulation, and Metabolism,* are meant to convey the breadth of Kjell's interest in physiology. The contributors to this volume have in common their interest and expertise in cardiopulmonary physiology as well as their association with Kjell as former students and colleagues.

The volume begins with a completely nonscientific but fascinating glimpse at Kjell, the man and the artist. This is followed by an overview of the kinds of physiology that interested Kjell, i.e., adaptational, environmental, and ecological physiology. The chapters of the first section of the volume are devoted to metabolism and biochemical adaptations to hypoxia and to the metabolic cost of locomotion. The next section, "Gas Exchange," conveys the breadth of Kjell's interest in respiratory function in species spanning the animal kingdom, including structure–function relationships and control systems. Kjell was first and foremost a circulatory physiologist, so the dominance of this area in the last three sections is appropriate. He pioneered in the area of circulatory shunts, air-breathing fishes, circulatory control systems, diving physiology, and blood gas transport, the primary topics of the last three sections.

The editors of this volume all met Kjell when we were beginning our careers in science. His enthusiasm and energy were contagious. His mark on us, on his many colleagues around the world, and on the field of physiology is indelible. We hope that this book portrays a sampling of his interests that may inspire other young scientists to follow unchartered paths, as he did.

**Stephen C. Wood**
**Roy E. Weber**
**Alan R. Hargens**
**Ronald W. Millard**

# CONTENTS

**Part Three    CIRCULATION: ENVIRONMENT, ONTOGENY,
AND EXERCISE**

**Part Five       CIRCULATION: COMPARATIVE STUDIES**

# CONTRIBUTORS

**Michael Axelsson, Ph.D.** Department of Zoophysiology, University of Göteborg, Göteborg, Sweden

**Warren W. Burggren, Ph.D.***  Professor, Department of Zoology, University of Massachusetts, Amherst, Massachusetts

**Michael de Burgh Daly** Department of Physiology, Royal Free Hospital School of Medicine, London, England

**Robert Elsner, Ph.D.** Professor Emeritus, Institute of Marine Science, University of Alaska, Fairbanks, Alaska

**Hans Gesser, Ph.D.** Lecturer, Department of Zoophysiology, University of Aarhus, Aarhus, Denmark

**Mogens L. Glass, Ph. D.** Professor, Department of Physiology, Faculdade de Medicina de Ribeirão Preto, University of São Paulo, São Paulo, Brazil

**Gordon Grigg, Ph.D., DSc.** Professor, Department of Zoology, The University of Queensland, Queensland, Australia

**Alan R. Hargens, Ph.D.** Chief, Space Station Project Scientist, Life Science Division, NASA—Ames Research Center, Moffett Field, California

**Peter W. Hochachka, Ph.D., F.R.S.C.** Professor, Department of Zoology and Division of Sports Medicine, Faculty of Science and Faculty of Medicine, University of British Columbia, Vancouver, British Columbia, Canada

---

*Present affiliation:* Professor, Department of Biology, University of Las Vegas, Las Vegas, Nevada.

*xvii*

**Susanne Holmgren**   Associate Professor, Comparative Neuroscience Unit, Department of Zoophysiology, University of Göteborg, Göteborg, Sweden

**Kjell Johansen, Ph.D.**†   Department of General and Animal Physiology, University of São Paulo, São Paulo, Brazil

**C. Barker Jørgensen, DSc.**   Professor Emeritus, Zoophysiological Laboratory A, August Krogh Institute, Copenhagen, Denmark

**Gary M. Malvin, Ph.D.**   Oxygen Transport Program, Lovelace Medical Foundation, Albuquerque, New Mexico

**Charlotte P. Mangum, Ph.D.**   Professor, Department of Biology, College of William and Mary, Williamsburg, Virginia

**Arthur W. Martin, Ph.D.**   Professor Emeritus, Department of Zoology, University of Washington, Seattle, Washington

**Attilio Maseri**   Department of Cardiology, Hammersmith Hospital, London, England

**Ronald W. Millard, Ph.D.**   Professor, Department of Pharmacology and Cell Biophysics and Department of Internal Medicine, University of Cincinnati College of Medicine, Cincinnati, Ohio

**William K. Milsom, Ph.D.**   Professor, Department of Zoology, University of British Columbia, Vancouver, British Columbia, Canada

**Stefan Nilsson, Ph.D.**   Professor, Comparative Neuroscience Unit, Department of Zoophysiology, University of Göteborg, Göteborg, Sweden

**Rüdiger J. Paul, Ph.D.**   Assistant Professor, Zoological Institute, University of Düsseldorf, Düsseldorf, Germany

**Steven F. Perry, Ph.D.***   Associate Professor, Department of Biology, Universität Oldenburg, Oldenburg, Germany

---

†Deceased.
*Present affiliation:* Respiratory Physiology Research Group, University of Calgary, Calgary, Alberta, Canada.

**Knut Pettersson, Ph.D.**   Assistant Professor, Cardiovascular Research Laboratories, AB Hässle, Mölndal, Sweden

**Johannes Piiper, M.D.**   Professor, Department of Physiology, Max Planck Institute for Experimental Medicine, Göttingen, Germany

**Otakar Poupa, M.D., M.D.h.c., DSc.**   Professor Emeritus, Department of Clinical Physiology, University of Göteborg, Göteborg, Sweden

**Dean F. Rigel, Ph.D.**   Instructor, Department of Pharmacology and Cell Biophysics and Department of Surgery, University of Cincinnati College of Medicine, Cincinnati, Ohio

**Peter Scheid, M.D., Ph.D.**   Professor, Department of Physiology, Ruhr University Bochum, Bochum, Germany

**Bodil Schmidt-Nielsen, Dr. phil.**   Adjunct Professor, Department of Physiology, University of Florida College of Medicine, Gainesville, Florida

**C. Richard Taylor, Ph.D.**   Alexander Agassiz Professor of Zoology, Museum of Comparative Zoology, Harvard University, Cambridge, Massachusetts

**Roy E. Weber, Ph.D.**   Professor, Zoophysiology Laboratory, Institute of Zoology and Zoophysiology, University of Aarhus, Aarhus, Denmark

**Francis C. White**   Department of Pathology, University of California, San Diego, School of Medicine, La Jolla, California

**Stephen C. Wood, Ph.D.**   Senior Scientist, Oxygen Transport Program, Lovelace Medical Foundation, Albuquerque, New Mexico

# Kjell
## The Artist

**OTAKAR POUPA**

University of Göteborg
Göteborg, Sweden

> I have always spelled Hell
> with a capital H
> often god in small letters.
> I wonder why?
> But find no answer
>
> *K. Johansen, Observations (1985)*

Late in the autumn of 1972 I was called by Kjell, who had something to do in Göteborg. I admired his work, but had never met him personally. It was one year after he returned to Europe from the United States to build up his institute in Århus. I was settled in Göteborg as fellow of Swedish Medical Research Council after my emigration from Czechoslovakia in 1968. My research dealt, in part, with comparative cardiology. His aim was to start similar research in Århus, and I was more than happy to help. Our cooperation became even deeper when my co-worker and friend Hans Gesser was invited to Århus as a permanent member of the staff. God bless this telephone call, since it started not only my regular stay in Århus, but also our close friendship.

*1*

In those days Kjell was a Hemingway-like bearded man, full of energy and enthusiasm. His charisma emanates even from a rather bleached snapshot photo I took when he opened the shell of the turtle to get the heart sample from this miraculous animal, about which the old man Santiago when fishing the great marlin in the Stream says, "Most people are heartless about turtles because a turtle's heart will beat for hours after he has been cut up and butchered" (Hemingway, 1965). It was really so: we had to wait 15 hr before the isometric heart strip stopped developing force under complete anoxia. The Århus institute developed rapidly to the paradise of comparative physiological research where it was possible to get even very exotic animal material, and we soon extended our experiments with cardiac anoxia. Heart strips of African *Varanus* contributed to the plot, comparing anoxic tolerance of myocardium from hagfish (*Myxine glutinosa*—one of the Kjell's favorites) to human myocardium (Fig. 1).

This was the beginning of our research in comparative cardiology. But as Claude Bernard pointed out (Bernard, 1945), the human mind dealing with experimental work has two faces: When entering the laboratory leave your fantasy in the cloakroom, but do not forget to take it on again when leaving the institute building. For creative experimental work, the free fantasy of an artist is of the same value as critical unbiased scientific logic. Kjell's mind had this rare ambiguity, and I would not wonder if his multifaceted genius would have allowed him to become a painter or a poet of the same caliber as he was a scientist. Plastic art was another source of pleasure we shared. Soon after our first scientific meeting, we introduced ourselves as painters. After that, we painted a lot together and were regular visitors of exhibitions and galleries. One of them we favored was Silkeborg—not far from Århus. This small Danish town has a remarkable artistic history. The COBRA-group was started there. It was initiated and guided by a village teacher and autodidact, Asger Jorn. Artists from Copenhagen, Brussels, and Amsterdam (CO-BR-A), such as Appel, Corneille, Alechinsky, Lucebert, closely allied by Dubuffet, Fautrier, and others, met there. They painted together and discussed the future of the culture in postwar Europe. The school building was changed to the art museum exhibiting the Asger Jorn collection of contemporary art, which recently moved to a masterly adapted group of country houses in the outskirts of the town. Silkeborg owns a further rarity: The greatest picture of Dubuffet painted al fresco on the facade of a renting house close to the place. During one visit, Kjell made a snapshot of it and decided to place me at the wall to show the comparative size of the painting (Fig. 2).

Through the years of our expeditions, Kjell's art experience was stepwise transformed. Since our first meeting, he would send me postcards from all corners of the world. They were usually a reproduction of some painting he had just seen and admired, and in verso he wrote his comments. I collected them and Figure 3 shows some selected pieces that illustrate the evolution of his artistic feeling (see color plate, facing page 8).     The first one is dated Christmas 1972.

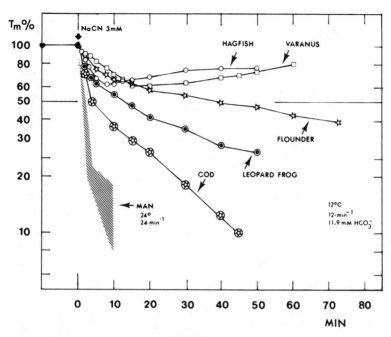

**Figure 1** Cardiac anoxic tolerance in different vertebrates. Isometric strips of cardiac muscle developing force (ordinate) when respiratory (mitochondrial) ATP production was inhibited by cyanide.

As a purebred Norwegian he admired Edvard Munch. This imprinting influenced his further step to more expressive imagination, Emil Nolde. I remember his excited description of Nolde's museum in Flensburg, to which, regretfully, I could not travel with him. Nolde's strong expression, burning colors, and themes of sea, clouds, and exotic flowers, fascinated him. Through Nolde's art he found his way to the nonfigurative painting and sculpture from which he discovered unlimited possibilities to express emotions by form and color, a free space for limitless experimentation. Among many other things, it was the mysterious colored light, that attracted him to the lyricism of Marc Rothko. These are only a few examples and a sober description of a private artistic facet of Kjell's personality. Behind every postcard is a hidden charisma of our shared expectations of the next challenge, next surprise, which the art would offer to our sensors tuned to high sensibility.

But there is no light without shadows: one has to pay for highlights of creative sensitivity by an increased vulnerability of the mind. Depressions came as an unavoidable consequence. During the dark periods of life, there is not much one can do: patience and understanding are the only remedies. Sometimes

**Figure 2**  Dubuffet: Fresco at the wall of the renting house in Silkeborg (Denmark). Photograph taken by K. Johansen in early spring 1976.

it was music that could be of some help in the nights of solitude—Mozart especially. Under one such period of depression, his letter was accompanied by a group of poems called *Observations* and *Reflections*. It was dated 17.1.85, and the poems were written in English and Norwegian. Here are some fragments:

I have always spelled Hell
with a capital H
often god in small letters
I wonder why?
But find no answer.

* * *

The magpies are my artists,
the snow makes them into black fragments
on the naked frostwhite treelimbs.
I watch them through my iced window.

* * *

It is still dark at eight,
lights flicker, move and pass
each other on the distant highway
toward east.
Light on the way to work
or someone they love.
Soon daylight
will wipe them out.

* * *

Is it possible to long
for something you never knew?
Like finding a colour
you never saw.
To see inside a beating heart.
To kiss an unknown woman's breast.

* * *

For years I have not read any prose,
only poetry.
My souls orgasms
have come from painting(s).
Now I read a fascinating novel
by Axel Sandemose,

A Dane who became Norwegian.
now dead as all famous men.
"The past is a dream"
is the novel.
Never have I seen language
used with such eloquence.
I underline the passages
I want to remember.
I have been through so much
that I cannot recall
Where can it be?
Let me discover it,
describe it, paint it.
A diary?
No I shall never write it!

* * *

I no longer wonder
what most men are like.
I know I am different.

* * *

While time goes at snailspeed
I have won a battle
within myself
a battle with doubts
about my identity,
my self respect.
The blue-grey ice
in the corners of my window
is melting,
so is my feeling of guilt.

Poetry was a new facet of Kjell's mind I discovered late in our friendship. It was bitter and dry, but pure and not at all pessimistic, although calling *de profundis*.

In the last period of his life, Kjell discovered the art of Paul Klee. It was a good choice. Klee's calm but assiduous strain for synthesis of subjective, emotional sources and the objective means of art (Read, 1972), his unsatiable curiosity and experimentation, and the magic of the unknown, which challenges both artists and scientists as their common driving force to permanent investigation, suited Kjell's mercurylike intellect. A special kind of serenity of mind that one feels when diving in Klee's paintings helped him to bridge over periods of depressions, the frequency of which alarmingly increased. It is significant that his last postcard in my collection (Christmas 1986) is a reproduction of Klee's picture.

In October 1986, I met Kjell for the last time. In those months we were in permanent contact, preparing a new project to study the transformation of the lacunary blood–supplied primitive spongious myocardium to the coronary-supplied compact cardiac muscle, as seen in birds and mammals. In other words, we tried to see and follow the birth of coronaries. This was a challenging task, and Kjell produced all his admirable witchcraft to get the grant for it.* In his spare time, he was experimenting with a new pictorial technique. He called it x-ray collage. As a background he used x-ray pictures of various natural objects (remember it was x-ray techniques he used for his first scientific studies when trying to understand the blood flow in the evolutionary first right–left compartmentalized heart). These transparent gray basic forms he combined with patches of films of shining colors and, in this way, he created compositions of brilliant beauty, which one can observe both in normal illumination and as transparencies. One of those artifacts he presented to me as a gift for my 70th birthday in Århus, October 23rd, where we met to have a 1-day workshop with invited guests (R. Zak, Chicago; A. Waldenström, Uppsala; H. Gesser, Århus and others) to discuss their individual contributions to the future project.

Kjell's effort to get the grant was successful, and in early spring 1987, we had all begun to work. He left for a short trip to Southern France to prepare lectures for his United States tour. Before his departure, we had a long night call about the project. At the end he asked me what galleries to see there, and I recommended Palais Grimaldi, with excellent Picassos, in Antibes and especially Gallerie Maeght in Saint-Paul de Vence, if there would not be too much time to see other treasures. He tried to persuade me to follow him, but I could not accept the invitation, as the initial experiments of the project had just started. This was my last contact with him, and I do not know what he saw there. But in my fantasy, I see Kjell-Viking, a man grown from the firm granite of northern Europe, walking on the soft ground of the Mediterranean chalk-stone, covered

---

*Letter dated 13.10.86 read as follows: Dear Otakar—my great friend. You have been a senior authority in science for many decades and a wonderful friend for me for many years. I send you heartfelt wishes for the 17th. I hope the people who administrate the 15 million "kroner" for research have enough wisdom to grant us the funds we request. This would have the added importance of allowing us to be together more often. I have one of my x-ray collages waiting for your arrival here October 23. Keep swinging those golf clubs to keep your body young. Your mind and spirit will never get old. Your friend Kjell.

by a pineneedle carpet, admiring the golden explosions of flowering mimosa that filled the air with seducing mellow perfume. The man stubbornly trying to achieve the synthesis of pure logic and colorful sensuality, to find equilibrium between left and right halves of his neopallium, to reconcile physics and metaphysics—the aim and goal that for centuries all great and noble European minds have tried to achieve.

The day was crisp under cloudless sky when the telephone rang: Kjell was found dead. Through the window I saw on the sky's blue emptiness a jet very high flying to the unknown harbor with a white tail of vapor in the windless space: there somewhere is perhaps the cold aluminum coffin with a dead body inside. I opened the book and started to read: "Then they began to climb and they were going to the east it seemed, and then it darkened and they were in a storm, the rain so thick it seemed like flying through a waterfall, and then they were out and Compie turned his head and grinned and pointed and there, ahead, all he could see, as wide as all the world, great, high, and unbelievably white in the sun, was the square top of Kilimanjaro. And then he knew that there was where he was going" (Hemingway; 1967).

I stopped reading. Wasn't it his voice I heard, "To hell with sentiments. Let's have a beer"?

### References

Bernard, C. (1945). *Introduction a l'Etude de la Medecine Experimentale*. Constant Bourquin Editeur, Geneve.

Hemingway, E. (1965). *The Old Man and the Sea*. Scribner & Sons, New York, p. 28.

Hemingway, E. (1967) The snows of Kilimanjaro. In *The Essential Hemingway*. Penguin, New York, P. 463.

Read, H. (1972) *A Concise History of Modern Painting*. Revised Edition. Thames and Hudson, London.

**Figure 3** Postcards sent to the author by K. Johansen showing works of his favorite painters. Top left: Edvard Munch: *Nude with Red Hair*. Sin (litho) 1901. Top right: Emil Nolde: *Muhlr (Windmill)*. 1924. Bottom left: Mark Rothko: *Light Red Over Black*. 1957. Bottom right: Paul Klee: *Flora in the Sand*. 1927.

# 1

## Adaptational, Environmental, and Ecological Physiology
### A Case for Hierarchical Thinking

**C. BARKER JØRGENSEN**

August Krogh Institute
Copenhagen, Denmark

Kjell Johansen introduced his August Krogh lecture at the International Physiology Congress in 1986 by citing August Krogh's (1929) statement that "for a large number of problems there will be some animal of choice or a few such animals on which it can be most conveniently studied," and he considered this statement to epitomize the very essence of comparative physiology. But he added as a profession of his own ". . . the animals' environment and the constraint it offers should also be of a paramount consideration in organismic physiology" (Johansen, 1987).

These two statements cover animal physiology from the general level to the levels of adaptational and environmental physiology. Kjell Johansen's interests were definitely in these latter, higher levels, as revealed by the lecture, which John Krogh, in a commemorative speech, calls his testament (Krogh, 1988).

The very title of the August Krogh lecture: *The World as a Laboratory*, shows Kjell Johansen's attitude toward animal physiology. This attitude he identified with that of August Krogh, when he advocated the study of comparative physiology for its own sake by referring to "animal mechanisms and adaptations of exquisite beauty and the most surprising character."

Kjell Johansen expresses the same feelings when he refers to the lungfish, estivating in his chunk of mud on his desk for more than 7 years, as a revelation in suspended animation.

Kjell Johansen characterized his own work as "research in comparative environmental physiology," and his lecture provides examples of how animals have adapted to cope with their environments, typically extreme ones, as met in the Arctic and Antarctic; in a tropical, underground thermostat; at hypoxic conditions in the Amazon; during drought and starvation. His research on physiological adaptations to extreme environments carried an important field within comparative animal physiology to a zenith.

What I want to call attention to is use of the concepts of adaptational and environmental physiology as synonymous. This is not special to Kjell Johansen, it has today become the conventional use of the terms. Moreover, the concept of ecological physiology is increasingly being used synonymously with environmental physiology, and the choice of terms is often opportunistically determined, rather than the result of conceptual considerations.

The question, therefore, arises whether the concepts do differ in content and nature, or only in origin, later developments showing them to be redundant terminologies. To answer this question we should trace the origin and development of the concepts.

## I. Origin and Development of Concepts

Until the post-Darwinian 19th century, physiology practiced on animals was basically human physiology. The human body and its functions could be studied directly to only a limited extent, but animals could be used as substitutes. This old belief that functional features are common to humans and animals became of special importance during the 19th century, when physiology definitely became experimental. As early as 1840, Dumeril stressed the importance of the frog to physiology, enumerating the discoveries that had been made on this animal. The list included almost all known physiological functions. And in 1865, Claude Bernard wrote that "the intelligent choice of an animal offering a happy anatomical arrangement is often essential to the success of an experiment and to the solution of an important physiological problem" (Bernard, 1957), as also realized by later physiologists, for example, August Krogh in his 1929 lecture (Jørgensen, 1983).

During the second half of the 19th century, however, animal physiology became established as a branch of physiology in its own right, along with the establishment of comparative anatomy. This development was greatly furthered by the acceptance of Darwinism. The comparative anatomy offered important contributions in support of the theory of evolution. The study of the morphology of homologous structures and organs served to establish phylogenetic relationships between animal groups. Animal physiologists studied the function of analogous structures and organs, and the field became known as comparative physiology. Often the overlap between comparative anatomy and comparative physiology was great, as indicated by the concept "functional morphology." At the level of interpretation, function as well as structure of animals were strongly influenced by the old concept of adaptation. With the establishment of Darwinism, physiological and morphological adaptations acquired an evolutionary perspective, and comparative adaptational physiology flourished in the laboratories at the science faculties, concurrently with human physiology in the laboratories of the medical schools.

With the growing understanding of the normal functions of the human body, physiologists also became interested in the functional capacities of the body and its organs. How does the body react on heavy impacts? This environmental physiology attempted to answer questions, such as, how does man maintain homeostasis at high or low temperatures? at low oxygen tensions? at high altitudes in the mountains or during flight? at high pressures during diving? at water deprivation? at high work loads or work to exhaustion? and so on. Environmental physiologists, thus, studied how the human body reacts to "stress" and survives extreme conditions. This period saw the development of highly sophisticated techniques in the physiological studies, simultaneously with an increasing understanding of the physiological processes at the cellular and biochemical levels.

Also animal physiologists became interested in how animals survive under extreme conditions. Presumably, this interest was often inspired by the developing field of human environmental physiology. Typically, this branch of animal physiology is characterized by a high professional standard. It obviously builds on the classic physiological tradition as it evolved at all levels, from biophysics to cell biology and organ physiology (Dill, 1964).

The emphasis among animal physiologists on adaptations to extreme and "harsh" environments not only reflected the interests of human physiologists in the reactions of the human body when exposed to such environments, it also fitted conventional concepts of the general relationship between animals and their environment. Adaptational and environmental physiology differentiated and matured during the period of Darwinism, when evolution through natural selection spelled "struggle for life" and "survival of the fittest," reflecting traits in the economical and social life of liberalist England.

Such concepts may have helped direct these new physiologies toward the means by which organisms survive in harsh and hostile environments. One may speculate how animal physiology would have developed on a pre-Darwinian background, for which the organisms and their environment interacted harmoniously according to the Creator's will, or on a neo-Darwinian background for which natural selection operates through differential survival within populations. Perhaps emphasis would have been on the interplay between organism and environment, carrying environmental physiology from the organism-centered level to the ecosystem level of organization. This level has hardly yet been reached by the adaptational and environmental physiologies, as evolved from classic organism-centered animal physiology.

It is this difference in levels that distinguishes adaptational, environmental, and ecological physiology. *Adaptational physiology* focuses on the functional properties of the organs that enable the organism to survive. *Environmental physiology* primarily focuses on the whole organism, on how it copes with the uncertainties of the environment, often considered within the framework of "stress." *Ecological physiology* focuses on the interplay between organism and environment, considered as the functional unit within the ecosystem. The use of "adaptational," "environmental," and "ecological" as qualifying adjectives in animal physiology, therefore, requires thinking in terms of levels of organization. There is, however, no tradition for such hierarchical thinking among animal physiologists. It may even be discouraged. Krogh referred to this in his address to the International Physiology Congress, in 1929. I should like once more to quote from this address: "Too many experiments and observations are being made and published and too little thought is bestowed upon them," in accord with a contemporary statement in instructions for medical writers "that what is needed in scientific papers is facts and again facts and still more facts. I venture to disagree emphatically with this statement. Facts are necessary, of course, but unless fertilized by ideas, correlated with other facts, illuminated by thought, I consider them as material only for science." I wonder whether the emphasis on attitudes among physiologists has changed substantially during the intervening 60 years.

Facts are necessary, but, to contribute to our understanding of nature, they must be interpreted, and the proper interpretation depends upon the choice of the reference frame that can place into perspective the raw results obtained. Feibleman (1954) formulated the process as follows: "For an organization of any given level, its mechanism lies at the level below and its purpose at the level above." I may illustrate by an example.

The main interest of most participants in our "Kjell Johansen Memorial Symposium" is presumably the mechanisms by which organisms secure the delivery of oxygen from the ambient medium—air or water—to the body. I have, therefore, chosen an example from the field of respiratory physiology: ventilation in filter-feeding bivalves.

## II. Ventilation in Filter-Feeding Bivalves: Hierarchical Interpretation

Early experiments showed that rates of ventilation and oxygen consumption were closely correlated (Fig. 1). The relationship was interpreted conventionally in

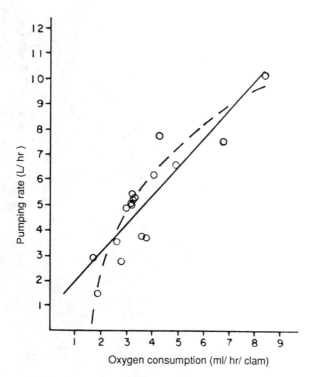

**Figure 1** Relationship between rates of water pumping and oxygen consumption in the hard clam *Mercenaria mercenaria,* which Hamwi and Haskin (1969) interpreted as indicating that the clams regulate ventilation according to oxygen requirements. The relationship is expressed in the regression line. Verduin (1969) drew the dashed line to indicate that Hamwi and Haskin's data expressed costs of water pumping. (From Verduin, 1969.)

terms of a direct causality. However, there was disagreement over the direction of the cause–effect relationship. According to Hamwi and Haskin (1969), the clams regulate the ventilation to meet the animals' need for oxygen. Verduin (1969) reinterpreted the same data as expressing the energetic costs of ventilation. Oxygen uptake at zero ventilation was obtained by extrapolation. Bayne et al. (1976) adopted Verduin's interpretation, confirming the results in experiments on mussels.

Experiments on the relationship between oxygen uptake and oxygen tension in mussels showed different patterns. In some mussels, the relation was linear, in others, curved (see Fig. 2). Also these results were interpreted at the organismic level as indicating that mussels may, or may not, regulate their oxygen consumption. The two types of relationship were identified with active and standard

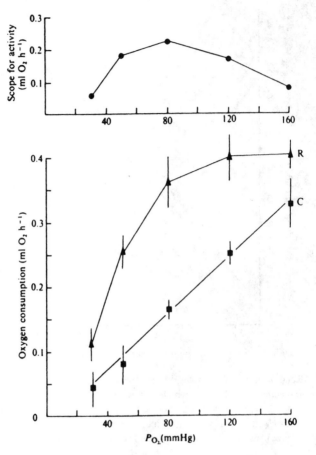

**Figure 2**   Two types of relationship between rates of oxygen consumption and oxygen tensions in the mussel *Mytilus edulis*. The linear relationship is interpreted as indicating nonregulating individuals; the hyperbolic relationship, regulating individuals. The nonregulating condition is assumed to express standard metabolic rates; the regulating condition, active metabolic rates. The numerical differences between the two relationships are interpreted as "scope for activity." (From Bayne et al., 1976.)

metabolic rates, the difference between the two constituting the scope for activity (Bayne et al., 1976; Shumway, 1982).

An interpretation of the relationship between oxygen consumption and ventilation in terms of metabolic costs of water transport is doubtful because it implies that these costs represent a major part of the total energy expenditure. Actual measurements and estimates show, however, that the costs of water

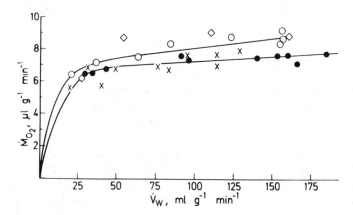

**Figure 3** Relationships between mass specific rates of oxygen consumption and ventilation in naturally ventilating mussels (●, ○, x) and artificially ventilated (◊), including the entire range of the ventilatory capacity. (From Jørgensen et al., 1986.)

transport in filter-feeding bivalves, as well as other ciliary filter feeders, are marginal (Clemmesen and Jørgensen, 1987).

Any interpretation that is based on physiological control of oxygen consumption is questionable, because it implies the existence of control mechanisms; but, there is good evidence that such mechanisms do not exist. At a constant perfusion rate of the mussel's mantle cavity, the rate of oxygen consumption was independent of the blood circulation and of the presence of the gills (Famme, 1981; Famme and Kofoed, 1980). Thus, the gills lacked any importance as respiratory organs. The undifferentiated surfaces of the mantle cavity serve as respiratory surfaces. In filter-feeding bivalves the gills are feeding structures, responsible for processing the ambient water, including retention of food particles and their transfer to the mouth.

This function is disregarded in the literature on the relationships between oxygen consumption, ventilation, and oxygen tension. The evolutionary transition of the gills from respiratory organs to feeding structures involved a drastic increase in ventilatory capacity of the organism. Therefore, in establishing the relationship between oxygen consumption and ventilation, it is crucial to assess to what degree the capacity for water transport has been utilized under the experimental conditions. When the ventilatory rates include the entire range from low to maximum, the relationship became hyperbolic, as shown in Figure 3 (Jørgensen et al., 1986). Accordingly, the steep increase in oxygen consumption with increasing ventilation is restricted to the lower end of the range. Previous studies were restricted to this part of the range, which represents rates of water processing in mussels under adverse conditions.

It may be concluded, therefore, that interpretations of oxygen consumption in terms of energetic costs of ventilation or physiological regulation of metabolic rates are ad hoc interpretations, lacking biological meaning. The relationship between oxygen consumption and ventilation can be explained in terms of resistance to oxygen diffusion across the boundary layer at the interphase between the through current and mantle surfaces, we well as within the tissues of the body. At low-flow rates the boundary layer is thick, whereas the diffusional pathways within the tissues tend to be short, because most of the oxygen that diffuses into the tissues is consumed peripherally (Jørgensen et al., 1986). Oxygen consumption, thereby, tends to be determined by the diffusional resistance across the boundary layer and, consequently, approaches proportionality with oxygen tension in the water. At increasing flow rates, the thickness of the boundary layer decreases, and diffusion through the tissues becomes correspondingly important in determining the relationship between oxygen consumption and flow rate.

The relationship may be considered a consequence of the transfer of oxygen uptake from the gills to other parts of the mantle cavity, that is, the substitution of a site structurally adapted for efficient diffusional uptake of oxygen by inefficient sites, at which the thickness of the diffusive boundary layer is small compared with the thickness of the laminar currents passing the surface. Consequently, only small fractions of the oxygen carried with the ventilatory currents are available for respiration. Hence, it is misleading to speak about rates of water transport as being grossly overdimensioned in filter-feeding bivalves for the respiratory purposes that water pumping also serves. The small fraction of oxygen available to the animal requires a large flow rate before diffusion through the boundary layer ceases to be limiting for oxygen consumption. The correlations observed between respiration and ventilation in filter-feeding bivalves, as well as in other filter feeders, thus reflect physical conditions of viscous flow and diffusive boundary layers, and interpretations in terms of physiological regulation may be generally misleading when applied to respiration in filter feeders.

The primary physiological import of water pumping in filter-feeding bivalves is to secure food in amounts that enable the organism to exploit its potential for growth under optimal environmental conditions. This is achieved by a water-processing capacity that is adapted to the level of food—the phytoplankton—in the ambient water. The capacity for water processing is thus the evolutionary result of the interplay between the organism and its environment. Understanding the nature of the relationships between respiration and ventilation in filter feeders, therefore, requires hierarchical thinking.

### References

Bayne, B. L., Thompson, R. J., and Widdows, J. (1976). Physiology: I. In *Marine Mussels: Their Ecology and Physiology*. Edited by B. L. Bayne. Cambridge, Cambridge University Press, pp. 121–206.

Bernard, C. (1957). *Introduction to the Study of Experimental Medicine*. Translated by H. C. Green. New York, Dover Press, p. 117.

Clemmesen, B., and Jørgensen, C. B. (1987). Energetic costs and efficiencies of ciliary filter feeding. *Mar. Biol., 94:445–449*.

Dill, D. B., ed. (1964). *Handbook of Physiology*. Section 4: Adaptation to the Environment. Washing, D.C., American Physiological Society.

Dumeril, A.M.C. (1840). Notice historique sur les decouvertes faites dans les sciences d'observation par l'etude de l'organisation des Grenouilles. *Ann. Sci. Nat. Zool., 13*:65–75.

Famme, P. (1981). Haemolymph circulation as a respiratory parameter in the mussel, *Mytilus edulis* L. *Comp. Biochem. Physiol., 69A*:243–247.

Famme, P., and Kofoed, L. H. (1980). The ventilatory current and ctenidial function related to oxygen uptake in declining oxygen tension by the mussel *Mytilus edulis* L. *Comp. Biochem. Physiol., 66A*:161–171.

Feibleman, J. K. (1954). Theory of integrative levels. *Br. J. Phil. Sci., 5*:59–66.

Hamwi, A., and Haskin, H. H. (1969). Oxygen consumption and pumping rates in the hard clam *Mercenaria mercenaria*: A direct method. *Science, 163*:823–824.

Jørgensen, C. B. (1983). Ecological physiology: Background and perspectives. *Comp. Biochem. Physiol., 75A*:5–7.

Jørgensen, C. B., Møhlenberg, F., and Sten-Knudsen, O. (1986). Nature of relation between ventilation and oxygen consumption in filter feeders. *Mar. Ecol. Prog. Ser., 29*:73–88.

Johansen, K. (1987). The August Krogh Lecture: The world as a laboratory. In *Advances in Physiological Research*. Edited by H. McLennan, J. R. Ledsome, C. H. S. McIntosh, and D. R. Jones. New York, Plenum Press, pp. 377–396.

Krogh, A. (1929). Progress of physiology. *Am. J. Physiol., 90*:243–251.

Krogh, J. O. (1988). Minnetale over professor dr. philos. Kjell Johansen. In *Norske Videnskaps-Akademi, Årbok 1987*. Oslo, Universitetsforlaget, pp. 255–259.

Shumway, S. E. (1982). Oxygen consumption in oysters: An overview. *Mar. Biol. Lett., 3*:1–23.

Verduin, J. (1969). Hard clam pumping rates: Energy requirements. *Science, 166*:1309–1310.

# Part One

**METABOLISM**

# 2

## Principles of Physiological and Biochemical Adaptation

High-Altitude Man as a Case Study

**PETER W. HOCHACHKA**

University of British Columbia
Vancouver, British Columbia, Canada

## I. Introduction

Many comparative physiologists and biochemists realize that the concept of the unity of biochemical structures and physiological functions creates an enormous problem for biology: How does one account in mechanistic terms for the almost unimaginable diversity (and obvious success in wildly different environments) of living things on this planet? In a recent review, four principles were suggested as fundamental to, and capable of, resolving the paradox. These included (1) the principle of conservation of critical sequences in both regulatory and structural genes, (2) the principle of unique assembly of parts by means of unique or tissue-specific and temporal activation of regulatory loci, (3) the principle of genetic innovation by mechanisms internal or external to the genome, and (4) the principle of adaptation by selection for favorable alleles of structural or regulatory genes or for favorable genetic innovations (Hochachka, 1988a). For biologists, it is the last—adaptation—that lies at the very heart of the issue and is most crucial for resolving it. Although there are numerous behavioral and morphological examples of biological adaptation (see Schluter et al., 1985, for an interesting example), adaptations at the biochemical and physiological levels are not easily established. Endler (1986) supplies several explanations of why this is so (we will see an example later in our discussion of man at high altitude), but in my opinion the main reason is to be found in the nature of research in these disciplines: *the emphasis and focus is upon mechanism of function, not mechanism of evolution and adaptation.*

In one of his last major lectures, Kjell Johansen (1987), explained how, as a scientist, he worked in a framework dominated by (1) the August Krogh principle (Krogh, 1929; Krebs, 1975) and by (2) the constraints imposed by the environment in shaping the physiology and biochemistry of animals. Working on animals particularly well-designed for unraveling physiological function means working on animals adapted for life in specific environments. Kjell Johansen, a master at recognizing which animals were best suited for researching which problems, realized that his research strokes cut two ways: *at the physiological functions under study and at the adaptational processes that exaggerated the expression of those physiological functions in the first place.* The aim of this paper is to illustrate this approach with a study of high-altitude adaptation in humans.

## II. The Basic Problem and Strategy of Study

Even if $O_2$ availability declines with decreasing barometric pressure, man is able to meet the $O_2$ demands of resting aerobic metabolism (about $0.2$ mmol $\cdot$ kg$^{-1}$ $\cdot$ min$^{-1}$ of $O_2$), even on earth's highest mountains. The demands of aerobic exercise, however, are not as easily satisfied at high altitude because of a progressive drop in metabolic scope for activity. At low altitudes, the *scope for activity* (defined as the difference between basal and maximum metabolic rates) for most mammals and humans is about tenfold (Taylor et al., 1980). Altitude (or hypobaric hypoxia) reduces maximum aerobic metabolism in humans by so much that, at first, it was predicted that the scope for activity at altitudes equivalent to the peak of Mount Everest would be vanishingly close to zero. That is why many scientists were perplexed when Peter Habeler and Reinhold Messner, elite climbers with no exceptional aerobic metabolic capacities (Oelz et al., 1986), scaled Mount Everest, in 1978, without supplementary $O_2$, an achievement that led to two scientific reviews aimed at explaining this improbable event and refocusing our attention on high-altitude performance (Sutton et al., 1983; West, 1983). Later studies showed that lowlanders achieving these activity levels in hypobaric hypoxia that is equivalent to the top of Mount Everest must sustain reductions in metabolic scopes down to one-sixth to one-fifth of normoxic maximum values (Sutton et al., 1988). Thus, the exercise capacities under hypobaric hypoxia, even of individuals as motivated as the Habelers and Messners of this world, are seriously compromised.

On an interspecies comparative scale, such feats of man are puny and unimpressive. The common sparrow can fly horizontally at over 7000-m altitude, whereas the bar-headed goose, a rather dull-looking animal, routinely flies over Mount Everest at estimated altitudes in excess of 10,000 m (Fedde, 1985). Similarly, the Andean llama's $\dot{V}O_2$max is unaffected by reductions in inspired $O_2$ tensions so severe that $PaO_2$ values are equivalent to those of man on the peak of Mount Everest (C. R. Taylor, personal communication). Numerous additional studies of mammals and birds show that it is clearly within the vertebrate adaptive range to be able to profoundly compensate for reduced $O_2$ availability of high-altitude environments. If animals can achieve this, why not man? The possibility that high-altitude peoples have become adapted through phylogenetic time to permit an acceptably high scope for activity, despite hypobaric hypoxia, has long intrigued laymen and scientists alike (see Baker, 1976). Yet, despite much effort to establish if this is possible, a consensus has not emerged; in fact, just the opposite situation of two extreme views prevails.

The view that peoples indigenous to high-altitude environments are, indeed, biologically different from lowlanders, because they are better adapted to hypobaric hypoxia, is widely held by laymen; all of us who have traveled to high mountains have experienced or have heard of anecdotal evidence suggesting improved performance capacities of native highlanders compared with lowlanders. However, this view was not placed on a scientific basis until Monge (1948) published a small book collating the historical and physiological evidence favoring altitude adaptation of highland natives. Monge's synthesis stimulated numerous subsequent studies of the $O_2$-transport system of Andean natives, much of which implicitly suggested that the exercise performance and oxidative metabolism of native highlanders were less perturbed by hypobaric hypoxia than they were in lowlanders (see, e.g., Hurtado, 1964; Kollias et al., 1968; Way, 1976). Nevertheless, whether or not these differences in exercise capacities under hypoxic conditions could be ascribed strictly to adaptive and unchangeable biological characteristics could not be definitely established. The remaining uncertainty after these studies encouraged an alternative point of view; namely, that high-altitude natives do not differ from lowland individuals in any fundamental way. Instead, this view argues that selective pressures have not been intense enough (and there has been inadequate geologic time) for fixation of unique high-altitude-adapted genotypes. Besides, it is argued that, even if this had occurred, the flow of genetic information between highlanders and lowlanders would obliterate the opportunity of demonstrating the adaptation (Cruz-Coke, 1976). Thus, this view assumes that any observed differences are reasonably modest and arise because of short-term adjustments to hypoxia, to training, or to other environmental influences, such as nutrition. Although this interpretation may represent a minority view today, nonetheless, it is quite widely held (see, e.g., Heath and Williams, 1981).

We believe that this controversy has remained unresolved to this day because of several theoretical and experimental difficulties. First, although the use of exercise stress to expose highlander-versus-lowlander differences is widely acknowledged, a most important problem arises from inabilities to separate and define "true" biological adaptations as distinct from other (e.g., training) effects. Second, in the past, minimal advantage has been taken of extensive comparative studies of animals. Third, much of the literature on indigenous high-altitude peoples is based on studies carried out under trying field conditions or in underdeveloped countries, where control of parameters may be almost impossible and where technological support systems may be lacking.

To circumvene some of these problems, we organized a study of exercise metabolism and physiology of Quechua natives based on a three-pronged strategy: (1) The study was designed to allow separation of acute, intermediate-term, and long-term adaptations (Prosser, 1986; Hochachka and Somero, 1984). This put us in a position to identify so-called true biological adaptations and to gain insight into their underlying mechanisms. (2) The study was designed to take advantage of the matching of $O_2$ fluxes at various steps or links in the path of $O_2$ from atmosphere to mitochondria, to help sort out relative plasticity (relative rates of adjustment possible) for different steps in the process. Finally, (3) the study was designed as a modern laboratory research program, rather than as a field expedition with limited experimental possibilities. In this context, six Quechua Indians, born and living essentially all of their lives in the valleys, plains, and mountains of the La Raya area of Peru, at altitudes ranging from 3600 to 4500 m, volunteered to fly to Vancouver, Canada to participate in a 6-week deacclimation study.

As perhaps could have been anticipated from animal studies (see Taylor et al., 1987), we found that some processes in gas exchange and metabolism appeared to be the end result of long-term (developmental or genetic) adaptation; some functions displayed acclimation or deacclimation capacities; and still others, displayed acute adaptational capacities. For example, several functional features of the lung were measurably unique and distinctly different from homologous lung functions in lowlanders (Jones et al., 1990), yet showed no change on deacclimation. Our initial interpretation is that these functions (or steps in the path of $O_2$) in high-altitude-adapted Quechuas are long-term developmental or genetic adaptations, analogous to interspecies scaling adaptations studied in detail by Taylor and Weibel and their co-workers (Taylor et al., 1987). As a result of such adaptations, the hypoxia sensitivity of maximum aerobic metabolism (of $\dot{V}O_2$max in Andean natives, tested under conditions equivalent to 4200-m altitude, is one-third to one-fifth that for lowlanders; this characteristic also showed essentially no deacclimation over a 6-week period at sea level (Hochachka et al., 1991). Several similar conclusions arose from functional studies of the heart at rest and at work (McKenzie et al., 1991) and in the metabolic properties of skeletal muscles. The latter system was particularly instructive; hence, we will focus most of the rest of our discussion upon it.

## III. Muscle Metabolic Homeostasis During Exercise

One of the most useful sources of information about metabolic homeostasis during exercise in humans is the plasma lactate concentration profile during exercise and recovery. Large perturbations in plasma lactate pools are clearly indicative of serious mismatch between muscle energy demands and $O_2$ fluxes [between muscle adenosine triphosphate (ATP) demands and the capacity to supply ATP through aerobic metabolic pathways]. The usual situation in lowlanders during incremental $\dot{V}O_2max$ tests is for plasma lactate concentrations to remain stable for about the first half of the test, but these values begin to rise at about 50% of maximum work; at fatigue, plasma concentrations in excess of 10–12 mM are not at all uncommon, and higher values are commonly seen in well-trained athletes. When such lowlanders exercise under hypoxic conditions, they form more lactate (for any given power output) than in normoxia. This metabolic response is common in many animals under $O_2$-limiting conditions; it is interpreted as an attempt to make up the energy deficit caused by $O_2$ insufficiency and is a special expression of the Pasteur effect (see Hochachka et al., 1991; Hochachka and Guppy, 1987).

The behavior of Andean natives differs strikingly from this standard metabolic pattern. At all exercise intensities to fatigue, plasma lactate concentrations are notably lower than in lowlanders. Curves of plasma lactate concentration versus power output in watts, in effect, are right-shifted, such that, at fatigue, plasma lactate values are in the 5-mM range, or less than half those seen in lowlanders (Hochachka et al., 1991). Although the data indicate that $O_2$ fluxes to working muscles are more closely balanced with ATP demands in Andeans than in lowlanders, they are perplexing for an obvious reason: despite the hypobaric hypoxia of La Rayan atmosphere, *Quechua natives produce less, rather than more, lactate for a given power output.* This kind of metabolic response, known as the lactate paradox (West, 1986; Hochachka, 1988b), was first described for Andean natives over 50 years ago (Edwards, 1936). In lowlanders, this metabolic characteristic is an acclimation; it requires about 10–20 days at altitude to be expressed (Green et al., 1989; West, 1986), and it deacclimates along a similar time course on descent. Andean Quechuas, in contrast, express the lactate paradox even 6 weeks after descent and, indeed, after 6 weeks of reacclimation to high altitude (C. Stanley, personal communication). Thus, we conclude that it, too, is a fixed metabolic property, which we tentatively term the *perpetual lactate paradox* (Hochachka et al., 1991). Because it is an expression of oxidative metabolism (a part of the last link in the path of oxygen from air to mitochondria) that seems fixed and does not deacclimate, we also assume that it is a developmental or genetic level adaptation.

Although the adaptive significance of the lactate paradox at high altitude is well recognized (Edwards as long ago as 1936 realized that the excessive production and accumulation of lactate are counterproductive), the molecular mechanisms underlying these unique regulatory interactions between aerobic and anaerobic metabolism have remained a mystery for some 50 years. Phosphate-31 nuclear magnetic resonance spectroscopy (NMRS) studies using a calf muscle ergometer arranged for function within a 1-m, 1.5-T magnet allowed us to examine mechanisms underlying the lactate paradox (Matheson et al., 1991).

Earlier, Cerretelli et al. (1982) and West (1986) hypothesized that high-altitude-adapted individuals might display a more labile intracellular muscle pH; they reasoned that an inordinately large decrease in muscle pH for a given power output would serve to inhibit glycolysis, presumably by phosphofructokinase inhibition. If real, this process could easily account for the lactate paradox. Our NMRS measurements clearly rule out that alternative: if anything, skeletal muscle in Quechuas displays more stable intracellular pH for a given power output than in lowlanders, and this difference is retained during work while breathing hypoxic gas mixtures to simulate the La Rayan atmosphere (Matheson et al., 1991).

Instead of differences in muscle pH homeostasis, we hypothesize that differences in ATP demand–ATP supply coupling lie at the heart of the lactate paradox (Hochachka, 1988b; Hochachka et al., 1991; Matheson et al., 1991). We hypothesize that the difference between skeletal muscle metabolism in Quechuas and in lowlanders is analogous to the difference between cardiac and skeletal muscles, but that the difference is less extreme. In cardiac muscle, energy demand and energy supply functions are so closely balanced that large changes in work rate are achieved with minimal or no changes in concentrations of high-energy phosphate metabolites and with minimal or no lactate production (see Hochachka, 1988b, for literature in this area). In contrast, in working skeletal muscle, change in power output is usually accompanied by changes in high-energy phosphate metabolites and, particularly, in the phosphorylation potential (Connett and Honig, 1989). The latter is widely considered to supply kinetic and thermodynamic drive for oxidative metabolism and, thereby, to account for the large increase in $\dot{V}O_2$ that skeletal muscle can sustain during work. What is often overlooked or underemphasized is that the same metabolite signals that turn on oxidative metabolism serve (kinetically and thermodynamically) to activate glycolysis. That is why aerobically working skeletal muscle generates lactate in proportion to the power output, in contrast with cardiac muscle, which produces no lactate at all under these conditions. Given this spectrum of metabolic organization (from the classic situation, as exemplified by the dog gracilis to the cardiac muscle situation), we consider that high-altitude *acclimation* in Caucasian lowlanders moves skeletal muscle metabolic organization toward the cardiac end of the spectrum (Hochachka, 1988b) and that *in high-altitude-adapted Quechuas, the mechanism allowing closer ATP demand–ATP supply coupling has improved even further* (Hochachka et al., 1991; Matheson et al., 1991). Because this key regulatory component in the final link of the path of $O_2$ in vivo can no longer acclimate or deacclimate in Quechua natives, we tentatively conclude that it, too, represents a true, long-term (developmental or genetic) adaptation. What is more, if the central feature (tight energy demand–energy supply coupling) of this analysis is correct, it implies that a given power output in Quechua natives can be sustained by lower $O_2$ fluxes than in lowlanders; that is, energy coupling is more stable because muscle work is more efficient.

Energetic efficiency of muscle work in these kinds of studies is operationally defined as the ratio of metabolic power output/net metabolic power input, both expressed in watts per kilogram, and determined for whole-body submaximal and maximal exercise. By this definition, Andean Quechuas, exercising at maximum rates in normoxia or hypoxia, display energetic efficiencies of about 30%, similar to the values obtained under our experimental conditions for elite lowlander athletes (Hochachka et al., 1991). In contrast, major differences between Quechuas and lowlanders appear when submaximal work rates are compared. Under normoxia, the efficiency of submaximal exercise by Quechuas is about 1.5 times that of lowlanders, whereas under hypoxic conditions, it is nearly a full twofold greater (Hochachka et al., 1991). Compared with lowlanders under hypoxic conditions, *the Andean natives are behaving as if they are able to get about 1.5 times as much work out of a given amount of oxygen and carbon fuel.* Whereas the energetic advantages of being able to get nearly two times more power output from a given amount of $O_2$ and fuel (ultimately, from a given amount of ATP) may immediately account for more stable energy demand–energy supply coupling and for lower lactate accumulation at fatigue in Andean natives than in lowlanders, they do not yield insight into underlying mechanisms. How are we to account for such large differences in apparent energetic efficiency of submaximal exercise in the two groups?

## IV. The Thyroid Hormone Connection in High-Altitude Adaptation

To put this issue in context, it should be emphasized that although we were able to plausibly account for the lactate paradox purely on the basis of metabolic regulation theory (Hochachka, 1988b), we were unable to complete our model of exercise metabolism in Quechuas until we discovered their improved efficiency of muscle work (Hochachka et al., 1991). Two earlier literature observations— an inverse relationship between altitude adaptation and thyroid function and one between energetic efficiency and thyroid hormones—then supplied us with the clues needed to piece together the final parts of the high-altitude adaptation puzzle. Both in hypothyroid humans and in animal models, energetic efficiency (assessed by the amount of ATP used/power output sustained) is substantially higher than in euthyroid or hyperthyroid states; that is, muscle work is more efficient in hypothyroidy, and this advantage is particularly large and easily measurable at submaximal work rates, in both animals (Leijendekker et al., 1983) and humans (Wiles et al., 1979). Although the lactate paradox, per se, has not been described in this physiological state, the so-called anaerobic threshold is lowered in hyperthyroid patients (Kendrick et al., 1988), which suggests that, for a given level of work, reduced lactate accumulation and hypothyroidy may well be correlated. Furthermore, it is known that perfused hindlimb preparations in hypothyroid rats produce less lactate in response to a given stimulus than do muscles from euthyroid or hyperthyroid individuals (van Hardeveld and Clausen, 1984). Since, additionally, there is well-established evidence of compromised thyroid hormone function in high-altitude-adapted animals (see Heath and Williams, 1981), we are encouraged to hypothesize that muscle function in Quechuas behaves as if it were modestly hypothyroid. Because of the variety of critical roles played by thyroid hormones (van Hardeveld, 1986), and because total thyroxine ($T_4$), triiodothyronine ($T_3$), and thyroid-stimulating hormone (TSH) concentrations in the plasma of Quechuas are in the normal range (Hochachka et al., 1991), we believe that the only way the energetic advantages of hypothyroidy could be reaped at the level of working muscles without seriously compromising other thyroid functions would be through *down regulation of muscle responsiveness (or sensitivity) to thyroid hormones*. In such an event, muscles of Andean natives could behave as if they were in a hypothyroid environment, even if plasma supplies of $T_4$ and $T_3$ were in the normal or near-normal range, a situation, in fact, commonly found in thermogenic tissues under conditions of thyroid-mediated calorigenesis (Bianco and Silva, 1988). Although muscular fatigue is a well-known leading symptom in hypothyroid patients, it is noteworthy that the metabolic activation caused by cold exposure in Quechuas is measurably blunted compared with Caucasian lowlanders (the metabolic activation rate is reduced by about half; Little and Hanna, 1978). Although unexplained in the original study, this result is understandable and, indeed, is predictable on the basis of our model because of the crucial role played by thyroid hormones in cold-stimulated calorigenesis. Finally, if the reduced thyroid sensitivity extends not only to skeletal and cardiac muscle, but also to smooth muscle, we would anticipate modified vasoconstrictor and vasodilator responses. These, in fact, are known: First, in our studies (Hochachka et al., unpublished data) we observed that in response to hypoxia, the muscles of Quechuas seem to be relatively better oxygenated than in lowlanders; this result is interpreted to indicate a reduced responsiveness to exercise-induced catecholamines owing to reduced thyroid sensitivity of the smooth muscle of arterioles (Henley et al., 1987). Second, hypoxia-induced hypertension, a potentially serious medical problem in lowlanders during prolonged exposure to high altitude, is known to be attenuated in high-altitude-adapted people and may well be attributable, at least in part, to reduced thyroid sensitivity of pulmonary arterial smooth muscle (Henley and Tucker, 1987; Henley et al., 1987).

If, for heuristic reasons, we assume that muscle work in Andean natives is energetically more efficient (down regulation of $T_3$ sensitivity need not be assumed), we are still left with the question of mechanisms allowing improved efficiency. This problem is not yet fully resolved either in animals models or in humans, but we consider that the most plausible possibility involves the coupling efficiency of sarcoplasmic reticulum (SR) $Ca^{2+}$ ATPases. In hypothyroidy, the $Ca^{2+}$–ATP coupling stoichiometry approaches 2, the theoretical maximum, whereas in euthyroidy and, especially, in hyperthyroidy, it falls drastically; as a result more ATP must be expended for this critical function in muscle contraction–relaxation cycles (for literature in this area, see van Hardeveld, 1986). Since $Ca^{2+}$ cycling between the SR and the cytosol during contraction–relaxation cycles may require 30–50% of the cell ATP being turned over during muscle work in the euthyroid state, decreasing this energy cost by favoring energetically efficient $Ca^{2+}$ ATPase isoforms could greatly increase muscle work efficiency in Quechua natives. Currently, however, we are aware of no data on thyroid hormone-binding capacities, $T_4$ metabolism, or $Ca^{2+}$ ATPase stoichiometries for muscles of Andean natives, so whether or not these represent sites of bio-chemical adaptation to high altitude remain open questions.

## V. The Interplay Between Time and Adaptation

The data summarized in the foregoing make it clear that the adaptive responses available to Quechua natives when exposed to hypoxia depend upon the time available for the response and emphasize a biological principle well known to comparative physiologists and biochemists; namely, that there is an intricate interplay between time and adaptational strategies (options or mechanisms) available to organisms when facing specific hostile environmental parameters. Biologists define long-term or phylogenetic adaptations to a given environmental parameter as processes that compensate for its direct effects and that are so selectively advantageous that they may become developmentally or genetically fixed and unchangeable. For hypobaric hypoxia, a *long-term adaptation* is defined as any structure or function contributing to circumventing or compensating for reduced amounts of $O_2$ in the inspired air. Our study identifies several such characteristics. These include relatively elevated lung diffusion capacity (Jones et al., 1991), improved energetic efficiency of working muscles, and, as a result, closer energy demand–energy supply coupling, reduced perturbation of high-energy phosphate metabolites and $pH_i$ during work to fatigue, and the lactate paradox (low levels of lactate for any given work rate despite reduced $O_2$ in the inspired air). Additionally, we expect that reduced responsiveness of skeletal (cardiac and smooth) muscles to thyroid hormone may be included in this list of properties or functions that represent stable high-altitude adaptations. Any such characteristics expressed in Quechuas imply that their selective advantages are large enough to have become widespread in the population within the 300 or so generations through which these people have been known to be living at 3000 m or higher (Baker, 1976). Furthermore, if the return to normoxia does not impose an alternate and severe selective pressure, *such characteristics should, by definition, be expressed whether the individuals bearing them are living at high or at low altitude* (i.e., they should not deacclimate). That may be why comparisons of indigenous highland natives to those recently arrived at sea level, as is often done in studies of this problem (see Baker, 1976) may not yield any useful information.

A point of emphasis is that these adaptations need not be universal solutions to high-altitude problems faced by humans and, therefore, may not be found in other high-altitude populations, such as those in the Himalayas or in highland regions of Africa. The possibility *that a given environmental problem can be solved differently by different animals is widely recognized in biology* (see Hochachka and Somero, 1984), but this seems to be largely overlooked in research on high-altitude adaptation in humans. Our impression is that attempts at directly comparing high-altitude populations in widely separated geographic regions should be made with these possibilities in mind.

Whereas the foregoing characteristics seem to be genetically or developmentally fixed, several responses are more plastic and can be adjusted through acclimation. In biology, *acclimations* (or acclimatizations) are defined as short- or intermediate-term mechanisms that compensate for direct effects of the environment. Biologists usually define acclimations as operating within time frames that are fractions of the life cycle of organisms in question. With respect to hypobaric hypoxia, an acclimation is defined as any structural or functional adjustment that occurs within a fraction of the organism's life cycle that compensates for the debilitating effects of reduced $O_2$ availability. Usually, acclimatory mechanisms operate over periods of days to weeks (see Prosser, 1986; Hochachka and Somero, 1984). Any such processes available to Quechuas on transition from high to low altitudes (or vice versa) would be expected (1) to be expressed over a time course of days to weeks and (2) to be reversible. An example of this kind of adaptation involves the changes in hematocrit or red blood cell mass. As reported previously in numerous studies, the hematocrit changes as a function of altitude exposure time, reaching a stable new value over a period of a few weeks (see Winslow and Monge, 1987). We observed the same phenomenon (McKenzie et al., 1991), but the studies now available are not detailed enough to know if the kinetics of the response are the same in Quechuas as they are in lowlanders. As indicated in Figure 1, the *acclimatory potential is in theory itself under genetic control. Hence, it is not surprising to find that a metabolic characteristic, such as the lactate paradox, is reversible in lowlanders, but is seemingly fixed in Quechua natives.*

Finally, another way in which Quechua natives differ from lowlanders is

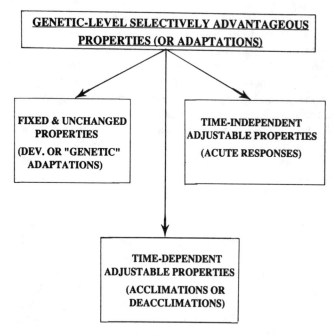

**Figure 1** A diagrammatic summary of the interplay between time and adaptational processes allowing "tuning-up" or adjusting various links in the path of $O_2$ from the atmosphere to mitochondria to compensate for reduced $O_2$ availability in the inspired air. The diagram emphasizes that all three time courses of adaptation ultimately are, at least to a degree, genetically based. That may be one reason why lowlander Caucasians may differ from Andean natives in their responses to acute hypoxic exposure, in their capacities to acclimate over periods of days to weeks, and in their long-term relatively fixed adaptations. For example, in lowlanders, the lactate paradox behaves like a metabolic acclimation, whereas in Quechuas, it appears to be a metabolic adaptation, largely unchangeable, presumably because its genetic components are fixed through long-term processes of natural selection. The diagram also emphasizes that, in principle, the same biological endpoint or goal—compensating for reduced $O_2$ availability—could be achieved in various ways. This implies that not all high-altitude-adapted people necessarily solve the hypoxia problems of their high-altitude environment the same way and that comparisons of peoples indigenous to geographically widely separated high-altitude regions should be made with caution.

in their responses to acute hypoxia. Biologists define *acute adaptations* as those that can be turned on essentially instantaneously as mechanisms compensating for environmental change. Here, the time frame is usually considered to be seconds to minutes (hours at the most), only an infinitely small fraction of the organism's life cycle. For hypobaric hypoxia, biologists would define an acute adaptation as one that rapidly compensates for reduced $O_2$ availability. The Pasteur effect (activation of anaerobic glycolysis to make up for any energy deficit due to $O_2$ lack) might be considered an acute adaptation. Any given function showing acute adaptation in Quechuas by definition would not be seriously perturbed on transition from normoxia to hypoxia (or would be perturbed less than in lowlanders). The lactate paradox is an interesting acute adaptational difference between Quechuas and Caucasian lowlanders: lowlanders cannot express the lactate paradox in response to a brief exposure to hypoxia, whereas, in contrast, Quechuas express it at any stage from brief to long-term exposure to hypoxia. Similarly, the two groups differ strikingly in the way brief hypoxia influences maximum aerobic metabolism: In lowlanders, exposure to hypoxia equivalent to the La Raya atmosphere depresses $\dot{V}o_2$max by about 30%, whereas in Quechuas, the depression is one-third to one-fifth as large (Hochachka et al., 1991). As in the acclimatory response (see Fig. 1), the genetic framework determines the acute adaptational response to hypoxia (lowlanders being some two- to fivefold more sensitive to hypoxia than are Quechuas). Thus, it is evident that, although it is common to refer only to the first of the foregoing categories as true genetic adaptation, this is just a convenient shorthand. The biochemical components allowing acclimations or acute adaptations are, themselves, determined genetically (Hochachka and Somero, 1984). In this sense, acute adaptations and acclimations are genetically based, just as are long-term or phylogenetic adaptations; the big difference is that they are, by definition, more plastic. For hypobaric hypoxia, the kind and range of acute or acclimatory adaptations possible in Quechua natives may be different from those in lowlanders, presumably because these mechanisms, per se, are genetically determined.

## Acknowledgments

This paper is dedicated to Kjell Johansen, friend, colleague, and coexpeditionary biologist. As fate would have it, just before his death, Kjell Johansen and I were discussing a cooperative research program on the physiology and biochemistry of high-altitude hypoxia in animals indigenous to both lowlands and high-mountain environments. The work I have summarized in this essay is a logical extension of our original plans and is the main reason I have chosen it as the data set around which to explore the nature of physiological and biochemical adaptation.

This work was supported by NSERC (Canada) in grants to PWH; additional support was provided by MRC (Canada) to P. S. Allen, G. O. Matheson, and D. C. McKenzie and by AHFMR (Alberta) to G. O. Matheson and P. S. Allen. The work would not have been possible without the enthusiastic cooperation of our six Quechua volunteers and our collaborators in Peru: Julio Sumar-Kalinowski and C. Monge.

## References

Baker, P. T. (1976). The adaptive fitness of high-altitude populations. In *The Biology of High-Altitude Peoples*. Cambridge, Cambridge University Press, pp. 317–350.

Bianco, A. C., and Silva, J. E. (1988). Cold exposure rapidly induces virtual saturation of brown adipose tissue nuclear $T_3$ receptors. *Am. J. Physiol.*, **255**:E496–E503.

Cerretelli, P., Veicsteinas, A., and Marconi, C. (1982). Anaerobic metabolism at high altitude: The lactacid mechanism. In *High Altitude Physiology and Medicine*. Edited by W. Brendel and R. A. Zink. New York, Springer Verlag, pp. 94–102.

Connett, R. J., and Honig, C. R. (1989). Regulation of $O_2$ consumption in red muscle: Do current biochemical hypotheses fit in vivo data. *Am. J. Physiol.*, **256**:R898–R906.

Cruze-Coke, R. (1976). A genetic description of high-altitude populations. In *The Biology of High-Altitude Peoples*. Cambridge, Cambridge University Press, pp. 47–63.

Edwards, H. T. (1936). Lactic acid in rest and work at high altitude. *Am. J. Physiol.*, **116**:367–375.

Endler, J. A. (1986). *Natural Selection in the Wild*. Princeton, Princeton University Press.

Fedde, M. R., Faradi, F. M., Kilgore, D. L., Cardinett, G. H. III, and Chatterjee, A. (1985). Cardiopulmonary adaptations in birds for exercise at high altitude. In *Circulation, Respiration, and Metabolism*. Edited by R. Gilles. Berlin, Springer-Verlag, pp. 148–163.

Green, H. J., Sutton, J., Young, P., Cymerman, A., and Houston, C. S. (1989). Operation Everest II: Muscle energetics during maximal exhaustive exercise. *J. Appl. Physiol.*, **66**:142–150.

Heath, D., and Williams, D. R. (1981). *Man at High Altitude*. London, Churchill–Livingstone, pp. 1–347.

Henley, W. N., and Tucker, A. (1987). Hypoxic moderation of systemic hypertension in the spontaneously hypertensive rat. *Am. J. Physiol.*, **252**:R554–R561.

Henley, W. N., Tucker, A., Tran, T. N., and Stager, J. M. (1987). The thyroid and hypoxic moderation of systemic hypertension in the spontaneously hypertensive rat. *Aviat. Space Environ. Med.*, **58**:559–567.

Hochachka, P. W. (1988a). The nature of evolution and adaptation: Resolving the unity–diversity paradox. *Can. J. Zool.*, **66**:1146–1152.

Hochachka, P. W. (1988b). The lactate paradox: Analysis of underlying mechanisms. *Ann. Sports Med.*, **4**:146–151.

Hochachka, P. W., and Guppy, M. (1987). *Metabolic Arrest and the Control of Biological Time*. Cambridge, Mass., Harvard University Press, pp. 1–227.

Hochachka, P. W., and Somero, G. N. (1984). *Biochemical Adaptation*. Princeton, Princeton University Press, pp. 1–537.

Hochachka, P. W., Stanley, C., Matheson, G. O., McKenzie, D. C., Allen, P. S., and Parkhouse, W. S. (1991). Metabolic and work efficiencies during exercise in Andean natives. *J. Appl. Physiol.,* **70**:1720–1730.

Hurtado, A. (1964). Animals in high altitudes: Resident man. In *Handbook of Physiology,* Section 4, Adaptation to the Environment. Washington, D.C., American Physiological Society, pp. 843–860.

Johansen, K. (1987). The August Krogh Lecture: The world as a laboratory. Physiological insights from nature's experiments. In *Advances in Physiological Research.* Edited by H. McLennan, J. R. Ledsome, C. H. S. McIntosh, and D. R. Jones. New York, Plenum Press, pp. 377–396.

Jones, R., Man, P. S. F., Matheson, G. O., Parkhouse, W. S., Allen, P. S., and Hochachka, P. W. (1990). Lung volumes and regional ventilation and perfusion in Andean natives after 2 and 37 days at low altitude. *Resp. Physiol.,* (in press).

Kendrick, A. H., O'Reilly, J. F., and Laszlo, G. (1988). Lung function and exercise performance in hyperthyroidism before and after treatment. *Q. J. Med.,* **88**:615–627.

Kollias, J., Buskirk, E. R., Akers, R. F., Prokop, E. K., Baker, P. T., and Picon-Reategui (1968). Work capacity of long-time residents and newcomers to altitude. *J. Appl. Physiol.,* **24**:792–799.

Krebs, H. (1975). The August Krogh principle: For many problems there is an animal on which it can be most conveniently studied. *J. Exp. Zool.,* **194**:221–226.

Krogh, A. (1929). The progress in physiology. *Am. J. Physiol.,* **90**:243–251.

Leijendekker, W. K., van Hardeveld, C., and Kassenaar, A. A. A. H. (1983). The influence of the thyroid state on energy turnover during tetanic stimulation in the fast-twitch (mixed-type) muscle of rats. *Metabolism,* **32**:615–621.

Little, M. A., and Hanna, J. M. (1976). The response of high altitude populations to cold and other stresses. In *The Biology of High-Altitude Peoples.* Edited by P. T. Baker. Cambridge, Cambridge University Press, pp. 251–298.

Matheson, G. O., Allen, P. S., Hanstock, C., Gheorghiu, D., Ellinger, D. C., McKenzie, D. C., Stanley, C., Parkhouse, W. S., and Hochachka, P. W. (1991). Skeletal muscles metabolism and work capacity: A $^{31}$P NMR study of Andean natives and lowlanders. *J. Appl. Physiol.,* **70**:1963–1970.

McKenzie, C. D., Goodman, L. S., Davidson, B., Nath, C. C., Matheson, G. O., Parkhouse, W. S., Hochachka, P. W., Allen, P. S., Stanley, C., and Amman, W. (1991). Functional and structural cardiovascular adaptations in high altitude adapted natives after 6 weeks exposure to sea level. *J. Appl. Physiol.,* **70**:2650–2653.

Monge, C. (1948). *Acclimatization in the Andes.* Baltimore, Johns Hopkins University Press.

Oelz, O., Howald, H., Di Prampero, P. E., Hoppeler, H., Claassen, H., Jenni, R., Buhlmann, A., Ferretti, G., Bruckner, J.-C., Veicsteinas, A., Gussoni, M., and Cerretelli, P. (1986). Physiological profile of world-class high-altitude climbers. *J. Appl. Physiol.,* **60**:1734–1742.

Prosser, C. L. (1986). *Adaptational Biology: Molecules to Organisms.* New York, John Wiley & Sons, pp. 1–784.

Schluter, D., Price, T. D., and Grant, P. R. (1985). Ecological character displacement in Darwin's finches. *Science,* **227**:1056–1059.

Sutton, J. R., Jones, N. L., and Pugh, L. G. C. E. (1983). Exercise at altitude. *Annu. Rev. Physiol.,* **45**:427–437.

Sutton, J. R., Reeves, J. T., Wagner, P. D., Groves, B. M., Cymerman, A., Malconian, M. K., Rock, P. B., Young, P. M., Walter, S. D., and Houston, C. S. (1988). Operation Everest II: Oxygen transport during exercise at extreme simulated altitude. *J. Appl. Physiol.,* **64**:1309–1321.

Taylor, C. R., Maloiy, G. M. O., Weibel, E. R., Langman, V. A., Kamau, J. M. Z., Seeherman, H. J., and Heglund, N. C. (1980). Design of mammalian respiratory system. III. Scaling maximum aerobic capacity to body mass: Wild and domestic mammals. *Respir. Physiol.,* **44**:25–37.

Taylor, C. R., Karas, R. H., Weibel, E. R., and Hoppeler, H. (1987). Adaptive variation in the mammalian respiratory system in relation to energetic demand: II. Reaching the limits to oxygen flow. *Respir. Physiol.,* **69**:7–26.

van Hardeveld, C. (1986). Effects of thyroid hormones on oxygen consumption, heat production, and energy economy. In *Thyroid Hormone Metabolism.* Edited by G. Hennemann. New York, Marcel Dekker, pp. 579–608.

van Hardeveld, C., and Clausen, T. (1984). Effect of thyroid status on $K^+$-stimulated metabolism and $^{45}Ca$ exchange in rat skeletal muscle. *Am. J. Physiol.,* **247**:E421–E430.

Way, A. B. (1976). Exercise capacity of high altitude Peruvian Quechua Indians migrant to low altitude. *Hum. Biol.,* **48**:175–191.

West, J. B. (1983). Climbing Mt. Everest without oxygen: An analysis of exercise during extreme hypoxia. *Respir. Physiol.,* **52**:265–279.

West, J. B. (1986). Lactate during exercise at extreme altitudes. *Fed. Proc.,* **45**:2953–2957.

Wiles, C. M., Young, A., Jones, D. A., and Edwards, R. H. T. (1979). Muscle relaxation rate, fibre-type composition, and energy turnover in hyper- and hypothyroid patients. *Clin. Sci.,* **57**:375–384.

Winslow, R. M., and Monge, C. (1987). *Hypoxia, Polycythemia, and Chronic Mountain Sickness.* Baltimore, Johns Hopkins University Press, pp. 1–231.

# 3

# Aspects of Poikilotherm Myocardial Function During Hypoxia

**HANS GESSER**

University of Aarhus
Aarhus, Denmark

## I. Introduction

Cellular adaptation of vertebrate heart muscle to conditions such as oxygen availability is of particular interest, since uninterrupted cardiac function is of paramount importance to the animal.

This paper addresses the cellular mechanisms underlying the effects of oxygen lack and inhibited cellular respiration on the contractile activity in myocardial tissue, with emphasis on the situation in poikilothermic vertebrates. It should remembered, however, that reactions seen in isolated tissue or cell preparations are generally strongly modified in the heart in vivo (e.g., Farrell, 1984). Furthermore, a study of cellular mechanisms frequently requires that the experimental perturbations incurred (for instance, hypoxia) are exaggerated, compared with the situation in vivo. The present review extends previous reviews with a similar scope (Gesser, 1985; Poupa, 1976).

## II. Causes of Myocardial Oxygen Lack

In adult mammals and birds, the myocardium is considered to be almost exclusively aerobic. Neonatal mammalian myocardium shows increased tolerance to oxygen lack (e.g., Jarmakani et al., 1979), which may be of importance during parturition, when gas exchange is severely restricted. Furthermore, cardiac hypoxia probably occurs regularly in diving species of mammals and birds. In other species, however, during adulthood, hypoxia is almost exclusively associated with pathological conditions. This situation may be radically different in poikilothermic vertebrates, for both anatomical and environmental reasons. Apart from the thin endothelium of the inside of the heart wall, the tissue of the heart of homoiotherms consists of densely packed cells supplied by a well-developed coronary system. In the poikilotherm heart, however, the fraction of the cardiac wall consisting of this "compact"-type tissue, which is supplied by coronaries carrying blood directly from the gas exchanger, lungs, or gills, varies from about zero, as in the flounder, to about 70%, as in big eye tuna (Santer and Greer Walker, 1980). Within one species, the Atlantic salmon, it varies from about zero to 30% depending on the developmental state (Poupa et al., 1974). The rest of the heart wall consists of so-called spongy tissue (i.e., a network of thin trabeculae). This tissue lacks coronaries and depends on blood pumped through the heart lumen for its supply of $O_2$, and for removal of waste products. Accordingly, it is nourished by systemic venous blood. Fishes show this particularly clearly because of their single-circuit circulation in which the heart is placed just before the gills. Hence, somewhat paradoxically from a functional point of view, the $O_2$ supply to the spongy part of the heart should relate inversely to the activity level of the animal. The $O_2$ supply of the heart muscle may, however, be improved by circulatory shunts carrying arterial, well-oxygenated blood (Randall, 1985).

The cardiac $O_2$ supply is, however, also likely to vary in response to environmental conditions. Water breathers, in particular, may be exposed to low and varying $Po_2$ values (Dejours, 1975). For instance, the flounder may be exposed to values as low as 20 torr (Muus, 1967). Furthermore, it may burrow to depths of 15 cm in sand, which probably further lowers $Po_2$ (Fletcher, 1975). Although adaptations exist for extracting and delivering $O_2$ to the cells under these conditions (Steffensen et al., 1982; Weber and de Wilde, 1975), cellular $O_2$ availability is still likely to be lower than in animals exposed to atmospheric $Po_2$. However, in some cases, it is unclear if any adaptive value can be ascribed to a high myocardial tolerance to oxygen lack. Hence, it is unclear why the tolerances recorded for reptiles appear to be higher than for any other poikilotherm group (Poupa, 1976; Gesser and Poupa, 1978).

## III.  Metabolic Capacities and Contractility During Hypoxia

In most myocardial preparations, oxygen lack or an inhibition of cell respiration, for instance, by cyanide, is followed by a decrease in twitch force or contraction. Simultaneously, resting tension tends to rise (contracture), owing to interaction between actin and myosin in diastole. Figure 1 depicts the changes in twitch

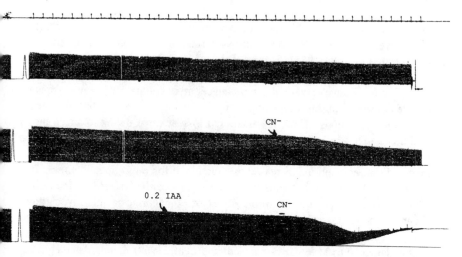

**Figure 1** Isometric force development of ventricle tissue of rainbow trout during inhibition of cellular respiration by 2-mM sodium-cyanide either alone or in combination with 0.2-mM sodium iodoacetate (IAA). Three strips were isolated from one heart, arranged for recording of isometric force, and stimulated electrically to contraction at 0.2 Hz, in three parallel setups (e.g., Purup-Hansen and Gesser, 1987). One served as control (upper trace), one was exposed to cyanide (middle trace) and one to iodoacetate and cyanide (bottom trace). Iodoacetate was applied 15 min before cyanide.

force and diastolic tension that typically follow upon impairment of cellular energy liberation. Apart from the degree and type of metabolic impairment imposed, the extent of these effects depends, as may be expected, largely on the species (e.g., Poupa, 1976). This can be illustrated by the situation in marine fishes, for which the duration of a full aerobic block required to lower isometrically recorded twitch force by 50% in isolated ventricular strips varied from about 5 to 50 min. During these periods, no significant contracture appeared. Not surprisingly, the decrease in twitch force was inversely related to the ratio of the capacities of glycolytic and oxidative phosphorylation, assessed in terms of the activity of pyruvate kinase and cytochrome oxidase, respectively. This ratio was taken to reflect the extent to which an inhibited oxidative energy liberation could be counterbalanced by glycolysis (Gesser and Poupa, 1974).

## IV.  Regulation of Contractility During Hypoxia

The foregoing result could suggest that glycolysis is maximally activated following an inhibition of oxidative phosphorylation. If this were so, the positive inotropic effects, for example, of catecholamines or of elevations in extracellular calcium concentrations ($Ca_o$), should be strongly suppressed during such an inhibition. This seems to be true for the mammalian myocardium, in which these effects were much smaller under anaerobic than under aerobic conditions (e.g., Nielsen and Gesser, 1983). However, in the poikilotherm heart, the situation can be quite different.

The force developed by the trout and eel myocardium can be approximately doubled by epinephrine (adrenaline), not only under aerobic, but also under anaerobic, conditions. Thus, the fractional loss of force owing to anaerobiosis is little changed by epinephrine (Gesser et al., 1982). This situation may be modified by other control factors, however. In similar experiments on the flounder myocardium, epinephrine increased the fraction of force lost upon hypoxia. This accentuated loss of force seems to be due to myocardial release of adenosine, which lowers the positive inotropic effect of epinephrine in this myocardium (Lennard and Huddart, 1989). Since many situations involving oxygen lack result in an elevated catecholamine level, and since mammalian heart muscle is irreversibly damaged by severe hypoxia (Jennings et al., 1969), Lennard and Huddart (1989) interpreted this effect as a mechanism to counteract an imbalance between energy demand and energy liberation during oxygen lack. However, this mechanism may not be present in all species, as it was not observed in trout and eel.

The positive inotropic action of epinephrine depends largely on an enhanced influx of $Ca^{2+}$ during excitation. As should be expected, an elevation of $Ca_o$ had an effect similar to epinephrine on trout myocardium in which cell respiration had been blocked, except that the force lost, in relative terms, was somewhat lower in 5 mM than in 1 mM $Ca^{2+}$ (Gesser and Höglund, 1988). Thus, the positive inotropic effect of elevated $Ca_o$ was larger under anaerobic than aerobic conditions. The situation was different for the rat myocardium. Here, in contrast with that under aerobic conditions, the anaerobic force development was not substantially stimulated by an elevation of $Ca_o$ from 1.25 to 5 mM (Nielsen and Gesser, 1983).

The stimulation of anaerobic force development of trout myocardium following elevation of $Ca_o$ is energetically supported by an enhanced glycolytic rate, as judged from lactate production (Nielsen and Gesser, 1984a). This indicates that glycolysis is not necessarily fully activated upon blockage of the aerobic metabolism. Instead, there seems to be a reserve capacity, which is activated by catecholamines or elevations of $Ca_o$. Together, these observations show that many poikilotherms are able to control force development, even during severe hypoxia.

Catecholamines and $Ca_o$ are of particular interest with regard to the effect of oxygen lack on myocardial tissue. For instance, oxidative phosphorylation of the spongy tissue of the fish heart is likely to be reduced because of oxygen lack in situations that require a high physical activity involving an elevated catecholamine level.

Furthermore, evidence exists that the $Ca_o$ is increased following hypoxia or intense physical exercise. The diving turtle provides a striking example of this, as its plasma $Ca^{2+}$ concentration shows a tenfold increase under prolonged periods of severe hypoxia. It should be noted, though, that most of the $Ca^{2+}$ so released to the plasma is complexed with lactate (Jackson and Heisler, 1982). Furthermore, the total plasma $Ca^{2+}$ of several vertebrates with bony skeletons has been reported to be augmented after intense physical activity. Thus, the plasma levels of $Ca^{2+}$ in trout increased by about 70% (Ruben and Bennett, 1981). Some controversy, however, exists. In another study, the $Ca^{2+}$ activity (i.e., the "free" $Ca^{2+}$) of trout blood plasma increased by 16% as a result of physical exhaustion, whereas the total plasma $Ca^{2+}$ level remained unchanged. Neither the activity nor the total concentration of plasma $Ca^{2+}$ was significantly affected by sustained exercise, acidosis, or hypoxia (Andreasen, 1985). The reason for this difference is obscure, although it can be speculated that some subspecific taxa may contain larger stores of mobilizable $Ca^{2+}$ than others. Even though it is still unclear whether or not in vivo changes in extracellular $Ca^{2+}$ occur, experimental changes of $Ca_o$ provide a mean of changing both the $Ca^{2+}$ uptake during excitation and the $Ca^{2+}$ content of intracellular structures taking part in the excitation–contraction (E–C) coupling. This is of physiological interest, since the force developed by the heart in vivo is regulated primarily by the amount of $Ca^{2+}$ in this coupling.

## V. Calcium-Activated Force and the Cellular Energy State

Anaerobic levels of adenosine triphosphate (ATP) and phosphocreatine (PCr) in the trout myocardium were not significantly changed by elevation of $Ca_o$, in spite of increased contractility (Nielsen and Gesser, 1984a; Purup-Hansen and Gesser, 1987). Unchanged ATP and PCr levels suggest that the enhanced glycolysis following increased calcium availability is due to a direct effect of $Ca^{2+}$ on the glycolytic enzymes, rather than to the classical Pasteur effect, which involves a lowered cytoplasmic energy state. It is known that $Ca^{2+}$ has a direct influence on the activity of several enzymes implicated in the cellular energy liberation. The presence of such effects under aerobic conditions is indicated by the finding that both the PCr level and force development were higher at 5 than at 1.25 mM $Ca^{2+}$ (Purup-Hansen and Gesser, 1987).

Typically, hypoxia induces only a marginal drop in ATP, although force development is drastically depressed (e.g., Purup-Hansen and Gesser, 1987). This suggests that developed force does not directly relate to the cellular energy state. Here, however, the problems associated with an assessment of the energy state should be discussed. It has long been known that myocardial force may fall drastically as a result of oxygen deprivation, whereas there is no substantial change in the cellular ATP level (e.g., Kammermaier et al., 1982). This finding leads to the idea that the energy liberated on hydrolysis of ATP not only depends on the concentration of "free" ATP, but also on that of "free" ADP and inorganic phosphate ($P_i$) according to the equation:

$$G = G_o - R \cdot T \cdot \ln (ATP/ADP \cdot P_i) \tag{1}$$

(e.g., Kammermaier et al., 1982).

The calculation of the last term is complicated because the substances involved occur in the mitochondria as well as in the cytoplasm. Furthermore, only a minor fraction of cellular ADP is free (i.e., not bound to different structures), and it cannot be measured directly by any available method. Related to these circumstances, the cytoplasmic phosphorylation potential was calculated from the creatine kinase (CK)-catalyzed reaction: PCr + ADP + $H^+ \rightarrow$ Cr + ATP, which is thought to be close to equilibrium under most (Matthews et al., 1982), but not all (Saks et al., 1984), physiological conditions. Moreover, PCr and Cr are localized almost exclusively in the cytoplasm. If one assumes that the CK reaction is in equilibrium and that pH is unchanged, the cytoplasmic ratio of ATP/ADP should be proportional to PCr/Cr.

In one approach to the problem of assessing the concentration of "free" phosphate in the cytoplasm, it is assumed that this phosphate stems mainly from hydrolysis of PCr. Therefore, as an approximation, its concentration can be set equal to that of Cr, that is $Cr_{tot}$ − PCr (e.g., Kammermaier et al., 1982; Meyer, 1988). As a result $\ln(ATP/ADP \cdot Pi)$ in the cytoplasm can be assessed by $\ln[PCr/(Cr_{tot} - PCr)^2]$. This expression, in turn, varies approximately linearly with the PCr value, when the fraction of creatine that is phosphorylated (i.e., $PCr/Cr_{tot}$) is between 0.7 and 0.3 (Meyer, 1988). This interval covers the physiologically important values reasonably well.

With an aerobic block, an increase in $Ca_o$ will stimulate twitch force development, in spite of an unchanged PCr level, and thus, presumably, in spite of an unchanged cytoplasmic phosphorylation potential. This effect of $Ca_o$ was also seen in trout myocardial tissue subjected to full inhibition of both glycolysis and oxidative phosphorylation. Despite that no rephosphorylation of the high-energy phosphates, ATP and PCr, was possible, an elevation of $Ca_o$ from 1.25 to 5 mM was followed by a significant augmentation of the twitch force developed at a given PCr level. An increased $Ca^{+2}$ availability raises the fraction of actin sites that can partake in cross-bridge formation. Conceivably, therefore, the system at a given phosphorylation potential is pushed to an enhanced force development (Purup-Hansen and Gesser, 1987).

## VI.  Contracture Under a Depressed Metabolism

Suppression of cellular energy liberation, as observed under inhibition of oxidative phosphorylation, is frequently associated with an elevation of the resting tension (see Fig. 1) or a shortening of the resting length. Measurement of heat production strongly suggests that formation of rigor complexes is the main cause, as the heat associated with a diastolic tension raised by applying a metabolic inhibition is considerably lower than that produced as a result of $K^+$ depolarization (Holubarsch et al., 1982). It is, however, unclear whether the formation of rigor complexes is the sole reason, or whether contracture can also be attributed to inefficient removal of cytoplasmic $Ca^{2+}$ during diastole. Measurements of intracellular $Ca^{2+}$ activity have provided conflicting results. Smith and Allen (1988) found that the increase in resting tension in ferret papillary muscle, following a total metabolic block, occurred without any change in cellular $Ca^{2+}$ activity as measured with aequoerin. At variance with this, Eisner et al. (1989), working with isolated rat heart myocytes, found that metabolic inhibition elicited contracture, which was preceded by augmented cellular $Ca^{2+}$ activity, as measured with Fura-2. At the beginning of its development (but not later), the contracture was diminished when extracellular $Ca^{2+}$ was removed. Similar results have been recorded by Barry et al. (1987) with cultured chick myocardial cells. In particular, it was noted that the contracture could not be exclusively related to an augmented $Ca^{2+}$ activity. These investigators, therefore, suggested that the hydrolysis of ATP and, thereby, the formation of rigor complexes, are enhanced by, but not unconditionally dependent on, an increased cellular $Ca^{2+}$ activity.

For the trout myocardium subjected to a full metabolic block, the twitch force was stimulated by an elevation of $Ca_o$ from 1.25 to 5 mM. This indicates that more $Ca^{2+}$ enters and, accordingly, has to be handled by the cell. In spite of this, however, the resting tension at a given PCr was not affected by the difference in $Ca_o$. Therefore, it appears that $Ca^{2+}$ regulation functions also at a substantially lowered cellular energy state (Purup-Hansen and Gesser, 1987).

The varying results for the effect of metabolic inhibitions are points of concern. Accordingly, some disagreement exists over the methods for measuring the cellular $Ca^{2+}$ activity (Eisner et al., 1989). Furthermore, and of more general interest, isolated cells and multicellular preparations appear to give qualitatively different results. This might be due to a difference in their energy demand and, consequently, in the rate of energy degradation, as well as in the extracellular diffusion conditions (Eisner et al., 1989).

## VII. Glycolysis and the Relationship Between Contractility and Energy

The relationship between force development and PCr level is influenced by $Ca_o$ and, thus, presumably by the amount of activator $Ca^{2+}$. As shown for trout heart, it is also influenced by glycolytic activity, but only at lowered PCr concentrations. Accordingly, the force development relative to the PCr concentration is not affected by an inhibition of glycolysis with iodoacetate, provided the cellular respiration is left intact, whereas it is lowered when cell respiration is partly or fully inhibited (Purup-Hansen and Gesser, 1987; Hartmund and Gesser, 1991). Assuming that PCr gives a reasonable estimate of the cytoplasmic phosphorylation potential, glycolysis appears to have positive inotropic effects that cannot be directly related to the cellular energy state.

The reason for this effect is unclear. Evidence for a compartmentalization of cellular energy liberation in such a way that glycolysis specifically supports membrane active transport processes comes particularly from studies of smooth muscle, but also from cardiac muscle (reviewed by Paul, 1989). Allen and Orchard (1983) found that, in ferret papillary muscle, the transient increase in intracellular $Ca^{2+}$ activity following excitation was not significantly affected by inhibition of cellular respiration, whereas it was strongly suppressed by concomitant glycolytic block. However, the results obtained with trout myocardium (Purup-Hansen and Gesser, 1987; Hartmund and Gesser, 1991) cannot immediately be interpreted in terms of cellular ion regulation, as the resting tension relative to the PCr level was strikingly higher in the presence than in the absence of a glycolytic block. Some caution should be exercised, though, since the significance of cellular ion balance for resting tension is unclear.

An effect of glycolytic inhibition, as noted in the trout heart, may also indicate that the CK-catalyzed reaction alone cannot counteract a decrease in ATP and an increase in ADP under conditions in which the PCr levels is lowered. The effect of glycolytic inhibition on the phosphorylation potential may be accentuated at the ATPase sites. Of the three substances (ATP, ADP, and $P_i$) that determine the phosphorylation potential, the free concentration of ADP is most likely to be the main cause for lowering this potential when the ATPase activity is enhanced. Because of its low value, the ADP concentration may have to increase severalfold to obtain a concentration gradient at which ADP will diffuse away from the ATPase sites at the same rate that it is formed. The ATP concentration may have to fall only by some small percentage to reach the new steady state at which influx balances consumption.

Hence, the basic assumption may not always be valid for using PCr to assess the cytoplasmic phosphorylation potential. This suggestion is supported by Saks et al. (1984), who presented evidence that a fall in PCr concentration (i.e., in the substrate level) lowers the creatine kinase activity to such an extent that the CK-catalyzed reaction no longer is in equilibrium. In a situation for which the alternative possibility of regenerating ATP in the cytoplasm (i.e., by glycolysis) is suppressed, the cytoplasmic phosphorylation potential when assessed as PCr, therefore, would be overestimated. In support of this interpretation, the level of ATP relative to that of PCr was lower with a combination of glycolytic and aerobic inhibition than with inhibition of the aerobic metabolism alone. Possibly, this effect could be due to an influence of glycolysis on intracellular pH (pH$_i$), but it was not changed significantly by attempts to vary the pH$_i$ by changes in P$CO_2$ (Hartmund and Gesser, 1991).

The relationship between the glycolytic capacity and the activity of CK in hearts from different vertebrates is now being examined in light of the observation that glycolysis is relatively more important to myocardial energy liberation in poikilotherms than in homoiotherms (Driedzic et al., 1987).

To conclude, the relationship between the contractile activity and the cellular energy state under different conditions is still obscure, mainly because the cytoplasmic phosphorylation potential cannot be directly measured because of the difficulty in determining free ADP.

Evidence exists, however, that the depressed contractility that commonly follows the onset of hypoxia is, to a large extent, due to those direct effects of phosphate metabolites that are not exerted through the phosphorylation potential.

## VIII. Hypoxic Contractility and the Importance of Inorganic Phosphate

A recent study (Godt and Nosek, 1989) shows that a reduction of energy released at the hydrolysis of ATP ($-G_{ATP}$), comparable with that occurring in hypoxic cardiac tissue, enhanced rather than inhibited $Ca^{2+}$-activated force development of rabbit cardiac muscle in which the cells had been "skinned" (i.e., made permeable for ATP, $Ca^{2+}$, and such). In contrast, however, the elevation of "free" phosphate (P$_i$) concentration associated with reduction of phosphorylation potential in the living cell may have, by itself, a substantial negative effect (Godt and Nosek, 1989). This is in accordance with previous studies also on skinned myocardial tissue. Increases in P$_i$ from zero to 20 mM depress maximal $Ca^{2+}$-activated force (i.e., the force at saturation levels of $Ca^{2+}$; Herzig and Rüegg, 1977; Kentish, 1986) and $Ca^{2+}$ sensitivity of the myofilament (Kentish, 1986). The mechanism for lowering $Ca^{2+}$ sensitivity is unclear (Kentish, 1986). For the maximal $Ca^{2+}$-activated force, P$_i$ is released upon the formation of those actin–myosin bonds that cause the main part of the force production. Evidence exists that this formation is reversible; hence, it should be diminished by a mass action effect upon an elevation of P$_i$ (Hibberd et al., 1985).

The P$_i$ in mammalian myocardium may raise by a factor of three to ten, within the range of 2–20 mM, upon several oxygen lack (e.g., Dawson, 1983). If we take the trout myocardium as an example of a poikilotherm species, the increase in P$_i$ should be about the same in relative terms, whereas the concentration range should be somewhat lower (Purup-Hansen and Gesser, 1987; Hartmund and Gesser, 1991). In intact tissue, P$_i$ commonly increases as a result of a hydrolysis of PCr, so that PCr decreases by a similar amount. This decrease will probably counteract the P$_i$ elevation effect. Thus, the negative effect of P$_i$

on force generation in skinned myocardial tissue is diminished at low PCr levels, probably because the lowered ATP regeneration by the CK reaction counteracts the breaking of cross-bridges. A fall in PCr concentration would, therefore, tend to offset the action of an elevated $P_i$ level (Mekhfi and Ventura-Clapier, 1988). For intact heart tissue, however, evidence has been obtained that the decreases in contractility following impairment of cellular metabolism are, to a large extent, due to an elevation of $P_i$ concentration (e.g., Marban and Kusuoka, 1987). On balance, therefore, it seems that elevation of $P_i$ concentration is a main cause of the lowered $Ca^{2+}$-activated force development that commonly follows hypoxia. In reducing cross-bridge formation (Hibberd et al., 1985), however, an elevated $P_i$ level should counteract the development of "rigor" contractures. Accordingly, the latter may still be a consequence of a decrease in the free energy of ATP hydrolysis. Hence, the causes of the decrease in twitch contraction and the tendency to contracture during hypoxia may differ.

## IX. Excitation–Contraction Coupling During Oxygen Lack

The decrease in energy released by ATP hydrolysis upon inhibition of cell respiration cannot be disregarded as a cause of the depressed twitch force development. Even though a decreased phosphorylation potential does not have to act directly on the contractile system, it may lower the $Ca^{2+}$ activity involved in the electromechanical coupling and, thereby, the activation of the contractile system.

Studies on preparations of mammalian myocardium provide evidence both for and against the possibility that the transient increase in the intracellular $Ca^{2+}$ activity following excitation is suppressed in step with oxidative phosphorylation. The shorter action potentials during severe oxygen lack support this hypothesis, suggesting that sarcolemmal influx of $Ca^{2+}$ during excitation is diminished (e.g., McDonald and MacLeod, 1973). In addition, it has been suggested that inhibition of cell respiration impairs the sarcoplasmic reticulum (SR) function and reduces the amount of activator $Ca^{2+}$ (Griese et al., 1988). Strong support was also provided by the finding of Eisner et al. (1989) that the effect of cyanide on the shortening of isolated rat heart cells upon excitation varied in parallel with the size of the transient increase in $Ca^{2+}$ levels. On the other hand, Allen and Orchard (1983) found that the transient $Ca^{2+}$ increase was not affected by inhibition of cell respiration in papillary muscles of rat, cat, and ferret.

A large positive inotropic action of elevated $Ca_o$ levels on the anaerobically working myocardium of trout or eel could be taken to indicate that the force development is lowered as a result of a reduction in the amount of activator $Ca^{2+}$. It should, however, be noted that aerobic force development at a given $Ca_o$ concentration is always higher than the anaerobic one (e.g., Nielsen and

Gesser, 1983), although the difference appears to be somewhat diminished as the $Ca_o$ level is elevated (Gesser and Höglund, 1988).

Other experiments with the myocardium of trout provide evidence that the force loss following inhibition of cell respiration is not due to an impairment of E–C coupling. Thus, the duration of the action potential was not influenced by inhibition of oxidative phosphorylation, except for an initial, transient decrease. A similar result was obtained when the action potential was recorded at high $K_o^+$ levels to block the initial $Na^+$ current and, thereby, accentuate its $Ca^{2+}$-dependent part. It should be noted that the corresponding twitch force fell by about 70% after inhibition of cell respiration. Neither does the SR appear to play a role in trout, since the force loss caused by a block of aerobic metabolism was not affected by either ryanodine or caffeine, which both inhibit SR function, but by different mechanisms (Gesser and Höglund, 1988).

The possibility that E–C coupling becomes more, instead of less, efficient upon inhibition of cellular respiration should also be considered, however. Thus, mitochondrial function is not solely restricted to energy liberation, but probably also extends to cellular $Ca^{2+}$ regulation. The mitochondria are not likely to contribute to the beat-to-beat regulation of $Ca^{2+}$ activity, but may influence the $Ca^{2+}$ content of cellular structures, which do so (Fry et al., 1987). The E–C coupling of the trout heart evidently does not depend crucially on SR function (Gesser and Höglund, 1988; Hove-Madsen and Gesser, 1989), but alternatively, may involve $Ca^{2+}$-binding sites at the inside of the sarcolemma (Lüllman and Peters, 1977). From this, it could be speculated that the amount of activator $Ca^{2+}$ bound to sarcolemmal stores is enlarged in the myocardium exposed to anaerobic conditions, when mitochondria are likely to release $Ca^{2+}$ (e.g., Jundt et al., 1975). As an alternative to being bound to the sarcolemma, for instance, the $Ca^{2+}$ released may remain free in the cytoplasm and cause an elevation of diastolic $Ca^{2+}$ activity. As suggested by Bers (1987), the elevation, although too small to activate the contractile system, may add to the transient increase in $Ca^{2+}$ activity upon excitation and, thereby, enhance force development.

In conclusion, no unequivocal statement can be made about the extent to which inhibition of cellular respiration affects force development through effects on cellular $Ca^{2+}$ regulation. The possibility exists that the extent varies among species.

Such a variation may relate to the SR as well as to sensitivity of the membrane channels to lowered ATP concentrations. For the latter possibility, the sarcolemma appears to contain a $K^+$ channel that is activated by decreases in ATP levels, shortening the action potential (Weiss and Lamp, 1987). Furthermore, it should be recalled that the heart of poikilotherms is more dependent on glycolysis than that of homoiotherms (Driedzic et al., 1987), and that this pathway has been suggested to be of specific importance to membrane processes (e.g., Paul, 1989). Hence, in addition to species differences, variations in response may depend on the experimental conditions that influence glycolytic activity and diffusion.

## X. Hypoxic Contractility and Its Dependence on Intracellular pH

The changes in contractility following inhibition of oxidative phosphorylation have frequently been ascribed to concomitant changes in $pH_i$. These changes may vary both in direction and magnitude, although most studies report a decrease (i.e., cellular acidification). The following reactions are particularly important for $pH_i$ of the hypoxic myocardium. Anaerobic glycolysis, by producing lactic acid and hydrolysis of ATP to ADP, tends to depress $pH_i$, whereas rephosphorylation of ADP to ATP at the cost of PCr consumes hydrogen ions and works in the opposite direction (e.g., Kushmerick, 1985).

Under anaerobic conditions, $pH_i$ should thus depend on these reactions, the cellular buffer capacity, and the mechanisms to transport hydrogen ions across the sarcolemma. Furthermore, by their influence on sarcolemmal concentration gradients, the extracellular diffusion conditions are of crucial importance to sarcolemmal transport processes. Hence, there are many possible explanations for the variations in $pH_i$ reported. Furthermore, attention should be paid to variations in power output and, thereby, in ATP hydrolysis (e.g., Eisner et al., 1989). However, the common observation with multicellular preparations, including atrial and ventricular strips, papillary muscles, and whole hearts, is that $pH_i$ falls or stays unchanged following inhibition of aerobic metabolism. A fall in $pH_i$ should, at least, primarily depress contractility. This follows from experiments with skinned myocardial preparations, which demonstrate that an elevation of the hydrogen ion activity lowers both the $Ca^{2+}$-sensitivity and the force developed at saturating $Ca^{2+}$ concentrations (Fabiato and Fabiato, 1978). Furthermore, cellular acidosis is likely to lower the cellular energy liberation insofar as it depresses glycolytic activity (e.g., Steenbergen et al., 1977). Most studies accordingly demonstrate a negative effect of acidosis on cardiac contractile activity under anaerobic conditions (e.g., Bing et al., 1973; Nielsen and Gesser, 1984b), whereas this situation may be reversed in aerobically working preparations (Gesser and Poupa, 1983). According to recent studies, however, it is unlikely that the loss of contractility, which, with some exceptions (e.g., Eisner et al., 1989), follows inhibition of cellular respiration, is solely due to intracellular acidification. Thus, as evident from results on skinned myocardial tissue, the decrease in $pH_i$ measured by Allen et al. (1985) following inhibition of cellular respiration is too small to explain the concomitant fall of contractility. Furthermore, the twitch force of trout myocardial tissue declined by about 70% during anaerobic conditions, although no change in $pH_i$ could be recorded with the DMO method (Nielsen and Gesser, 1984a). An unchanged $pH_i$ may tentatively be explained by a much lower myocardial energy turnover in the trout than in mammals. In addition, the myocardial cell generally tends to be smaller (i.e., to possess a higher surface/volume ratio) in poikilothermic than in homoiothermic vertebrates (Kilarsky, 1967). Given these differences, lactic acid should be produced at a lower rate and excreted more efficiently in the anaerobic myocardium of trout than in that of mammals (Nielsen and Gesser, 1984a).

Concerning a possible cellular acidosis induced by oxygen lack, the myocardial cell does not depend solely on its own activity, but also on the blood supplying it. This blood may vary in quality. Apart from being low in oxygen, it may be high in carbon dioxide and lactic acid, particularly in exercising fish, because of the single-circuit circulation in which the heart pumps venous blood. However, the myocardium of other vertebrates, as, for example, diving mammals, may also experience combined oxygen lack and acidosis. Moreover, environmental conditions may have an influence. For example, fishes inhabiting stagnant waters rich in vegetation may experience periods with low oxygen concentrations in combination with a high carbon dioxide level because of plant respiration (Dejours, 1975).

The negative effect of acidosis on contractility and, thus, on energy demand, has been suggested to counteract irreversible impairments of the myocardium under oxygen lack (Bing et al., 1973). This hypothesis is related to that of Lennard and Huddart (1989) ascribing a protective effect to the adenosine-dependent lowering of the potency of epinephrine in the hypoxic flounder heart. However, anaerobic force development may also be stimulated by acidosis. The force of the myocardium of eel, in which cellular respiration was inhibited, was significantly higher during hypercapnia than during normocapnia, provided the extracellular $Ca_o$ concentration approximated that in vivo. As the $Ca_o$ level was elevated, the effect of hypercapnia under anaerobic conditions was transformed from positive to negative (Nielsen and Gesser, 1984b). A positive action of hypercapnic acidosis on anaerobic performance is probably mediated by cellular $Ca^{+2}$ regulation. Comparative studies have provided evidence that, apart from its primarily negative effect on the contractile system (Fabiato and Fabiato, 1978), intracellular acidosis may increase the $Ca^{2+}$ available for contraction. In all myocardia examined, elevation of $P_{CO_2}$ resulted in a loss of contractility. In some, however, the loss was transient and followed by recovery to values that sometimes surpassed the prehypercapnic ones. This recovery has been suggested to be due to release of intracellular $Ca^{+2}$ stores. Support of this hypothesis is provided by the finding of an enhanced cellular efflux of $Ca^{2+}$, which probably indicates an increased intracellular activity of $Ca^{2+}$ (e.g., Gesser and Poupa, 1983). Some indirect evidence suggests that a release of mitochondrial $Ca^{2+}$ is involved (Gesser and Poupa, 1978). Involvement of the mitochondria is in accordance with the fact that $Ca^{2+}-H^+$ exchange appears to occur across the mitochondrial membrane (e.g., Fry et al., 1987). Tentatively, acidosis may cause a transfer of $Ca^{2+}$ from the mitochondria to some compartment involved directly in the E–C coupling and in a stimulation of twitch force development.

Thus, for instance, heart function in fishes inhabiting waters that experience large and inverse changes in $Po_2$ and $Pco_2$ may be protected from the primarily negative effects of oxygen lack by concomitant hypercapnic acidosis, as suggested by experiments with the eel heart.

## XI. Conclusions

Except for some recent results with isolated myocardial cells, oxygen lack has been found to depress the controllable contractility of heart muscle. This appears, on one hand, as a decrease in the transient excitation-dependent contraction and, on the other, as a tendency to a contracture. Strong evidence exists that the first effect is largely due to an elevation of $P_i$ in the cytoplasm as a result of a net hydrolysis of PCr. The contracture that frequently follows severe hypoxia seems to be mainly due to formation of rigor complexes, which may be enhanced by possible disturbances of cellular $Ca^{2+}$ regulation, causing an elevation of the cellular $Ca^{2+}$ activity.

Cellular acidification may also contribute. Primarily, acidosis depresses contractility by a direct action on the contractile proteins. However, some results suggest that this effect may be offset and even overcompensated by an enhancement of $Ca^{2+}$ in E–C coupling. Mitochondrial $Ca^{2+}$ stores should be considered here, as they may be released by acidosis.

Anaerobic contractility is supported by glycolysis; therefore, it was not astonishing to find a positive correlation between enzymatic capacity for this pathway and anaerobic contractility. The relationship between contractility and the cellular energy state is not clear, however. In particular glycolysis may protect contractility in a way that does not immediately relate to the cellular level of high-energy phosphates.

Although the mechanisms at play probably are qualitatively similar, the degree to which hypoxia affects myocardial contractility varies greatly among species. The highest abilities to maintain a controllable myocardial activity during hypoxia seem to be found in poikilothermic vertebrates.

This difference may depend on a higher glycolytic capacity, a lower energy turnover rate, and smaller cells (i.e., a higher surface/volume ratio) in cardiac muscle of poikilotherms. Furthermore, possible differences in E–C coupling as concerns the importance of structures like the SR and the mitochondria should be considered.

In some cases, these differences in hypoxic tolerance can be ascribed to environmental and anatomical conditions. In others, the adaptive significance is obscure. Conceivably it may sometimes be a side effect of differences that have an adaptive value not related to hypoxic tolerance.

## References

Allen, D. G., and Orchard, C. H. (1983). Intracellular calcium concentration during hypoxia and metabolic inhibition in mammalian ventricular muscle. *J. Physiol.*, **339**:107–122.

Allen, D. G., Morris, P. G., Orchard, C. H., and Pirolo, J. S. (1985). A nuclear magnetic resonance study of metabolism in the ferret heart during hypoxia and inhibition of glycolysis. *J. Physiol.*, **361**:185–204.

Andreasen, P. (1985). Free and total calcium concentrations in the blood of rainbow trout, *Salmo gairdneri*, during "stress" conditions. *J. Exp. Biol.*, **118**:111–120.

Barry, W. H., Peeters, G. A., Rasmussen, C. A., and Cunningham, M. J. (1987). Role of changes in $[Ca^{2+}]_i$ in energy deprivation contracture. *Circ. Res.*, **61**:726–734.

Bers, D. M. (1987). Mechanisms contributing to the cardiac inotropic effect of Na pump inhibition and reduction of extracellular Na. *J. Gen. Physiol.*, **90**:479–504.

Bing, O. H. L., Brooks, W. W., and Messer, J. V. (1973). Heart muscle viability following hypoxia: Protective effects of acidosis. *Science*, **180**:1297–1298.

Dawson, M. J. (1983). Nuclear magnetic resonance. In *Cardiac Metabolism*. Edited by A. J. Drake-Holland and M. I. M. Noble. Chichester, John Wiley & Sons, pp. 309–337.

Dejours, P. (1975). *Principles of Comparative Physiology*. Amsterdam, North-Holland Publishing Co.

Driedzic, W. R., Sidell, B. D., Stowe, D., and Branscombe, R. (1987). Matching of vertebrate cardiac energy demand to energy metabolism. *Am. J. Physiol.*, **252**:R930–R937.

Eisner, D. A., Nichols, C. G., O'Neill, S. C., Smith, G. L., and Valdeolmillos, M. (1989). The effects of metabolic inhibition on intracellular calcium and pH in isolated rat ventricular cells. *J. Physiol.*, **411**:393–418.

Fabiato, A., and Fabiato, F. (1978). Effects of pH on the myofilaments and the sarcoplasmic reticulum of skinned cells from cardiac and skeletal muscles. *J. Physiol.*, **276**:233–255.

Farrell, A. (1984). A review of cardiac performance in the teleost heart: Intrinsic and humoral regulation. *Can. J. Zool.*, **62**:523–536.

Fletcher, G. L. (1975). The effect of capture "stress" and storage of whole blood on the red blood cells, plasma proteins, glucose and electrolytes of the winter flounder. *Can. J. Zool.*, **53**:197–206.

Fry, C. H., Harding, D. P., and Mounsey, J. P. (1987). The effects of cyanide on intracellular ionic exchange in ferret and rat ventricular myocardium. *Proc. R. Soc. B*, **230**:53–75.

Gesser, H. (1985). Effects of hypoxia and acidosis on fish heart performance. In *Circulation, Respiration and Metabolism*. Edited by R. Gilles. Berlin, Springer-Verlag.

Gesser, H., and Höglund, L. (1988). Action potential, force and function of the sarco-plasmic reticulum in the anaerobic trout heart. *Exp. Biol.*, **47**:171–176.

Gesser, H., and Poupa, O. (1974). Relations between heart muscle enzyme pattern and directly measured tolerance to anoxia. *Comp. Biochem. Physiol.*, **48**:97–104.

Gesser, H., and Poupa, O. (1978). The role of intracellular $Ca^{2+}$ under hypercapnic acidosis of cardiac muscle: Comparative aspects. *J. Comp. Physiol.*, **127**:307–313.

Gesser, H., and Poupa, O. (1983). Acidosis and cardiac muscle contractility: Comparative aspects. *Comp. Biochem. Physiol.*, **76A**:559–566.

Gesser, H., Andreasen, P., Brams, P., and Sund-Laursen, J. (1982). Inotropic effects of adrenaline on the anoxic or hypercapnic myocardium of rainbow trout and eel. *J. Comp. Physiol.*, **147**:123–128.

Godt, R. E., and Nosek, T. M. (1989). Changes of intracellular milieu with fatigue or anoxia depress contraction of skinned rabbit skeletal and cardiac muscle. *J. Physiol.*, **412**:155–180.

Griese, M., Perlitz, V., Jüngling, E., and Kammermaier, H. (1988). Myocardial per-formance and free energy of ATP-hydrolysis in isolated rat hearts during graded hypoxia, reoxygenation and high $K^+$-perfusion. *J. Mol. Cell. Cardiol.*, **20**:1189–1201.

Hartmund, T., and Gesser, H. (1991). ATP, creatine phosphate, and mechanical activity in rainbow trout myocardium under inhibition of glycolysis and cell respiration. *J. Comp. Physiol.*, **160**:691–697.

Herzig, J. W., and Rüegg, J. C. (1977). Myocardial crossbridge activity and its regulation by $Ca^{2+}$, phosphate and stretch. In *Myocardial Failure*. Edited by G. Riecker, A. Weber, and J. Goodwin. International Boehringer Mannheim Symposiun, Berlin, Springer-Verlag, pp. 41–51.

Hibberd, M. G., Dantzig, J. A., Trentham, D. R., and Goldman, Y. E. (1985). Phosphate release and force generation in skeletal muscle fibres. *Science*, **228**:1317–1319.

Holubarsch, C., Alpert, N. R., Goulette, R., and Mulieri, L. A. (1982). Heat production during hypoxic contracture of rat myocardium. *Circ. Res.*, **51**:777–786.

Hove-Madsen, L., and Gesser, H. (1989). Force frequency relation in the myocardium of rainbow trout. Effects of $K^+$ and adrenaline. *J. Comp. Physiol.*, **159B**:61–69.

Jackson, D. C., and Heisler, N. (1982). Plasma ion balance of submerged anoxic turtles at 3°C: The role of calcium lactate formation. *Respir. Physiol.*, **49**:159–174.

Jarmakani, J. M., Nakamishi, T., and Jarmakani, R. N. (1979). Effect of hypoxia on calcium exchange in neonatal mammalian myocardium. *Am. J. Physiol.*, **237**:H612–H619.

Jennings, R. B., Sommers, H. M., Herdson, P. B., and Kaltenbach, J. B. (1969). Ischaemic injury of myocardium. *Ann. N. Y. Acad. Sci.*, **156**:61–78.

Jundt, H., Porzig, H., Reuter, H., and Stucki, J. W. (1975). The effects of substances releasing intracellular $Ca^{2+}$-ions on sodium dependent calcium efflux from guinea-pig auricles. *J. Physiol.*, **246**:229–253.

Kammermaier, H., Schmidt, P., and Jüngling, E. (1982). Free energy change of ATP hydrolysis: A causal factor of early hypoxic failure of the myocardium? *J. Mol. Cell. Cardiol.*, **14**:267–277.

Kentish, J. C. (1986). The effects of inorganic phosphate and creatine phosphate on force production in skinned muscles from rat ventricle. *J. Physiol.*, **370**:585–604.

Kilarsky, W. (1967). The fine structure of striated muscles in teleosts. *Z. Zellforsch.*, **79**:562–580.

Kushmerick, M. J. (1985). Patterns in mammalian muscle energetics. *J. Exp. Biol.*, **115**:165–177.

Lennard, R., and Huddart, H. (1989). Purinergic modulation of cardiac activity in the flounder during hypoxic stress. *J. Comp. Physiol.*, **159B**:105–114.

Lüllman, H., and Peters, T. (1977). Plasmolemmal calcium in cardiac excitation–contraction coupling. *Clin. Exp. Pharmacol. Physiol.*, **4**:49–57.

Marban, E., and Kusuoka, H. (1987). Maximal $Ca^{2+}$ activated force and myofilament $Ca^{2+}$-sensitivity in intact mammalian hearts. Differential effects of inorganic phosphate and hydrogen ions. *J. Gen. Physiol.*, **90**:609–623.

Matthews, P. M., Bland, J. L., Gadian, D. G., and Radda, G. K. (1982). A $^{31}$P-NMR saturation transfer study of the regulation of creatine kinase in the rat heart. *Biochim. Biophys. Acta,* **721**:312–320.

McDonald, T. F., and MacLeod, D. P. (1973). Metabolism and electrical activity of anoxic ventricular muscle. *J. Physiol.*, **229**:559–582.

Mekhfi, H., and Ventura-Clapier, R. (1988). Dependence upon high-energy phosphates of the effects of inorganic phosphate on contractile properties in chemically skinned rat cardiac fibres. *Pflügers Arch.*, **411**:378–385.

Meyer, R. A. (1988). A linear model of muscle respiration explains monoexponential phosphocreatine changes. *Am. J. Physiol.*, **254**:C548–C553.

Muus, B. J. (1967). *The Fauna of Danish Estuaries and Lagoons.* Copenhagen, Andr. Fred. Host., p. 316.

Nielsen, K. E., and Gesser, H. (1983). Effects of $[Ca]_o$ on contractility in the anoxic cardiac muscle of mammal and fish. *Life Sci.*, **2**:1437–1442.

Nielsen, K. E., and Gesser, H. (1984a). Energy metabolism and intracellular pH in trout heart muscle under anoxia and different $[Ca^{2+}]_o$. *J. Comp. Physiol.*, **154**:523–527.

Nielsen, K. E., and Gesser, H. (1984b). Eel and rainbow trout myocardium under anoxia and/or hypercapnic acidosis with changes in $[Ca]_o$ and $[Na]_o$. *Mol. Physiol.*, **5**:189–198.

Paul, R. J. (1989). Smooth muscle energetics. *Annu. Rev. Physiol.*, **51**:331–349.

Poupa, O. (1976). Some trends of the natural defense against cardiac anoxia. *Acta Med. Scand. Suppl.*, **587**:47–56.

Poupa, O., Gesser, H., Jonsson, S., and Sullivan, L. (1974). Coronary supplied compact shell of ventricle myocardium in salmonids: Growth and enzyme pattern. *Comp. Biochem. Physiol.*, **48**:85–96.

Purup-Hansen, S., and Gesser, H. (1987). Extracellular $Ca^{2+}$, force and energy state in cardiac tissue of rainbow trout. *Am. J. Physiol.*, **253**:R838–R847.

Randall, D. (1985). Shunts in fish gills. In *Alfred Benzon Symposium 21.* Edited by K. Johansen and W. Burggren, Copenhagen, Munksgaard.

Ruben, J. A., and Bennett, A. F. (1981). Intense exercise, bone structure and blood calcium levels in vertebrates. *Nature,* **291**:411–413.

Saks, V. A., Ventura-Clapier, R., Huchva, Z. A., Preobrazhensky, A. N., and Emelin, I. V. (1984). Creatine kinase in regulation of heart function and metabolism. Further evidence for compartmentation of adenine nucleotides in cardiac myofibrillar and sarcolemmal coupled ATPase–creatine kinase systems. *Biochim. Biophys. Acta,* **803**:254–264.

Santer, R. M., and Greer Walker, M. (1980). Morphological studies on the ventricle of teleost and elasmobranch hearts. *J. Zool. Lond.,* **190**:259–272.

Smith, G. L., and Allen, D. G. (1988). The effects of metabolic blockade on intracellular calcium concentration in isolated ferret ventricular muscle. *Circ. Res.,* **62**:1223–1236.

Steenbergen, C., Deleuw, G., Rich, T., and Williamson, J. R. (1977). Effects of acidosis and ischaemia on contractility and intracellular pH of rat heart. *Circ. Res.,* **41**:849–858.

Steffensen, J. F., Lomholt, J. P., and Johansen, K. (1982). Gill ventilation and oxygen extraction during graded hypoxia on two ecologically distinct species of flatfish, the flounder and the plaice. *Environ. Biol. Fish.,* **7**:157–163.

Weber, R. E., and de Wilde, J. A. M. (1975). Oxygenation properties of haemoglobins from the flatfish, plaice and flounder. *J. Comp. Physiol.,* **101**:99–110.

Weiss, J. N., and Lamp, S. T. (1987). Glycolysis preferentially inhibits ATP sensitive channels in isolated guinea pig cardiac myocytes. *Science,* **238**:67–69.

# 4

# Cost of Running Springs

## C. RICHARD TAYLOR

Museum of Comparative Zoology
Harvard University
Cambridge, Massachusetts

## I. Introduction

Large animals literally bounce as they run or hop along the ground (Alexander, 1988). This is perhaps most obvious in a kangaroo, but it is equally true for humans, ostriches, horses, and other runners. During each stride the animals are airborne. As they land, their muscles and tendons are stretched and energy is stored in muscle–tendon "springs." This stored elastic energy is recovered as they take off and become airborne again. If these springs were optimally designed, only the first few hops or strides would require a large input of mechanical energy from the muscles to accelerate the animal upward and forward. The subsequent strides could rely mainly on the alternate storage and recovery of energy in the springs to sustain a constant speed. The animal would approximate a bouncing ball, or perhaps it might be easier to envisage it as a pogo stick, with a coiled spring being alternately compressed and expanded. This would lead one to expect running should be a very inexpensive mode of locomotion, yet it is a much more expensive way of covering a distance than flying or swimming, despite the spring mechanism (Schmidt-Nielsen, 1972). Why does it take so much energy to run?

The explanation lies in an important difference between the ball and coil spring, on one hand, and the muscle–tendon spring, on the other. The ball and coil are "passive" springs, whereas the muscle–tendon springs are "active." The muscles must be turned on and generate force to operate the spring, and this consumes metabolic energy. Even if these springs were "perfect" and could store and recover all of the mechanical energy changes, their operation would still involve an energetic cost to the animal. The high costs of running, compared with those of swimming and flying, indicate that these costs are substantial.

In this paper I examine the idea that the cost of generating muscular force to operate these springs sets the energetic cost of running. After reviewing the evidence for springs, I propose a simple model, based on common properties of vertebrate striated muscles, to predict the cost of operating the springs in running animals. Then I test the value of the model by comparing its predictions with measurements of the metabolic rate of running animals: over a range of speeds and body size; when they carry loads; and when they run up hills.

## II. Evidence for Running Springs

The classic studies of running humans by Cavagna and co-workers (1964) demonstrated the importance of springs in conserving energy. They measured the energy changes of the center of mass and calculated the amount of energy that the muscles and their tendons would have to supply to lift and accelerate the body during each stride. When they compared this value with the chemical energy that muscles consumed (measured as oxygen consumption), they found that they could account for only one-third to one-half of the mechanical energy at high speeds. They concluded that the other one-half to two-thirds of the energy was supplied by storage and recovery in springs. These studies were extended to a variety of large birds and mammals, including turkeys, rheas, monkeys, dogs, rams, spring hares, and kangaroos (Cavagna et al., 1977), and the conclusions were the same. Recovery of elastic energy from "muscle–tendon springs" appears to be a general mechanism for conserving energy in running animals.

Alexander and his colleagues have provided direct evidence for the importance of springs in hopping animals (Ker et al., 1986). They have calculated that about 40% of the energy changes of the center of mass are alternately stored and recovered in the tendons of a hopping kangaroo (Alexander and Jayes, 1983) by using measurements of force, displacement, and the spring constant of the tendon. Furthermore, models of locomotion treating running animals as simple spring–mass systems do a remarkably good job of explaining how the mechanical properties of locomotion change as a function of size and speed (Alexander, 1988; Cavagna et al., 1988; McMahon et al., 1987). There can be little doubt of the importance of muscle–tendon springs in running animals.

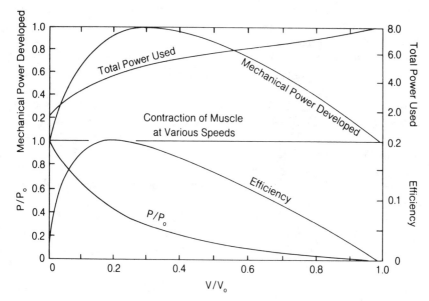

**Figure 1** Hill's classic explanation of how muscles work efficiently during locomotion can also be used to explain how they could operate economically to generate force. See text for discussion of the figure and a definition of the parameters that are plotted. (After Hill, 1950.)

## III. Cost of Generating Spring Force

All vertebrates use basically the same machines for generating force—striated skeletal muscles—resulting in some fundamental similarities in the amount of force they can generate and in the energy cost of generating this force. These similarities and their implications for muscle performance during running were considered by Hill (1950). He assumed that the muscles were "working" at maximal efficiency, providing the mechanical energy to sustain a constant speed for a minimal energetic cost. If we change his assumptions, letting the springs conserve the mechanical energy and muscles generate force to operate the springs at a minimal cost, we can use the same approach to predict how cost of running will change with speed and size.

Hill started his logical argument with the force velocity curve (Fig. 1). The curve is similar for skeletal muscles when force (P) and velocity (V) are normalized to isometric force, $P_0$, and maximum shortening velocity, $V_0$ (i.e., $P/P_0$ versus $V/V_0$). It shows that a muscle generates its highest force when it is active without shortening (i.e., isometrically). Force falls as the muscle shortens at faster velocities, until it generates no force at its fastest velocity. Hill calculated the mechanical power output of the muscles simply by multiplying force by velocity over the range of velocities, and this is included in the figure. This shows that muscles produce their maximal power at about 0.3 of its maximum shortening velocity. Hill also included values for the rate of energy consumption on the plot. This enabled him to calculate efficiency [the ratio of mechanical power developed/total power used (i.e., metabolic power)]. He concluded that vertebrate muscles reach nearly the same maximal efficiency of about 20% for converting chemical energy into mechanical work, and this occurs at about 0.2 of its maximum velocity when the muscle develops about 0.4 of its maximum force (see Fig. 1). Similar maximal efficiencies are found in humans for activities, such as bicycling, running up hills, or powering a human-powered aircraft, indicating that this relationship applies to muscles as they are used by animals in their normal activities.

It follows from this logic that when muscles operate at maximal efficiency, their rate of mechanical power development and their rate of energy consumption, $\dot{E}_m$, will be directly proportional to the maximum shortening velocity of the active muscle fibers:

$$\dot{E}_m \propto V_0 \tag{1}$$

This proportionality will be true for any particular ratio of $V/V_0$; however the proportionality constant will change dramatically as the relative shortening velocity changes.

Now, let us change our assumptions about what the muscles of running animals are doing, and use the same logic to develop a relationship for the energy cost of operating springs economically. The muscles have to generate force so that the spring can be stretched and shortened, but they do not have to shorten. Figure 1 shows that the rate of energy consumption is lowest and the greatest force is developed when the muscle does not shorten, and $V/V_0$ is zero (i.e., isometric). The rate of energy consumption increases, whereas force falls as velocity increases from zero to $0.2\ V_0$. A unit force can be developed at about one-fourth the rate of energy consumption when the muscle shortens at very slow velocities, close to isometric, compared with $0.2\ V_0$ at which it performs work most efficiently. Thus, if we want to build an economical muscle–tendon spring system, we should design it so that the muscles operate at very slow velocities, close to isometric. This would minimize the rate of energy consumption for operating the springs.

## IV. Cost of Running Springs

Now let us try to develop a simple relationship for estimating the rate of energy consumption of a running animal, assuming that most of the energy is consumed to generate force to operate springs, and that muscles operate economically at very slow velocities at which this cost is minimized. For simplicity, we will start by assuming that muscle force is directly proportional to the force exerted on the ground, $F_g$, and the amount of energy consumed is directly proportional to the force. Then using Equation (1), the energy consumption rate of the running animal's muscles when they are "on" generating force, $\dot{E}_m$, will be

$$\dot{E}_m \propto F_g \cdot V_0 \tag{2}$$

Muscles generate this force during the time the feet are in contact with the ground during each stride, $t_c$. Faster fibers will be required to generate the force over a shorter $t_c$ and, as a first approximation, it is reasonable to assume that the maximum shortening velocity, $V_0$ of the active fibers, is proportional to the intrinsic rate of force development, $1/t_c$.

$$V_0 \propto 1/t_c \tag{3}$$

This is important because we can easily measure $t_c$ of running animals, whereas the maximum shortening velocity, $V_0$ of the active fibers, is difficult, if not impossible, to measure. Now we can use the proportionalities of Equations (2) and (3) to write a simple equation for $\dot{E}_m$ in terms of parameters we can measure:

$$\dot{E}_m = k \cdot F_g \cdot 1/t_c \tag{4}$$

If we assume the spring will only be "on" and consuming energy during the fraction of the stride that the foot is in contact with the ground, and "off" when it is in the air, then the average rate of energy consumption of the animal over a complete stride, $\dot{E}_{run}$, is

$$\dot{E}_{run} = \dot{E}_m \cdot t_c/t_s \tag{5}$$

Furthermore, the average force applied to the ground over a stride is approximately equal to the weight of the animal, $F_{bw}$, because most of the force is applied in the vertical direction, overcoming the forces of gravity. This is true for all speeds and all sizes of animals. Our bouncing animal exerts this force during $t_c$ and spends the rest of the stride airborne. The force applied to the ground has to be high enough to compensate for the time in the air so that the average force over time of the stride, $t_s$, is equal to body weight:

$$F_g = F_{bw} \cdot t_s/t_c \tag{6}$$

The effects of $t_c/t_s$ on $F_g$ and $\dot{E}_{run}$ cancel each other, and by combining Equations (4), (5), and (6), we obtain a simple relationship expressing $\dot{E}_{run}$ in terms of body weight and time of contact:

$$\dot{E}_{run} = k \cdot F_{bw} \cdot 1/t_c \tag{7}$$

According to our model the value of k will be determined by the ratio of

$V/V_0$ and will be a constant only for the same relative shortening velocities of the active muscle. From Figure 1, we can see that the cost of generating force and the value for k will increase from a minimal value when $V/V_0$ is zero (isometric) to a value about four times as great when muscles operate at $0.2\ V_0$ and perform mechanical work most efficiently.

Let us use these equations to consider what happens to rate of energy consumption, $t_c$, and average force applied to the ground during $t_c$ over a series of strides as an animal increases speed. First let us have an animal double its speed by increasing stride frequency while keeping the ratio of $t_c/t_s$ constant at 0.5 (Fig. 2). The average force during the contact is twice the body weight, and it is the same at the two speeds. Energy is consumed at twice the rate at the higher speed because $\dot{E}_m$, doubles as $1/t_c$, intrinsic rate of force generation, doubles. In both cases, the energy is being consumed during half of the stride, and the rate of energy consumption during the time the muscle is "on" is twice the rate averaged over a stride. Now, let us consider what would happen if an animal doubles its speed by increasing stride length while keeping stride frequency constant and decreasing the ratio of $t_c/t_s$ from 0.5 to 0.25. The average force during the contact is doubled, from two to four times body weight. Although energy is consumed at four times the rate during $t_c$ (since both $F_g$ and $1/t_c$ are doubled) the muscle is "on" for one-fourth, instead of one-half the stride. In both cases the rate of energy consumption of the running animal averaged over a complete stride is doubled.

## V. Testing the Model

This very simplistic way of looking at the cost of running springs is useful because it makes testable predictions. The rate of energy consumption per unit weight of running animals changes by four- to fivefold with speed; by tenfold at the same speed in different-sized animals; by at least 30% by having an animal carry weights; and triples as dogs run up a steep incline. How well does the spring model account for these large differences in rates of oxygen consumption?

### Test 1:  Changes in $E_{run}$ with Speed and Size

To test this model, R. Kram, N. Heglund and I (unpublished observations) have recently compared the rate of energy consumption (measured as oxygen consumption) and $1/t_c$, using a wide range of speeds in ponies, dogs, and ground squirrels to obtain large differences in $\dot{V}O_2/M_b$. Both $\dot{V}O_2/M_b$ and $1/t_c$ increase linearly with speed in the pony over the range of trotting and galloping speeds the animals can sustain aerobically (Fig. 3). The force generation constant, k, (Eq. 7) is simply $\dot{V}O_2/M_b$ (expressed in watts) divided by the intrinsic rate of

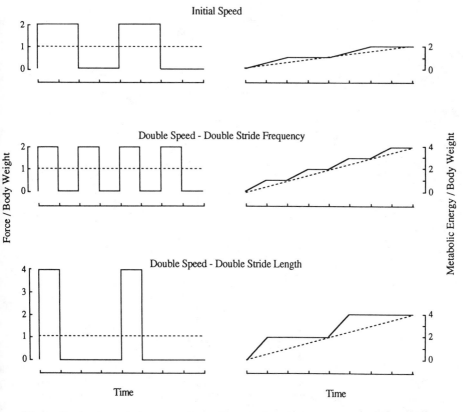

**Figure 2** A schematic representation to illustrate how force applied to the ground and metabolic energy consumption change as an animal doubles speed: by doubling stride frequency (top panel compared with middle); and by doubling stride length (top panel compared with bottom). The energy consumed during the time the foot is on the ground is given by the solid lines (right panels) and their slope is rate of energy consumption. The average energy consumed during an entire stride is plotted as a dotted line. The slope of this line is what one would measure as rate of energy consumption in a running animal (see text for discussion).

force generation. The bottom panel shows this ratio is a constant over the entire range of speeds, having a value of about 2 J/kg. The metabolic rate increases as the same linear function of $1/t_c$ in trotting and galloping animals, regardless of speed or size (Fig. 4). The slope of this relationship, k, is 2 J/kg. These findings agree with the predictions of the model over a 15-fold difference in $\dot{V}O_2/M_b$ and $1/t_c$.

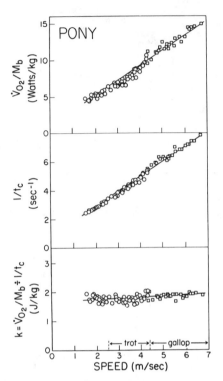

**Figure 3** Mass-specific rate of oxygen consumption ($\dot{V}_{O_2}/M_b$, top), and 1/time of contact of a foot during a stride (average of the four feet) ($1/t_c$, middle), both increase linearly with speed in the pony. The ratio of the two (bottom) is the force generation constant, k [see Eq. (7) of text]. The nearly constant k of 2 J/kg over the entire range of speeds indicates that the muscle is operating at the same fraction of maximal shortening velocity (see text). The circles represent trotting, the squares galloping measurements.

### Test 2: Carrying Weights

Running animals increase their metabolic rate when they carry weights, and this provides another test of our model. Is the force generation constant changed by carrying weights? The metabolic rate of animals running weighted and un-weighted at the same speed increases in direct proportion to increase in total weight that must be supported (Taylor et al., 1980). A 10% increase in weight increases the metabolism by 10%, a 20% increase by 20%, and so on. This direct proportionality was found at different speeds in the rats, dogs, humans, and ponies. The footfall pattern, stride frequency, and $t_c$ were measured in dogs and did not change when the weights were carried. Consequently, the force

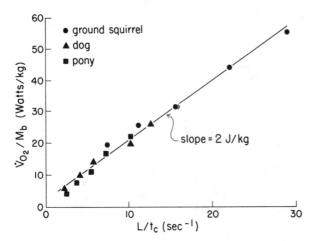

**Figure 4** Rate of mass-specific oxygen consumption ($\dot{V}_{O_2}/M_b$) increases linearly with 1/time of contact of a foot during a stride (average of the four feet)($1/t_c$). Values from small 200-g ground squirrels, intermediate-sized 25-kg dogs, and large 110-kg ponies follow the same relationship. The slope of this relationship (2 J/kg) is the force generation constant for running quadrupeds of Equation (7). The figure shows k independent of speed or (animal) size (see text for discussion).

generation constant, k, was the same, 2 J/kg, whether the animals ran with or without the weight (Table 1).

### Test 3: Do Animals Run the Springs Economically?

We have assumed in our model that the cost of generating the force is minimized by operating at slow shortening velocities relative to the maximum shortening

**Table 1** Cost of Carrying Weights[a]

| Load | $\dot{E}_{run}$ (Ws) | = | k (J/kg) | × | $1/t_c$ (sec$^{-1}$) | × | $F_{bw}$ (incl. load) (kg) |
|---|---|---|---|---|---|---|---|
| 30% body weight | 324 | | 2 | | 4.5 | | 36 |
| Unloaded | 252 | | 2 | | 4.5 | | 28 |
| Ratio | 1.3 | | 1 | | 1 | | 1.3 |

[a]Metabolic rate of running dogs increases in direct proportion to the increase to the weight they support, whereas the force generation constant, k, and $1/t_c$ remain the same. Values are given for dogs trotting at 2.4 m/sec carrying loads of 30% of body weight.

**Table 2**  The Cost of Generating Force[a]

| Incline (°) | $\dot{E}_{run}$ (Ws) | = | k (J/kg) | × | $1/t_c$ (sec$^{-1}$) | × | $F_{bw}$ (kg) |
|---|---|---|---|---|---|---|---|
| level | 252 | | 2.0 | | 4.5 | | 28 |
| up 12° incline | 616 | | 5.0 | | 4.4 | | 28 |

[a]The force generation constant, k, is much larger when dogs run up an incline than when they run on the level. The dogs running up the incline had an efficiency of 0.22, indicating their muscles were operating at about 0.2 $V_0$. The same average force can be generated most economically, for about one-third the cost, (k of 1.7) while active muscles do not shorten. The k of dogs running on the level is close 1.7, indicating they are operating at slow velocities, near isometric. A smaller k indicates slower shortening velocities (see text for discussion). The time over which the force was applied and the magnitude of the force were approximately the same when dogs ran at the same speed (2.4 m/sec) on the level and up the incline.

velocity. Kimberly Mar, an undergraduate in my laboratory, designed an experiment to test this assumption. She ran dogs up a steep (12%) incline at 2.4 m/sec and obtained efficiencies for lifting the center of mass of 0.22, close to the maximum mechanical efficiency of muscle. As illustrated in Figure 1, these high efficiencies are achieved at about 0.2 $V_0$ where the value of k is about four times larger than that for the isometric muscle. She found that the value of k was 5.0 J/kg when the muscles performed work efficiently, compared with 2 J/kg during level running (Table 2). This supports the idea that cost of generating force in running animals is minimized by operating muscles at slow velocities.

## VI.  Conclusions

Running animals bounce along the ground conserving energy in muscle–tendon springs. A simple equation is derived from common properties of vertebrate muscles to estimate the metabolic cost of generating force to operate these springs economically. This simple equation works remarkably well in predicting how metabolic rate of running quadrupeds changes with speed, body size, and weighting. The close agreement between prediction and measurement of metabolic rate provides strong support for the ideas that the energetic cost of running is determined by the cost of generating force. We also present evidence to support the idea that cost is minimized by operating the muscles at slow velocities.

### Acknowledgment

Preparation was supported by a National Institutes of Health Grant (2 R01 AR 18140-13) to C. R. Taylor.

## References

Alexander, R. McN. (1988). *Elastic Mechanisms in Animal Movement.* Cambridge, Cambridge University Press.

Alexander, R. McN., and Jayes, A. S. (1983). A dynamic similarity hypothesis for the gaits of quadrupedal mammals. *J. Zool.*, **201**:135–153.

Cavagna, G. A., Franzetti, P., Heglund, N. C., and Willems, P. (1988). The determinants of the step frequency in running, trotting and hopping in man and other vertebrates. *J. Physiol.*, **399**:81–982.

Cavagna, G. A., Heglund, N. C., and Taylor, C. R. (1977). Mechanical work in terrestrial locomotion: Two basic mechanisms for minimizing energy expenditure. *Am. J. Physiol.*, **233**:R243–261.

Cavagna, G. A., Saibene, F. P., and Margaria, R. (1964). Mechanical work in running. *J. Appl. Physiol.*, **19**:249–256.

Hill, A. V. (1950). The dimensions of animals and their muscular dynamics. *Sci. Prog.*, **38**:209–230.

Ker, R. F., Dimery, N. J., and Alexander, R. McN. (1986). The role of tendon elasticity in hopping in a wallaby (*Macropus rufogriseus*). *J. Zool. A*, **208**:417–428.

McMahon, T. A., Valiant, G., and Frederick, E. C. (1987). Groucho running. *J. Appl. Physiol.*, **62**:2326–2337.

Schmidt-Nielsen, K. (1972). Locomotion: Energy cost of swimming, flying and running. *Nature*, **177**:222–228.

Taylor, C. R., Heglund, N. C., McMahon, T. A., and Looney, T. R. (1980). Energetic cost of generating force during running: A comparison of large and small animals. *J. Exp. Biol.*, **86**:9–18.

# Part Two

## GAS EXCHANGE

# 5

# Modeling of Gas Exchange in Vertebrate Lungs, Gills, and Skin

**JOHANNES PIIPER**

Max Planck Institute for
Experimental Medicine
Göttingen, Germany

**PETER SCHEID**

Ruhr University Bochum
Bochum, Germany

## I. Introduction

Under *modeling* we mean understanding and explanation of observed gas exchange variables on the basis of the various anatomical structures of the external gas exchange organs, the physicochemical properties of the respiratory media and blood, and the physiological parameters such as ventilation and blood perfusion.

We shall first present a generalized schema that applies to all vertebrate gas exchange organs (lungs, gills, and skin) and discuss the properties, relevant for transport of $O_2$ and $CO_2$, of the external respiratory media (air and water) as well as of blood (see Sect. II). The transfer process of respiratory gases between the medium and blood by diffusion has a central importance. Therefore, particular attention is given to the factors determining the extent of diffusion limitation in equilibration of capillary blood with the medium in respiratory organs (see Sect. III). The various gas exchange organs (fish gills, avian lungs, mammalian lungs, and amphibian skin) and their respective models (countercurrent, crosscurrent, ventilated pool, and open system) are briefly introduced, and the efficiency limits of the models are discussed (see Sect. IV). Particular emphasis is placed on consideration of functional inhomogeneities that occur

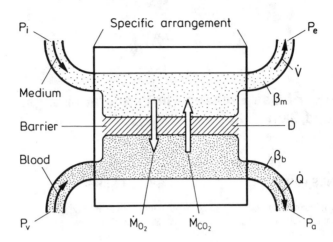

**Figure 1** General model for gas exchange models in vertebrates. For symbols, see text. (After Piiper and Scheid, 1982).

because not all the multiple parallel units of gas exchange organs (such as alveoli, parabronchi, gill secondary lamellae) are equal in their ventilation, perfusion, or diffusion conditions. The models for analysis of ventilation–perfusion inequalities that have been elaborated for mammalian lungs may be adjusted to other systems (see Sect. V).

Only selected references are cited, and the interested reader should consult two recent volumes of the present review series (Chang and Paiva, 1989; Wood, 1989). The reader is also referred to more detailed review papers published on related topics by the authors of this report (Piiper, 1982; Piiper and Scheid, 1977; 1982; 1989.

## II.  Models, Properties, and Processes

### A.  General Model

The general model for a vertebrate gas exchange organ (Fig. 1) comprises 1) convective transport by medium (air or water) flow, 2) diffusive exchange across a barrier between medium and blood, and 3) convective transport by blood flow. For a quantitative analysis, the following quantities and relationships are required:

*Transfer rates,* in particular $O_2$ uptake, $\dot{M}O_2$, and $CO_2$ output, $\dot{M}CO_2$.
*Flow* of the medium or ventilation, $\dot{V}$, and blood flow or perfusion, $\dot{Q}$.

*Concentrations,* C, in the medium and in blood (it is appropriate to employ the same definition and units for medium and blood, e.g., mM/L).

*Partial pressures,* P; the conventional unit is torr ($=$ mm Hg), although the SI unit kilopascal (kPa) is increasingly used (1 kPa $=$ 7.5 torr).

*Capacitance coefficient or effective solubility,* $\beta$, defined as increment of concentration per increment of partial pressure ($\beta = \Delta C/\Delta P$) (Piiper et al., 1971). For the gas phase, $\beta$ is equal for all (ideal) gases, and equal to $1/(RT)$ (R, gas constant; T, absolute temperature). For inert gases in water and blood and for $O_2$ in water, $\beta$ is equal to physical solubility. For the respiratory gases $O_2$ and $CO_2$ in blood, $\beta$ is equivalent to the slope of the (effective) dissociation curves (i.e., plots of concentration versus partial pressure).

*Transport equations.* Convective transport (of $O_2$, $CO_2$, or other gases) by ventilation and by perfusion, and diffusive transport between the external medium and blood, are described by the following relationships (i, inspired medium; e, expired medium; v, incoming, venous blood; a, exiting, arterialized blood; m, medium; b, blood):

$$\dot{M} = \dot{V} \cdot (Ci - Ce) = \dot{V} \cdot \beta m \cdot (Pi - Pe) \tag{1}$$

$$\dot{M} = \dot{Q} \cdot (Ca - Cv) = \dot{Q} \cdot \beta b \cdot (Pa - Pv) \tag{2}$$

$$\dot{M} = D \cdot (Pm - Pb) \tag{3}$$

Equation (3) defines the diffusing capacity (transfer factor), D, of the barrier separating blood from the external medium (Pm $-$ Pb, mean medium-to-blood partial pressure difference).

*Conductance,* G, is defined as transfer rate per effective partial pressure difference (its reciprocal is resistance). The following basic relationships for ventilatory (vent), perfusive (perf), and diffusive (diff) conductances are obtained from the transport equations:

$$G_{vent} = \dot{V} \cdot \beta m \tag{4}$$

$$G_{perf} = \dot{Q} \cdot \beta b \tag{5}$$

$$G_{diff} = D \tag{6}$$

## B. External Medium: Water Versus Air Breathing

In comparing air and water breathing the capacitance coefficients ($\beta$) of the medium for $CO_2$ and $O_2$, are the decisive factors. For air (gas phase), $\beta$ is equal for all (ideal) gases. For water, $\beta$ for $O_2$ and $CO_2$ are markedly different, the ratio $\beta CO_2/\beta O_2$ being about 30 (the exact figure is dependent on temperature, salinity, and buffering). The ratio $\beta$ (water)/$\beta$ (gas) is close to unity for $CO_2$, but only 0.033 for $O_2$. These relationships have the following consequences for external gas exchange (Rahn, 1966; Dejours, 1981; 1988):

1.  To achieve the same $G_{vent}$ for $O_2$, water breathers must ventilate much more than air breathers.
2.  Since $\beta CO_2$ is about equal for water and air, the increased ventilation with water breathing means a proportionately increased $G_{vent}$ for $CO_2$, whereby $P_{CO_2}$ is markedly diminished in expired water and in arterial blood. This is the primary reason for the large discrepancy in arterial $P_{CO_2}$ between the mammals (about 40 torr) and fish (about 1–4 torr).
3.  According to the Henderson–Hasselbach equation, a much higher pH is expected in water-breathing animals, compared with air breathers. In reality, however, there is little difference in blood pH between air and water breathers (when compared at the same temperature), because the apparent hyperventilation in water breathers is compensated for by a relatively low blood bicarbonate concentration (see Dejours, 1988).

For the ideal models, $\beta$ is the only significant property of the medium for gas transfer. In real gas exchange organs, however, a number of other properties are important. These include the following:

*Diffusion* properties, characterized by the diffusion coefficient, $d$, or Krogh's diffusion constant, $K = d \cdot \alpha$ ($\alpha$, solubility), determine the development of partial pressure gradients within the medium (e.g., in interlamellar water in fish gills; in surrounding air or water in skin breathing; stratification in mammalian lungs).

*Viscosity,* $\eta$, is a major determinant of the mechanical resistance to respiratory medium flow.

*Density,* $\rho$, determines the inertia of the medium and is, therefore, of importance in respiratory flow variations within the respiratory cycle. Since K is much smaller, and $\eta$ and $\rho$ are much higher in water than in air, water breathing is generally more costly; that is, it requires more energy per volume of medium respired than does air breathing (e.g., Scheid, 1987).

### C.  Internal Transport Medium: Blood

*Oxygen Transport*

The equilibrium of $O_2$ and hemoglobin in blood is usually described by plots of $O_2$ saturation of hemoglobin, $S_{O_2}$, against $P_{O_2}$. For an analysis of convective $O_2$ transport by circulation, however, the plot of $O_2$ concentration, $C_{O_2}$, against $P_{O_2}$ is the adequate representation, and it is the slope of this curve that constitutes

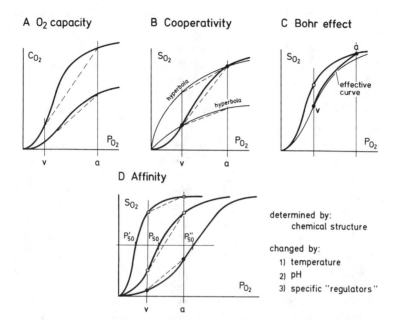

**Figure 2** Oxygen dissociation curve and influencing parameters. In each graph, $O_2$ content in blood ($C_{O_2}$) is on the ordinate, $P_{O_2}$ on the abscissa a and v denote arterial and venous $P_{O_2}$. (A) The $O_2$ capacity is lower in blood with lower hemoglobin concentration. The dashed lines connect corresponding points of $C_{O_2}$ and $P_{O_2}$ in arterial and venous blood: slope is βb. (B) The cooperativity of the hemoglobin subunits results in higher βb compared with non-cooperative binding (hyperbola; e.g., in myoglobin). (C) Bohr effect results in effective dissociation curve that is steeper than that at the pH of either the arterial or the venous blood. (D) Moving the curve to the left or right, thereby changing $P_{50}$ to $P_{50}'$ or $P_{50}''$ changes the slope βb between the given arterial $P_{O_2}$ and the venous $P_{O_2}$.

the decisive parameter. This slope is termed the *capacitance coefficient*, βb, for $O_2$.

The value of βb for $O_2$ is determined, and may be modified, by several factors, that are partly relevant as adapting mechanisms for $O_2$ transport (Fig. 2).

1. *Concentration* of hemoglobin in blood defines the maximum value of chemically bound $O_2$, the $O_2$ capacity (see Fig. 2A). βb for $O_2$ is nearly proportional to the $O_2$ capacity.

2. *Cooperativity:* The stepwise association of $O_2$ to the four hemoglobin subunits increases the $O_2$ affinity of the remaining subunits (positive cooperativity). The equilibrium of the hemoglobin–$O_2$ equilibrium can empirically be described by the relationship

$$\log [S_{O_2}/(1 - S_{O_2})] = n \cdot \log (P_{O_2}/P_{50}) \tag{7}$$

where $P_{50}$ is the $Po_2$ for $So_2 = 0.5$; and n, the Hill coefficient. In many cases, n is nearly constant in the $So_2$ range from about 0.2 to 0.95. In mammalian blood, n is typically about 2.5–3. The shape of the $O_2$ dissociation curve determines n; thus, a hyperbolic curve yields n = 1, a sigmoid $O_2$ dissociation curve, n > 1 (see Fig. 2B). For constant $P_{50}$, the slope of the $O_2$ dissociation curve in its middle range increases with n.

3. The *$O_2$ affinity,* expressed by the $P_{50}$ ($Po_2$ for $So_2 = 0.5$) determines the $Po_2$ range in which $\beta$ reaches its maximum (see Fig. 2D). It is primarily determined by the chemical structure of the hemoglobin and may be modified by 1) temperature (increase in temperature increases $P_{50}$); 2) pH (increase in pH lowers $P_{50}$); 3) specific regulatory substances that combine reversibly with hemoglobin, such as $CO_2$, 2,3-diphosphoglycerate (DPG), inositol pentaphosphate (IPP), adenosine triphosphate (ATP), and guanosine triphosphate (GTP). These substances occur in different concentrations in the red blood cells of various animals. For the usually occurring sigmoid-shaped $O_2$ dissociation curves, $\beta$ is maximum in a range somewhat lower than $P_{50}$; and for a given Pa and Pv, the concentration difference (Ca − Cv) is highest for Pa > $P_{50}$ > Pv. In man (and other mammals), in which these relationships are best known, $Po_2$ in mixed venous blood at rest ($\approx$ 40 torr) is definitely higher than $P_{50}$ ($\approx$ 27 torr), but in heavy exercise mixed venous $Po_2$, and particularly muscle venous $Po_2$, drop clearly below $P_{50}$. Apparently the $P_{50}$ value is adjusted to allow optimum conditions for circulatory $O_2$ transport during heavy exercise.

4. Increasing acidity decreases the $O_2$ affinity of hemoglobins (*Bohr effect*). The Bohr factor, B, depends on $So_2$ and is usually given for half saturation: $B_{50} = dlogP_{50}/dpH$. For mammalian blood, $B_{50}$ is in the range between $-0.4$ and $-0.8$. The physiologically most important regulator of blood acidity is $CO_2$. Changing $Pco_2$ gives rise to changes in pH and, thus, to the physiological Bohr effect by which venous blood, with a relatively high $Pco_2$, displays a lower affinity than arterial blood (see Fig. 2C). The "physiological" $\beta b$ for $O_2$ is, thus, increased above the value for constant $Pco_2$. Since $CO_2$, aside from its effect through pH, exerts an additional, specific effect on the $O_2$ affinity, a $CO_2$ Bohr factor may be discerned from a fixed acid Bohr factor, the latter being smaller than the former.

### Carbon Dioxide Transport

The $\beta b$ value for $CO_2$ is considerably higher than that for $O_2$, and this results mainly from reversible formation of bicarbonate with increasing $Pco_2$ by the buffering action of nonbicarbonate buffers of blood (hemoglobin, plasma proteins, phosphates). Effects on $CO_2$ binding are exerted by temperature, the acid–base status, and the $O_2$ saturation of hemoglobin. Of particular physiological importance is the Haldane effect (decreased $CO_2$ affinity by increased hemoglobin

$O_2$ saturation), which increases the physiological $\beta b$ for $CO_2$ considerably over that for constant $O_2$ saturation.

## III. Diffusion and Perfusion

### A  Diffusive Equilibration and Equilibration Coefficient

Many times gases are transferred, across a tissue barrier, between a medium of (relatively) constant composition and flowing blood. This is particularly evident for mammalian lungs and for cutaneous gas exchange. For a basic understanding and evaluation, use can be made of a very simple model that contains the basic variables and demonstrates their interaction (Piiper and Scheid, 1981). The model is composed of a uniform medium (alveolar) space that is separated from a blood stream of uniform velocity by a homogeneous, flat diffusion barrier (Fig. 3). It is assumed that transfer (of any gas) by diffusion is perpendicular across the barrier, that there is instantaneous mixing with a cross-sectional element of blood, and that transport by blood is by square-front bulk flow with negligible axial diffusion. In steady state, the diffusive and convective transport rates are equal in any element, dx:

$$(P_A - P_C) \cdot dD = \dot{Q} \cdot \beta b \cdot dP_C \tag{8}$$

($P_A$, alveolar gas partial pressure; $P_C$, partial pressure in capillary blood in the element considered; $dP_C$, partial pressure difference between inflow and outflow of the blood element corresponding to the element of diffusing capacity, dD). Integration of Equation (8) from the mixed venous end ($\bar{v}$) to a point, x, along the capillary of length $x_0$ yields:

$$\frac{P_A - P_C(x)}{P_A - P\bar{v}} = \exp \left\{ - \frac{D}{\dot{Q} \, \beta b} \cdot \frac{x}{x_0} \right\} \tag{9}$$

This equation describes the exponential decrease of the difference $P_A - P_C(x)$ along the capillary, the exponent being proportional to $D/(\dot{Q} \cdot \beta b)$. For the extent of equilibration reached at the end of the capillary ($x = x_0$), one obtains:

$$\frac{P_A - P_a}{P_A - P\bar{v}} = \exp \left\{ - \frac{D}{\dot{Q} \, \beta b} \right\} \tag{10}$$

This relationship is of fundamental importance and shows that the extent of alveolar–capillary equilibration is determined by the ratio, $D/(\dot{Q} \cdot \beta b)$, which has been termed *equilibration coefficient* by Scheid and Piiper (1989). The higher the value of $D/(\dot{Q} \cdot \beta b)$, the more complete is the equilibration reached in end-capillary blood; it is immaterial whether a high $D/(\dot{Q} \cdot \beta b)$ is achieved by high D or low $\dot{Q}$ or low $\beta b$, or by a combination of the three.

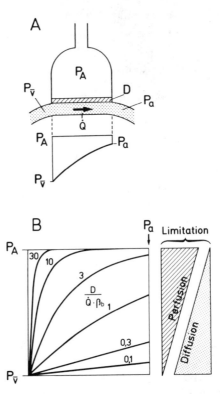

**Figure 3** Diffusion–perfusion limitation in alveolar–capillary gas transfer. (A) Model of alveolus with capillary and the $P_{O_2}$ profile in capillary blood from mixed venous ($P\bar{v}$) to arterial (= end-capillary) value (Pa), thus approaching alveolar $P_{O_2}$ (PA). (B) Profiles of $P_{O_2}$ in capillary blood for various values of the equilibration coefficient, $D/(\dot{Q} \cdot \beta b)$. Small values of this coefficient mean prevalent diffusion limitation; large values, perfusion limitation. (After Piiper and Scheid, 1981).

## B.  Overall Conductance and Component Conductances

The total conductance for alveolar gas exchange, $G_{tot}$, may be defined by the relationship,

$$G_{tot} = \dot{M}/(PA - P\bar{v}) \tag{11}$$

Its components are the diffusive conductance, equal to the diffusing capacity, D, and the perfusive conductance, defined as $\dot{Q} \cdot \beta b$

$$\dot{Q} \cdot \beta b = \dot{M}/(Pa - P\bar{v}) \tag{12}$$

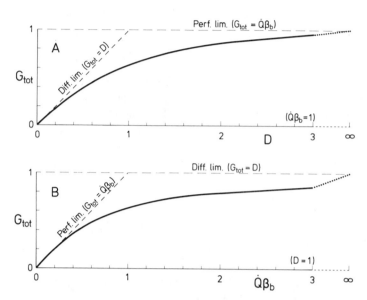

**Figure 4** Total conductance, $G_{tot}$, as function of diffusive conductance, D (A), and perfusive conductance, $\dot{Q} \cdot \beta b$ (B). The limiting cases of pure perfusion and diffusion limitation are marked by broken lines. (After Piiper and Scheid, 1981.)

Combination of Equations (10), (11), and (12) yields:

$$G_{tot} = \dot{Q} \cdot \beta b \left[ 1 - \exp \left\{ -\frac{D}{\dot{Q} \, \beta b} \right\} \right] \tag{13}$$

It is evident that for $D \to \infty$, $G_{tot} = \dot{Q} \cdot \beta b$ (perfusion limitation) and for $\dot{Q} \cdot \beta b \to \infty$, $G_{tot} = D$ (diffusion limitation). The dependence of $G_{tot}$ on D at constant $\dot{Q} \cdot \beta b$ is shown in Figure 4A, and on $\dot{Q} \cdot \beta b$ at constant D, in Figure 4B. Note the following: 1) At very low values of D, $G_{tot} = D$ (diffusion limitation); but when D is increased, $G_{tot}$ increases less than D (combined diffusion and perfusion limitation); and at very high D, $G_{tot}$ becomes independent of D (perfusion limitation). 2) At very low $\dot{Q} \cdot \beta b$, $G_{tot} = \dot{Q} \cdot \beta b$ (perfusion limitation); when $\dot{Q} \cdot \beta b$ is increased, $G_{tot}$ increases less than $\dot{Q} \cdot \beta b$ (combined perfusion and diffusion limitation), and at very high $\dot{Q} \cdot \beta b$, $G_{tot}$ is independent of $\dot{Q} \cdot \beta b$, being determined solely by D (diffusion limitation).

Several parameters may be used to describe diffusion and perfusion limitation in quantitative terms (Piiper and Scheid, 1981; 1983). The simplest is the "extent of limitation," L, which denotes the relative reduction in $G_{tot}$, from the limiting value it would attain without the respective limitation, to its actual value. The extent of diffusion limitation, $L_{diff}$, is thus given by $(P_A - P_a)/(P_A - P\bar{v})$ in Equation (10).

## C.  Diffusion–Perfusion Limitation for Various Gases

According to Fick's diffusion law, the diffusing capacity D is determined, by the following properties of the diffusion barrier: the diffusion coefficient ($d$), the solubility ($\alpha$), the surface area (A), and the thickness (h),

$$D = d \cdot \alpha \cdot A/h \tag{14}$$

For the $D/(\dot{Q} \cdot \beta b)$ ratio one obtains,

$$\frac{D}{\dot{Q} \cdot \beta b} = \frac{d \cdot \alpha}{\beta b} \cdot \frac{A}{h \cdot \dot{Q}} \tag{15}$$

This relationship reveals that it is not the diffusion coefficient ($d$) alone, but the product $d \cdot \alpha/\beta b$ that determines the diffusion–perfusion behavior of gases for any given geometry (A/h) and blood flow ($\dot{Q}$).

The diffusion coefficient, $d$, for gases in tissues or water is approximately inversely proportional to the square root of the molecular mass of the gas (Graham's law; cf., Kawashiro et al., 1975). Thus the $d$ values for very light gases (like $H_2$) and very heavy gases (like $SF_6$) are expected to differ by a factor of about 8.

The $\alpha/\beta b$ ratio should be near unity for all inert gases (except for highly lipid-soluble gases, for which $\alpha/\beta b$ may be above unity) (cf., Meyer et al., 1980). But for gases chemically bound in blood, the $\beta b$ value may be greatly increased over its physical solubility in blood, $\alpha b$. With appropriate Pa and Pv and blood dissociation curves one obtains by the relationship,

$$\frac{\beta b}{\alpha b} = \frac{Ca - Cv}{\alpha b \cdot (Pa - Pv)} \tag{16}$$

the following values for the $\beta b/\alpha b$ ratio: $CO_2$ 10; $O_2$ in normoxia, 30; $O_2$ in hypoxia, 170; CO in hypoxia, 40,000. Accordingly, the $\beta b/\alpha b$ ratio shows a much greater variability among gases than the diffusivity, $d$.

For the exchange of gases that are chemically bound in blood, the reaction rate of chemical binding may be limiting. As a first approximation, this could be taken into account by reducing the diffusivity, $d$, by a (dimensionless) coefficient, r ($< 1$), to an apparent diffusivity, $d_{app}$:

$$d_{app} = d \cdot r \tag{17}$$

Thus, the effective $D/(\dot{Q} \cdot \beta b)$ for chemically bound gases may be further reduced, compared with inert gases.

In Figure 5 the equilibration coefficient $D/(\dot{Q} \cdot \beta b)$ of alveolar–capillary

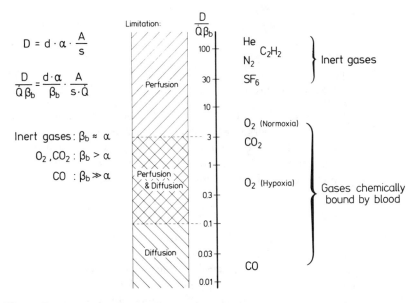

**Figure 5** Diffusion–perfusion limitation in alveolar–capillary transfer of various gases. The $D/(\dot{Q} \cdot \beta b)$ ratio is plotted on logarithmic scale, and the values expected for various gases in gas transfer in mammalian lungs are indicated as well as the limiting processes. (After Piiper and Scheid, 1981.)

transfer is estimated for various gases in human lungs. The basis for this estimate is $D_{O_2} = 60$ ml $\cdot$ min$^{-1}$ $\cdot$ torr$^{-1}$ (Meyer et al., 1981), $D_{CO_2} = 200$ ml $\cdot$ min$^{-1}$ $\cdot$ torr$^{-1}$ (Piiper et al., 1980), and approximate relative $\alpha$, $\beta b$, and $d$ values. The main features are the following:

The transfer of all inert gases is practically not diffusion limited.
$O_2$ and $CO_2$ transfer extends from predominant perfusion limitation to the range of combined diffusion and perfusion limitation.
CO transfer is almost exclusively diffusion (and reaction) limited.

### D. Pulmonary Oxygen Uptake in High-Altitude Hypoxia

The alveolar–capillary equilibration deficit in the physiologically interesting situation of deep hypoxia, when pulmonary $O_2$ uptake is limited by both perfusion and diffusion, can be analyzed particularly well using the $D/(\dot{Q} \cdot \beta b)$ concept. This is because 1) $\beta b$, the slope of the $O_2$ dissociation curve, is large producing small $D/(\dot{Q}\beta b)$ and, therefore, pronounced effects of diffusion limitation; 2) $\beta b$

is relatively independent of $Po_2$ (the blood $O_2$ dissociation curve between Pa and P$\bar{v}$ is nearly linear); 3) the disturbing effects of functional inhomogeneities are of reduced importance.

An analysis, based on the values reported by Cerretelli (1976) on members of the Italian 1973 Mount Everest expedition in the base camp (altitude 5350 m) led to the following conclusions (cf., Piiper and Scheid, 1981; 1983).

1.  There is considerable diffusion limitation as shown by the $L_{diff}$ values: 0.12 at rest, 0.64 during maximum $O_2$ uptake exercise.
2.  In resting conditions, the limiting role of perfusion in $O_2$ transport is quantitatively more important than that of pulmonary diffusion; but, in heavy exercise, diffusion limitation becomes predominant.

### E. Cutaneous Gas Exchange in Amphibians

Cutaneous gas exchange occurs to a certain extent in all vertebrates, but is of particular importance in amphibians (cf., Feder and Burggren, 1985). It is best studied in lung-less, gill-less salamanders in which all gas transfer takes place through the body skin and buccopharyngeal mucosa.

From comparative measurements of the equilibration kinetics of soluble inert gases in living and dead specimens of exclusively skin-breathing salamanders (Gatz et al., 1975), the $D/(\dot{Q} \cdot \beta b)$ ratio for cutaneous transfer of Freon 22 was estimated at 0.42–0.63, showing combined diffusion and perfusion limitation. But the extrapolated $D/(Q \cdot \beta b)$ ratio for $O_2$ and $CO_2$ yielded values showing predominant diffusion limitation. The observed dependence of $O_2$ uptake upon the ambient $Po_2$ was in agreement with the diffusion-limited nature of $O_2$ transfer. Moreover, the estimated $Do_2$ was in reasonable accordance with the $Do_2$ derived from morphometric measurements (Piiper et al., 1976).

More recently, it has been shown, however, that plethodontid salamanders are capable of increasing their $O_2$ uptake during exercise several times above the resting level (Withers, 1980; Feder, 1985; Full, 1985). This is difficult to explain without the assumption of a substantial increase in D. Similarly, studies by Burggren and Moalli (1984) and Malvin and Hlastala (1986) have shown that in frogs the skin conductance for gases can change, apparently by regulation of the number of perfused capillaries. A recent study, however, indicates that gas conductance of frog skin can change without changes in the number of perfused capillaries, apparently by changes in blood flow (Malvin and Hlastala, 1989).

### IV. Various Gas Exchange Organs and their Models

The functional properties of gas exchange organs of vertebrates—gills, skin, and lungs—can be described in terms of four models (Piiper and Scheid, 1972;

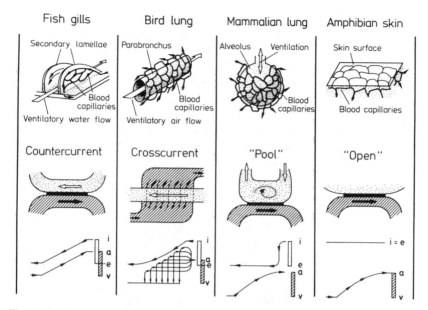

**Figure 6** Models for gas exchange organs in vertebrates and partial pressures in medium (water or air) and blood. The profiles in medium, between the entrance to (i) and the exit from (e) the organ, as well as in blood, between venous (v) and arterial (a) values, are indicated. (After Piiper and Scheid, 1982.)

1975; 1977; 1982). The functional anatomy and the models is shown in Figure 6.

### A. Fish Gills

The rows of secondary lamellae carried by the gill filaments form a fine sieve for respiratory water. Gas exchange takes place in the blood lacunae of the secondary lamellae, which receive venous blood from the ventral aorta and send the arterialized outflow into the arterial system. The anatomical arrangement is such that water and blood flow in opposite directions (*countercurrent model*).

### B. Amphibian Skin

Skin breathing is important in all extant amphibians, being the only alley of gas exchange in those salamanders (terrestrial and aquatic) that possess neither lungs nor gills. Gas exchange takes place in the dense subepidermal capillary network (*open model*), the inflow to which is from the arterial system; additionally, in anurans, from a branch of the pulmonary arch carrying venous blood. The oxygenated cutaneous blood flows into the venous system.

### C.  Avian Lungs

The lungs are formed by several parabronchi (or tertiary bronchi), in parallel arrangement, most of which connect the mediodorsal secondary bronchi with the medioventral secondary bronchi. Air passes through the parabronchi, unidirectionally both during inspiration and expiration in the major part of the lungs, bidirectionally in a smaller part (neopulmo). Gas exchange takes place in the periparabronchial tissue, consisting of an interwoven network of air capillaries and blood capillaries. The simplest model adequate for gas transfer in avian lungs is the serial multicapillary, or *crosscurrent model* (Scheid and Piiper, 1972; Scheid, 1979).

### D.  Mammalian Lungs

The airways of mammalian lungs constitute a highly branching system of numerous orders of bronchi, leading to bronchi with alveoli and, finally, to alveolar ducts, the walls of which are entirely made up of alveoli surrounded by a blood capillary network. Since the renewal fraction of alveolar gas per breath is small, the variations in the composition of alveolar gas are relatively small and, for a simplified analysis, a constant composition of alveolar gas may be assumed (*ventilated pool model*). The same functional model may be used for the lungs of amphibians and some reptiles; however, in lungs of other reptiles there is a marked tendency to develop nonalveolated regions, resembling avian air sacs (Duncker, 1978).

### E.  Comparison of Models: Gas Exchange Efficiency

The decisive parameter for the overall gas exchange performance of a gas exchange organ, or its model, is the *total conductance,* defined as transfer rate divided by the inspired–venous partial pressure difference, $G_{tot} = M/(Pi - Pv)$. A comparison of $G_{tot}$ for the various models yields the picture shown in Figure 7. The following decreasing order of gas exchange efficiency is obtained for the models (the *infinite pool* model is a limiting case, resulting from all models when $G_{vent}$ approaches infinity): countercurrent > crosscurrent > ventilated pool. Figure 7 also shows that the differences in efficiency between the models are largest with good diffusion conditions ($G_{diff}$ large to infinity).

　　The reason for the adoption of a certain type of gas exchange organ by the different vertebrate groups cannot be sought in the gas exchange requirements alone. Nevertheless, the following factors appear to play a role.

1.　As water breathing is energetically costly (see foregoing), it is important for fishes to use the scarce dissolved $O_2$ as effectively as possible. This is achieved by the countercurrent arrangement.
2.　Birds, many of which are capable of sustained flight at high altitudes,

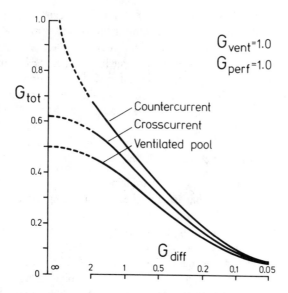

**Figure 7** Total exchange conductance, $G_{tot}$, as a function of the diffusive conductance, $G_{diff}$, for the three (finite) models of Figure 6.

require particularly efficient gas exchange organs. However, the higher tolerance of hypoxia in birds, compared with mammals, probably results from an interaction of multiple, as yet unknown, factors besides the efficient crosscurrent type gas–blood arrangement in avian lungs (Shams and Scheid, 1987).

## V. Limitations to the Applicability of the Models

The models have been analyzed on the basis of simplifying assumptions (Piiper and Scheid, 1972; 1975; 1977; 1982). When these simple models are applied to experimental gas exchange data, one usually finds a much lower efficiency than expected. This may result from strong diffusion limitation, but it may also be due to a number of complicating factors discussed in the following sections.

### A. Unsteady State

The simplified models are applicable to steady-state gas exchange only. But, in reality, ventilation is always cyclic (with the possible exception of ram ventilation in swimming fish), and blood flow is always pulsatile. In spite of this, in animals breathing regularly and not too slowly (which usually holds for mammals, birds, fish) ventilation and blood flow may, with sufficient accuracy, be modeled as being continuous. In amphibians and reptiles, however, very slow or periodic breathing (groups of breaths preceded and followed by apneic periods) is common (reviewed by Glass and Wood, 1983). In such cases, more elaborate models containing capacitances for $O_2$ and $CO_2$ have to be used for analysis of gas exchange and transport (Piiper, 1982). In diving air breathers, capacitances attain prominent importance as measures for the availability of $O_2$ and for storage of $CO_2$.

### B. Medium Flow and Composition

Applicability of the models rests on partial pressure data in medium entering (Pi) and leaving the gas exchange area (Pe). While sampling of gas or water entering (PI) or leaving the animal (PE) is relatively easy, the relation of the partial pressures thus obtained to those at the gas exchange area depends on structural and functional parameters.

Lungs are connected to the external body surface by conducting airways in which little or no gas exchange takes place and which, therefore, constitute a respiratory dead space. In mammals, the effect of this (anatomical) dead space on pulmonary gas exchange is usually taken into account by using alveolar partial pressures (PA) and by defining an effective or alveolar ventilation, calculated as the difference between the total ventilation and dead space ventilation.

Since in bird lungs there is no mixing pool comparable with the mammalian alveolar space, application of the concept of dead space is problematic (Scheid et al., 1989). Moreover, the relation of Pi and Pe to PI and PE is complex and depends on the airflow pattern in the lung. According to direct sampling (Powell et al., 1981), Pe is close to P in end-expired gas or in clavicular air sac gas. A proper estimation of Pi, however, is complex. Caudal air sac gas (for expiratory phase) and a mixture calculated from inspired and reinhaled dead space gas (for inspiratory phase) may be used, but the effect of neopulmonic gas exchange remains a problem (Scheid et al., 1989).

Fish are sometimes said to have the advantage of having no dead space because their ventilation is unidirectional. But water flow bypassing the inter-lamellar spaces would functionally correspond to (alveolar) dead space ventilation, and water moving fast in the central stream through the interlamellar spaces may contribute very little to gas exchange and, accordingly, act as dead space ventilation as well. Here, and in many other instances, there is a transition from "diffusion limitation" to "dead space ventilation."

### C. Blood Flow and Composition

It follows from the general arrangement of the circulatory system and its connection with the respiratory organ that only in fish, birds, and mammals is systemic arterial blood essentially identical in composition with the blood leaving the respiratory organ and that the extent of respiratory organ perfusion is close to that of body perfusion (cardiac output). Even in fish, there is anatomical and functional evidence for several kinds of accessory vascular pathways, some of which act as shunts (reviewed by Laurent, 1984).

In reptiles and amphibians, with their incomplete separation of the right and left heart, shunting is always expected to occur and to reduce arterial $P_{O_2}$. Further complications arise in amphibians because part of the skin is supplied with arterialized blood from systemic arterial branches and part by venous blood through the pulmocutaneous artery. Arterialized skin blood enters the venous system. In the lungless plethodontids, in which skin (and buccal mucosa) is the only site of gas exchange, the circulatory system is secondarily simplified into a system in which the gas exchange organ is in parallel to the systemic capillaries (in contrast with fish, birds, and mammals) and in which all organs, including skin, receive blood of the same composition (Gatz et al., 1975).

## VI. Functional Inhomogeneities

All gas exchange organs consist of numerous units (secondary lamellae in fish gills, alveoli and lobuli in mammalian lungs, parabronchi in avian lungs) that are funtionally arranged in parallel. It can be stated quite generally that if any two of the variable influencing the conductances (e.g., ventilation, blood flow, or diffusive conductance) are differently distributed among the units (functional inhomogeneity) the total gas exchange efficiency of the system is reduced compared with equal distribution (functional homogeneity). Identification and quantitative assessment of the effects of inhomogeneities (unequal distribution of ventilation or diffusing capacity to blood flow) is usually a difficult task. If the inhomogeneities are neglected or if their extent is underestimated, the diffusion conductance may be undervalued by a large factor.

### A. Unequal Distribution of Ventilation to Perfusion

*Mechanism of Reduced Gas Exchange Efficiency*

A mammalian lung model in which alveolar ventilation ($\dot{V}_A$) is unequally distributed to blood flow ($\dot{Q}$), whereby different parallel regions have different ratios of $\dot{V}_A/\dot{Q}$, has reduced gas exchange efficiency and, thus, yields alveolar–arterial differences for $O_2$ and $CO_2$ (AaD) in the absence of diffusion limitation. The basic mechanism for generation of AaD is the flow-weighted mixing of gas and blood. The higher the $\dot{V}_A/\dot{Q}$ ratio in a given unit, the higher $P_{O_2}$, and the lower $P_{CO_2}$, in alveolar gas and arterialized blood of this region, and vice versa for lower $\dot{V}_A/\dot{Q}$. The "mixed" alveolar gas is biased to regions with high $\dot{V}_A/\dot{Q}$ and, hence, with high $P_{O_2}$ and low $P_{CO_2}$, because it constitutes a venti-

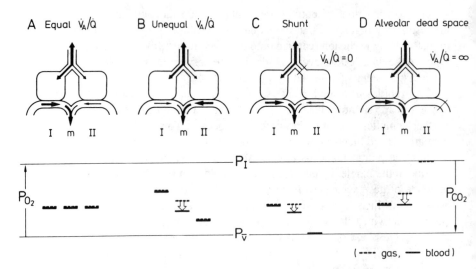

**Figure 8** Schematic explanation of alveolar–arterial differences (AaD) caused by un-equal distribution of $\dot{V}A$ to $\dot{Q}$. Indicated are compartments I and II with their gas and blood partial pressures (below) as well as the P values in mixed gas and blood (m). The AaD, visualized by open arrows, are qualitatively similar, but quantitatively different for $O_2$ and $CO_2$. (A) Equal distribution, no AaD. (B) Unequal $\dot{V}A/\dot{Q}$ distribution, AaD because of different flow-weighting of gas and blood. (C) Shunt; compartment II has no ventilation, its existing blood is unchanged mixed venous blood. (D) Alveolar dead space; compart-ment II has no blood flow, its ventilation is alveolar dead space ventilation, adding unchanged inspired gas to gas expired from compartment I. (After Piiper and Scheid, 1989.)

lation-weighted average. Conversely, "mixed" arterial blood is biased to regions with low $\dot{V}A/\dot{Q}$ and, hence, with low $P_{O_2}$ and high $P_{CO_2}$, because of perfusion-weighted mixing. The result is a higher $P_{O_2}$ and a lower $P_{CO_2}$ in expired alveolar gas than in exiting arterial blood (Fig. 8B), despite the fact that $P_{CO_2}$ and $P_{O_2}$ in alveolar gas and arterialized blood are equal in every lung region.

Extreme cases of $\dot{V}A/\dot{Q}$ inequality are 1) compartment with zero $\dot{V}A/\dot{Q}$, the perfusion of which is venous admixture or shunt (see Fig. 8C); 2) compart-ment with infinite $\dot{V}A/\dot{Q}$, the ventilation of which is alveolar dead space venti-lation (see Fig. 8D).

### Ideal Alveolar Gas and Three-Compartment Model

Although the alveolar–arterial $P_{O_2}$ and $P_{CO_2}$ differences are the important con-sequences and measures of $\dot{V}A/\dot{Q}$ inequality, there are problems in obtaining the proper alveolar gas values. The end-tidal gas as a measure for average alveolar gas becomes questionable when 1) there is a large regional variation of $P_{CO_2}$

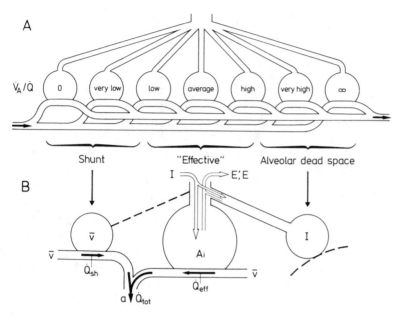

**Figure 9** Continuous $\dot{V}_A/\dot{Q}$ distribution (A) and the three-compartment equivalent model (B). For details, see text. (After Piiper and Scheid, 1989.)

and $P_{O_2}$ (as in diseased human lungs); 2) there is no clear alveolar plateau, but $P_{CO_2}$ rises and $P_{O_2}$ falls during the expiration (this may be due to sequential emptying, i.e., lung regions, usually with high $P_{CO_2}$ and low $P_{O_2}$, expire last); 3) the breathing frequency is very high (problems in recording) or very low (unsteady state).

In all such cases an "ideal alveolar" gas composition can be indirectly obtained (Riley and Cournand, 1949; 1951; Rahn, 1949). The *ideal alveolar* gas is the alveolar gas that an ideal lung (i.e., homogeneous lung without diffusion limitation) would have with the same alveolar ventilation, blood flow, inspired gas, and mixed-venous blood. It can be derived graphically or algebraically, and it yields a functional (analogous) three-compartment model (Fig. 9B), which is composed of 1) a compartment effective in gas exchange, with complete gas–blood equilibration; 2) a shunt compartment representing the venous admixture that is equivalent to perfusion of underventilated lung regions and produces the $P_{O_2}$ difference between the ideal alveolar gas and arterial blood; 3) an alveolar dead space compartment, the ventilation of which has the same effect as ventilation of underperfused lung regions, engendering the $P_{O_2}$ difference between end-expired ideal alveolar gas.

The analysis is applicable to reptiles and amphibians as far as their lungs can be visualized as a mixed-pool system, and their inhomogeneity as $\dot{V}/\dot{Q}$ inhomogeneity. But a relatively regular breathing is a prerequisite. Moreover, the effect of a true intracardiac right-to-left shunt should be separated from effects arising in lungs.

In birds, the lungs of which operate on the basis of the crosscurrent system, it must be considered that in ideal conditions (homogeneous lungs) a negative end-expired to arterial $P_{O_2}$ difference is expected to occur, so that equality of both $P_{O_2}$ values may indicate presence of inhomogeneities. An analysis of $\dot{V}/\dot{Q}$ maldistribution using a two-compartment model has been performed in the duck by Burger et al. (1979).

### Detection of Continuous Distributions of $\dot{V}_A$ to $\dot{Q}$

Distinction between low $\dot{V}_A/\dot{Q}$ and shunt, and between high $\dot{V}_A/\dot{Q}$ and alveolar dead space ventilation, and estimation of the real extent of $\dot{V}_A/\dot{Q}$ inhomogeneity has been made possible by use of multiple inert gases of different solubility in blood (Farhi, 1967). The gases are best infused intravenously, whereby a steady state is achieved (Wagner et al., 1974; Hlastala, 1984).

The method is based on inert gas elimination by an ideal lung, which can be described by the following relationship that shows the arterial/mixed venous partial pressure ratio, termed *retention*, $P_a/P_{\bar{v}}$, for inert gases to depend only on the partition coefficient, $\lambda$, and on $\dot{V}_A/\dot{Q}$:

$$\frac{P_a}{P_{\bar{v}}} = \frac{\lambda}{\lambda + \dot{V}_A/\dot{Q}} \tag{18}$$

This means that 1) a gas of given $\lambda$ is the more efficiently eliminated (less retained: $P_a/P_{\bar{v}}$ smaller) the higher the $\dot{V}_A/\dot{Q}$ ratio; 2) at a certain $\dot{V}_A/\dot{Q}$ ratio, the gas with higher $\lambda$ is less efficiently eliminated (more retained). It follows for use of several gases of different $\lambda$:

1.  For an ideal lung, $P_a$ ($= P_A$) for gases of different $\lambda$ will follow the curve determined by Equation (18) (Fig. 10A).
2.  For a lung with $\dot{V}_A/\dot{Q}$ inhomogeneity (see Fig. 10B), the $P_{c'}$ ($= P_a$) curve will be displaced to the left whereas $P_A$ will be displaced to the right. The quantitative deviations from the behavior of the homogeneous lung allow estimation of the extent and pattern of $\dot{V}_A/\dot{Q}$ inhomogeneity.
3.  In a lung with (anatomical) shunt and (anatomical and alveolar) dead space ventilation, but no further $\dot{V}_A/\dot{Q}$ inhomogeneity (see Fig. 10C), gas and blood values in the gas-exchanging compartment are equal ($P_A = P_{c'}$). A shunt reduces the ($P_{\bar{v}} - P_a$), difference for all gases by a constant factor, and for very low $\lambda$, when $P_{c'} = 0$ ($= P_I$) in

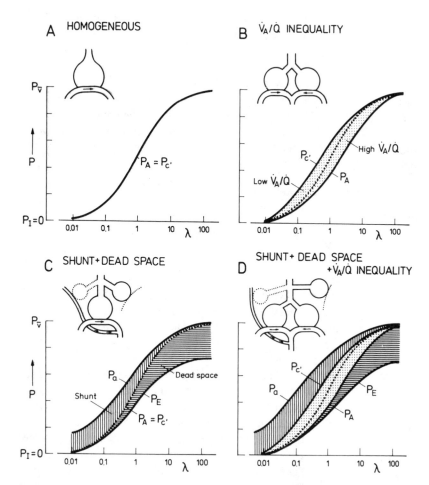

**Figure 10** Multiple inert gas elimination in alveolar lungs. Partial pressure (ordinate) plotted against inert gas solubility (gas–blood partition coefficient λ; abscissa) in the homogeneous lung (A) or in lungs with various types of functional parallel inhomogeneity (B–D). For details, see text. (After Piiper and Scheid, 1989.)

ventilated regions, the fractional shunt becomes identical with the retention, Pa/Pv̄. Dead space ventilation reduces the PA values for all gases by a constant factor; for very high λ, when PA = Pv̄, the fractional dead space ventilation is given by 1 − PE/Pv̄ (where E refers to mixed expired gas).

Using six gases of suitable λ (from < 0.01, SF$_6$, to > 100, acetone) and applying particular numerical procedures, continuous V̇A to Q̇ distributions (including shunt and dead space ventilation) have been determined in laboratory animals and in normal and diseased humans (reviewed by West, 1977; Hlastala, 1984). In spite of very high accuracy requirements and laborious techniques, the method has now been successfully introduced into physiological and clinical pulmonary function laboratories.

The method has been applied with remarkable success to the domestic duck. Here, the evaluation must be based on a (nondiffusion-limited) cross-current model (Powell and Wagner, 1982a,b). It should be noted that the method is not applicable in water breathing because, here, inert cases covering a wide range in the blood–water partition coefficient (rather than the blood–gas partition coefficient) are required, but not available.

### B. Other Functional Inhomogeneities

Besides the $\dot{V}_A/\dot{Q}$ inhomogeneity, other kinds of inhomogeneity have been considered for mammalian lungs and may well be expected to occur in other exchange organs.

#### Inequality of D/($\dot{Q}$ · βb)

It was shown in the foregoing that the equilibration coefficient $D/(\dot{Q} \cdot \beta b)$ determines the extent of equilibration of pulmonary capillary blood with alveolar gas in mammalian lungs. The effect of unequal $D/(\dot{Q} \cdot \beta b)$ is to reduce the overall gas transfer, because a decrease of $D/(\dot{Q} \cdot \beta b)$ diminishes gas transfer more than an increase of the ratio enhances it. The extreme case of $D/(\dot{Q} \cdot \beta b)$ = 0 leads to shunt (Piiper, 1961a). There are several factors that are expected to produce some local variability of this ratio. 1) Capillary length may vary considerably among parallel lung units. A short capillary is bound to have low D, high $\dot{Q}$ (owing to reduced resistance to flow), and a short transit time. In the extreme case, this unit may act as a shunt. 2) The thickness of the gas–blood barrier may vary, particularly with incipient alveolar edema. 3) Pulmonary capillary blood flow is known to vary regionally owing to variable distension by hydrostatic pressure. 4) Variations of hematocrit are known to occur in the microcirculation, the branch with smaller resistance and higher flow receives disproportionately more red blood cells and, thus, has a higher βb.

An evaluation of the alveolar gas exchange inefficiency in terms of $D/\dot{Q}$ inequality was attempted in anesthetized dogs when the alveolar–arterial differences appeared not to fit the expectation for $\dot{V}/\dot{Q}$ inequality (Piiper et al., 1961). Generally, there may occur both $\dot{V}_A/\dot{Q}$ and $D/(\dot{Q} \cdot \beta b)$ inequality in lungs. Here, the gas exchange behavior of lungs may be analyzed in terms of a two-dimensional $\dot{V}_A/\dot{Q}$ and $D/(\dot{Q} \cdot \beta b)$ "field" (Piiper, 1961b).

#### Unequal Distribution of Gas-Phase Conductance

In recent years, asymmetric lung airway models (i.e., with asymmetric pattern of branching and highly varying lengths of the airway branches) have received

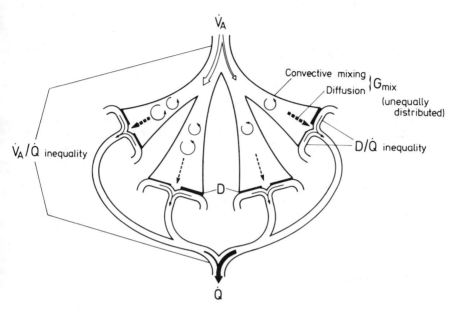

**Figure 11** Schematic representation of combination of various inhomogeneities, including $\dot{V}_A/\dot{Q}$ and $D/\dot{Q}$ inequality, as well as mixing deficiencies in the gas phase (stratification).

attention to explain the slope of the alveolar plateau for inert test gases with low solubility (see foregoing) (e.g., Paiva and Engel, 1984). In terms of function, this means essentially local variation of diffusion resistance in the gas phase.

Corresponding models have been devised to explain experimental results in anesthetized dogs in which the sloping alveolar plateau was measured for several insoluble inert gases of different diffusivity (Meyer et al., 1983; Hook et al., 1985). The experimental data could be simulated by a two-compartment model in which low $\dot{V}_A/V_A$ was associated with a low ratio of the gas-phase-mixing conductance, $G_{mix}/V_A$, and delayed emptying during expiration.

### Combined Inhomogeneities

The aforementioned and other inhomogeneities are expected to occur simultaneously. This would make their identification and estimation of their relative contributions to the overall gas exchange inefficiency a difficult task. In Figure 11 a schematized hypothetical model for a mammalian lung with $\dot{V}/\dot{Q}$, $D/\dot{Q}$, and gas-mixing inhomogeneities is shown. Research aimed at analysis of gas exchange in mammalian lungs on the basis of similar models is under way and in planning. Applicability in modified form to other gas exchange organs should be examined.

## VII.  General Conclusion

The function of external gas exchange organs of vertebrates (lungs, skin, gills) can be analyzed using very simple models that comprise ventilation, medium–blood diffusion, blood flow, and the anatomical–functional arrangement. Besides the flow rates of medium and blood, the effective solubilities (capacitance coefficients) of $O_2$ and $CO_2$ are of equal importance in determining gas transport. The role of diffusion in limiting gas exchange is often difficult to evaluate. The fact that the gas exchange performance is less efficient than that predicted from modeling and from morphometric values is due to discrepancies between the simple models and real organs. Important are difficulties in isolating the medium and blood flow through the respiratory organ proper and various kinds of functional inhomogeneities.

## References

Burger, R. E., Meyer, M., Graf, W., and Scheid, P. (1979). Gas exchange in the parabronchial lung of birds: Experiments in unidirectionally ventilated ducks, *Respir. Physiol.*, **36**:19–37.

Burggren, W. W., and Moalli, R. (1984). "Active" regulation of cutaneous gas exchange by capillary recruitment in amphibians: Experimental evidence and a revised model for skin respiration. *Respir. Physiol.*, **55**:379–392.

Cerretelli, P. (1976). Limiting factors to oxygen transport on Mount Everest. *J. Appl. Physiol.*, **40**:658–667.

Chang, H. K., and Paiva, M., eds. (1989). *Respiratory Physiology: An Analytical Approach.* (*Lung Biology in Health and Disease.* Vol. 40. Edited by C. Lenfant.) New York, Marcel Dekker.

Dejours, P. (1981). *Principles of Comparative Respiratory Physiology*, 2nd ed. Amsterdam, Elsevier.

Dejours, P. (1988). *Respiration in Water and Air*. Amsterdam, Elsevier.

Duncker, H.-R. (1978). General morphological principles of amniotic lungs. In *Respiratory Function in Birds, Adult and Embryonic.* Edited by J. Piiper. Heidelberg, Springer-Verlag, pp. 2–15.

Farhi, L. E. (1967). Elimination of inert gas by the lung. *Respir. Physiol.*, **3**:1–11.

Feder, M. E. (1985). Effects of thermal acclimation on locomotor energetics and locomotor performance in a lungless salamander. *Physiologist*, **28**:342.

Feder, M. E., and Burggren, W. W. (1985). Cutaneous gas exchange in vertebrates: Design, patterns, control, and implications. *Biol. Rev.*, **60**:1–45.

Full, R. J. (1985). Exercising without lungs: Energetics and endurance in a lungless salamander, *Plethodon jordani. Physiologist*, **28**:342.

Gatz, R. N., Crawford, E. C., Jr., and Piiper, J. (1975). Kinetics of inert gas equilibration in an exclusively skin-breathing salamanders, *Desmognathus fuscus*. *Respir. Physiol.*, **24**:15–29.

Glass, M. L., and Wood, S. C. (1983). Gas exchange and control of breathing in reptiles. *Physiol. Rev.*, **63**:232–260.

Hlastala, M. P. (1984). Multiple inert gas elimination technique. *J. Appl. Physiol.*, **56**:1–7.

Hook, C., Meyer, M., and Piiper, J. (1985). Model simulation of single-breath washout of insoluble gases from dog lung. *J. Appl. Physiol.*, **58**:802–811.

Kawashiro, T., Campos Carles, A., and Piiper, J. (1975). Diffusivity of various inert gases in rat skeletal muscle. *Pflügers Arch.*, **359**:219–230.

Laurent, P. (1984). Gill internal morphology. In *Fish Physiology*. Vol. 10A. Edited by W. W. Hoar and D. J. Randall. Orlando, Academic Press, pp. 73–183.

Malvin, G. M., and Hlastala, M. P. (1986). Regulation of cutaneous gas exchange by environmental $O_2$ and $CO_2$ in the frog. *Respir. Physiol.*, **65**:99–111.

Malvin, G. M., and Hlastala, M. P. (1989). Effects of environmental $O_2$ on blood flow and diffusing capacity in amphibian skin. *Respir. Physiol.*, **76**:229–242.

Meyer, M., Tebbe, U., and Piiper, J. (1980). Solubility of inert gases in dog blood and skeletal muscle. *Pflügers Arch.*, **384**:131–134.

Meyer, M., Scheid, P., Riepl, G., Wagner, H. J., and Piiper, J. (1981). Pulmonary diffusing capacities for $O_2$ and CO measured by a rebreathing technique. *J. Appl. Physiol.*, **51**:1643–1650.

Meyer, M., Hook, C., Rieke, H., and Piiper, J. (1983). Gas mixing in dog lungs studied by single-breath washout of He and $SF_6$. *J. Appl. Physiol.*, **55**:1795–1802.

Paiva, M., and Engel, L. A. (1984). Model analysis of gas distribution within human lung acinus. *J. Appl. Physiol.*, **56**:418–425.

Piiper, J. (1961a). Unequal distribution of pulmonary diffusing capacity and the alveolar–arterial $Po_2$ differences: Theory. *J. Appl. Physiol.*, **16**:493–498.

Piiper, J. (1961b). Variations of ventilation and diffusing capacity to perfusion determining the alveolar–arterial $O_2$ difference: Theory. *J. Appl. Physiol.*, **16**:507–510.

Piiper, J. (1979). Series ventilation, diffusion in airways and stratified inhomogeneity. *Fed. Proc.*, **38**:17–21.

Piiper, J. (1982). Respiratory gas exchange at lungs, gills and tissues: Mechanisms and adjustments. *J. Exp. Biol.*, **100**:5–22.

Piiper, J., and Scheid, P. (1972). Maximum gas transfer efficacy of models for fish gills, avian lungs and mammalian lungs. *Respir. Physiol.*, **14**:115–124.

Piiper, J., and Scheid, P. (1975). Gas transport efficacy of gills, lungs and skin: Theory and experimental data. *Respir. Physiol.*, **23**:209–221.

Piiper, J., and Scheid, P. (1977). Comparative physiology of respiration: Functional analysis of gas exchange organs in vertebrates. In *Respiration Physiology* II. Edited by J. G. Widdicombe. *Int. Rev. Physiol. Ser.*, **14**:219–253.

Piiper, J., and Scheid, P. (1981). Model for capillary–alveolar equilibration with special reference to $O_2$ uptake in hypoxia. *Respir. Physiol.*, **46**:193–208.

Piiper, J., and Scheid, P. (1982). Models for a comparative functional analysis of gas exchange organs in vertebrates. *J. Appl. Physiol.*, **53**:1321–1329.

Piiper, J., and Scheid, P. (1983). Comparison of diffusion and perfusion limitations in alveolar gas exchange. *Respir. Physiol.,* **51**:287–290.

Piiper, J., and Scheid, P. (1989). Gas exchange: Theory, models, and experimental data. In *Comparative Pulmonary Physiology.* Edited by S. C. Wood. (Lung Biology in Health and Disease. Vol. 39. Edited by C. Lenfant). New York, Marcel Dekker, pp. 369–416.

Piiper, J., Haab, P., and Rahn, H. (1961). Unequal distribution of pulmonary diffusing capacity in the anesthetized dog. *J. Appl. Physiol.,* **16**:491–506.

Piiper, J., Dejours, P., Haab, P., and Rahn, H. (1971). Concepts and basic quantities in gas exchange physiology. *Respir. Physiol.,* **13**:292–304.

Piiper, J., Gatz, R. N., and Crawford, E. D., Jr. (1976). Gas transport characteristics in an exclusively skin-breathing salamander, *Desmognathus fuscus* (Plethodontidae). In *Respiration of Amphibious Vertebrates.* Edited by G. M. Hughes. New York, Academic Press, pp. 339–356.

Piiper, J., Meyer, M., Marconi, C. and Scheid, P. (1980). Alveolar–capillary equilibration kinetics of $^{13}CO_2$ in human lungs studied by rebreathing. *Respir. Physiol.,* **42**:29–41.

Powell, F. L., and Wagner, P. D. (1982a). Measurement of continuous distributions of ventilation–perfusion in non-alveolar lungs. *Respir. Physiol.,* **48**:219–232.

Powell, F. L., and Wagner, P. D. (1982b). Ventilation–perfusion inequality in avian lungs. *Respir. Physiol.,* **48**:233–24.

Powell, F. L., Geiser, J., Gratz, R. K., and Scheid, P. (1981). Airflow in the avian respiratory tract: Variations of $O_2$ and $CO_2$ concentrations in the bronchi of the duck. *Respir. Physiol.,* **44**:195–213.

Rahn, H. (1949). A concept of mean alveolar air and the ventilation–blood flow relationships during pulmonary gas exchange. *Am. J. Physiol.,* **158**:21–30.

Rahn, H. (1966). Aquatic gas exchange: Theory. *Respir. Physiol.,* **1**:1–12.

Riley, R. L., and Cournand, A. (1949). "Ideal" alveolar air and the analysis of ventilation–perfusion relationships in the lungs. *J. Appl. Physiol.,* **1**:825–847.

Riley, R. L., and Cournand, A. (1951). Analysis of factors affecting partial pressures of oxygen and carbon dioxide in gas and blood of the lungs: Theory. *J. Appl. Physiol.,* **4**:77–101.

Scheid, P. (1979). Mechanisms of gas exchange in bird lungs. *Rev. Physiol. Biochem. Pharmacol.* **86**:137–186.

Scheid, P. (1987). Cost of breathing in water- and air-breathers. In *Comparative Physiology: Life on Land and in Water.* Edited by P. Dejours, L. Bolis, C. R. Taylor, and E. Weibel (Fidia Research Series, Vol. 9). Berlin, Springer-Verlag, pp. 83–92.

Scheid, P., and Piiper, J. (1989). Blood–gas equilibration in lungs and pulmonary diffusing capacity. In *Respiratory Physiology: An Analytical Approach.* Edited by H. K. Chang and M. Paiva. (Lung Biology in Health and Disease, Vol. 40. Edited by C. Lenfant). New York, Marcel Dekker, pp. 453–497.

Scheid, P., Fedde, M. R., and Piiper, J. (1989). Gas exchange and air-sac composition in the unanaesthetized, spontaneously breathing goose. *J. Exp. Biol.,* **142**:373–385.

Shams, H., and P. Scheid (1987). Respiration and blood gases in the duck exposed to normocapnic and hypercapnic hypoxia. *Respir. Physiol.*, **67**:1–12.

Wagner, P. D., Laravuso, R. B., Uhl, R. R., and West, J. B. (1974). Continuous distributions of ventilation–perfusion ratios in normal subjects breathing air and 100% $O_2$. *J. Clin. Invest.*, **54**:54–68.

West, J. B. (1977). Ventilation–perfusion relationships. *Am. Rev. Respir. Dis.*, **116**:919–943.

Withers, P. C. (1980). Oxygen consumption of plethodontid salamanders during rest, activity, and recovery. *Copeia* **1980**:781–786.

Wood, S. C., ed. (1989). *Comparative Pulmonary Physiology: Current Concepts.* (Lung Biology in Health and Disease. Vol. 39, Edited by C. Lenfant, New York, Marcel Dekker.

# 6

## Ventilatory Responses to Hypoxia in Ectothermic Vertebrates

**MOGENS L. GLASS**

Faculdade de Medicina de Ribeirão Preto
University of São Paulo
São Paulo, Brazil

## I. General Introduction

Oxygen transport in vertebrates occurs in four steps: 1) convection of the respired medium (air or water) to the gas exchanger; 2) diffusion from the respired medium to blood; 3) convective transport by the blood; 4) diffusion from blood to tissue. Altered conditions for $O_2$ transport may cause adjustments in all steps of this cascade. For example, a decreased ambient $O_2$ concentration (i.e., environmental hypoxia) will usually cause an increased ventilation of the gas exchanger, with concomitant augmentation of its diffusive conductance. In addition, perfusion of the gas exchanger may increase, combined with a larger $O_2$-carrying capacity and affinity of the blood (cf. Dejours, 1981).

In some species, respiratory responses are combined with altered behavior in the form of an escape maneuver to avoid $O_2$-poor environments. Alternatively, preference of a lower body temperature may decrease metabolic demands, thereby, alleviating $O_2$-transport problems (cf. Wood and Glass, 1991).

The present chapter focuses on ventilatory responses to hypoxia and their control. These responses are important in acute hypoxia because they are immediate, whereas days may be required to complete adjustments of the $O_2$-carrying properties of the blood (cf. Weber, 1982). The discussion of ventilation will be supplemented with some basic information on concomitant regulations involving other steps of the $O_2$ cascade. This serves to clarify the relative role of ventilation and the context in which the ventilatory responses occur.

Preceding a more specific discussion, it may be useful to consider one of "the fundamental equations of respiratory physiology" (Dejours, 1981), which states that:

$$(\dot{V}/\dot{V}O_2) \cdot EO_2 \cdot CI_{O_2} = 1$$

where $\dot{V}$ is ventilation of the gas exchanger, $\dot{V}O_2$ is $O_2$ uptake, $EO_2$ is fraction of $O_2$ extracted from the inspired gas, and $CI_{O_2}$ is the inspired $O_2$ concentration. This relationship implies that extraction or ventilation or both, must increase to maintain $O_2$ uptake, when the inspired $O_2$ concentration declines. The potential for enhancing $EO_2$ is often limited and, consequently, an inverse relationship between ventilation and ambient $O_2$ concentration is predicted if $O_2$ uptake is maintained at a constant level. Such "hyperbolic" curves for the (ventilation–$CI_{O_2}$) relationship have been recorded from all vertebrate groups (cf. Dejours, 1981), and indicate that the ventilatory responses usually maintain $O_2$ uptake. In some species, however, ventilation increases only to a certain level. which is not exceeded with further reductions of $CI_{O_2}$ (Burggren and Cameron, 1980). In other species, ventilatory responses may be inversely related to $CI_{O_2}$, but still be insufficient to maintain $O_2$ transport (Johansen et al., 1967; Steffensen et al., 1982). In these latter instances $\dot{V}O_2$ may decline as a liner function of decreasing $CI_{O_2}$. Species showing this pattern are known as *$O_2$ conformers*, whereas species maintaining a constant $\dot{V}O_2$ over a wide range of environmental $O_2$ concentrations are considered *$O_2$ regulators* (Rantin and Johansen, 1984).

Evident from the equation is the beneficial effect of a low metabolism under conditions of environmental hypoxia: $O_2$ uptake can be sustained with a smaller ventilation. The $O_2$ uptake of an ectothermic vertebrate is often an order of magnitude lower than for a similar-sized mammal or bird and can be substantially reduced by decreased temperature (Else and Hulbert, 1981; Herbert and Jackson, 1985). As will be emphasized in this chapter, temperature is a key variable for respiration in ectothermic vertebrates because it affects metabolism as well as $O_2$-affinity of the blood. Consequently, the general background for respiratory regulation changes with temperature.

The various ectothermic vertebrate groups will be considered in this chapter, although the limited space available will not allow a complete review of the extensive literature. Some themes will not be discussed, although they are important. These include the combined effects of hypoxia and exercise on ventilation. Also, the relative effects of hypoxia on tidal volume and respiratory frequency are sparingly mentioned. Currently, the available information is too scarce for an adequate general discussion of such topics. The focus of the chapter is to compare ventilatory responses to hypoxia in air and water breathers. In particular, differences suggested by recent studies will be pointed out.

## II. Water Breathers

As often stated in the literature, aquatic gas exchange is characterized by a low $O_2$ availability, relative to that of air (cf. Rahn, 1966). For example, at 20°C, the $O_2$ capacitance of air is 30 times larger than the value for distilled water (see Boutilier et al., 1984; for solubility tables). Moreover, large fluctuations in aquatic $O_2$ concentration may occur on a daily, as well as an annual, basis. This phenomenon may receive increasing attention in coming years owing to pollution-induced decreases of $O_2$ concentrations in fresh and coastal waters. The effects of ambient hypoxia on respiration in fish has become a theme of more than academic interest. Solutions to pollution-induced problems in the aquatic environment must involve a knowledge of respiratory regulation in fish, particularly in relation to $O_2$ transport. Moreover, such information is highly relevant to aquaculture.

Ventilatory responses play a major role for fish in $O_2$-poor waters. Fish possess an $O_2$-oriented control of breathing. Gill ventilation is little involved in acid–base regulation, which can be achieved by ion transfer mechanisms (cf. Heisler, 1986). Unfortunately, an ideal method for routine measurement of gill ventilation is not yet available, but previous studies provide a rather consistent picture. When in well-aerated water, fish usually maintain a high $Eo_2$ (often exceeding 50%) (cf. Johansen, 1982), which sets a narrow limit to increases of extraction, implying a necessity of increased ventilation in response to hypoxia if $O_2$ uptake is maintained. Many teleost fish possess a large potential for increasing ventilation relative to normoxic values, because ventilation is periodic (i.e., bursts of breathing activity alternate with breath holding (Gehrke and Fielder, 1988; Roberts and Rowell, 1988). Hypoxia often induces a transition from periodic to continuous breathing, with a concomitant larger tidal volume (Lomholt and Johansen, 1979).

Hypoxia-induced increases of ventilation are substantial in some fish species. For example, the white sucker, *Catostomus commersoni*, may increase ventilation nearly 40-fold in response to severe hypoxia (Saunders, 1982). The magnitude of responses seems to correlate with mode of life of the species, as exemplified by a study on two species of burrowing flatfish that inhabit different water depths (Steffensen et al., 1982). Plaice (*Pleuronectes platessa*) occur at depths between 10 and 50 m, whereas the flounder (*Platichthys flesus*) inhabits more shallow coastal waters, which are characterized by large diurnal fluctuations in $O_2$ availability, with hypoxic conditions occurring at dawn ($Pw_{O_2}$ down to 20 mm Hg). This time of day corresponds to a period of activity in flounder (Kerstens et al., 1979). Steffensen et al. (1982) found that, in well-aerated water, ventilation was the same for both species, but that hypoxia caused the flounder to increase ventilation markedly more than the plaice. As a consequence, $O_2$ uptake was better maintained in the former species. This correlates well with the ability of flounder to inhabit more hypoxic environments.

As a curious fact, the ventilatory response to ambient hypoxia in fish is not accompanied by any substantial increase of gill perfusion. Instead, a hypoxic bradycardia develops along with an augmentation of stroke volume. As the combined consequence of both changes, perfusion is the same as for normoxic conditions, or even slightly decreased (Garey, 1970; Farrell, 1981; Randall, 1982; Pettersson and Johansen, 1982). This lack of an increased blood flow may not be critical to $O_2$ transport. An analysis by Scheid and Piiper (1976) showed that gas exchange in the dogfish, *Scyliorhinus stellaris*, is markedly more limited by ventilation and diffusion than by perfusion of the gills, and consistent data exist for the carp (Itazawa and Takeda, 1978). As pointed out by Scheid and Piiper this implies that increases of ventilation much more effectively promote $O_2$ transport than would an equivalent rise in perfusion. A study on rainbow trout deserves mention in this context. Iwama et al. (1987) altered and controlled gill water flow and found a large fall in $Pa_{O_2}$, if flow was reduced below 100 ml/min.

Rather severe hypoxic conditions have been applied in most studies. This may well serve to achieve large responses, but as a disadvantage, information is lacking on hypoxic thresholds. Interesting aspects may have been overlooked, because indications are that relatively small decreases of water $Po_2$ may cause rather large ventilatory responses (Burggren and Cameron, 1980; Rantin and Johansen, 1984). In comparison, much larger decreases of inspired $Po_2$ are required to achieve such responses in air-breathing vertebrates (Fig. 1). This is consistent with the low $O_2$ content of water, relative to that of air (cf. Dejours, 1981; and see equation in the general introduction).

Two aspects of ventilatory control have been difficult to assess for hypoxic responses in fish. The first concerns the specific stimulus causing the responses to hypoxia. The second concerns the number and locations of $O_2$ receptors involved. Candidates for the stimulus include arterial or water $Po_2$ ($Pa_{O_2}$, $Pw_{O_2}$), $O_2$ saturation of the blood ($Sa_{O_2}$), or blood $O_2$ content ($Ca_{O_2}$). A study on rainbow trout suggested that $Ca_{O_2}$ was the adequate stimulus because an inverse relationship was found between gill ventilation and $Ca_{O_2}$. In addition, hypercapnia caused a reduction in $Ca_{O_2}$ whereas $Pa_{O_2}$ remained constant. This reduction was accompanied by increased ventilation (Smith and Jones, 1982; reviewed by Randall, 1982), but recent studies indicate a more complicated picture.

Glass et al. (1990) measured ventilatory responses to ambient hypoxia in

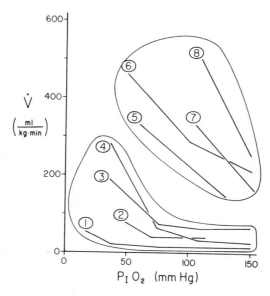

**Figure 1**   Ventilatory responses to decreased inspired $Po_2$ as shown for selected air- (1 to 4) or water-breathing (5–8) vertebrates: (1, 4) northern painted turtle, *Chrysemys picta bellii* (1:20°C; 4:30°C) (Glass et al., 1983); (2) monitor lizard, *Varanus exanthematicus* (35°C) (Glass et al., 1979); (3) toad, *Bufo paracnemis* (32°C) (Kruhøffer et al., 1987); (5) starry flounder, *Platichthys stellaris* (9–11°C) (Watters and Smith, 1973); (6) erythrinid teleost, *Hoplias malebaricus* (20°C) (Rantin and Johansen, 1984); (7) channel catfish, *Ictalurus punctatus* (18°C) (Burggren and Cameron, 1980); (8) carp, *Cyprinus carpio* (20°C) (Glass et al., 1990). See text for further explanation.

carp while monitoring blood gases. Large increases of ventilation occurred without any decrease in $Sa_{O_2}$ on $Ca_{O_2}$, in part because hyperventilation decreased pHa, causing a higher $O_2$ affinity of the blood from the Bohr effect. It seems unlikely that the stimulus to breathing can be basically different in two species of teleost fish, and further research may be required. As an additional complication, hypoxia-induced decreases of $Pa_{O_2}$ in carp were small and inconsistent, whereas ventilatory responses were large and well-defined relative to $Pw_{O_2}$. This implies that a response curve for ventilation versus $Pa_{O_2}$ will be unconventionally steep, lacking any clear dose–response relationship. This finding suggests involvement of nonarterial receptor sites.

Recent work on $O_2$-receptor location improved the understanding of ventilation–$Pa_{O_2}$ relationships in fish. Studying the yellowfin tuna (*Thunnus albareces*) Milsom and Brill (1986) obtained in vitro recordings of afferent impulses from the tenth cranial nerve, which innervates the first gill arch. This approach was motivated by the possible homology between the artery of this arch and the carotid artery, at which the mamallian carotid body $O_2$ receptors are located (Butler et al., 1977). Some of the studied fibers of the tenth cranial nerve of tuna responded to alterations of $Po_2$ in the bathing medium containing the preparation. Likewise, changes in $Po_2$ of the perfusate affected impulse frequency of some fibers, even when changes in the $Po_2$ of the bathing medium were ineffective. Differential sensitivity of different sites to the $Po_2$ of perfusate and external medium may provide a background for interpretation of ventilatory responses: the important point being that a decreased $Pw_{O_2}$ may stimulate ventilation, independently of changes in $Pa_{O_2}$.

More locations for $O_2$ receptors in fish have been suggested and, in part, documented (reviewed by Randall and Daxboeck, 1984). In addition, differences may exist between species. Nevertheless, the study on tuna is important because it reports on receptors that discharge with an $O_2$ sensitivity equal to that of carotid body receptors in mammals. The study was conducted at 25°C, and a higher temperature would probably have increased their sensitivity farther. On this background, the receptors seem good candidates for playing a dominant role in control of breathing. Moreover, their location suggests a widespread occurrence, provided the homology with mammalian receptors.

Randall (1987) pointed to a further complication for evaluation of ventilatory responses to hypoxia. An increased circulating catecholamine level could possibly stimulate ventilation. Evidence against a major role of this mechanism is that cessation of a severely hypoxic condition causes a nearly instantaneous return of ventilation to normoxic values (Lomholt and Johansen, 1979). This would rather indicate involvement of fast-responding $O_2$ receptors.

Relatively few studies address the effects of temperature on ventilatory regulation in fish, and available data are inconsistent. Gehrke and Fielder (1988) measured the effects of combined changes in $Pw_{O_2}$ and water temperature on breathing frequency in the spangled perch (*Leiopotherapon unicolor*) and reported a depression of responses by low temperature. In contrast, Spitzer et al. (1969) observed a depression of the frequency response to hypoxia if bluegill sunfish (*Lepomis macrochirus*) were maintained at high temperature. These divergent results could be caused by different temperature acclimation ranges of the species. A study on *Oreochromis niloticus* (Cichlidae) reports that ventilatory responses to hypoxia were considerable when studied at temperatures between 20 and 35°C, corresponding to the range encountered in the natural habitats of the species (Fernandes and Rantin, 1989) (Fig. 2). Consistently, Glass et al. (1990) have measured ventilatory responses to moderate hypoxia in carp at 15 and 25°C. Substantial responses occurred at both tempertures, with consequent reduction of $Pa_{CO_2}$ to half of the normoxic value when $Pw_{O_2} \sim 75$ mm Hg. In both carp and *Oreochromis*, ventilation decreased with reduced temperature, but the responses to hypoxia were substantial, regardless of temperature, if considered as a percentage relative to normoxic baseline values. This can be regarded

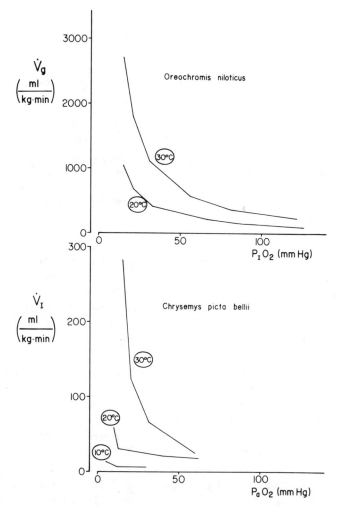

**Figure 2** Comparison of ventilatory responses to hypoxia at different temperatures. Responses are markedly depressed at low temperature in a reptile, the turtle *Chrysemys picta bellii*, whereas responses are better maintained at reduced temperature in the cyclic fish *Oreochromis niloticus*. For reasons explained in the text the responses of *Chrysemys* are related to Pa$_{O_2}$, whereas PI$_{O_2}$ is applied for *Oreochromis*. Notice the different scales of the ordinates. (Based on Glass et al., 1983, for *Chrysemys*; Fernandes and Rantin, 1989, for *Oreochromis*.)

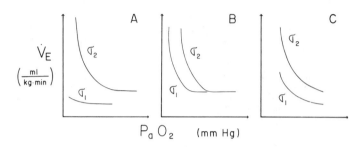

**Figure 3** Schematic presentation of possible ventilatory responses to hypoxia at decreased temperature: (A) Reduction of responses (sensitivity and threshold); (B) low temperature shifts the threshold for responses to the left, but the "gain" of the responses is independent of temperature; (C) Decreased temperature shifts the baseline down while the threshold and gain are independent of temperature. See text for further discussion.

as a proportionate reduction of ventilatory events when temperature decreases, whereas a depression of ventilatory responses implies a disproportionate reduction of ventilatory responses relative to baseline values (Fig. 3).

Fundamental differences in $O_2$ regulation between fish and ectothermic air breathers are indicated by the effects of temperature on $Pa_{O_2}$. Both in trout (Randall and Cameron, 1973) and carp (Andersen et al., in preparation; Glass et al., 1990) the values for $Pa_{O_2}$ are independent of temperature (Fig. 4), implying a declining $Sa_{O_2}$, when blood $O_2$ affinity decreases with rising temperature. Conversely, amphibians and reptiles tend to maintain a constant temperature-independent saturation, which causes a rise in $Pa_{O_2}$ with rising temperature (cf. Wood, 1982; 1984; (see Fig. 4). Unfortunately for consistency Watters and Smith (1973), studying the starry flounder, measured a twofold increase of $Pa_{O_2}$ with a rise of temperature from 15 to 36°C. Further studies seem needed to achieve a more complete picture.

A special aspect of ventilatory regulation in fish concerns *ram ventilation*, which is a term coined for passive irrigation of gills while breathing movements are absent. Passive ventilation can be achieved by keeping an open mouth during swimming or by adequate orientation in a fast current. Transition from active to ram ventilation in trout depends on swimming speed. In turn, the swimming speed that must be achieved for transition depends on ambient $Po_2$ (Steffensen, 1985): A higher swimming speed is required to obtain sufficient ventilation if $Pw_{O_2}$ is low. This response occurs in the skipjack tuna, *Katsuwonis pelamis*, which increases swimming speed as an inverse function of ambient $Po_2$ (Gooding et al., 1981). This $O_2$ dependence of ram ventilation also applies to the shark-sucker, *Echeneis naucrates*, which may enjoy passive ventilation through transportation by its host. In this species the combined effects of ambient $Po_2$ and

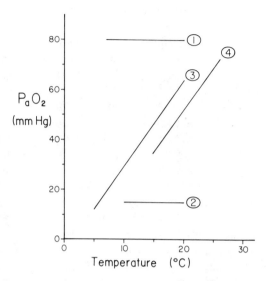

**Figure 4** The effects of temperature on $Pa_{O_2}$ in (1) rainbow trout, *Salmo gairdneri* (Randall and Cameron, 1973); (2) carp, *Cyprinus carpio* (Glass et al., 1990); (3) northern painted turtle, *Chrysemys picta bellii* (Glass et al., 1983); (4) toad, *Bufo paracnemis* (Kruhøffer et al., 1987). See text.

swimming speed of the host determine conditions for transition (Steffensen, 1985).

In conclusion, fish possess ventilatory responses to hypoxia that match species-specific demands. These responses are not accompanied by corresponding increases of gill perfusion. The underlying specific $O_2$ stimulus is still uncertain, whereas progress has been made in establishing receptor location. Arterial $P_{O_2}$ may remain constant, regardless of body temperature, and relatively large ventilatory responses to hypoxia are also maintained at lower temperatures.

## III. Air-Breathing Fish

Numerous fish species belonging to different groups are equipped with organs for air breathing. Most of these inhabit tropical and subtropical lakes and rivers. Such organs may consist of pouches extending from the branchial cavity, as in the snakehead fish, *Channa argus* (Ishimatsu and Itazawa, 1983). Alternatively, regions of the gastrointestinal tract may be modified to perform gas exchange (e.g., *Hypostomus regani*; Favaretto et al., 1980). Proper lungs are present in extant representatives of several ancient groups (For a review and information on further types of air-breathing organs see Johansen, 1970; Burggren et al., 1985).

The assembly of "air-breathing fish" is highly inhomogeneous from a phylogenetic viewpoint. The members include ancient forms, such as the *Polypteriformes*, which belong to the chondrosteans, an extant group of actinopterygians with ancient traits that are not present in their relatives, the modern teleost fish (Carroll, 1988). Included are also the lungfish (*Dipnoi*), which may be more closely related to ancestors of amphibians than to teleost fish (Waehneldt et al., 1987). Uniform regulatory patterns can hardly be expected, given this phylogenetic diversity. Examples of differences will be presented in the following discussion, but general trends will also be pointed out. As the main theme, the effects of aquatic hypoxia will be considered in relation to control of breathing.

Some species may rely predominantly on gill ventilation, provided there is a high $Pw_{O_2}$. *Polypterus* sp. are equipped with ventrally positioned and bilateral elongate lungs, arising from the eosophagus. These lungs are not ventilated when *P. senegalus* is maintained in well-aerated water. Pulmonary ventilation becomes important only with progressively decreasing $Pw_{O_2}$. Total $O_2$ uptake is kept constant regardless of $Pw_{O_2}$, because air breathing compensates for a reduced aquatic $O_2$ uptake (Babiker, 1984). *Polypterus* in anoxic water depends exclusively on pulmonary ventilation and, concomitantly, it avoids losing significant amounts of $O_2$ from skin and gills to anoxic water, implying a "shutdown" of branchial exchange (Lomholt and Glass, 1987). The Australian lungfish (*Neoceratodus forsteri*) provides another example of this type of bimodal control of breathing. It possesses lungs, which are homologous with those of terrestrial vertebrates. Johansen and associates (1967) found that, in spite of the potential for pulmonary breathing, this species relies exclusively on gas exchange by its well-developed gills, provided that $Pw_{O_2}$ is sufficiently high. Moderate decreases of $Pw_{O_2}$ are compensated for by an increased branchial ventilation. The onset of additional pulmonary ventilation requires decreases of $Pw_{O_2}$ to less than 90 mm Hg. Concomitantly with development of pulmonary ventilation, the perfusion of the lungs constitute a larger fraction of total cardiac output.

In contrast with the situation in *Polypterus* and *Neoceratodus*, some species maintain an aerial ventilation that depends little on $Pw_{O_2}$. This applies to *Channa argus*, which inhabits fresh waters of temperate East Asia. Under normoxic conditions at 25°C, as much as 60% of its $O_2$ uptake is obtained by air breathing. Aerial ventilation is little affected by changes in $Pw_{O_2}$, whereas decreased $Po_2$ of the gas contained in the air-breathing organ causes marked increases of aerial ventilation (Glass et al., 1986). This pattern also applies to the African lungfish (*Protopterus aethiopicus*), which possesses a combination of lungs and reduced gills (Johansen and Lenfant, 1968). As a general trend, species with heavy dependence on air breathing combined with a reduced branchial respiration will not change aerial ventilation much in response to variations in $Pw_{O_2}$ (cf. Johansen,

1970). Conversely, species equipped with well-developed gills may depend little on air breathing if $Pw_{O_2}$ is sufficiently high. In such species the frequency of air ventilation often rises steeply with decreases of $Pw_{O_2}$. This situation applies to *Trichogaster* (Burggren, 1979), *Lepisosteus* (Smatresk and Cameron, 1982), *Piabucina* (Graham et al., 1977), and *Synbrancus* (Bicudo and Johansen, 1979).

Johansen and colleagues (1970) studied the effects of decreased $Pw_{O_2}$ on gas exchange in the bowfin (*Amia calva*), a holostean fish, possessing a well-developed gill as well as an effective air-breathing organ. This study provides examples of interaction between aquatic and aerial gas exchange. For example, at 20°C, a steep increase of aerial ventilation coincided with a decrease of $Pw_{O_2}$ to about 50 mm Hg. Concomitantly, the frequency of gill ventilation was reduced. The authors (Johansen et al., 1970), also studied the effect of increasing temperature on the "gain" of ventilatory responses to decreased $Pw_{O_2}$. A rising temperature markedly enhanced the effect of $Pw_{O_2}$ on aerial ventilation in accordance with larger demands for $O_2$. An amplifying effect of temperature on ventilatory responses to hypoxia is also typical of amphibians and reptiles (see later sections).

As mentioned earlier, the water-breathing fish lack any marked response to environmental hypercapnia (cf. Dejours, 1981). Likewise, fish with bimodal breathing will usually not increase aerial ventilation much if $CO_2$ is inhaled into the air-breathing organ. This applies to the Cuchia eel (*Amphipnous cuchia*), which increases ventilation only when an inspired $PCO_2$ exceeds 30 mm Hg (Lomholt and Johansen, 1974). A low $CO_2$ sensitivity of aerial ventilation also characterizes *Trichogaster* (Burggren, 1979) and *Channa argus* (Glass et al., 1986). In contrast, marked ventilatory responses to inspiration of hypoxic gases occur in the same species. In *Channa* these responses were enhanced by a rise of temperature (Glass et al., 1986).

## IV. Pulmonary Breathing: Amphibians and Reptiles

An ectothermic air breather may never inhale hypoxic gases. Hypoxic exposure occurs only in species in special habitats, such as high altitude or subterranean spaces (Abe and Johansen, 1987). Ventilation, however, is not regulated relative to ambient $Po_2$, but relative to $O_2$ receptors, probably screening arterial blood (see later). An efficient and practical way to study the function of this regulatory system is to decrease $Pa_{O_2}$ by inspiration of hypoxic gas mixtures. The foregoing statement may provide new insights to those who doubt the biological significance of hypoxia experiments just because amphibians and reptiles are unlikely to climb Mount Everest.

Both amphibians and reptiles increase pulmonary ventilation in response to a decreased inspired $Po_2$ ($PI_{O_2}$). Relatively large decreases may be required to cause ventilatory responses, and the regulatory system may seem less sensitive than in fish (see Fig. 1). It should be noted, however, that the chemical control of breathing in anuran amphibians and reptiles is markedly oriented toward acid–base regulation (cf. Dejours, 1981). A ventilatory response to hypoxia will reduce $Pa_{CO_2}$, thereby decreasing the acid–base-related drive to breathing. This may act as a "brake" on the ventilatory responses to hypoxia, until substantial decreases of $Pa_{O_2}$ have occurred. That an $O_2$-mediated drive to breathing exists also during inspiration of air at sea level can be shown by applying a brief episode of pure $O_2$ inhalation. A transient reduction of ventilation follows $O_2$-inhalation in reptiles (Glass and Johansen, 1976, Benchetrit et al., 1977; Glass et al., 1978). These responses show that part of the normoxic chemical drive to breathing arises from $O_2$ receptors.

Both amphibians and reptiles ventilate the lungs in a periodic manner during which breath holding alternates with breathing activity, which may consist of a single breath or a bout of several consecutive breaths (cf. Shelton and Boutilier, 1982). Reptiles initiate breathing activity by expiration, whereas inspiration precedes breath holds, and their ventilation occurs through a suction pump mechanism (Glass and Wood, 1983). The breathing patterns of amphibians may be more complicated owing to positive-pressure filling of the lungs by means of the buccal pump. Successive inspirations may stepwise inflate the lungs without interposed expirations. Conversely, a stepwise deflation may take place. Such patterns alternate with breaths consisting of both inspiration and expiration (Jones, 1982; Boutilier, 1988). The periodic pattern as well as the buccal pump ventilation in amphibians represent additional features of ventilation that may be modified in response of hypoxia. Consequently, a full description of the ventilatory responses to hypoxia requires more than a simple analysis in terms of respiratory frequency and tidal volume.

Amphibians may obtain a substantial fraction of total $O_2$ uptake through cutaneous respiration. In particular, this applies to urodeles, which may accomplish most of their uptake through the skin, with this cutaneous fraction being most important at low temperature (Feder and Burggren, 1985). The lungless salamanders (*Plethodontidae*) obtain their total uptake exclusively by skin respiration (Piiper et al., 1976). Recent research has emphasized the skin as a regulated site of gas exchange, at which redirection of blood flow or capillary recruitment may occur (Feder and Burggren, 1985; Boutilier et al., 1986; Malvin and Hlastala, 1986). Nevertheless, the statement still seems valid that responses to altered metabolic conditions in amphibians rely predominantly on changes in pulmonary ventilation, whereas the skin assumes a more passive role (Gottlieb and Jackson, 1976).

Consistently, amphibians increase ventilation in response to rising temperature and also when exposed to ambient hypoxia. Toews (1971) studied control of breathing in the salamander, *Amphiuma tridactylum*, which was kept free-swimming and equipped with a catheter to monitor pulmonary volume and intrapulmonary gas pressures. Diving time could be modulated by manipulation of intrapulmonary $P_{O_2}$, whereas $CO_2$ increases within the physiologically relevant range did not shorten dives. These results reflect the presence of $O_2$ receptors and also the major role of cutaneous $CO_2$ elimination. Volume receptors also appear involved in control of breathing in *Amphiuma*. A surfacing maneuver could be interrupted by injection of a sufficient amount of $N_2$ into the lungs, upon which the salamander would return to the bottom without breathing at the surface. The lungs of *Amphiuma* will shrink during dives, because $O_2$ is taken up from the lungs, whereas the $CO_2$ produced will be stored in tissue or removed to the water, rather than being eliminated to the lungs. Consequently, a regulation based on both pulmonary shrinkage and $O_2$ depletion seems efficient. These characteristics reflect a highly aquatic mode of life and correlate with a rather "piscine" mode of regulation.

Adult anuran amphibians accomplish only a minor fraction of $O_2$ uptake by skin respiration ($< 20\%$ of total), but about half of total $CO_2$ elimination (Feder and Burggren, 1985). This more important role of the lungs in gas exchange is reflected in ventilatory responses to both hypoxia and acid–base disturbances (Boutilier, 1988). In normoxic *Bufo marinus*, buccal movements may occur without any accompanying ventilation of the lungs. Such buccal cycles are scarce during hypoxia, whereas pulmonary ventilations become more frequent, with inflation sequences constituting a predominant feature (Boutilier and Toews, 1977). Ventilation was measured by a face mask technique in the related *B. paracnemis*, in which hypoxia caused an increase in the number of breathing episodes per unit time. Moreover, pulmonary inflations and deflations became predominant features of the breathing pattern (Kruhøffer et al., 1987).

Anuran amphibians also increase ventilation considerably, if arterial pH is decreased by inspiration of hypercapnic gases (Macintyre and Toews, 1976; Boutilier et al., 1979a; Jones, 1982). Curiously, *B. marinus* may enter a state of estivation, during which the frequency of breathing decreases, whereas $Pa_{CO_2}$ rises. In this condition, the hypercapnic drive to breathing seems depressed. Moreover, $Pa_{O_2}$ also decreases to lower values, apparently without stimulating ventilation (Boutilier et al., 1979b).

Acid–base-related receptors are not well studied in amphibians, whereas $O_2$ receptors have been located to the aortic arch in *B. vulgaris*. Additionally, the carotid labyrinth may be involved in chemoreceptive functions (Ishii et al., 1985a). The specific $O_2$ stimulus for ventilation has not been identified. Likewise, the thermal sensitivity of receptor output needs to be evaluated. This is particularly relevant, because low temperature (15°C) may abolish ventilatory responses to hypoxia in *B. paracnemis*, which otherwise responds markedly at 25–32°C (Kruhøffer et al., 1987). Such low-temperature depression of ventilatory responses also occurs in reptiles, as will be discussed later.

Cutaneous gas exchange accounts for only a low percentage of total gas exchange in terrestrial reptiles, whereas some aquatic forms may achieve about 30% of $O_2$ uptake through the skin. Carbon dioxide is eliminated predominantly by the lungs (temperatures 20–30°C; review by Feder and Burggren, 1985). Consequently, pulmonary ventilation determines both $O_2$ uptake and $CO_2$ output. Reptiles may also substantially readjust cardiovascular function in response to hypoxia. For example, the tortoise *Testudo pardalis* and the side-necked turtle *Pelomedusa subrufa*, both African species, increased cardiac frequency as well as stroke volume, whereby increases in pulmonary perfusion exceeded those in ventilation (Burggren et al., 1977). At higher temperatures, the ventilation of reptiles is inversely related to $PI_{O_2}$ and responses are substantial (cf. Jackson, 1973; Glass and Wood, 1983). Oxygen receptors for these regulations have been located to the aortic and pulmonary arches and also to the truncal region of turtles (Ishii et al., 1985b). Carotid body receptors have not been identified with any certainty, and they are probably absent in reptiles. The presence of a receptor site in the pulmonary arches is supported by Benchetrit and co-workers (1977), studying the tortoise *Testudo horsfieldi*. The receptors need to be further characterized, however, and work on nonchelonian species is desirable.

Reptiles regulate acid–base status by ventilatory adjustments and often respond markedly to $CO_2$ inhalation (cf. Jackson et al., 1974; Glass et al., 1979). Central receptors for $[H^+]$ regulation have been documented for the turtle *Pseudemys scripta* (Hitzig and Jackson, 1978). Peripheral $CO_2$ receptors may also exist (Benchetrit and Dejours, 1980), and lizards possess pulmonary and upper airway $CO_2$ receptors, the role of which is not well established in relation to the control of breathing (cf. Ballam, 1985).

Arterial $PO_2$ often increases markedly with rising temperature in amphibians and reptiles (Wood et al., 1981; Glass et al., 1983; Kruhøffer et al., 1987; Boutilier et al., 1987) (see Fig. 4). This effect is well explained through model considerations by Wood (1982). Venous admixture to the arterial blood (right-to-left shunt) occurs in both groups, the anatomical basis being a continuity of ventricular chambers (cf. Ishimatsu et al., 1988). This shunt prevents full arterial saturation. If one assumes a relatively constant venous admixture, in spite of changing temperature, the arterial saturation will also be maintained at a certain level. In this situation, a rising temperature will increase in vivo $PO_2$ (Wood, 1982). The temperature dependence of $Pa_{O_2}$ has some possible consequences for control of breathing.

As first established for reptiles (Jackson, 1973; Benchetrit et al., 1977; Glass et al., 1983) and later for amphibians (Kruhøffer et al., 1987) the ventilatory responses to hypoxia are markedly enhanced by rising temperature (see Fig. 2). This is meaningful from a functional viewpoint, because high temperature correlates with larger metabolic demands: The larger the demand for $O_2$, the more vigorous are the responses to maintain its delivery to the gas exchanger. Conversely, low temperature may markedly depress metabolism. The freshwater turtle, *Chrysemys picta bellii*, may hibernate under ice for 3 months or more. Under the conditions of 3°C and anoxia the metabolism of this turtle decreased to 0.6% of the aerobic rate at 20°C (Jackson and Heisler, 1982; Herbert and Jackson, 1985).

Jackson (1973) pointed out that a relatively low $O_2$ extraction ($EO_2$) of reptiles at decreased temperature will provide a potential for increases of $EO_2$, which will reduce the need for ventilatory responses to ambient hypoxia. Conversely, an elevated normoxic $EO_2$ at high temperature will imply that ventilatory responses are required to alleviate the effects of hypoxia. This explains the responses well in relation to gas exchange. Alternatively, Wood and Hicks (1985) attempted an analysis in terms of the regulated variable, suggesting arterial saturation as a candidate. This choice was motivated by an earlier study on the northern painted turtle (*C. picta belii*) (Glass et al., 1983), which documented a simple relationship between $P_{50}$ (half saturation pressure) of blood and the thresholds for ventilatory responses to hypoxia. The $P_{50}$ increased from 5 mm Hg at 10°C to 28 mm Hg at 30°C. Concomitantly, the threshold for ventilatory responses rose from 5 to 30 mm Hg, which points to saturation as a key variable.

The increased $O_2$ affinity of blood at low temperature certainly reduces the impact of hypoxic conditions. Also beneficial is a high $PA_{O_2}$ which can be inferred from the already mentioned reduced $EO_2$. In amphibians and reptiles, low temperature is also associated with decreases in $PA_{O_2}$ and, consequently $Pa_{CO_2}$, causing a systematic increase of pHa. This has been hypothesized to reflect a conservation of net charge on plasma protein systems ("alphastat-regulation"; Reeves, 1972). The required decrease in $Pa_{CO_2}$ must be accompanied by an elevated $PA_{O_2}$, because

$$PA_{O_2} \simeq PI_{O_2} - PA_{CO_2}/RE$$

where RE is the pulmonary gas exchange ratio (simplified alveolar gas exchange equation). This requirement, combined with a decrease of $Pa_{O_2}$ at low temperature (Wood, 1982) implies that the difference $(PA - Pa)_{O_2}$ is markedly dependent on temperature, as has been confirmed for *C. picta*, in which it may exceed 100 mm Hg at 10°C (Glass et al., 1985). This leaves a large reserve for reduction of $PA_{O_2}$ before any effect on pulmonary venous saturation will be apparent. Conversely, even under normoxic conditions the $(PA - Pa)_{O_2}$ difference may be critically low at high temperature as indicated by effects on the $(Pa_{O_2}/TA)$ relationship: $Pa_{O_2}$ may not increase further with rising temperature, but will remain the same, or even fall (Wood, 1982; Glass et al., 1983). In this situation, a small reduction of $PA_{O_2}$ may become critical and, consistently, large ventilatory responses serve to minimize reductions of $PA_{O_2}$ and maintain an adequate saturation.

It may seem an inviting and simple suggestion that a maintained arterial saturation provides a key to ventilatory responses, but alternative interpretations are possible. Ideally, a $P_{50}$-related shift of thresholds for responses would conform to the relationship of Figure 3B. The actual responses, however, are better represented by Figure 3A, which also includes a depressed "gain" of responses at decreased temperature. This could indicate that low temperature simply depresses $O_2$-receptor output, which, in turn, is reflected in the magnitude of ventilatory responses. This point of view receives some support from data on the temperature dependence of impulse frequency from the carotid body $O_2$ receptors in cats. Substituting impulse frequency for ventilation, relationships very similar to those of Figure 3A are obtained, although these receptors are considered sensitive to $P_{O_2}$ and not to saturation (Lahiri and Gelfand, 1981). Further studies on $O_2$ receptors in amphibians and reptiles seem needed to evaluate relationships between $O_2$-receptor output and ventilation.

## V. General Discussion and Conclusions

To conclude this chapter, some generalizations will be attempted concerning hypoxia-induced ventilatory responses, comparing water and air breathers among ectothermic vertebrates. Generalizations are risky, because data are scarce and often inconsistent. The present author has been confronted, at times, with the view that a respiratory problem has already been studied, although data may be available for only one or two of the usually studied species. Clearly, rainbow trout is not typical of all teleost fish, and *Bufo marinus* does not represent the "general amphibian," since divergent patterns may result from different phylogenetic backgrounds and modes of life. With this reservation, the sketching of some broad conclusions will be attempted.

1.  Both in amphibians and reptiles the arterial $P_{O_2}$ increases with rising temperature, owing to a relatively constant arterial $O_2$ saturation, except at the highest temperatures. Arterial $P_{O_2}$ in teleost fish may remain constant and independent of temperature, implying a fall in $S_{O_2}$ when temperature rises. These data for the pulmonary breathers seem well established and can be accounted for on a theoretical basis (Wood, 1982). Similar data are scarce for teleost fish, for which a theoretical framework is not available to explain temperature effects on $P_{aO_2}$.

2.  Amphibians and reptiles possess arterial $O_2$ receptors, whereas $O_2$ receptors may, in part, be monitoring ambient $O_2$ in teleost fish. Further work is needed, however, concerning receptor locations, specific $O_2$ stimulus, and temperature influences on receptor output.

3.  The decreases of $P_{IO_2}$ required to cause ventilatory responses are generally smaller in teleost fish than in amphibians and reptiles. This difference is meaningful, considering the substantially lower $O_2$ con-

tent of water relative to that of air. The same argument applies to the following point.

4. Teleost fish may maintain substantial responses to ambient hypoxia at low temperatures, whereas decreased temperature depresses the hypoxic drive to breathing in amphibians and reptiles. This may correlate with an insignificant role in fish of ventilatory acid–base regulation, which orients the responses toward $O_2$ transport.

The foregoing conclusions may fit currently available data, but revisions are likely to be required when more species are studied, in particular using better techniques for ventilation measurement. Ideally, studies should include ventilation measurements, along with a complete analysis of blood $O_2$ and acid–base characteristics. Graded hypoxia should be applied, and the time course of responses should be evaluated for each degree of hypoxia. Moreover, the temperature dependence of responses should be assessed.

## Acknowledgments

The author wants to acknowledge his late friend and teacher, Kjell Johansen, for numerous discussions that have been highly useful in writing this chapter.

## References

Abe, A. S., and Johansen, K. (1987). Gas exchange and ventilatory responses to hypoxia and hypercapnia in *Amphisbaena alba* (Reptilia: Amphisbaenia). *J. Exp. Biol.* **127**: 159–172.

Babiker, M. M. (1984). Development of dependence on aerial respiration in *Polypterus senegalus* (Cuvier). *Hydrobiologia*, **110**:351–363.

Ballam, G. O. (1985). Breathing response of the tegu lizard to 1–4% $CO_2$ in the mouth and nose or inspired into the lungs. *Respir. Physiol.*, **62**:375–386.

Benchetrit, G., Armand, J., and Dejours, P. (1977). Ventilatory chemoreflex drive in the tortoise, *Testudo horsfieldi*. *Respir. Physiol.*, **31**:183–191.

Benchetrit, G., and Dejours, P. (1980). Ventilatory $CO_2$ drive in the tortoise *Testudo horsfieldi*. *J. Exp. Biol.*, **87**:229–236.

Bicudo, J. E. P. W., and Johansen, K. (1979). Respiratory gas exchange in the air-breathing fish, *Synbranchus marmoratus*. *Environ. Biol. Fishes*, **4**:55–64.

Boutilier, R. G. (1988). Control of arrhythmic breathing in bimodal breathers: Amphibia. *Can. J. Zool.*, **66**:6–19.

Boutilier, R. G., and Toews, D. P. (1977). The effect of progressive hypoxia on respiration in the toad *Bufo marinus*. *J. Exp. Biol.*, **82**:331–344.

Boutilier, R. G., Glass, M. L., and Heisler, N. (1986). The relative distribution of pulmocutaneous blood flow in *Rana castesbeiana*: Effects of pulmonary or cutaneous hypoxia. *J. Exp. Biol.*, **126**:33–36.

Boutilier, R. G., Glass, M. L., and Heisler, N. (1987). Blood gases, and extracellular/intracellular acid–base status as a function of temperature in the anuran amphibians *Xenopus laevis* and *Bufo marinus*. *J. Exp. Biol.*, **130**:13–25.

Boutilier, R. G., Heming, T. A., and Iwama, G. K. (1984). Appendix: Physicochemical parameters for use in fish physiology. In *Fish Physiology*, Vol. 10A. Edited by W. S. Hoar and D. J. Randall. Orlando, Fla., Academic Press, pp. 73–183.

Boutilier, R. G., Randall, D. J., Shelton, G., and Toews, D. P. (1979a). Acid–base relationships in the blood of the toad, *Bufo marinus* I. The effects of environmental $CO_2$. *J. Exp. Biol.*, **82**:331–344.

Boutilier, R. G., Randall, D. J., Shelton, G., and Toews, D. P. (1979b). Acid–base relationships in the blood of the toad, *Bufo marinus* III. The effects of burrowing. *J. Exp. Biol.*, **82**:357–365.

Burggren, W. W. (1979). Bimodal gas exchange during variation in environmental oxygen and carbon dioxide in the air breathing fish. *Trichogaster trichopterus*. *J. Exp. Biol.*, **82**:197–213.

Burggren, W. W., and Cameron, J. N. (1980). Anaerobic metabolism, gas exchange and acid–base balance during hypoxic exposure in the channel catfish. *Ictalurus punctatus*. *J. Exp. Zool.*, **213**:405–416.

Burggren, W. W., Glass, M. L., and Johansen, K. (1977). Pulmonary ventilation: Perfusion relationships in terrestrial and aquatic chelonian reptiles. *Can. J. Zool.*, **55**:2024–2034.

Burggren, W., Johansen, K., and McMahon, B. (1985). Respiration in phylogenetically ancient fishes. In *Evolutionary Biology of Primative Fishes*. Edited by R. E. Forman, A. Gorbman, J. M. Dodd, and R. Olsson. New York, Plenum Press, pp. 217–252.

Butler, P. J., Taylor, E. W., and Short, S. (1977). The effect of sectioning cranial nerves V, VII, IX, and X on the cardiac response of dogfish *Scyliorhinus canicula* L. to environmental hypoxia. *J. Exp. Biol.*, **69**:233–245.

Carroll, R. L. (1988). *Vertebrate Palaeontology and Evolution*. New York, Freeman and Company.

Dejours, P. (1975; 1981). *Principles of Comparative Respiratory Physiology*, 1st and 2nd ed. Amsterdam, North-Holland Publishing Co.

Else, P. L., and Hulbert, A. J . (1981). Comparison of the "mammal machine" and the "reptile machine": Energy production. *Am. J. Physiol.*, **240**:R3–R9.

Farrell, A. P. (1982). Cardiovascular changes in the unanaesthetized lingcod (*Ophiodon elongatus*) during short-term, progressive hypoxia dn spontaneous activity. *Can. J. Zool.*, **60**:933–941.

Favaretto, A. L. V., Petenusci, S. O., Lopes, R. A., and Sawaya, P. (1981). Effect of exposure to air on haematological parameters in *Hypostomus regani* (Pisces: Loricariidae), teleost with aquatic and aerial respiration. I. Red cells. *Copeia*, **1981**:918–920.

Feder, M. E., and Burggren, W. W. (1985). Cutaneous gas exchange in vertebrates, design, patterns, control and implications. *Biol. Rev.*, **60**:1–45.

Fernandes, M. N., and Rantin, F. T. (1989). Respiratory responses of *Oreochromis niloticus* (Pisces, Cichlidae) to environmental hypoxia under different thermal conditions. *J. Fish Biol.*, **35**:509–519.

Garey, W. (1970). Cardiac output of the carp (*Cyprinus carpio*). *Comp. Biochem. Physiol.*, **33**:181–189.

Gehrke, P. C., and Fielder, D. R. (1988). Effects of temperature and dissolved oxygen on heart rate, ventilation rate and oxygen consumption of spangled perch, *Leiopotherapon unicolor* (Günther 1859), Percoidei, Teraponidae). *J. Comp. Physiol. B*, **157**:771–782.

Glass, M. L., and Johansen, K. (1976). Control of breathing in *Acrochordus javanicus*, an aquatic snake. *Physiol. Zool.*, **49**:328–339.

Glass, M. L., and Wood, S. C. (1983). Gas exchange and control of breathing in reptiles. *Physiol. Rev.*, **63**:232–261.

Glass, M. L., Andersen, N. A., Kruhøffer, M., Williams, E. M., and Heisler, N. (1990). Combined effects of environmental $Po_2$ and temperature on ventilation and blood gases in the carp (*Cyprinus carpio* L.). *J. Exp. Biol.*, **148**:1–17.

Glass, M. L., Boutilier, R. G., and Heisler, N. (1983). Ventilatory control of arterial $Po_2$ in the turtle *Chrysemys picta bellii*: Effects of temperature and hypoxia. *J. Comp. Physiol.*, **151**:145–153.

Glass, M. L., Boutilier, R. G., and Heisler, N. (1985). Effects of body temperature on respiration, blood gases and acid–base status in the turtle *Chrysemys picta bellii*. *J. Exp. Biol.*, **114**:37–51.

Glass, M. L., Burggren, W. W., and Johansen, K. (1978). Ventilation in an aquatic and a terrestrial chelonian reptile. *J. Exp. Biol.*, **72**:165–179.

Glass, M. L., Wood, S. C., Hoyt, R. W. and Johansen, K. (1979). Chemical control of breathing in the lizard, *Varanus exanthematicus*. *Comp. Biochem. Physiol. G*, **2A**: 999–1003.

Glass, M. L., Ishimatsu, A., and Johansen, K. (1986). Responses of aerial ventilation to hypoxia and hypercapnia in *Channa argus*, an air-breathing fish. *J. Comp. Physiol. B*, **156**:425–430.

Gooding, R. M., Neil, W. H., and Dizon, A. E. (1981). Respiration rates and low-oxygen tolerance limits in skipjack tuna, *Katsuwonus pelamis. Fish. Bull.* **79**:31–48.

Gottlieb, G., and Jackson, D. C. (1976). Importance of pulmonary ventilation in respiratory control in the bullfrog. *Am. J. Physiol.*, **230**:608–613.

Graham, J. B., Kramer, D. L., and Pineda, E. (1977). Respiration of the air breathing fish *Piabucina festae*. *J. Comp. Physiol.*, **122**:295–310.

Heisler, N. (1986). Mechanisms and limitations of fish acid–base regulation. In *Fish Physiology: Recent Advances*. Edited by S. Nilsson and S. Holmgren. London, Croom Helm, pp. 24–49.

Herbert, C. V., and Jackson, D. C. (1985). Temperature effects on the responses to prolonges submergence in the turtle *Chrysemys picta bellii*. II. Metabolic rate, blood acid–base ionic changes, and cardiovascular function in aerated and anoxic water. *Physiol. Zool.*, **58**:670–681.

Hitzig, B. M., and Jackson, D. C. (1978). Central chemical control of breathing in the unanesthetized turtle. *Am. J. Physiol.*, **235**:R257–R264.

Ishii, K., Ishii, K., and Kusakabe, T. (1985a). Chemo- and baroreceptors innervation of the aortic trunk of the toad *Bufo vulgaris*. *Respir. Physiol.*, **60**:365–375.

Ishii, K., Ishii, K., and Kusakabe, T. (1985b). Electrophysiological aspects of reflexogenic area in the chelonian, *Geoclemmys reevesii*. *Respir. Physiol.*, **59**:45–54.

Ishimatsu, A., and Itazawa, Y. (1983). Differences in blood oxygen levels in the outflow vessels of the heart of an air-breathing fish, *Channa argus*: Do separate blood streams exist in a teleosteam heart? *J. Comp. Physiol.*, **149**:435–440.

Ishimatsu, A., Hichs, J. W., and Heisler, N. (1988). Analysis of intracardiac shunting in the lizard, *Varanus niloticus:* A new model based on blood oxygen levels and microsphere distribution. *Respir. Physiol.*, **71**:83–100.

Itazawa, Y., and Takeda, T. (1978). Gas exchange in carp gills in normoxic and hypoxic conditions. *Respir. Physiol.*, **35**:263–269.

Iwama, G. K., Boutilier, R. G., Heming, T. A., Randall, D. J., and Mazeaud, M. (1987). The effects of altering gill water flow on gas transfer in rainbow trout. *Can. J. Zool.*, **65**:2466–2470.

Jackson, D. C. (1973). Ventilatory response to hypoxia in turtles at various temperatures. *Respir. Physiol.*, **18**:178–187.

Jackson, D. C., and Heisler, N. (1982). Plasma ionic balance of submerged anoxic turtles at 3°C: The role of calcium lactate formation. *Respir. Physiol.*, **49**:159–174.

Jackson, D. C., Palmer, S. E., and Meadow, W. L. (1974). The effects of temperature and carbon dioxide breathing on ventilation and acid–base status of turtles. *Respir. Physiol.* **20**:131–146.

Johansen, K. (1970). Air breathing in fishes. In *Fish Physiology*, Vol 4. Edited by W. S. Hoar and D. J. Randall. New York, Academic Press, pp. 361–411.

Johansen, K. (1982). Respiratory gas exchange of vertebrate gills. In *Gills*. Edited by D. F. Houlihan, J. C. Rankin, and T. J. Shuttleworth. Soc. Exp. Biol. Ser. 16. Cambridge, Cambridge University Press, pp. 99–128.

Johansen, K., and Lenfant, C. (1968). Respiration in the African lungfish *Protopterus aethiopicus*. *J. Exp. Biol.*, **49**:453–468.

Johansen, K., Hanson, D., and Lenfant, C. (1970). Respiration in a primitive air breather, *Amia calva*. *Respir. Physiol.*, **9**:162–174.

Johansen, K., Lenfant, C., and Grigg, G. C., (1967). Respiratory control in the lungfish, *Neoceratodus foresteri* (Krefft). *Comp. Biochem. Physiol.*, **20**:835–854.

Jones, R. M. (1982). How toads breathe: Control of air flow to and from the lungs by the nares in *Bufo marinus*. *Respir. Physiol.*, **49**:251–265.

Kerstens, A., Lomholt, J. P., and Johansen, K. (1979). The ventilation, extraction and uptake of oxygen in undisturbed flounders, *Platichthys flesus*: Responses to hypoxia acclimation. *J. Exp. Biol.*, **83**:169–179.

Kruhøffer, M., Glass, M. L., Abe, A. S., and Johansen, K. (1987). Control of breathing in an amphibian *Bufo paracnemis*: Effects of temperature and hypoxia. *Respir. Physiol.*, **69**:267–275.

Lahiri, S., and Gelfand, R. (1981). Mechanisms of acute ventilatory responses. In *Regulation of Breathing*, part II. Edited by T. F. Hornhein. New York, Marcel Dekker, pp. 773–843.

Lomholt, J. P., and Glass, M. L. (1987). Gas exchange of air-breathing fishes in near-anoxic water. *Acta Physiol. Scand.*, **129**:45A.

Lomholt, J. P., and Johansen, K. (1974). Control of breathing in *Amphipnous cuchia*, and amphibious fish. *Respir. Physiol.*, **21**:325–340.

Lomholt, J. P., and Johansen, K. (1979). Hypoxia acclimation in carp—how it affects $O_2$-uptake, ventilation, and $O_2$ extraction from water. *Physiol. Zool.*, **52**:38–49.

Macintyre, D. H., and Toews, D. P. (1976). The mechanisms of lung ventilation and the effects of hypercapnia on respiration in *Bufo marinus*. *Can. J. Zool.*, **54**:1364–1374.

Malvin, E. M., and Hlastala, M. P. (1986). Effects of lung volume and $O_2$ and $Co_2$ content on cutaneous gas exchange in frogs. *Am. J. Physiol.*, **251**:R941–R946.

Milsom, W. K., and Brill, R. W. (1986). Oxygen sensitive afferent information arising from the first gill arch of yellowfin tuna. *Respir. Physiol.*, **66**:193–203.

Pettersson, K., and Johansen, K. (1982). Hypoxic vasoconstriction and the effects of adrenaline on gas exchange efficiency in fish gills. *J. Exp. Biol.*, **97**:263–272.

Piiper, J., Gatz, R. N., and Crawford, E. C., Jr. (1976). Gas transport characteristics in an exclusively skin-breathing salamander, *Desmognathus fuscus* (Plethodontidae). In *Respiration of Amphibious Vertebrates*. Edited by G. M. Hughes, London, Academic Press, pp. 339–356.

Rahn, H. (1966). Aquatic gas exchange: Theory. *Respir. Physiol.*, **1**:1–12.

Randall, D. (1982). The control of respiration and circulation in fish during exercise and hypoxia. *J. Exp. Biol.*, **100**:275–288.

Randall, D. J. (1987). Control of ventilation in fish during hypoxia. *Physiologist*, **30**:168.

Randall, D. J., and Cameron, J. N. (1973). Respiratory control of arterial pH as temperature changes in rainbow trout *Salmo gairdneri*. *Am. J. Physiol.*, **225**:997–1002.

Randall, D. J., and Daxboeck, C. (1984). Oxygen and carbon dioxide transfer across fish gills. In *Fish Physiology*, Vol. 10A. Edited by W. S. Hoar and D. J. Randall. Orlando, Academic Press, pp. 263–314.

Rantin, F. T., and Johansen K. (1984). Responses of the teleost *Hoplias malabaricus* to hypoxia. *Environ. Biol. Fishes*, **11**:221–228.

Reeves, R. B. (1972). An imidazole alphastat hypothesis for vertebrate acid–base regulation: Tissue carbon dioxide content and body temperature in bullfrogs. *J. Appl. Physiol.*, **40**:752–761.

Roberts, J. L., and Rowell, D. M. (1988). Periodic respiration of gill-breathing fishes. *Can. J. Zool.*, **66**:192–190.

Saunders, R. L. (1962). The irrigation of gills in fishes II Efficiency of oxygen uptake in relation to respiratory flow activity and concentrations of oxygen and carbon dioxide. *Can J. Zool.*, **40**:817–862.

Scheid, P., and Piiper, J. (1976). Quantitative functional analysis of branchial gas transfer: Theory and application to *Scyliorhinus stellaris* (Elasmobranchii). In *Respiration of Amphibious Vertebrates*. Edited by G. M. Hughes. London, Academic Press, pp. 17–38.

Shelton, G., and Boutilier, R. G., (1982). Apnoea in amphibians and reptiles. *J. Exp. Biol.*, **100**:245–273.

Smatresk, N., and Cameron, J. N. (1982). Respiration and acid–base physiology of the spotted gar, a bimodal breather. I. Normal values and the response to severe hypoxia. *J. Exp. Biol.*, **96**:263–280.

Smith, F. M., and Jones, D. R. (1982). The effect of changes in blood oxygen carrying capacity on ventilation volume in the rainbow trout (*Salmo gairdneri*). *J. Exp. Biol.*, **97**:325–334.

Spitzer, K. W., Marvin, D. E., Jr., and Heath, A. G. (1969). The effect of temperature on the respiratory and cardiac response of the bluegill sunfish to hypoxia. *Comp. Biochem. Physiol.*, **30**:83–90.

Steffensen, J. F. (1985). The transition between branchial pumping and ram ventilation in fishes: Energetic consequences and dependence on water oxygen tension. *J. Exp. Biol.*, **114**:141–150.

Steffensen, J. F., Lomholt, J. P., and Johansen, K. (1982). Gill ventilation and $O_2$ extraction during graded hypoxia in two ecologically distinct species of flatfish, the flounder (*Platichthys flesus*) and the plaice (*Pleuronectes platessa*). *Environ. Biol. Fishes*, **7**:157–163.

Toews, D. P. (1971). Factors affecting the onset and termination of respiration in the salamander, *Amphiuma tridactylum. Can. J. Zool.*, **49**:1231–1237.

Waehneldt, T. V., Matthiew, J.-M., Malotka, J., and Joss, J. (1987). A glycosylated proteolipid protein is common to CNS myelin of recent lungfishes (Ceratodidae, Lepidosirenidae). *Comp. Biochem. Physiol.*, **88B**:1209–1212.

Watters, K. W., and Smith, L. S. (1973). Respiratory dynamics of the starry flounder *Platichthys stellatus* in response to low oxygen and high temperature. *Marine Biol.*, **19**:133–148.

Weber, R. E. (1982). Intraspecific adaptation of hemoglobin function in fish to environmental oxygen availability. In *Exogeneous and Endogeneous Influences on Metabolic and Neural Control*, Vol. 1. Biochemistry. Edited by A. D. F. Addink and N. Spronk, Oxford, Pergamon Press, pp. 87–102.

Wood, S. C. (1982). The effect of oxygen affinity on arterial $Po_2$ in animals with central vascular shunts. *J. Appl. Physiol.*, **53**:R1360–R1364.

Wood, S. C. (1984). Cardiovascular shunts and oxygen transport in lower vertebrates. *Am. J. Physiol.*, **247**:R3-R14.

Wood, S. C., and Glass, M. L. (1991). Respiration and thermoregulation of amphibians and reptiles. In *Physiological Strategies for Gas Exchange and Metabolism*. Edited by A. J. Woakes, M. K. Grieshaber, and C. R. Bridges. Cambridge, Cambridge University Press, pp. 107–124.

Wood, S. C., and Hicks, J. W. (1985). Oxygen homeostasis in vertebrates with cardiovascular shunts. In *Cardiovascular shunts: Phylogenetic, Ontogenetic and Clinical Aspects*. (Alfred Benzon Symposium 21). Edited by K. Johansen and W. W. Burggren. Copenhagen. Munksgaard, pp. 354–367.

Wood, S. C., Johansen, K., Glass, M. L., and Hoyt, R. W. (1981). Acid–base regulation during heating and cooling in the lizard *Varanus exanthematicus. J. Appl. Physiol.*, **50**:779–783.

# 7

## Control of Breathing in Hibernating Mammals

**WILLIAM K. MILSOM**

University of British Columbia
Vancouver, British Columbia, Canada

One of the most fascinating strategies employed by birds and mammals faced with the extreme metabolic stress of living in a cold climate is to abandon homeothermy and to reduce metabolic rate and, thereby, body temperature ($T_b$) as ambient temperature ($T_a$) declines. There is a progression in mammals from species that lower metabolic rate and $T_b$ only slightly (a state of torpor) to those in which $T_b$ remains only a few degrees above $T_a$, down to levels of 3–5°C (deep hibernation) (see Lyman, 1982a, for review). It should be stressed that this spectrum of change does not represent a varying state of hypothermia by the usual definition. *Hypothermia* refers to an abnormal situation in which $T_b$ is depressed and can only be reelevated by exogenous heat. *Hibernation*, on the other hand, is a natural process in which the "set-point" for thermoregulation is reduced and from which animals rewarm using only endogeneous heat (Heller, 1979). As such, hibernation is an intermittent event, with all species exhibiting bouts of periodic arousal during which metabolic rate and $T_b$ spontaneously regain euthermic levels, before falling again to the levels characteristic of deep hibernation, repeatedly demonstrating the nature of this controlled physiological process (Lyman, 1982b). From evidence in studies of thermoregulation, hibernation is believed to be homologous with slow-wave sleep, involving similar, albeit more extreme, physiological changes (Heller and Glotzbach, 1977).

*119*

As animals enter hibernation, dramatic changes occur in their breathing patterns (Fig. 1), as well as in the relative importance of various respiratory stimuli, indicative of substantial change in respiratory control. Detailed respiratory studies of the animals that enter deep hibernation, however, have been limited to those few species that are easy to obtain or rear in captivity. As a consequence, the following discussion is based on data obtained from only a handful of mammalian species and, thus, all generalizations that arise from such restricted information should be treated with due caution. These studies, however, have produced intriguing results that have given rise to several speculative hypothesis, as well as to more questions than they have answered.

## I. Ventilatory Responses and Control in the Euthermic State

Most species of hibernating mammals are also fossorial. Their burrows provide them with added insulation from the environment, as well as protection during the period of extreme vulnerability while in hibernation. At such times, these animals are moribund and capable of only slow uncoordinated movements; arousal from this state can take hours. While these animals are euthermic, however, their burrows also create a hypoxic, hypercarbic environment. Diffusive exchange between burrow gas and outside air is slow, and levels of $CO_2$ up to 6% and $O_2$ down to 14% for burrow gas composition have been frequently reported (reviewed by Tenney and Boggs, 1986). Fossorial animals show respiratory adaptations that are believed to be in response to life under such chronic conditions. There is no data to suggest that fossorial animals that hibernate are any different in this from fossorial animals that do not hibernate, but some of these adaptations to burrow dwelling have been considered "preadaptations" for hibernating and, as such, are worthy of note.

In general, both metabolic rate and minute ventilation ($\dot{V}E$) are reduced in burrowing animals under resting conditions (breathing air) compared with nonburrowing species (Fig. 2). Hudson and Deavers (1973) report that nighttime (i.e., resting) oxygen consumption ($\dot{V}O_2$) in eight species of ground squirrels can be described by the equation $\dot{V}O_2(ml/hr) = 3.24$ body weight$^{0.66} \pm 0.12$. The values for metabolic rate that this equation produces are only 60% of those reported for other, nonfossorial mammals of comparable size. McNab (1979) has extended these observations to a number of other burrowing mammals and confirmed these results for fossorial mammals larger than 80-g body mass. Smaller species, below 60-g body mass, do not appear to conform to this trend (Geiser, 1988). In conjunction with the reductions in resting metabolic rate and associated $\dot{V}E$ seen in larger fossorial species, arterial $PO_2$ values (60–75 torr) are significantly lower and $PCO_2$ values (45–55 torr) higher than standard mammalian values (Burlington et al., 1969; Darden, 1972; Chapman and Bennett, 1975). Both bicarbonate levels and noncarbonic buffer levels have been reported

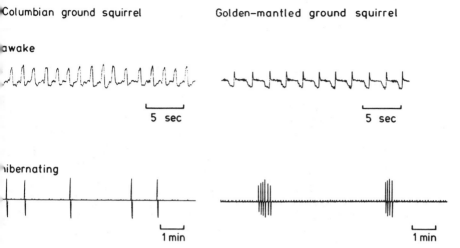

**Figure 1** Plethysmograph/pneumotachograph traces to illustrate the breathing patterns in two species of ground squirrel during euthermia and hibernation.

as elevated in some species of fossorial animals (Burlington et al., 1969; Chapman and Bennett, 1975; MacLean, 1978, 1981), but not all and, accordingly, pH values may or may not be reduced below standard mammalian values.

The low $\dot{V}E$ and resulting high $Pa_{CO_2}$ observed in fossorial animals while breathing air suggests that their $CO_2$ response threshold must be elevated, and this is borne out by experimental evidence. Accompanying this elevation in ventilatory set-point is a reduction in ventilatory sensitivity ($\Delta\dot{V}E/\Delta P_{CO_2}$) to hypercapnia (Darden, 1972; MacLean, 1978; Holloway and Heath, 1984; McArthur and Milsom, 1991a) (see Fig. 2). Hayward (1966) originally suggested that this reduced sensitivity (increased tolerance) to $CO_2$ may develop in the young as a result of chronic exposure to hypercarbic conditions. A recent comparison of the ventilatory responses of mice and rats raised under both normal conditions and chronic hypercarbia (6% $CO_2$), however, suggests that the increased $CO_2$ tolerance shown by fossorial mammals is genetically, rather than developmentally, determined (Birchard et al., 1984). This is supported by the fact that both juvenile and adult golden-mantled ground squirrels housed under simulated burrow conditions for over 1 year showed similar hypoxic and hypercapnic ventilatory responses to animals housed in room air (Fig. 3; Webb and Milsom, 1991a).

There have been consistent reports of elevated hemoglobin $O_2$ affinity (lowered $P_{50}$) in fossorial mammals (Hall, 1965; Baudinette, 1974; Boggs et al., 1984; Maginnis et al., 1989). Evidence concerning other changes in $O_2$ transport

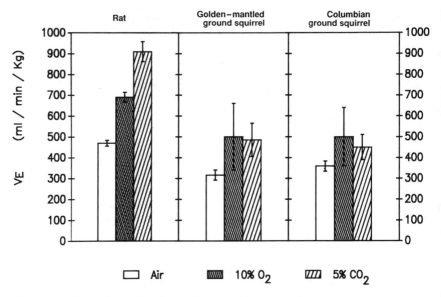

**Figure 2** Comparison of levels of minute ventilation recorded for awake ground squirrels and rats at $T_A$ = 20–22°C breathing air, 10% $O_2$ in $N_2$ or 5% $CO_2$ in air. (Rat data
from Cragg and Drysdale, 1983; from McArthur and Milsom, 1991a.)

properties of the blood, however, is largely inconsistent. There are reports demonstrating both no changes and increases in hemoglobin concentration, hematocrit, erythrocyte count, and blood volume in burrowing animals, compared
with nonburrowing species (see Boggs et al., 1984, for review).

The ventilatory responses of fossorial mammals to hypoxia have been
poorly studied, but available evidence indicates that neither $O_2$ response thresholds nor sensitivities differ from values reported in nonfossorial mammals (see
Fig. 2) (Holloway and Heath, 1984; Boggs et al., 1984; McArthur and Milsom,
1991a). What does appear to differ, at least in one species of hibernating ground
squirrel (golden-mantled ground squirrel; Webb and Milsom, 1991a), however,
is the origin of the reflex ventilatory response. Figure 3 also shows the results
of both acutely and chronically exposing animals that had undergone carotid
body denervation to hypoxic, hypercapnic gas mixtures similar to those recorded
under burrow conditions. It can be seen that, although the denervation did result
in a slight fall in resting minute ventilation, the animals still retained a strong
response to the gas mixture. Given the blunted nature of the $CO_2$ response, much
of this represents the hypoxic ventilatory response, indicating that the aortic
bodies or other receptor groups may play a much larger role in the hypoxic

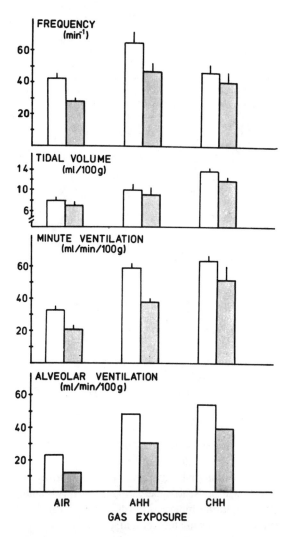

**Figure 3** Respiratory variables in intact (open bars) or carotid body denervated (filled bars) animals either breathing air (Air) or acutely (AHH) or chronically (CHH) breathing a hypoxic hypercapnic (17% $O_2$: 4% $CO_2$) gas mixture. (From Webb and Milsom, 1991a.)

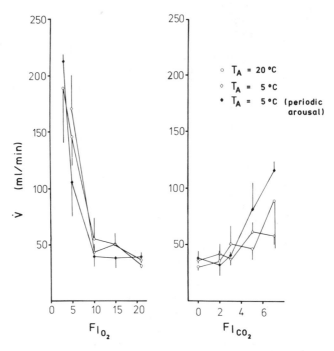

**Figure 4** Effects of decreasing $F_{I_{O_2}}$ (left) or increasing $F_{I_{CO_2}}$ (right) on $\dot{V}_E$ in Columbian ground squirrels under three conditions: awake at $T_A = 22°C$ (○); awake at $T_A = 5°C$ (◇); and during periodic arousal from hibernation at $T_A = 5°C$ (◆). (From McArthur and Milsom, 1991a.)

ventilatory response in this species than in other mammals (see also Fig. 10; the possible significance of this is discussed further in Sect. III).

Thus, in euthermic animals, hypoxia is a powerful respiratory stimulus, whereas the ventilatory response to hypercarbia is severely blunted. This situation is altered dramatically during hibernation (discussed later). It has been shown, however, that neither changes in ambient temperature nor season have any effect on either the thresholds or sensitivities of hibernating animals to hypoxia or hypercarbia (Fig. 4; McArthur and Milsom, 1991a). These data suggest that changes in respiratory sensitivity are associated with the physiological changes accompanying the entrance into hibernation, per se, and are not a consequence of the changes associated with preparation for hibernation.

Given the homology that has been drawn between hibernation and slow-wave sleep, it is interesting that the changes in breathing pattern that occur as hibernating animals enter sleep are similar to those recorded in other nonhibernating animals (Milsom et al., 1989; Phillipson and Bowes, 1986). Most notable

cr4a/8788

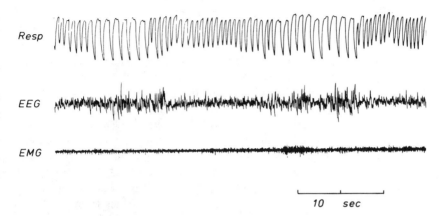

Resp

EEG

EMG

10 sec

**Figure 5** Recordings of respiratory impedance, EEG, and EMG activity obtained from a continuously instrumented golden-mantled ground squirrel during the early phases of slow-wave sleep. Note the waxing and waning of ventilation associated with changes in the contribution of slow-wave, high-voltage activity to the EEG. (From Milsom et al., 1989.)

is that respiratory amplitude increases and respiratory frequency decreases as animals enter slow-wave sleep and that waxing and waning is quite often visible in the respiratory pattern as animals fluctuate back and forth through different planes of slow-wave sleep (Fig. 5) reflecting the strong influence of "arousal" state on breathing pattern (Milsom et al., 1989).

## II. Ventilatory Control During Entrance into Hibernation

Almost all experiments on ventilatory control have concentrated on the steady state of deep hibernation, rather than the complex changes that occur during the transient states of entering into and arousing from hibernation. Nonetheless, a good deal of attention has been focused on the relationship between $\dot{V}E$ and metabolic rate during these states. The first indication that an animal is beginning to enter hibernation is generally a fall in respiratory frequency. This is accompanied by a fall in heart rate, followed by a decline in metabolic rate, and finally by a fall in $T_b$ (Lyman, 1958; Lyman and O'Brien, 1960; Strumwasser, 1960; Robertson et al., 1968; Wang and Hudson, 1970). The metabolic rate reaches the minimum values of deep hibernation long before $T_b$ completes its decline (Lyman, 1958).

During this process, arterial $P_{CO_2}$ declines and pH increases somewhat (Lyman and Hastings, 1951; Musacchia and Volkert, 1971; Tahti and Soivio, 1975). Despite this, there is a significant increase in $CO_2$ content owing to the increase in $CO_2$ solubility with decreasing temperature. Because of this and the change in neutral pH with temperature, the ratio of $[H^+]/[OH^-]$ in plasma increases (Malan et al., 1973; Malan, 1982). This represents a "relative respiratory acidosis." *Respiratory acidosis* has typically been defined in terms of the controlled variables involved in the regulation of ventilation under euthermic conditions in mammals and refers to a decrease in pH resulting from an elevation in $Pa_{CO_2}$ by hypoventilation (or an increase in inspired $CO_2$). In this instance, pHa and $Pa_{CO_2}$ appear to be maintained relatively constant. One consequence of this is that there must be a transient decrease in $\dot{V}_E/\dot{V}_{O_2}$ to allow the $CO_2$ content of the blood to increase in proportion to the increase in $CO_2$ solubility (which produces the concomitant increase in $[H^+]/[OH^-]$). This does not represent a hypoventilation in terms of the standard controlled variables (pHa and $Pa_{CO_2}$) used in the classic definition of respiratory acidosis. Appropriate terms to distinguish this respiratory-induced change in $[H^+]/[OH^-]$ caused by pH/$P_{CO_2}$ homeostasis with changing body temperature, from respiratory-induced changes in $[H^+]/[OH^-]$ owing to changes in pH/$P_{CO_2}$ at constant body temperature, remain to be defined. For the purpose of this paper, however, the former will be referred to as a *relative respiratory acidosis.**

Regardless of terms, the net effect will be to alter the homeostasis of the dissociation ratio of the predominant nonbicarbonate buffers, the imidazole groups of protein histidyl residues and, consequently, alter the electric charge-dependent properties of proteins, notably enzymes, altering their function. This may contribute to the metabolic depression associated with the entrance into hibernation. The degree of change in $[H^+]/[OH^-]$ seen in blood plasma is not transmitted to all tissues, however. The intracellular pH of such tissues as heart and liver increase markedly during hibernation, such that the ratio of $[H^+]/[OH^-]$ increases only slightly (Malan et al., 1985). This may serve to maintain proper enzyme function in these tissues and to restrict changes in the contractility of the heart as well as in the production and release of glucose, its primary source of energy,

---

*To emphasize the increase in $[H^+]/[OH^-]$ at a relatively constant pH as body temperature falls, Malan (1977) has promoted the format of reporting pH and $P_{CO_2}$ values as temperature-corrected (assuming a closed system) to 37°C. Thus, at 7°C, with an increase in $CO_2$ content from 29.2 to 43.7 mM/L in the European hamster, an in vivo pH of 7.46 and $P_{CO_2}$ of 37 torr would be reported as a temperature-corrected pH of 7.01 and a $P_{CO_2}$ of 160 torr. Not only does this add further confusion to an already complex issue, it is quite misleading, since these values in no way reflect the changes in $H^+$ activity or $CO_2$ diffusion gradient that actually exist. It is much simpler, and far less confusing, to report values at in vivo body temperature and to discuss acid–base changes in terms of changes in $[H^+]/[OH^-]$ or $H^+$ activity or the effects of acid–base changes in terms of their effect on the pK or dissociation ratio of different protein groups.

from the liver. The $[H^+]/[OH^-]$ ratio in skeletal muscle and brain, however, do increase significantly during entrance into hibernation, by an amount that could potentially cause metabolic rate to fall by 30–40% more than expected from changes in body temperature alone.

Consistent with this, in torpid squirrels, changes in body temperature accompanied by $CO_2$ retention affect $\dot{V}O_2$ more than changes that are not accompanied by $CO_2$ retention (Bickler, 1984). Thus, it has been argued that the reduction in metabolic rate during entrance into hibernation, as measured in many studies, exceeds that which would be expected from the fall in body temperature alone (i.e., $Q_{10} > 3.0$) (Malan, 1982). In a review of the literature, however, Geiser (1988) has shown that the effect of temperature on metabolic rate in hibernating animals is inversely proportional to body mass and, accordingly, $Q_{10}$ values for the fall in metabolic rate during hibernation approach and exceed 3.0 only for small animals. Since the mechanisms that underlie the process of hibernation appear to be common to all hibernators (it is highly unlikely that the effects of pH on metabolism are size-dependent), the significance of $Q_{10}$ values greater than 3.0 is far from clear (this is particularly so if one considers that the $Q_{10}$ for carotid body discharge in cats under basal conditions is 75.2!, Gallego et al., 1979). Furthermore, almost all of the literature values are based on the differences computed between hibernating animals and active, euthermic animals. Snapp and Heller (1981) have argued that, since hibernation is an extension of slow-wave sleep, comparisons should be made only between hibernating animals and sleeping, euthermic animals. When this is done, $Q_{10}$ values never exceed 3.0. It has been argued that the reduction in metabolism that occurs during sleep is also due to a respiratory acidosis (Malan, 1982), but even if this is so (which is far from clear), all further reductions that occur during the entrance into hibernation can be accounted for by the effects of changes in body temperature alone.

This latter argument aside, the balance of the data does argue for a role of relative respiratory acidosis in the metabolic depression associated with entrance into hibernation. It has even raised the suggestion that it may be the causal agent in this process; that is, the metabolic depression associated with the entrance into hibernation is the direct consequence of this relative respiratory acidosis. Thus, the primary event associated with the entrance into hibernation would be a reduction in ventilation, leading to $CO_2$ retention, acidosis, and then, metabolic depression (Malan et al., 1973; Malan, 1982; Bickler, 1984; Geiser, 1988). This latter claim is based on the trends outlined already: 1) ventilation and heart rate fall before recorded changes in metabolic rate or body temperature (Lyman and Chatfield, 1955) and, thus, 2) $\dot{V}E/\dot{V}CO_2$ is transiently reduced, $CO_2$ is retained in proportion to the increase in $CO_2$ solubility, and the ratio of $[H^+]/[OH^-]$ in plasma increases depressing metabolic functions. This could initiate the entrance into hibernation, either directly, by reducing general body metabolism (Malan et al., 1985) or, indirectly, by its depressant effect on central integrative process (Snapp and Heller, 1981).

Heller and his colleagues, however, have clearly shown that $T_b$ is actively regulated during entrance into hibernation. There is a gradual downshift of the set-point for temperature regulation. In most animals, the rate of fall in metabolic rate and $T_b$ tend to be somewhat faster than the decline in set-point, consequently, animals actively shiver during entrance to brake the rate of fall in $T_b$ (Heller, 1979). Thus, for the decrease in $\dot{V}E/\dot{V}CO_2$ to be the causal factor regulating metabolic rate and $T_b$ would require that changes in $\dot{V}E$ be the principal effector limb of the thermoregulatory reflex response to the change in $T_b$ set-point, superseding homeostatic regulation of arterial blood gases and pH.

Although the hypothesis seems attractive, this latter implication does not seem particularly plausible. Furthermore, several other factors argue against this hypothesis: 1) To begin with, owing to body mass, even changes in $\dot{V}E$ and heart rate from a reduction in metabolic rate will appear before the changes in $\dot{V}O_2$ and body temperature ($T_b$) which produce them; simply as a consequence of body stores and recording techniques. 2) Also, if animals are made hypothermic by artifically reducing $T_b$, and consequently, metabolic rate and $\dot{V}E$, one also sees an initial, small fall in $\dot{V}E/\dot{V}CO_2$ ($\simeq$ 20%) (Fig. 6a) (Osborne and Milsom, 1992). In fact, the decrease in metabolic rate produced when $\dot{V}E$ follows metabolic rate, which follows the decrease in $T_b$, appears no different from that which occurs in animals entering hibernation (see Fig. 6B) (Osborne and Milsom, 1992). 3) Finally, it should be noted that respiratory acidosis, produced by increasing $CO_2$ in inspired gas from zero to 6–8%, has no significant effect on metabolic rate in either euthermic or hibernating golden-mantled ground squirrels (Webb and Milsom, 1991a). It is conceivable that there is a slight metabolic depression that is masked by the increased metabolic demands associated with the higher levels of ventilation but, if so, it cannot be significant.

Thus, the question of whether changes in ventilation follow, or cause, the changes in metabolic rate during entrance into hibernation is still debated. As pointed out earlier, however, even if changes in ventilation are a consequence of changes in metabolism during entrance into hibernation, a relative respiratory acidosis will ensue which, although not the causal mechanism involved in initiating the entrance process, will contribute to the suppression of metabolism.

## III.  Ventilatory Responses and Control in Hibernation

The dramatic reduction in ventilation observed in hibernating mammals gives rise to two distinct respiratory patterns (see Fig. 1). In many species, a pattern of single breaths separated by periods of apnea in the range of 1–6 min is observed, whereas in others, episodes or bursts of continuous breathing are seen separated by longer periods of apnea, in the range of minutes to hours (see

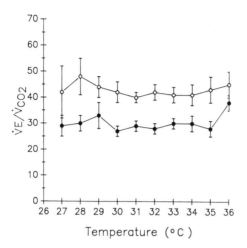

**Figure 6A** The relationship between the air convection requirement ($\dot{V}_E/\dot{V}_{CO_2}$) and body temperature for rats (open symbols) and golden-mantled ground squirrel (filled symbols) during experimentally induced hypothermia. (From Osborne and Milsom, 1992.)

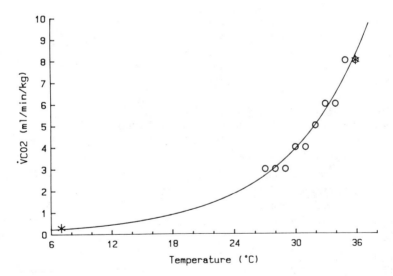

**Figure 6B** The relationship between metabolic rate ($\dot{V}_{CO_2}$) and body temperature for golden-mantled ground squirrels during experimentally induced hypothermia (open symbols) and for unanesthetized animals awake and hibernating (asterisk). (From Osborne and Milsom, 1992.)

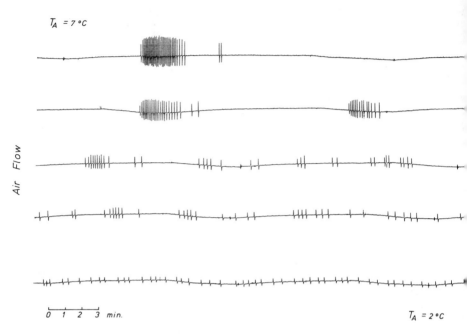

**Figure 7**   Airflow trace from a pneumotachograph on a hibernating, golden-mantled ground squirrel during the transition from episodic breathing at $T_A$ = 7°C to a single-breath, breathing pattern at $T_A$ = 2°C. The transition took several hours and traces are taken from random times during the transition. (From Webb and Milsom, 1991b.)

Lyman, 1982a; Malan, 1982, for reviews). The longest apneic period yet reported with this latter pattern is 150 min, observed in the European hedgehog, *Erinaceus europaeus* (Kristoffersson and Soivio, 1964). This bursting pattern has often been referred to as Cheyne–Stokes respiration and, although a waxing and waning of $V_T$ and f are sometimes seen during these breathing episodes, more often both $V_T$ and breath length are constant throughout.

There would appear to be a species difference between animals exhibiting these two patterns (see Malan, 1982, for review). It has been shown, however, that the golden-mantled ground squirrel exhibits the episodic breathing pattern down to a body temperature of ≃ 5°C, below which it exhibits the single-breath pattern (Fig. 7; Webb and Milsom, 1991b). The tidal volume, breathing frequency, and overall level of ventilation do not change significantly as body temperature is lowered from 7° to 4°C in this species, only the pattern of breathing (Fig. 8; Webb and Milsom, 1991b). In this same species, mild anesthesia during hibernation will also convert the episodic-breathing pattern to one of single breaths. These data, taken together with data obtained from similar studies in

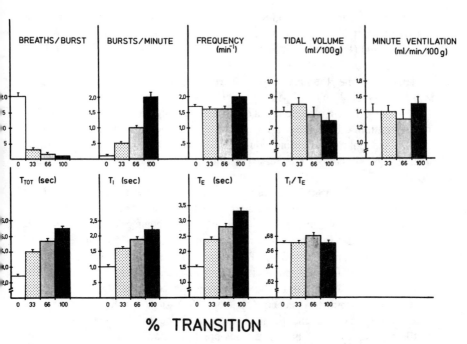

## % TRANSITION

**Figure 8**  Effects of decreasing ambient and body temperature on respiratory variables; breaths per burst, bursts per minute, respiratory frequency, tidal volume, minute ventilation, total breath duration ($T_{TOT}$), inspiratory duration ($T_I$), expiratory duration ($T_E$), and the ratio of $T_I/T_E$. 0% transition represents burst breathing at a $T_b$ of 8.6 ± 0.2°C and 100% transition represents single-breath breathing at a $T_b$ of 4.4 ± 0.5°C. (From Webb and Milsom, 1991b.)

reptiles (which also exhibit these same two breathing patterns) have been argued to indicate that the single-breath pattern is the basic pattern produced by the lower brain stem and that the episodic pattern seen in some species is the result of the action of supramedullary input acting on this basic pattern (Milsom, 1988). Anesthesia, low body temperatures (below 5°C in this species), and brain stem ablation at the pontomedullary junction (reptiles; Naifeh et al., 1971) remove this input and reveal the basic, single-breath pattern (Milsom, 1988). The significance of the two different patterns and their species distribution in both hibernating mammals and reptiles remain intriguing questions.

Intraspecies comparisons of animals that exhibit episodic-breathing patterns suggest that, the longer the period of apnea, the greater the number of breaths in the subsequent episode of breathing (Lyman, 1982a). Hence, in the golden hamster at 4°C, bursts of six to eight breaths are separated by apneic periods of

6.5–11 min (Kristoffersson and Soivio, 1966), whereas, in the garden dormouse at 4°C, bursts of 24–131 breaths (taking 1–8 min) are separated by apneic periods of 30–100 min (Pajunen, 1970). Within any given species, however, it is difficult to show any good correlation between the number of breaths in an episode and the length of either the previous or subsequent period of apnea (McArthur and Milsom, 1991b; Webb and Milsom, 1991b).

While breathing frequency and minute ventilation are greatly reduced during hibernation, tidal volume has been reported to either remain constant (golden-mantled and Columbian ground squirrels; McArthur and Milsom, 1991b; Webb and Milsom, 1991b) or to decrease (marmots; Endres and Taylor, 1930; Malan, 1973).

Given the intermittent nature of these breathing patterns, it is not surprising that blood gas concentrations and acid–base status have been reported to vary significantly. Malan et al (1973) reported arterial pH changes of 0.02–0.04 units over a 6-min apnea in a marmot, whereas Tahti and Soivio (1975) have reported changes in pH from 7.46 to 7.42, $Pa_{CO_2}$ from 27 to 35 torr, and $Pa_{O_2}$ from 120 to 10.5 torr over 50- to 70-min periods of apnea in the European hedgehog. The relatively small fall in pH in the hedgehog was consistent with a measured increase in bicarbonate concentration from 30.3 to 37.4 mEq/L during these periods of apnea. The picture that emerges is one of a dramatic change in ventilatory control from the continuous-breathing pattern, which ensured homeostatic blood gas concentrations in euthermic animals, to a periodic-breathing pattern, with resulting wide fluctuations in blood gas concentrations and plasma pH in hibernation. This latter situation closely resembles that seen in ectothermic vertebrates (Milsom, 1988).

In steady-state hibernation, the elevation in plasma $CO_2$ content and increase in the $[H^+]/[OH^-]$ ratio, referred to earlier as a relative respiratory acidosis are combined with a rise in arterial $Po_2$, maintained or decreased arterial $Pco_2$, and maintained or increased arterial pH. The latter reflect an overall increase in $\dot{V}e/\dot{V}co_2$ and, hence, by classic terms, a respiratory alkalosis (Stormont et al., 1939; Lyman and Hastings, 1951; Clausen, 1966; Kent and Pierce, 1967; Goodrich, 1973; Malan et al., 1973; Tahti and Soivio, 1975; Kreienbuhl et al., 1976). Thus, the $[H^+]/[OH^-]$ ratio has increased because of the increase in $CO_2$ solubility and, hence, content, but it is lower than it would have been if $Pco_2$ had been maintained constant. This only accentuates that the terms respiratory acidosis and alkalosis are relative to begin with and not particularly useful when applied to conditions under which the set-points for ventilatory control are changing.

### A. Effects of "Arousal" State

As mentioned earlier, hibernation is believed to be an extreme extension of slow-wave sleep (Heller and Glotzbach, 1977), and breathing pattern is strongly

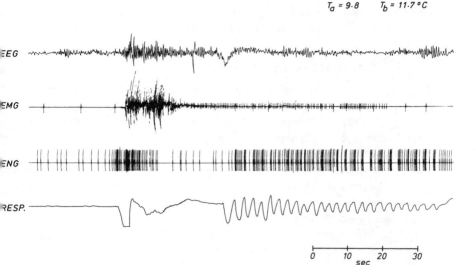

**Figure 9** Recordings of the EEG, EMG (the ECG is visible on the EMG trace), the ENG from a respiratory modulated neuron in the ventral respiratory center, and respiratory impedance in a hibernating golden-mantled ground squirrel. See text for details. (From Milsom et al., 1989.)

influenced by sleep state. Interestingly, on the basis of electroencephalographic (EEG) and electromyographic (EMG) recordings, golden-mantled ground squirrels hibernating at $\simeq$ 10°C spend roughly 7% of the time in a state that closely resembles wakefulness (Walker et al., 1977). These changes in central neural state are not expressed behaviorally; the animals continue to hibernate, with no external signs of activity. Preliminary data suggest that breathing episodes are always associated with these sporadic bouts of central "arousal". Figure 9 shows recordings of the EEG, EMG, electrocardiogram (ECG; superimposed on the EMG), and the electroneurogram (ENG), recorded from a respiratory unit in the ventral respiratory center of the medulla, and an impedance trace depicting respiratory movements, in a golden-mantled ground squirrel hibernating at 10°C during one of these periods of arousal. It can be seen that activity in the EEG and EMG occur first (along with movement of the body wall and intense discharge in the medullary neuron), followed by an episode of breathing, with an associated tachycardia. In the one animal for which such recordings were obtained, all such periods of arousal produced breathing episodes. On occasion, breathing episodes did occur without central arousal suggesting that it is not necessarily the stimulus to breath that triggers the change in central state. Although this data is far too preliminary to assign much significance, it does suggest that state-dependent changes in central neural activity, which appear to occur in a rhythmic fashion under some circumstances, may play a substantial role in the regulation of breathing pattern, at least under resting conditions.

### B. Hypoxic Ventilatory Responses

There have been reports indicating no change, an increase, or a decrease, in hemoglobin concentration, as well as in hematocrit, erythrocyte count, and blood volume of animals in hibernation (Svihla and Bowman, 1952; Bartels et al., 1969; Larkin et al., 1972; McLaughlin and Meints, 1972; Harkness et al., 1974; Temple and Musacchia, 1975; Maginniss et al., 1989). Overall the data suggest that there is an increase in $O_2$-storage capacity of the blood, but the true extent of this is far from clear. There are, however, consistent reports of a dramatic left shift in the oxyhemoglobin equilibrium curve (OEC) (Endres, 1930; Clausen and Ersland, 1968; Musacchia and Volkert, 1971; Maginniss et al., 1989). This shift is due to the interaction of several factors on hemoglobin binding to oxygen; temperature, pH (Bohr effect), and changing concentrations of organic phosphates. The effect of temperature is to dramatically increase hemoglobin–oxygen affinity, producing an extreme left shift in the OEC (Reeves, 1980). The Bohr effect (which may or may not be reduced during hibernation; Clausen and Ersland, 1968; Bartels et al., 1968; Kramm et al., 1975; Maginniss et al., 1989) reduces the affinity of Hb for $O_2$ as pH is lowered. Consistent reductions in 2,3-DPG and ATP concentrations have been reported in hibernating animals and have been shown to increase hemoglobin $O_2$ binding (Burlington and Whitten, 1971; Harkness et al., 1974; Tempel and Musacchia, 1975; Kramm et al., 1975; Maginniss et al., 1989). Maginnis et al., (1989) concluded that the net effect of these interactions was an 18% increase in Hb–$O_2$ affinity above that due to the effects of temperature alone. The overall shape of the Hb–$O_2$ equilibrium curve is now extremely steep, with blood being essentially fully saturated down to $Po_2$ levels of 15–25 torr and 50% saturated ($P_{50}$) at levels of 4.3–9 torr (Endres, 1930; Clausen and Ersland, 1968; Musacchia and Volkert, 1971; Maginniss et al., 1989).

Given the steepness and left shift of this equilibrium curve, a fall of Hb–$O_2$ saturation from 100 to 97% should reduce arterial $Po_2$ from $\simeq$ 80 to 15 torr in the thirteen-lined and golden-mantled ground squirrels. The removal of a further 50% of the $O_2$ content of this blood would then only reduce $Po_2$ a further 5–10 torr (Mussachia and Volkert, 1971; Maginniss et al., 1989). It is not surprising, therefore, that Tahti and Soivio (1975) reported that arterial $Po_2$ fell from 120 to 10.5 torr during periods of apnea of 50–70 min in the European hedgehog. Despite the extremely low values reported for arterial and venous $Po_2$, however, venous blood generally remains 60–70% saturated with $O_2$ (higher, in fact, than euthermic values) (Clausen and Ersland, 1968; Musacchia and

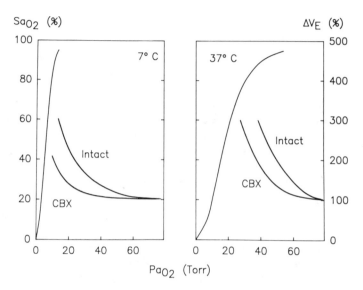

**Figure 10** The percentage change in $\dot{V}_E$ (right axis) and the arterial blood oxygen saturation ($Sa_{O_2}$, left axis) as a function of arterial $P_{O_2}$ in intact and carotid body denervated (CBX) golden-mantled ground squirrels during euthermia (right panel) and hibernation (left panel). (From Webb and Milsom, 1991a.)

Volkert, 1971), and tissue $P_{O_2}$ remains above the $P_{50}$ values reported for blood (Barr and Silver, 1972). This indicates that tissue oxygenation is adequate and that no anaerobiosis probably occurs. This is supported by reports that blood lactate levels remain normal during hibernation (Hanson and Johansson, 1961; Twente and Twente, 1968).

The dramatic shift in the Hb–$O_2$-dissociation curve will promote $O_2$ loading in the lung and should increase hypoxia tolerance in these animals. Few studies, however, have been made of $O_2$ responses in hibernating animals. In several studies, researchers were unable to elicit any ventilatory response to the administration of hypoxic gases (Saissy, 1815 cited in Svihla and Bowman, 1952; Heistand et al., 1950; Biörck et al., 1956; McArthur and Milsom, 1991b). In fact, if inspired levels of $O_2$ were reduced to 3–1%, respiratory depression and death would occur in some species before any significant respiratory stimulation or arousal occurred (Biörck et al., 1956; McArthur and Milsom, 1991b). In hibernating hedgehogs and golden-mantled ground squirrels, however, an hypoxic ventilatory response is present, and even remains (at least in the golden-mantled ground squirrel, although somewhat left shifted), following carotid body denervation (Fig. 10) (Tahti, 1975; McArthur and Milsom, 1991b; Webb and Milsom, 1991b). In Figure 10, the response curves for both intact and carotid body denervated golden-mantled ground squirrels (euthermic and hibernating)

(Webb and Milsom, 1991a) are plotted superimposed on the OEC determined for whole blood of this species at in vivo pH (Maginniss et al., 1989). This figure shows that the inflexion points of the hypoxic ventilatory response curves, particularly in the denervated animals, coincide with the inflexion points of the oxygen equilibrium curves. This correlation suggests that the hypoxic ventilatory responses of these animals may be more strongly correlated to changes in $O_2$ content than arterial $PO_2$. The presence of a strong ventilatory response following carotid body denervation, and previous reports suggesting that aortic bodies in mammals respond to changes in $O_2$ content (Hatcher et al., 1978; Lahiri et al., 1981), whereas carotid bodies do not, suggest that aortic bodies may play a more predominant role in this species. Similar correlations have been shown in reptiles (Glass et al., 1983), and it has been suggested that this may represent an adaptation in species that undergo wide fluctuations in $T_b$ and for whom $O_2$ content is a better indication of $O_2$ homeostasis than arterial $PO_2$ (Wood, 1984).

The reasons for the apparent species difference in the presence or absence of a hypoxic ventilatory response during hibernation are unclear. This may reflect species differences in either the input from carotid and aortic bodies (or other $O_2$ chemoreceptor inputs) in this response or in the central integration of this information. It would appear that in some species, however, because of the steepness of the left-shifted OEC, central hypoxic depression may develop before peripheral ventilatory stimulation.

### C. Hypercapnic Ventilatory Responses

During hibernation, all species retain their ventilatory responses to hypercapnia (Fig. 11). The threshold for eliciting a ventilatory response appears somewhat elevated in hibernating animals (ranging from 1 to 4% inspired $CO_2$) (Endres and Taylor, 1930; Lyman, 1951; Biörck et al., 1951; Tahti, 1975; McArthur and Milsom, 1991b; Webb and Milsom, 1991b). The sensitivities of the responses ($\Delta \dot{V}E/\Delta PCO_2$) are reduced in absolute terms, but if expressed in relative terms ($\Delta \dot{V}E/\Delta MCO_2$), sensitivity is actually greatly increased (Endres and Taylor, 1930; Biörck et al., 1956; Leitner and Malan, 1973; McArthur and Milsom, 1991b; Webb and Milsom, 1991b). Thus, if inspired levels of $CO_2$ are raised to 5–7%, continuous ventilation replaces intermittent breathing, and animals frequently begin to arouse from hibernation (Lyman, 1951; Biörck et al., 1956; Tahti, 1975; McArthur and Milsom, 1991b). As Figure 11 shows, the increase in $\dot{V}E$ is due to both increases in $VT$ and f. The increases in f stem from a decrease in the length of the period of apnea between breaths or episodes of breathing. There is very little change in the length of an individual breath.

These responses do not require intact carotid bodies in either euthermic or hibernating animals (see Fig. 11), emphasizing the relatively minor role of this chemoreceptor group in these animals and suggesting that central chemoreceptors may be exclusively involved in the hypercapnic ventilatory response.

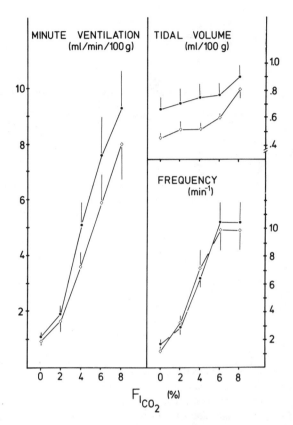

**Figure 11** Effects of increasing $F_{I_{CO_2}}$ on minute ventilation, tidal volume, and breathing frequency in hibernating, golden-mantled ground squirrels, both intact (filled symbols) and carotid body denervated (open symbols). (From Webb and Milsom, 1991b.)

In animals that exhibit the episodic-breathing pattern, it is still not clear what regulates the number of breaths in each breathing episode. Presumably, $CO_2$ plays a major role here as well. Certainly, the number of breaths per breathing episode goes up, along with the number of episodes per unit time, as the length of the periods of apnea decreases with increasing $P_{CO_2}$. Recent evidence suggests that mechanisms may also exist to optimize the rate of $CO_2$ excretion throughout each episode of breathing. Figure 12 depicts the changes in gas composition measured at the nose of a hibernating golden-mantled ground squirrel during a bout of hibernation ($T_b = 7°C$). Of particular note is that the end-expired $O_2$ concentration increases progressively throughout the breathing episode, whereas the $CO_2$ concentration falls, but at a slower rate. Figure 13 shows the progressive increase in the $O_2$ taken up and $CO_2$ excreted throughout

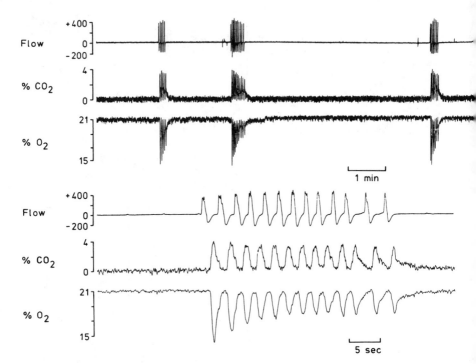

**Figure 12** Traces of pneumotachograph airflow and the fractional concentration of $CO_2$ and $O_2$ in expired air of a hibernating golden-mantled squirrel (7°C body temperature). The lower set of traces are on a faster time scale to illustrate the details of a single respiratory episode. (Voldstedlund and Milsom, unpublished.)

the episode depicted in the lower panel of Figure 12. Any straight line drawn through the origin on such a graph represents a constant rate of uptake or excretion. These curves show that the rate of $O_2$ uptake falls off progrssively after about the first four or five breaths in the episode. The rate of $CO_2$ excretion, however, increases over the first eight to ten breaths, presumably as $CO_2$ stores are moved from the tissues to the lungs, and it remains high until the last breath of the sequence. Thus, it appears that cardiorespiratory coupling and episode length may be regulated in such a way to maintain optimal (or at least high) rates of $CO_2$ excretion over the entire respiratory episode.

## IV.  Ventilatory Control During Arousal From Hibernation

The first overt sign of arousal from hibernation is usually an increase in ventilation. In some species, this is primarily due to an increase in VT (Malan et al.,

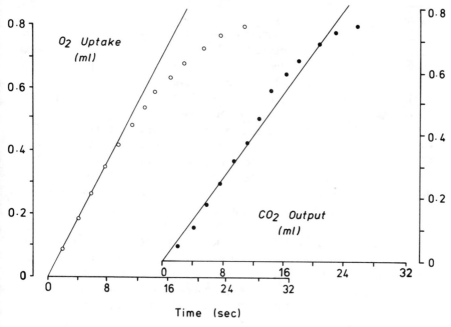

**Figure 13** The cumulative $O_2$ uptake (left axis, open symbols) and $CO_2$ output (right axis, filled symbols) derived for each successive breath (symbols) from the lower trace in Figure 12. (Voldstedlund and Milsom, unpublished.)

1973), whereas in others, it is due to an increase in breathing frequency (McArthur and Milsom, 1991b; Webb and Milsom, 1991b). These changes have been reported to precede the elevation of heart rate and metabolic rate, and breathing may even become continuous before any increase in $T_b$ is seen (Pajunen, 1970; Malan, 1982). It has recently been calculated that temperature-corrected pH may rise by 0.17 units during the first 15–30 minutes of arousal in European hamsters, whereas cheek pouch temperature in these animals only rose by 0.9°C (Malan et al., 1988). This is ten time greater than the increase in $[H^+]/[OH^-]$ that would have been expected based on the change in $T_b$ alone and would, the authors calculate, lead to excretion of up to 50% of the increase in $CO_2$ content that occurred during entrance into hibernation. Such a decrease in $[H^+]/[OH^-]$ would decrease the affinity of the mitochondrial uncoupling protein in brown adipose tissue for its inhibitor, GDP, and would facilitate thermogenesis, (Malan and Mioskowski, 1988). This evidence suggests that hibernating animals benefit not only from the depressing effects of $CO_2$-induced intracellular acidosis during entrance into hibernation, but by a rapid unloading of $CO_2$ stores, they also benefit from a rapid reversal of the acidosis-inhibiting effect on thermogenic tissue.

Once again, however, although these data suggest that the increase in ventilation during arousal contributes to the reversal of the metabolic depression associated with hibernation, the evidence does not support the concept that it is the causal agent involved in this process. Figure 14 illustrates the changes in EEG, EMG (and ECG superimposed on the EMG during the early part of the record), and respiration at the initiation of a bout of arousal in a golden-mantled ground squirrel. The initial breathing episode shown here is similar to those that were shown previously to accompany the occasional periods of central neural arousal (see Fig. 10); an increase in EEG activity followed by a burst of EMG activity, tachycardia, and an episode of breathing. In this instance, however, this is followed by cyclic increases in the slow-wave, high-voltage component of the EEG, massive bouts of shivering, and episodes of breathing. As arousal continues, breathing becomes continuous, but cyclic increases in slow-wave, high-voltage EEG activity still occur associated with episodes of shivering and, now, a waxing and waning of breathing (Fig. 15). Although still preliminary (data obtained from one animal), these data suggest that either ventilation follows metabolism in the usual fashion, or both ventilation and shivering thermogenesis may be coactivated at the initiation of the arousal from hibernation.

## V. Conclusions

Euthermic animals are fossorial and exhibit a normal hypoxic ventilatory response, but a severely blunted hypercapnic ventilatory response. Changes in arterial $P_{O_2}$ appear to be the primary respiratory stimulus. The thresholds and sensitivities of these responses are genetically determined and are not affected by extended changes in environmental gas composition and are not affected by the physiological changes associated with the preparation for hibernation.

In association with the fall in metabolic rate, which occurs during entrance into hibernation, is a fall in ventilation, which gives rise to intermittent breathing. It is suggested that the basic brain stem rhythm gives rise to a pattern of relatively evenly spaced single breaths. In some species, a supra-medullary input acts to convert this to an episodic-breathing pattern. In both cases, there seem to be separate thresholds for initiating and terminating breathing (i.e., blood gas and pH levels are regulated within a homeostatic "range" rather than at a constant level). In the episodic breathers, this range is wider, and breathing episodes are quite often associated with periods of central neural arousal.

Mainly because of the extreme effects of temperature on the OEC, wide fluctuations occur in blood $P_{O_2}$ levels during periods of apnea. The evidence suggests that the hypoxic ventilatory response in these animals may be more closely related to changes in the $O_2$ content of blood than in $P_{O_2}$ and that

**Figure 14** Recordings of the EEG, EMG (the ECG is visible superimposed on the EMG trace at the start of the record) and respiratory impedance of a golden-mantled ground squirrel at the initiation of arousal from hibernation (see text for details). (From Milsom et al., 1989.)

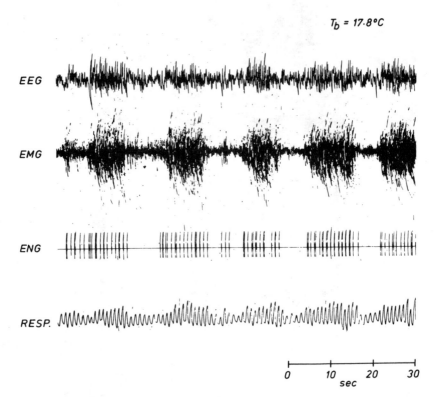

**Figure 15**  Recordings of the EEG, EMG, the ENG from a respiratory modulated neuron in the ventral respiratory center, and respiratory impedance in a golden-mantled ground squirrel during arousal from hibernation ($T_b$ = 11.7°C). This trace was obtained later in the same arousal episode illustrated in Figure 14. Note that the respiratory unit is recruited when respiratory amplitude increases during the periods of intense shivering and increased slow-wave, high-voltage EEG activity. (From Milsom et al., 1989.)

chemoreceptors other than those of the carotid body are involved in this response. Nonetheless, overall, the hypoxic ventilatory response appears greatly reduced or absent. Animals show an increase in their relative sensitivity to changes in $P_{CO_2}$ and pH, however, which now appear to represent the primary stimuli for respiration.

By their effects on the plasma $[H^+]/[OH^-]$ ratio during entrance into, and arousal from, hibernation, changes in ventilation appear to contribute significantly to the regulation of metabolic rate. It remains an intriguing question, however, as to whether ventilation follows metabolism or vice versa during these phases of the ventilatory cycle, or whether both are coregulated by a common mechanism.

The control of breathing in hibernating mammals is very similar to the control of breathing seen in all air-breathing, ectothermic vertebrates. This suggests that the generation and control of intermittent breathing is similar in all vertebrates in which metabolic rate is sufficiently reduced to preclude the need for continuous breathing.

## Acknowledgment

This work was supported by the NSERC of Canada. I wish to acknowledge the contribution of my graduate students whose advice, encouragement, and in many cases, as yet unpublished data, have gone into this paper. I would also like to thank my collaborators at Stanford University who assisted in the studies on the effects of "arousal state" on breathing pattern.

## References

Barr, R. E., and Silver, I. A. (1972). Oxygen tension in the abdominal cavity of hedgehogs during arousal from hibernation. *Respir. Physiol.*, **16**:16–21.

Bartels, H., Schmelzle, R., and Ulrich, S. (1969). Comparative studies of the respiratory function of mammalian blood. V. Insectivora: shrew, mole and non-hibernating hedgehog. *Respir. Physiol.*, **7**:278–286.

Baudinette, R. V. (1974). Physiological correlates of burrow gas conditions in the California ground squirrel. *Comp. Biochem. Physiol.*, **48A**:733–743.

Bickler, P. E. (1984). $CO_2$ balance of a heterothermic rodent: Comparison of sleep, torpor, and awake states. *Am. J. Physiol.*, **246**:R49–R55.

Biörck, G., Johansson, B., and Schmid, H. (1956). Reactions of hedgehogs, hibernating and non-hibernating, to the inhalation of oxygen, carbon dioxide, and nitrogen. *Acta Physiol. Scand.*, **37**:71–83.

Birchard, G. F., Gobbs, D. F., and Tenney, S. M. (1984). Effect of perinatal hypercapnia on the adult ventilatory response to carbon dioxide. *Respir. Physiol.*, **57**:341–347.

Boggs, D. F., Kilgore, Jr., D. L., and Birchard, G. F. (1984). Respiratory physiology of burrowing mammals and birds. *Comp. Biochem. Physiol.*, **77A**:1–7.

Burlington, R. F., Maher, T. J., and Sidel, C. M. (1969). Effect of hypoxia on blood gases, acid–base balance and in vitro myocardial function in a hibernator and a non-hibernator. *Fed. Proc.*, **28**:1042–1046.

Burlington, R. F., and Whitten, B. K. (1971). Red cell 2,3-diphosphoglycerate in hibernating ground squirrels. *Comp. Biochem. Physiol.*, **38A**:469–471.

Chapman, R. C., and Bennett, A. F. (1975). Physiological correlates of burrowing in rodents. *Comp. Biochem. Physiol.*, **51A**:599–603.

Clausen, G. (1966). Acid–base balance in the hedgehog *Erinaceus europaeus L.* during hibernation hypothermia, cooling and rewarming. *Arbok. Univ. Bergen, Mat.-Naturvitensk. Ser.* **6**:1–11.

Clausen, G., and Ersland, A. (1968). The respiratory properties of the blood of the hibernating hedgehog *Erinaceus europaeus L. Respir. Physiol.*, **5**:221–233.

Cragg, P. A., and Drysdale, D. B. (1983). Interaction of hypoxia and hypercapnia on ventilation, tidal volume and respiratory frequency in the anesthetized rat. *J. Physiol.*, **341**:477–493.

Darden, T. R. (1972). Respiratory adaptations of a fossorial mammal, the pocket gopher (*Thomomys bottae*). *J. Comp. Physiol.*, **78**:121–137.

Endres, G. (1930). Observations on certain physiological processes of the marmot—III, IV, and V. *Proc. R. Soc. Lond. Ser. B.*, **107**:241–247.

Endres, G., and Taylor, H. (1930). Observations on certain physiological processes of the marmot. II. The respiration. *Proc. R. Soc. Lond. Ser. B.*, **107**:230–240.

Gallego, R., Eyzaguirre, C., and Monti-Bloch, L. (1979). Thermal and osmotic responses of arterial chemoreceptors. *J. Neurophysiol.*, **42**:665–680.

Geiser, F. (1988). Reduction of metabolism during hibernation and daily topor in mammals and birds: Temperature effect or physiological inhibition. *J. Comp. Physiol., B.*, **158**:25–37.

Glass, M. L., Boutilier, R. G., and Heisler, N. (1983). Ventilatory control of arterial $Po_2$ in the turtle *Chrysemys picta bellii*: Effects of temperature and hypoxia. *J. Comp. Physiol. B.*, **151**:145–153.

Goodrich, C. A. (1973). Acid–base balance in euthermic and hibernating marmots. *Am. J. Physiol.*, **224**:1185–1189.

Hall, F. G. (1965). Hemoglobin and oxygen: Affinities in seven species of scuiridae. *Science*, **148**:1350–1351.

Hanson, A., and Johansson, B. W. (1961). Myocardial lactate concentration in guinea pigs, normothermic and hypothermic, and hedgehogs, in a hibernating and non-hibernating state. *Acta Physiol. Scand.*, **53**:137–141.

Harkness, D. R., Roth, S., and Goldman, P. (1974). Studies on the red blood cell oxygen affinity and 2,3-diphosoglyceric acid in the hibernating woodchuck (*Marmota monax*). *Comp. Biochem. Physiol.*, **48A**:591–599.

Hatcher, J. D., Chiu, L. K., and Jennings, D. B. (1978). Anemia is a stimulus to aortic and carotid chemoreceptors in the cat. *J. Appl. Physiol.*, **44**:696–702.

Hayward, J. D. (1966). Abnormal concentrations of respiratory gases in rabbit burrows. *M. Mammal.*, **47**:723–724.

Heistand, W. A., Rochold, W. T., Stemmler, F. W., Stullken, D. E., and Wiebers, J. E. (1950). Comparative hypoxic resistance of hibernators and non-hibernators. *Physiol. Zool.*, **23**:264–269.

Heller, H. C. (1979). Hibernation: Neural aspects. *Annu. Rev. Physiol.*, **41**:305–321.

Heller, H. C., and Glotzbach, S. F. (1977). Thermoregulation during sleep and hibernation. In *Environmental Physiology II* (International Review of Physiology. Vol. 15). Edited by D. Robertshaw. Baltimore, University Park Press.

Holloway, D. A., and Heath, A. G. (1984). Ventilatory changes in the golden hamster,

*Mesocricetus auratus*, compared with the laboratory rat, *Rattus norvegicus* during hypercapnia and/or hypoxia. *Comp. Biochem. Physiol.*, **77A**:267–273.

Hudson, J. W., and Deavers, D. R. (1973). Metabolism, pulmocutaneous water loss and respiration of eight species of ground squirrels from different environments. *Comp. Biochem. Physiol.*, **45A**:69–100.

Kent, K. M., and Pierce II, E. C. (1967). Acid–base characteristics of hibernating animals. *J. Appl. Physiol.*, **23**:336–340.

Kramm, C., Sattrup, G., Baumann, R., and Bartels, H. (1975). Respiratory function of blood in hibernating and non-hibernating hedgehogs. *Respir. Physiol.*, **25**:311–318.

Kreienbuhl, G., Strittmatter, J., and Ayim, E. (1976). Blood gases of hibernating hamsters and dormice. *Pflügers Arch.*, **366**:67–172.

Kristoffersson, R., and Soivio, A. (1964). Hibernation in the hedgehog *Erinacaeus europaeus*. Changes of respiratory pattern, heart rate and body temperature in response to gradually decreases or increasing ambient temperature. *Ann. Acad. Sci. Fenn. Ser. A4*, **82**:3–17.

Kristoffersson, R., and Soivio, A. (1966). Duration of hypothermia periods and type of respiration in the hibernating golden hamster, *Mesocricetus auratus* Waterh. Ann. Zool. Fenn., **3**:66–67.

Lahiri, S., Mulligan, E., Nichino, T., Mokashi, A., and Davies, R. O. (1981). Relative responses of aortic body and carotid body chemoreceptors to carboxyhemoglobinemia. *J. Appl. Physiol.*, **50**:580–586.

Larkin, E. C., Simmonds, R. C., Ulvedal, F., and Williams, W. T. (1972). Responses of some hematological parameters of active and hibernating squirrels (*Spermophilus mexicanus*) upon exposure to hypobaric and isobaric hyperoxia. *Comp. Biochem. Physiol.*, **43A**:757–770.

Leitner, L. M. and Malan, A. (1973). Possible role of the arterial chemoreceptors in the ventilatory responses of the anesthetized marmot to changes in inspired $P_{O_2}$ and $P_{CO_2}$. *Comp Biochem. Physiol.*, **45A**:953–959.

Lyman, C. P. (1951). Effect of increased $CO_2$ on respiration and heart rate of hibernating hamsters and ground squirrels. *Am. J. Physiol.*, **167**:638–643.

Lyman, C. P. (1958). Oxygen consumption, body temperature and heart rate of woodchucks entering hibernation. *Am. J. Physiol.*, **194**:83–91.

Lyman, C. P. (1982a). Entering hibernation. In *Hibernation and Torpor in Mammals and Birds*. Edited by C. P. Lyman, J. S. Willis, A. Malan, and L. C. H. Wang. New York, Academic Press.

Lyman, C. P. (1982b). The mystery of the periodic arousal. In *Hibernation and Torpor in Mammals and Birds*. Edited by C. P. Lyman, J. S. Willis, A. Malan, and L. C. H. Wang. New York, Academic Press.

Lyman, C. P., and Chatfield, P. O. (1955). Physiology of hibernation in animals. *Physiol. Rev.*, **35**:403–425.

Lyman, C. P., and Hastings, A. B. (1951). Total $CO_2$ of hamsters and ground squirrels during hibernation. *Am. J. Physiol.*, **167**:633–637.

Lyman, C. P., and O'Brien, R. C. (1960). Circulatory changes in the thirteen-lined ground squirrel during the hibernating cycle. *Bull. Mus. Comp. Zool.*, **124**:353–372.

Lyman, C. P., and O'Brien, R. C. (1963). Autonomic control of circulation during the hibernating cycle in ground squirrels. *J. Physiol. Lond.* **168**:477–499.

MacLean, G. S. (1978). Respiratory physiology of a semi-fossorial mammal *Tamias striatus*. *Physiologist*, **21**:75.

MacLean, G. S. (1981). Blood viscosity of two mammalian hibernators: *Spermophilus tridecemlineatus* and *Tamias striatus*. *Physiol. Zool.*, **54**:122–131.

Maginniss, L. A., Lo, G. S., and Milsom, W. K. (1989). Effects of hibernation on blood oxygen transport in golden mantled ground squirrels. *FASEB J.*, **3**:A234.

Malan, A. (1973). Ventilation measured by body plethysmography in hibernating mammals and poikilotherms. *Respir. Physiol.*, **17**:32–44.

Malan, A. (1977). Blood acid-base state at a variable temperature. A graphical representation. *Respir. Physiol.*, **31**:259–275.

Malan, A. (1982). Respiration and acid–base state in hibernation. In *Hibernation and Torpor in Mammals and Birds*. Edited by C. P. Lyman, J. S. Willis, A. Malan, and L. C. H. Wang. New York, Academic Press.

Malan, A., Arens, H., and Waechter, A. (1973). Pulmonary respiration and acid–base state in hibernating marmots and hamsters. *Respir. Physiol.*, **17**:45–61.

Malan, A., and Mioskowski, G. (1988). pH–temperature interactions on protein function and hibernation. GDP binding to brown adipose tissue mitochondria. *J. Comp. Physiol. B*, **158**:487–493.

Malan, A., Mioskowski, G., and Calgari, C. (1988). Time-course of blood acid–base state during arousal from hibernation in the European hamster. *J. Comp. Physiol. B*, **158**:495–500.

Malan, A., Rodeau, J. L., and Daull, F. (1985). Intracellular pH in hibernation and respiratory acidosis in the European hamster. *J. Comp. Physiol.*, **153**:251–258.

McArthur, M. D., and Milsom, W. K. (1991a). The effects of season and ambient temperature on ventilation and respiratory sensitivity of euthermic ground squirrels. *Physiol. Zool.*, **64**(4) (in press).

McArthur, M. D., and Milsom, W. K. (1991b). Effects of hypoxia and hypercapnia on the ventilatory patterns of awake and hibernating ground squirrels. *Physiol. Zool.*, **64**(4) (in press).

McLaughlin, D. W., and Meints, R. H. (1972). A study of hibernator erythropoietic responses to simulated high altitude. *Comp. Biochem. Physiol.*, **42A**:655–666.

McNab, B. K. (1979). The influence of body size on the energetics and distribution of fossorial and burrowing mammals. *Ecology*, **60**:1010–1021.

Milsom, W. K. (1988). Control of arrhythmic breathing in aerial breathers. *Can. J. Zool.*, **66**:99–108.

Milsom, W. K., Krilowicz, B., Grahn, D., Radeke, C., and Heller, H. C. (1989). Effects of "arousal state" on breathing pattern in sleeping and hibernating ground squirrels. In *Proceedings of the 6th International Hypoxia Symposium*. Edited by J. Sutten, J. Coates, and J. Remmers. New York, Benchmark Press.

Musacchia, X. J., and Volkert, W. A. (1971). Blood gases in hibernating and active ground squirrels: $HbO_2$ affinity at 6° and 38°C. *Am. J. Physiol.*, **221**:128–130.

Naifeh, K. H., Huggins, S. E., and Hoff, H. E. (1971). Effects of brain stem section on respiratory patterns of crocodilian reptiles. *Respir. Physiol.*, **13**:186–197.

Osborne, S., and Milsom, W. K. (1992). Effects of hypothermia on ventilation and ventilatory responses of rats and ground squirrels. (in preparation.)

Pajunen, I. (1970). Body temperature, heart rate, breathing pattern, weight loss and periodicity of hibernation in the Finnish garden dormouse *Eliomys quercinus L.* *Ann. Zool. Fenn.*, **7**:251–266.

Phillipson, E. A., and Bowes, G. (1986). Control of breathing during sleep. In *Handbook of Physiology*. Section 3, The Respiratory System. Vol. 2, Control of Breathing, part 1. Edited by A. P. Fishman, N. S. Cherniack, J. D. Widdicombe, and S. R. Geiger. Bethesda, American Physiological Society.

Reeves, R. B. (1980). The effect of temperature on the oxygen equilibrium curve of human blood. *Respir. Physiol.*, **42**:317–328.

Robertson, W. D., Yousef, M. K., and Johnson, H. D., (1968). Simultaneous recording of core temperature and energy expenditure during the hibernating cycle of *Mesocricetus auratus*. *Nature*, **219**:742–743.

Snapp, B. D., and Heller, H. C. (1981). Suppression of metabolism during hibernation in ground squirrels (*Citellus lateralis*). *Physiol. Zool.*, **54**:297–307.

Stormont, R. T., Foster, M. A., and Pfeiffer, C. (1939). Plasma pH, $CO_2$ content of the blood and "tissue gas" tensions during hibernation. *Proc. Soc. Exp. Biol. Med.*, **42**:56–59.

Strumwasser, F. (1960). Some physiological principles governing hibernation in *Citellus beecheyi*. *Bull. Mus. Comp. Zool.*, **124**:285–320.

Svihla, A., and Bowman, C. (1952). Oxygen carrying capacity of the blood of dormant ground squirrels. *Am. J. Physiol.*, **171**:479–481.

Tahti, H. (1975). Effects of changes in $CO_2$ and $O_2$ concentrations in the inspired gas on respiration in the hibernating hedgehog (*Erinaceus europas L.*) *Ann. Zool. Fenn.*, **12**:183–187.

Tahti, H., and Soivio, A. (1975). Blood gas concentration, acid–base balance and blood pressure in hedgehogs in the active state and in hibernation with periodic respiration. *Ann. Zool. Fenn.*, **12**:188–192.

Temple, G. E., and Musacchia, X. J. (1975). Erythrocyte 2,3-diphosphoglycerate concentrations in hibernating, hypothermic and rewarming hamsters. *Proc. Soc. Exp. Biol. Med.*, **148**:588–592.

Tenney, S. M., and Boggs, D. F. (1986). Comparative mammalian respiratory control. In *Handbook of Physiology*. Section 3. The Respiratory System. Vol. 2, Control of Breathing, Part 1. Edited by A. P. Fishman, N. S. Cherniack, J. G. Widdicombe, and S. R. Geiger. Bethesda, American Physiological Society.

Twente, J. A., and Twente, J. W. (1968). Concentrations of L-lactate in the tissues of *Citellus lateralis* after known intervals of hibernating periods. *J. Mammal.*, **49**:541–544.

Wang, L. C. H., and Hudson, J. W. (1970). Temperature regulation in normothermic and hibernating eastern chipmunks *Tamias striatus*. *Comp. Biochem. Physiol.*, **38A**:59–90.

Walker, J. M., Glotzbach, S. F., Berger, R. J., and Heller, H. C. (1977). Sleep and hibernation in ground squirrels (*Citellus* spp.): Electrophysiological observations. *Am. J. Physiol.*, **233**:R213–R221.

Webb, C. L., and Milsom, W. K. (1991a). The role of the carotid body in the control of breathing in euthermic and hibernating ground squirrels. *Respir. Physiol.* (submitted).

Webb, C. L., and Milsom, W. K. (1991b). Effects of changing body temperature on breathing pattern and ventilatory responses of the golden-mantled ground squirrel. *Respir. Physiol.* (submitted).

Wood, S. C. (1984). Cardiovascular shunts and oxygen transport in lower vertebrates. *Am. J. Physiol.*, **247**:R3–R14.

# 8

## Gas Exchange Strategies in Reptiles and the Origin of the Avian Lung

**STEVEN F. PERRY***

Universität Oldenburg
Oldenburg, Germany

McArthur and Wilson (1967) coined the term *strategy* to explain propagation patterns of island species, but the strategy concept can be applied equally well to cardiorespiratory physiology. Indeed, this concept also embodies lung morphology, as demonstrated later.

For the present purpose, *strategy* is defined as a set of connected processes seen in relationship to a specific goal. Although theoretically possible at any organizational level, a strategy is most readily seen at the level of the organism or organ system. That is, although it is possible to speak of the ecological strategy of a forest or the mitotic strategy of epithelial cells, the use of the word strategy in these contexts is not as intuitively clear as it is in the context of migratory, reproductive, metabolic, or, as in the present example, gas exchange strategy. The reason lies in the ultimate goal of all strategies: survival of the species. We can picture the survival of a species or of an individual and the role played by the processes of migration, reproduction, or gas exchange in relationship to this goal; but this picture disintegrates when we come to ecosystems or tissues.

If we examine more closely the processes involved in such strategies, we find that they are never purely functional. What is migration without organisms, or gas exchange without an anatomical interface between the external and internal

---

*Present affiliation:* University of Calgary, Calgary, Alberta, Canada.

milieu? Functions are there that structures may survive and vice versa. Thus, at the heart of the strategy concept lies the interaction of structure and function.

Gas exchange between the organism and the environment is one of the processes involved in metabolism. (The German word for metabolism, *Stoffwechsel,* literally "material exchange," expresses the exchange nature of metabolism even more clearly.) Thus, before we can consider gas exchange strategy we must take a closer look at the strategy of metabolism.

The immediate goal of all metabolic strategies is the same: the maintenance of an organism's vital processes. Among amniotes (reptiles, mammals, and birds) we recognize two main sets of patterns (i.e., strategies) for the use of metabolic energy. One of these strategies, which is typically observed in reptiles, is characterized by the direct dependence of the animal upon environmental sources for maintaining its body temperature, whereas the other, which is characteristic of mammals and birds, employs the heat generated as a by-product of metabolic processes to maintain a high, constant body temperature.

As seen from the viewpoint of a typical reptile, mammals and birds would appear to be energy wasters that must power oxygen-hungry metabolic machines to maintain the same body temperature that a reptile will reach with one-tenth as much oxygen consumption on a sunny day (Wood and Lenfant, 1976). For convenience, we will adopt the reptilian point of view and speak of "energy-saving" and "energy-wasting" metabolic strategies.

*Gas exchange strategy* is the set of processes involved in gas movement between the organism and its environment. As indicated in the foregoing, it has both physiological and morphological components. If we accept the premises that the gas exchange strategy of an organism is related in some characteristic way to its metabolic strategy, and that the morphological part of the gas exchange strategy bears some definite relationship to the physiological parts, then the structure of a lung can serve as an indicator of the gas exchange strategy and (less precisely) of the metabolic strategy of the organism.

Furthermore, if the phylogenetic relationships among the animals in question are known, it may be possible to use our knowledge of lung morphology and metabolic strategy together, according to the principle of mutual enlightenment, to reconstruct the probable gas exchange strategy of extinct animal groups. Fortunately, there is general consensus that the energy-wasting strategy must have evolved from an energy-saving one (Greenberg, 1980). In addition, it is generally accepted that birds and crocodilian reptiles are relatively closely related, whereas mammals occupy a rather isolated position among the amniotes (Hennig, 1983).

In this chapter we shall consider lung structure in reptiles in relation to its gas exchange function in the context of an overall strategy for survival of the individual. Then, from the admittedly largely hypothetical functional morphological construct established, we shall attempt to bridge the gap left by Cretaceous extinctions and link up with the functional morphology of the avian lung.

## I. Structural Types of Lungs and Gas Exchange Strategy

In keeping with their change in metabolic strategies, both mammals and birds have evolved high-performance respiratory systems. The fact that mammalian and avian lungs are morphologically different is not surprising in light of the great diversity in structural types of lungs found within the class Reptilia, from which both mammals and birds are derived (Fig. 1).

Lung structure shows more major variability among reptiles than in any other vertebrate class (Perry, 1989b). Most lizards and snakes have single-chambered or transitional lung types (Figs. 1 and 2); turtles; crocodilians, and platynotan lizards (in particular monitor lizards and gila monsters) have a complex, multichambered lung structure (see Figs. 1 and 2). But even within a small group, such as the monitor lizards, the structural diversity is so great that the lung has been employed as a taxonomic–systematic character (Becker et al., 1989). Could this structural diversity imply that there are an equally large number of gas exchange strategies among reptiles?

Two case studies among lizards illustrate the complexity of this problem. Monitor lizards are known for their ability to maintain a high level of aerobic activity (Bennett, 1972). Indeed, Kjell Johansen was among the first to notice the close matching of convection and perfusion in the lungs of the savanna monitor, *Varanus exanthematicus* (Wood et al., 1977), which is one of the "mammallike" attributes that characterize the respiratory physiology of this species. The authors concluded that the impressive aerobic capabilities of the monitor lizard could be best explained by the large surface area provided by its multichambered lungs (see Fig. 2).

A morphometric comparison (Perry, 1983) of the monitor lizard with the teju (*Tupinambis nigropunctatus*), its South American ecological equivalent that has single-chambered lungs, showed that the monitor lizard has, indeed, almost twice as much respiratory surface area (SAR) per unit body weight as does the teju. But the harmonic mean of the diffusion barrier from the lung to the capillary surface ($\tau$htR) is almost twice as great in the monitor lizard as in the teju. Thus, the anatomical diffusion factor (ADF = SAR/$\tau$htR), which is the anatomical component of diffusing capacity of lung tissue ($Dt_{O_2}$), was nearly identical in both species. Consideration of ADF and $Dt_{O_2}$ alone, then, does not explain the different gas exchange strategies of the multichambered monitor lung and the single-chambered teju lung.

From the Fick equation (follows) we see that the diffusing capacity represents a conductance, which determines how much gas can be transferred per

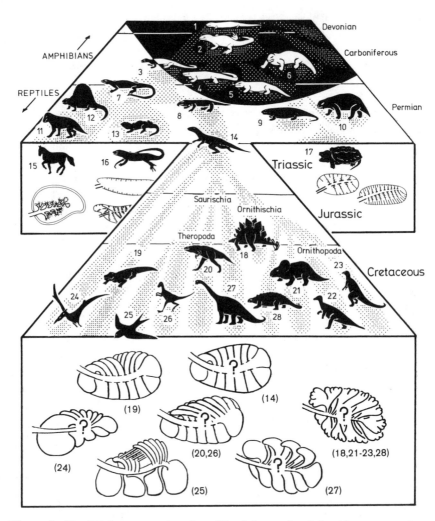

**Figure 1** Simplified representation of possible phylogenetic relationships among major groups of terrestrial, Paleozoic tetrapods and Mesozoic archosaurs. The white profiles against a black background represent those groups for which free-living larval stages have been demonstrated or are suspected. The origin of turtles (17) as a separate amniote group is tentative. Two unlabeled paths at the upper right lead to the Temnospondyli, Lepospondyli, and modern amphibians. 1, primitive anthroacosaurian labyrinthodonts; 2, Gephyrostegidae; 3, Captorhinomorpha; 4, Limnoscelidae; 5, Seymouriamorpha; 6, Diadectidae; 7, Romeriidae, 8, Captorhinidae; 9, Procolophonia; 10, Pareiasauria; 11,

unit time and mean "alveolar"–capillary partial pressure difference, $\overline{P_{A_{O_2}} - P_{C_{O_2}}}$:

$$\dot{M}_{O_2} = D_{O_2} \, (\overline{P_{A_{O_2}} - P_{C_{O_2}}})$$

Since we have established that $Dt_{O_2}$ is similar in a monitor lizard and a teju of the same body mass, for the monitor lizard to maintain a greater $\dot{M}_{O_2}$ than the teju, the monitor lizard must increase $\overline{P_{A_{O_2}} - P_{C_{O_2}}}$. This term is indicative of the ability of pulmonary blood to remove oxygen from lung air, a *small* value indicating an effective ventilation–perfusion matching. This paradoxical solution to the monitor lizards aerobic superiority is refuted by the demonstrated close ventilation–perfusion matching in the savanna monitor (Wood et al., 1977), as well as by the lack of such close matching in the teju (Hlastala et al., 1985). A more likely interpretation is that $Dt_{O_2}$ is not an adequate index of $D_{O_2}$; that is, that the morphometrically determined value does not completely reflect the dynamic physiological process.

In mammals and reptiles (see Chap. 6) $D_{O_2}$ does not remain constant, but increases with increasing $\dot{M}_{O_2}$. This phenomenon is usually explained by postulating that at the "alveolar" surface there is a stratified air layer, which constitutes an additional, morphometrically inaccessible diffusion barrier. Presumably, this stratified inhomogeneity becomes reduced at high levels of alveolar convection (see Chap. 5). It is thus possible that the multichambered lung of the monitor lizard is more effective in reducing stratified inhomogeneities at high ventilatory levels than is the single-chambered teju lung.

## II. Parenchymal Type and Gas Exchange Strategy

To test the foregoing hypothesis, we must take a closer look at the structure of the reptilian lung. In all structural types, the lung consists basically of a tissue-

Therapsida; 12, Pelycosauria; 13, Eosuchia; 14, Archosauria (*Euparkeria* as beginning of line); (14) presumed euparkerian lung type; 15, Mammalia with bronchoalveolar lung type; 16, Lepidosauria with lung types as in Figure 2; 17, Chelonia with multichambered lung type; 18, Stegosauria (Ornithischia); (18, 21–23, 28) presumed bronchoalveolarlike lung type of Ornithischia; 19, Crocodilia; (19), Crocodilian lung type; 20, Carnosauria (Saurischia: Theropoda), for presumed lung, see (26); 21, Ceratopsia, for presumed lung type, see (18); 22, Hadrosauridae (Ornithischia: Ornithopoda), for presumed lung type, see (18); 23, Iguanodontidae (Ornithischia: Ornithopoda), for presumed lung type, see (18); 24, Pterosauria; (24) presumed avianlike lung with cranial airsac; 25, Aves; (25), avian lung–airsac system. 26, Coelurosauria (Saurischia: Theropoda); (26), presumed carnosaurian/early coelurosaurian lung type; 27, Sauropoda; (27), presumed multisaccular sauropodian lung type; 28, Ankylosauria, for presumed lung type, see (18). (Modified after Perry, 1989b).

free central lumen surrounded by a parenchymal layer in which gas exchange tissue is found (see Fig. 2). In multichambered lungs, there are several central lumina: one for each chamber. The parenchymal structure can be quite variable, not only from species to species, but also within a single lung. In general, however, one type tends to predominate in a given lung.

We speak of three different types of parenchyma in reptilian lungs: *trabecular, edicular,* and *faveolar* (see Fig. 2; Duncker, 1978; Perry, 1983). In trabecular parenchyma, the bundles of smooth muscle and elastic tissue that form the core of the trabeculae lie against the inner lung wall. Since the trabeculae are interconnected, raising them above the lung wall results in a system of cubicles. If such a cubicle is wider than it is deep, we call it an *edicula,* which is a small niche in a wall where the Romans used to keep their house ikons. Or if the cubicle is deeper than it is wide, we call it a *faveolus,* which means small honeycomb (Duncker, 1978).

It is possible that the parenchymal type, rather than the structural type, of lung plays the decisive role in gas exchange strategy. It is, after all, the parenchyma, not the airways, that provides the gas exchange surfaces. Since the gas exchange surfaces in trabecular and edicular parenchymal types are readily accessible to moving air, they are compatible with a *convection-oriented gas exchange strategy* (Perry, 1985). On the other hand, faveolar parenchyma, in which only the upper portions are exposed to convective air movement, is indicative of a *diffusion-oriented gas exchange strategy.* (Discussion of the intermediate "confusion-oriented" condition will be left to the critics.)

We would expect that animals with predominantly edicular parenchyma could respond to changes in oxygen demand by increasing the efficiency of oxygen extraction, since increased ventilation would result directly in increased convection, which Kjell Johansen (1987), among others, has shown to be balanced on the perfusion side by a left-to-right cardiac shunt during breathing episodes (see Part Five of this volume for further references).

Differences in experimental protocol make it difficult to test this hypothesis on the basis of an available oxygen extraction data. In spite of extreme variability, the mean values from 15° to 35°C (Fig. 3) reveal a general tendency for animals with edicular parenchyma to extract a greater percentage of $O_2$ from the inspired air than do those with faveolar parenchyma. Furthermore, the increase of $O_2$ extraction at higher ambient temperatures also tends to be greater in species with edicular parenchyma.

If the gas exchange strategy depends only upon the type of parenchyma, what then is the functional significance of the structural type of lung? By using a simple geometric model of the multichambered lung of the red-eared turtle, *Pseudemys (Trachemys) scripta elegans* (Fig. 4), it is possible to estimate the primary surface area of the lung with and without intercameral septa. Because

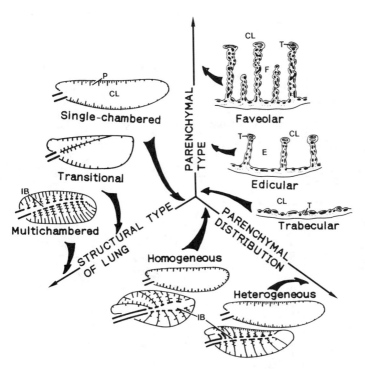

**Figure 2** Schematic representation of three variables in the macroscopic structure of reptilian lungs. Illustrating the *structural type of lung* are lung schemata of a scincid lizard (single-chambered), an iguanid lizard (transitional) and a sea turtle (multichambered); illustrating the *parenchymal distribution* are lung schemata of a teju lizard (homogeneous, upper) and a caiman (homogeneous, lower), as well as a scincid lizard (heterogeneous, upper) and a varanid lizard (heterogeneous, lower). The various *parenchymal types* can be found within a single heterogeneously partitioned lung, or they can be characteristic of an entire homogeneously partitioned lung. In general, even within a heterogeneous lung, a particular parenchymal type will predominate. (CL, central lumen of lung or chamber; E, edicula; F, faveolus; IB, intrapulmonary bronchus; P, parenchymal layer; T, smooth-muscular core of trabeculae.)

of the presence of these septa, the total surface area available for the elaboration of ediculae or faveoli is increased by 138%, compared with a single-chambered lung of the same volume. For sea turtles, monitors, and crocodiles, in which the chambers are tubular and more numerous than in the red-eared turtle, the primary surface area advantage from the multichambered structure is certainly greater. Thus, the combination of a multichambered primary structure and an

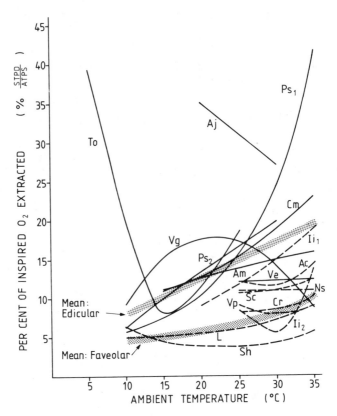

**Figure 3** Percentage of inspired $O_2$ extracted as a function of ambient temperature in reptiles. Solid lines represent species with primarily edicular parenchyma; dashed lines, species with primarily faveolar parenchyma. The green iguana (Ii, *Iguana iguana;* Ii$_1$ Giordano and Jackson, 1973; Ii$_2$ Perry, 1989d) has a transitional lung type with both edicular and faveolar parenchymal regions. **Primarily edicular:** Aj, elephant trunk snake, *Acrochordus javanicus* (Glass and Johansen, 1976); Am, American alligator, *Alligator mississippiensis* (Davies et al., 1982); Cm, green turtle, *Chelonia mydas* (Jackson et al., 1979); To, box turtle, *Terrapene ornata* (Glass et al., 1979); Ps, slider turtle, *Pseudemys (Trachemys) scripta* (Ps$_1$ Jackson, 1971; Ps$_2$ Jackson et al., 1974); Ve, savanna monitor, *Varanus exanthematicus* (Wood et al., 1978); Vg, Gould's monitor, *Varanus gouldii* (Bennett, 1972; 1973); **Primarily faveolar:** Ac, asp, *Aspis cerastes* (Dmi'el, 1972); Cr, Mediterranean colubrid snake, *Coluber ravergieri* (Dmi'el, 1972); L, emerald lizard, *Lacerta viridis* and Italian wall lizard, L. *sicula* (Nielsen, 1961); Ns, northern water snake, *Nerodia sipedon* (Perry, 1989d); Sc, desert colubrid snake, *Spalerosophis cliffordi* (Dmi'el, 1972); Sh, chuckwalla lizard, *Sauromalus hispidus* (Bennett, 1972; 1973); Vp, Palastine viper, *Vipera palastinae* (Dmi'el, 1972).

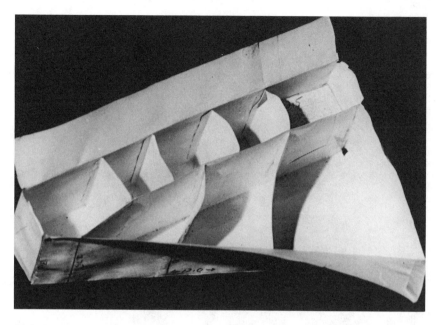

**Figure 4** Paper box model of a multichambered lung, based on that of the turtle, *Pseudemys (Trachemys) scripta*. The surface area available for the elaboration of parenchyma in this multichambered model exceeds by 138% that of a nonseptate, single-chambered lung of the same volume.

edicular parenchyma can result in both a large surface area and in a convection-oriented gas exchange strategy.

But this anatomical situation brings with it a physiological problem. Whereas, in the single-chambered lung, all ediculae communicate directly with the central lumen, in the multichambered lung, they communicate only with air stored in the individual chambers. In addition, not all chambers are equally accessible to tidal air movements. The dorsal and medial chambers in monitor lizards and turtles, for example, are virtually immobile owing to their firm attachment to the body wall, and the gas exchange function of their surfaces, however exposed they might appear, would be poor if the chambers that contain them could not be ventilated.

With use of radioactive xenon gas, Spragg et al. (1980) showed, in the red-eared turtle, that inspired gas becomes quickly and evenly distributed throughout the lung. During the breath-hold period the xenon (and presumably also oxygen) quickly disappears from the proximal region (near the intrapulmonary bronchus), but remains little changed in the saclike, distal regions of the chambers. What may happen during expiration is illustrated by experiments in which India ink

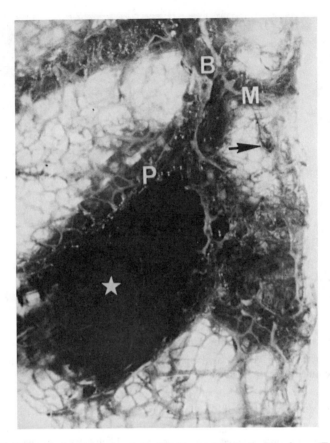

**Figure 5**    Frontally hemisected, gelatin-filled lung of the turtle *Pseudemys (Trachemys) scripta,* in which India ink has been forced out of the third lateral chamber (star) by a simulated expiratory maneuver before allowing the preparation to gel in an ice bath. Note that the ink is found in the proximal parenchyma (P), and in the medial chamber (M) at arrow, as well as in the intrapulmonary bronchus (B). Approximately twice natural size.

was injected into the distal portion of the third lateral chamber of warm, gelatin-filled lungs of dead turtles and pressed out in a simulated expiration. In the cooled, frontally hemisected preparation (Fig. 5), we see that the ink has re-ventilated the proximal exchange surfaces of the lateral chamber before leaving the lung by the intrapulmonary bronchus. In addition, some ink has crossed the intrapulmonary bronchus and entered the medial chambers. This ventilation of one chamber by another is termed *proxy ventilation.*

Of particular significance here are 1) that two-directional crosscurrent ventilation apparently occurs (see Chap. 5) proximally in the large chambers; 2) that gas is only slowly removed from the distal regions of the large chambers; and 3) that the small chambers of limited motility appear to be proxy ventilated.

Morphometric data for the turtle lung (Perry, 1978) are consistent with this functional model: the exchange surface is greater, the air–blood barrier is thinner, and the diffusion capacity (and ADF) are greater in proximal as opposed to distal regions of the large chambers. Only the distribution of respiratory capillaries remains regionally unchanged. In the savanna monitor, the picture is similar, except that the capillary density is greater proximally than distally within the individual chambers, and the barrier thickness remains constant (Perry, 1983).

The Nile crocodile, *Crocodylus niloticus,* has evolved yet another means to the same end (Perry, 1988; 1989a). Its lungs are characterized by long, tubular chambers dorsally and more saclike ones ventrally. In its microvascular structure the crocodile lung combines the modes of morphological specialization seen in the monitor and the turtle. The distal region of the homogeneously partitioned chambers displays a lower capillary density and a greater air–blood barrier thickness than does the proximal region.

It can hardly be coincidental that the multichambered lungs of these virtually unrelated reptiles (see Fig. 1) all demonstrate very similar patterns of specialization, which are consistent with a two-directional, crosscurrent exchange model: a high-ADF region proximally and a low-ADF region distally in the same chambers. Although the concept of the functional division of reptilian lungs and lung chambers into "exchange" and "mechanical/storage" regions is not new (see Wolf, 1933), the translation of these concepts into quantifiable entities, such as SAR, τhtR, and ADF, makes these findings interpretable for the first time in terms of gas exchange strategy.

A possible functional consequence of the observed morphological configuration is that low ADF in the distal portion of a given chamber precludes reventilation of the proximally located ediculae of that chamber with gas of lower $P_{O_2}$ than that contained just before expiration. Thus, the pulmonary venous $P_{O_2}$ should not fall during expiration. We propose that the two-directional crosscurrent model represents a functional improvement of the convection-oriented gas exchange strategy, but that further improvement is possible, as will be outlined in the next section.

## III. Honing the Crosscurrent Model: The Reptilian Way to the Avian Lung

The real "crosscurrent" masters are the birds, with their unidirectional flow in the paleopulmonic region of the lung (Scheid and Piiper, 1989). Cladistically speaking, crocodiles and birds are sister groups among the living archosaurs, and this common ancestry is, in part, betrayed by the similar structural plan of crocodilian and avian lungs: 1) Cranially four groups of monopodally branching, tubular chambers (medioventral bronchi; parabronchi in birds); 2) caudally, numerous groups of arching, tubular chambers (mediodorsal bronchi; parabronchi in birds); and 3) anastomoses where the chambers meet: parabronchial anastomoses in the avian paleopulmo; intercameral perforations in the crocodile.

The presence of intercameral perforations is not a compelling argument for unidirectional airflow in the crocodilian lung, as Wolf (1933) argued. They are much too rare for such an important function (Perry, 1988). More likely, their primary function is redistribution of air among chambers during breath-hold periods, which make up 80% of the time in a Nile crocodile resting at 25°C (Glass and Johansen, 1979). But they could become important in a constant, sinusoidal breather.

For the sake of argument, let us assume that birds originated during the Jurassic, that their common ancestor with crocodiles was a Triassic archosaur of euparkerian grade (see Fig. 1, No. 14), and that their immediate reptilian ancestor was a saurischian of coelurosaurian grade (see Fig. 1, No. 26).

In Figure 6, the euparkerian-grade lung is shown schematically to consist of the congruent features (see points 1–3, in the foregoing) of crocodilian and avian lungs. Note, that the most cranial chambers arch cranially, but that more caudal ones tend to extend straight out from the intrapulmonary bronchus, similar to the situation in the gila monster, which has rather archetypal multichambered lungs (Becker et al., 1989; Milani, 1894). As in the crocodile, a small number of perforations that permit intercameral air circulation during breath-hold periods are postulated for the euparkerian grade.

In the crocodilian-grade model, the caudal chambers arch caudally, thus to an even greater extent than in the euparkerian-grade model precluding direct caudocranial extrabronchial air circulation. All chambers are ventilated by muscular retraction and protraction of the liver, which moves the lungs back and forth in the conical chest cavity (Gans and Clark, 1976).

In the euparkerian and crocodilian models, pseudemys-like proxy ventilation of the dorsal chambers should be ineffective because of the tubular configuration of these chambers. Each chamber is self-ventilating. Thus, in keeping with the morphological correlates of the two-directional, crosscurrent exchange model, their distal regions must remain at low ADF.

The proposed early coelurosaurian-grade lung (see Fig. 6) differs in one crucial way from the crocodilian-grade: the caudally originating chambers make direct contact with their cranially originating counterparts. Perforations at the points of contact now result in a caudocranial, extrabronchial short-circuit. In the early stages of this development (see Fig. 6, early coelurosaurian grade), such connections would be of little consequence, since the chambers are still self-ventilating and must preserve a distal region of low ADF. Establishment of a proxy ventilation of these interconnected chambers, however, would allow the

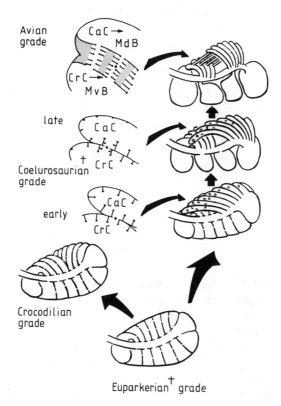

**Figure 6** Hypothetical pathway of evolution of the avian lung–airsac system, showing the relationship to the crocodilian lung. Euparkerian- and coelurosaurian-grade lungs are hypothetical constructs (compare Fig. 1). † Indicates extinct groups; *, perforations between chambers. These perforations are envisioned to play a crucial role in the stepwise evolution of the avian parabronchi, as indicated in the detail sketches of coelurosaurian- and avian-grade lungs. CrC and CaC are cranial and caudal chambers, which are connected with the respective regions of the intrapulmonary bronchus. MvB and MdB are avian medioventral bronchi and mediodorsal bronchi, which are proposed to evolve from CrC and CaC, respectively, as indicated by small arrows.

dorsal chambers to assume a completely respiratory function. A homogeneous distribution of ADF along their entire length is possible (see Fig. 6, late coelurosaurian grade).

This is the case in the avian lung, in which the cranial air sacs serve as a reservoir for air that has passed through the paleopulmo. If we assume the homology of the clavicular air sac of birds with the cranial saclike dilatation of the first lateral chamber of the crocodilian lung (Moser, 1904), then it is probable that a similar structure could have been used as a reservoir for expired air in the coelurosaurian-grade model. This storage region would lie distal to the exchange region just as required by the crosscurrent model, but, unlike the euparkerian and crocodilian models, a single chamber would now provide the storage volume for all other chambers.

From here, several paths could lead to the establishment of unidirectional airflow. The most likely of these is that the increasing dorsal attachment of the lung to the body wall results in a ventral diversion of the terminal saclike chamber. This bend, according to the analysis of Kuethe (1988), is instrumental in establishing the proxy ventilation role of the avian abdominal air sacs, which are presumably homologous to the terminal chamber in crocodiles (Moser, 1904; Perry, 1989b).

As the efficiency of proxy ventilation increases, the importance of the intercameral perforations would also increase: the parenchyma in the vicinity of the perforations would increase its ADF while the parenchyma on the opposite side of the chamber would degenerate accordingly (see Fig. 6, late coelurosaurian grade).

These hypothetical changes in the gas exchanger require matching changes in breathing mechanics, which, in turn, would allow further specialization of the exchanger until the stage of the avian parabronchus is reached (see Fig. 6). The accident of unidirectional flow thus results in a positive-feedback loop (Marayuma, 1963; Szarski, 1971; 1974; also compare Gutmann and Bonik, 1981), which is driven by a second, ecophysiological one: the ever-increasing efficiency of the respiratory system opens the door to new, aerobically demanding escape strategies and life-styles that, in turn, would place an increasing demand on the respiratory system.

We will never know the true origin of the avian respiratory system, and the euparkerian-grade and coelurosaurian-grade lungs remain hypothetical. Nevertheless, such evolutionary scenarios are of great heuristic value, since they test the capacity of our empirically generated models to predict missing parts of a structure–function complex. The exactness of the reconstruction becomes a test of our understanding of the existing models.

In the present example, it is easier to envision the staged transition of the crocodilianlike lung to a high-performance respiratory organ than it is to explain how the crocodile, in spite of the enormous potential of its respiratory and circulatory systems (see Chap. 18), has managed to achieve the lowest ADF per unit body mass of any reptile yet morphometrically evaluated (Perry, 1989c).

The convection-oriented gas exchange strategy presented by edicular parenchyma appears to explain the aerobic superiority of the monitor lizard. Edicular parenchyma, in combination with the multichambered lung, provides the prerequisites for two-directional crosscurrent ventilation and the evolution of a high-performance respiratory system. For this design, the sky is literally the limit. But if such lungs are so good, why are they lacking in most lizard families (Perry, 1983)?

## IV. Why Are There Still Single-Chambered Lungs?

There are two related complexes of possible answers to this difficult question. The first of these is that possibly not all reptiles are interested in having the sky as their limit; that is, there is some compelling "strategic" advantage offered by the single-chambered lung.

Even in the simplest of single-chambered lungs (e.g., as in the New Caledonian giant gecko *Rhacodactylus leachianus;* Perry et al., 1989b), all exchange surfaces have access to the whole body of stored air. When the animal walks, it swings its flank left and right. The air is shifted from lung to lung and the gas exchange surfaces are ventilated. But when it rests, which it does most of the time, the diffusion distance from the areas of lowest to highest $Po_2$ immediately increases to centimeter proportions and puts the brakes on $O_2$ uptake. Breathing episodes replenish and redistribute lung air during rest as required.

This system represents an incredibly simple and effective self-regulating system that is ideally suited for a classic energy saver. Although perhaps not explaining the origin of the single-chambered lung, this "pilot light" mechanism does provide a simple explanation for its presence in species with a low metabolic rate.

In more active species, the retention of the single-chambered lung could be due to a second phenomenon: the number of chambers being genetically programmed and established at an early developmental stage (Hesser, 1906; Broman, 1942). Metabolic stress at a later ontogenetic stage appears to modify only the parenchymal structure, as recently demonstrated by Hein and Perry (1989) in the tokay, *Gekko gecko.*

The tokay is an active, noctournal predator, and its lungs show a densely partitioned parenchyma, with a clearly heterogeneous distribution: faveolar cranially and trabecular caudally (Perry and Duncker, 1978). In response to persistent hypoxic stress (12% $O_2$ for 3–6 months) the lungs increase in volume. The parenchymal volume is doubled in all parts of the lung, but the surface area/volume ratio remains virtually unchanged (Hein and Perry, 1989). Thus, the lungs double their body mass-specific surface area in such a way that the exchange surfaces actually become less accessible to convection. The diffusion-oriented strategy is favored.

This adaptive developmental pattern is not as counterproductive as at first it may seem. As the faveoli deepen, there is a tendency toward an increase in the volume of nonvascular muscle of the interfaveolar septa: in the normoxic gecko lung, the septal muscle makes up only 1.5% of the total nonvascular pulmonary smooth muscle. After hypoxia, this increases to 4% (Hein and Perry,

1989). Although contraction of the trabecular muscle stretches the faveoli, septal muscle activity lowers them by throwing the wall into accordian pleats. In the highly specialized faveolar parenchyma of the teju lung, both muscle groups are of equal volume (Perry, 1983), whereas, in some snakes, the region of the interfaveolar septa nearest the central lumen is permanently pleated (S. F. Perry and R. M. Jones, unpublished observations).

These antagonistic smooth-muscle groups may contract in response to local hypoxia, possibly in connection with the activity of neuroepithelial bodies, which have been demonstrated in the tokay (Aumann and Perry, 1989) and in the red-eared turtle (Scheuermann et al., 1983), but not in the teju (Perry et al., 1989a). The exact nature of the relationship between endocrinelike cells of the lung and possible central control mechanisms of pulmonary smooth-muscular activity in reptiles remains to be elucidated. As elegant as these adjustment mechanisms may turn out to be in the long run, it is unlikely that they will suffice to change a single-chambered lung with faveolar parenchyma into a high-performance respiratory organ.

## V. The Bottom Line

In summary, there are three interdependent variables in the macroscopic structure of reptilian lungs (see Fig. 2): 1) *structural type,* 2) *parenchymal type,* and 3) *parenchymal distribution.* When we examine the first two relative to gas exchange, we discover certain structure–function correlations that are consistent with two different gas exchange strategies.

The single-chambered lung with edicular parenchyma appears to be the ideal, self-regulating lung for the typical energy saver with a low metabolic rate. The edicular surfaces are accessible to convective air movement (*convection-oriented gas exchange strategy*), but the surface area is severely limited by the single-chambered structural type of lung. In the face of an increased habitual metabolic demand, retention of the single-chambered primary lung structure could lead to the formation of faveolar parenchyma. As the faveoli deepen, the gas exchange surfaces become increasingly less accessible to convective air movement in the central lumen, resulting in the *diffusion-oriented gas exchange strategy.* Smooth-muscle activity in the faveoli can sporadically enhance ventilation, but the focus remains on the self-regulatory matching of $O_2$ supply and demand in the resting state.

Should the multichambered structural type be developed in the face of increased metabolic demand, the lung can achieve a large surface area while maintaining its edicular parenchyma and its associated convection-oriented gas exchange strategy. The two-directional crosscurrent model may make convection even more efficient in monitor lizards, turtles, and crocodiles. In the latter, it is possible to construct a functional morphological bridge to the unidirectional crosscurrent model of the avian paleopulmonic lung.

By postulating the existence of these strategies we have merely set up a series of hypotheses that must be more rigorously tested.

## References

Aumann, U., and Perry, S. F. (1989). Neuroepithelial bodies in normoxic and hypoxic geckos, *Gekko gecko*. In *Strategies of Physiological Adaptation. The Kjell Johansen Commemorative Symposium*. Edited by R. E. Weber and S. C. Wood. Copenhagen, August Krogh Institute, p. 1.

Becker, H. O., Böhme, W., and Perry, S. F. (1989). Die Morphologie der Lungen in der Gattung *Varanus* Merrum 1827 (Reptilia: Varanidae) und ihre Bedeutung für die Systematik der Varanidae. *Bonn Zool. Beitr.*, **40**:27–56.

Bennett, A. F. (1972). The effect of activity on oxygen consumption, oxygen debt, and heart rate in the lizards *Varanus gouldii* and *Sauromalus hispidus*. *J. Comp. Physiol.*, **79**:259–280.

Bennett, A. F. (1973). Ventilation of two species of lizards during rest and activity. *Comp. Biochem. Physiol.*, **46A**:653–671.

Broman, I. (1942). Über die Embryonalentwicklung der Chamäleonlunge. *Gegenbauers Morphol. Jahrb.*, **87**:490–532.

Davies, D. G., Thomas, J. L., and Smith, E. N. (1982). Effect of body temperature on ventilatory control in the alligator. *J. Appl. Physiol. Respir. Environ. Exerc. Physiol.*, **52**:114–118.

Dmi'el, R. (1972). Effect of activity and temperature on metabolism and water loss in snakes. *Am. J. Physiol.*, **223**:510–516.

Duncker, H.-R. (1978). General morphological principles of amniotic lungs. In *Respiratory Function in Birds, Adult and Embryonic*. Edited by J. Piiper. Heidelberg, Springer-Verlag, pp. 2–15.

Gans, C., and Clark, B. (1976) Studies on the ventilation of *Caiman crocodilus*. *Respir. Physiol.*, **26**:285–301.

Giordano, R. V., and Jackson, D. C. (1973). Effect of temperature on ventilation in the green iguana *(Iguana iguana)*. *Comp. Biochem. Physiol.*, **45A**:235–238.

Glass, M. L., Hicks, J. W., and Riedesel, M. L. (1979). Respiratory responses to long-term temperature exposure in the box turtle, *Terrapene ornata*. *J. Comp. Physiol.*, **131**:352–359.

Glass, M. L., and Johansen, K. (1976). Control of breathing in *Acrochordus javanicus*, an aquatic snake. *Physiol. Zool.*, **49**:328–340.

Glass, M. L., and Johansen, K. (1979). Periodic breathing in the crocodile *Crocodylus niloticus:* Consequences for the gas exchange ratio and control of breathing. *J. Exp. Zool.*, **208**:319–326.

Greenberg, N. (1980). Physiological and behavioural thermoregulation in living reptiles. In *A Cold Look at the Warm-Blooded Dinosaurs*. Edited by D. K. Thomas and E. C. Olson. (AAAS Symposium Series). Boulder, Colo. Westview Press, pp. 141–166.

Gutmann, W. F., and Bonik, K. (1981). *Kritische Evolutionstheorie.* Hildesheim, FRG, Gerstenberg-Verlag.

Hein, J., and Perry, S. F. (1989). Influence of chronic hypoxia on the lungs of the tokay, *Gekko gecko.* In *Strategies of Physiological Adaptation. The Kjell Johansen Commemorative Symposium.* Edited by R. E. Weber and S. C. Wood. Copenhagen, August Krogh Institute, p. 4.

Hennig, W. (1983). Stammesgeschichte der Chordaten. *Fortschr. Zool. Syst. Evolutionsforsch.,* **2**:1–208.

Hesser, C. (1906). Über die Entwicklung der Reptilienlunge. *Anat. Hefte,* **29**:277–308.

Hlastala, M. P., Standaert, T. A., Pierson, D. J., and Luchtel, D. L. (1985). The matching of ventilation and perfusion in the lung of the tegu lizard, *Tupinambis nigropunctatus. Respir. Physiol.,* **60**:277–294.

Jackson, D. C. (1971). The effect of temperature on ventilation in the turtle, *Pseudemys scripta elegans. Respir. Physiol.,* **12**:131–140.

Jackson, D. C., Kraus, D. R., and Prange, H. D. (1979). Ventilatory response to inspired $CO_2$ in the sea turtle: Effects of body size and temperature. *Respir. Physiol.,* **38**:71–81.

Jackson, D. C., Palmer, S. E., and Meadow, W. L. (1974). The effects of temperature and carbon dioxide breathing on ventilation and acid–base status of turtles. *Respir. Physiol.,* **20**:131–146.

Johansen, K., Abe, A. S., and Andresen, J. H. (1987). Intracardiac shunting revealed by angiocardiography in the lizard *Tupinambis teguixin. J. Exp. Biol.,* **130**:1–12.

Kuethe, D. O. (1988). Fluid mechanical valving of air flow in bird lungs. *J. Exp. Biol.,* **136**:1–12.

Maruyama, M. (1963). The second cybernetics: Deviation amplifying causal processes. *Am. Sci.,* **51**:164–179.

McArthur, R. H., and Wilson, E. O. (1967). *The Theory of Island Biogeography.* Princeton, N.J., Princeton University Press.

Milani, A. (1894). Beiträge zur Kenntnis der Reptilienlunge. I. Lacertilia. *Zool. Jahrb. Abt. Anat. Ontol.,* **7**:545–592.

Moser, F. (1904). Beiträge zur vergleichenden Entwicklungsgeschichte der Wirbeltierliunge. *Arch. Mikrosc. Anat. Entwicklungsgesch,* **60**:587–668.

Nielsen, B. (1961). On the regulation of respiration in reptiles. I. The effects of temperature and $CO_2$ on the respiration of lizards *(Lacerta). J. Exp. Biol.,* **38**:301–314.

Perry, S. F. (1978). Quantitative anatomy of the lungs of the red-eared turtle, *Pseudemys scripta elegans. Respir. Physiol.,* **35**:245–262.

Perry, S. F. (1983). Reptilian lungs. Functional anatomy and evolution. *Adv. Anat. Embryol. Cell Biol.,* **79**:1–81.

Perry, S. F. (1985). Functional anatomy and evolution of reptilian lungs. *Fortschr. Zool.,* **30**:379–382.

Perry, S. F. (1988). Functional morphology of the lungs of the Nile crocodile, *Crocodylus niloticus* (Laurenti). Nonrespiratory parameters. *J. Exp. Biol.,* **134**:99–117.

Perry, S. F. (1989a). Gas exchange strategy in the Nile crocodile: A morphometric study. *J. Comp. Physiol. B.,* **159**:761–769.

Perry, S. F. (1989b). Mainstreams in the evolution of vertebrate respiratory structures. In *Form and Function in Birds, Vol. 4*. Edited by A. S. King and J. McLelland. London, Academic Press, pp. 1–67.

Perry, S. F. (1989c). Morphometry of crocodilian lungs. *Prog. Zool.*, **35**:619–621.

Perry, S. F. (1989d). Structure and function of the reptilian respiratory system. In *Comparative Pulmonary Physiology. Current Concepts*. Edited by S. C. Wood. New York, Marcel Dekker, pp. 193–236.

Perry, S. F., and Duncker, H.-R. (1978). Lung architecture, volume and static mechanics of five species of lizards. *Respir. Physiol.*, **34**:61–81.

Perry, S. F., Aumann, U., and Maloney, J. E. (1989a). Intrinsic musculature and associated ganglion cells in a teiid lizard, *Tupinambis nigropunctatus* Spix. *Herpetologica*, **45**:217–227.

Perry, S. F., Bauer, A. M., Russell, A. P., Alston, J. T., and Maloney, J. E. (1989b). The lungs of the gecko *Rhacodactylus leachianus* (Reptilia: Gekkonidae): A correlative gross anatomical, light and electron microscopic study. *J. Morphol.*, **199**:23–40.

Scheid, P., and Piiper, J. (1989). Respiratory mechanics and air flow in birds. In *Form and Function in Birds, Vol. 4*. Edited by A. S. King and J. McLelland. London, Academic Press, pp. 369–391.

Scheuermann, D. W., de Groodt-Lasseel, M. H. A., Stilman, C., and Meisters, M. L. (1983). A correlative light-, fluorescence-, and electron-microscopic study of neuroepithelial bodies in the lung of the red-eared turtle, *Pseudemys scripta elegans*. *Cell Tiss. Res.*, **234**:249–269.

Spragg, R. G., Ackerman, R., and White, F. N. (1980). Distribution of ventilation in the turtle, *Pseudemys scripta elegans*. *Respir. Physiol.*, **42**:73–86.

Szarski, H. (1971). The importance of deviation amplifying circuits for understanding the course of evolution. *Acta Biotheor.*, **20**:158–170.

Szarski, H. (1974). L'importance des mécanismes de rétroaction positive au course de l'évolution. *Acad. Pol. Sci., Conf.* **107**:1–10. (Warsaw, Panstwowe Wydawnictwo Naukowe).

Wolf, S. (1933). Zur Kenntnis von Bau und Funktion der Reptilienlunge. *Zool. Jahrb. Abt. Anat. Ontol.*, **57**:139–190.

Wood, S. C., Johansen, K., and Gatz, R. K. (1977). Pulmonary blood flow, ventilation/perfusion ratio, and oxygen transport in a varanid lizard. *Am. J. Physiol.*, **233**:R89–R93.

Wood, S. C., Johansen, K., Glass, M. L., and Maloiy, G. M. O. (1978). Aerobic metabolism of the lizard *Varanus exanthematicus:* Effects of activity, temperature and size. *J. Comp. Physiol.*, **127**:331–336.

# 9

## Gas Exchange, Circulation, and Energy Metabolism in Arachnids

RÜDIGER J. PAUL

Zoological Institute
University of Düsseldorf
Düsseldorf, Germany

## I. Evolution

The arachnids, a class of arthropods in the subphylum Chelicerata, are a very old and large group in the animal kingdom, comprising about 37,000 species (Kükenthal and Renner, 1980). They include, among others, the scorpions (Scorpiones) and the spiders (Araneae). The latest paleontological studies (Kjellesvig-Waering, 1986) associate the scorpions closer to the extinct Eurypterida—which are related to the Xiphosura (horseshoe crabs)—than to the other terrestrial arachnids. The existence of book lungs, however, is still a characteristic of both scorpions and spiders. Obviously, the scorpions, which have been traced back to the Silurian (ca. 420 million years; a still earlier origin being very likely), originally had gills and were water breathers. First remnants of exclusively air-breathing scorpions date from no earlier than the Carboniferous (ca. 320 million years). There is evidence of the other terrestrial arachnids from the Lower Devonian (ca. 390 million years; Müller, 1981) and, as fossils show, there has not been much further change in the structure of their respiratory organs: the book

---

Dedicated to the late Bernt Linzen.

lungs (Fig. 1). In any event, the arachnids were among the first animals to conquer land and, thus, to carry on respiration in air.

## II. Morphology

The body of an arachnid is composed of an anterior part, the prosoma (plus extremities), and a posterior opisthosoma. In the spiders the first opisthosomal segment is of a narrow, stemlike structure (pedicel) separating prosoma and opisthosoma. The prosoma may be seen as the "animal" region, and the opisthosoma as the "vegetative" region (Paul et al., 1989a) containing the supporting organs: lungs, heart, digestive and central metabolic tissues, excretory and reproductive systems. The animal region bears the major sensory organs, the central nervous system (CNS), and systems for locomotion and for food acquisition as well as defense. A speciality in spiders is the hydraulic locomotory apparatus. Probably in all species of Araneae two essential articulations of the legs—femur-patella, tibia–metatarsus—are extended by hydraulic forces (e.g., Petrunkevitch, 1909; Ellis, 1944; Parry and Brown, 1959; Wilson, 1970); there are no extensor muscles in either joint. Contraction of the musculi laterales in the prosoma pulls down the carapace, thereby causing a decrease in prosomal volume and an increase in pressure in the hemolymph lumen (up to 480 torr; Stewart and Martin, 1974). This procedure shifts hemolymph toward the articulations in the legs, which leads to the desired extension. The reason for this mechanism may be an increase in muscle power, since the shift of the extensor action to the prosoma leaves space for more flexor muscles in the extremities (Anderson and Prestwich, 1975).

Gas exchange and transport in arachnids take place by book lungs or tracheae, or both, for respiration, a neurogenic heart (e.g., Wilson, 1967; Legendre, 1968; Sherman et al., 1969; Ude and Richter, 1974) and a closed arterial and an open venous vascular system (see Foelix, 1982) for perfusion. Book lungs are the exclusive respiratory organs in the phylogenetically older species. Scorpions have four pairs, the more ancient orthognathic spiders have two; and the more recent labidognathic spiders mostly have one pair, often with the second pair transformed into tracheae. In some families, there are only tracheae (Caponiidae, Symphytognathidae). In contrast with insect tracheae, they end openly, not contacting cells directly. This means that hemocyanin, the respiratory pigment in the hemolymph, has to take over oxygen transport to the tissues (Foelix, 1982). There is evidence that a tracheal system, with its ability to carry oxygen to the tissues without an intermediate perfusion, provides the more efficient way of oxygen transport (e.g., Levi, 1967; Bromhall, 1987).

The most characteristic gas exchange devices in arachnids are the book lungs. They are positioned ventrally at the opisthosoma (Figs. 2 and 3). A spiracle opens to the interior and widens into an atrium, from which a series of flat gas-

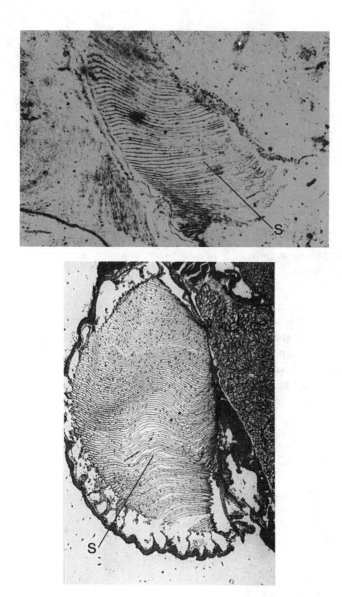

**Figure 1**  Longitudinal sections of book lungs (S, sacculi). Top: Fossil from the Lower Devonian. (From Claridge, M. F., and Lyon, A. G., 1961. Reprinted by permission from *Nature* 191:1190–1191, copyright © 1961 Macmillan Magazines Ltd.) Bottom: Book lung of *E. californicum.*

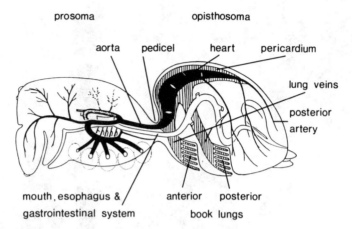

**Figure 2** Scheme of the arterial vascular system of an orthognathic spider. (Adapted from Foelix, 1982).

filled spaces lead anteriorly into the body. These sacculi (or lamellae) are kept from collapsing by small cuticular pillars. Gas-filled and hemolymph-filled spaces are arranged in sequence ("book" structure). Gas exchange with the hemolymph stream occurs across the walls of the sacculi, which consist of a chitinous layer about 0.2- to 0.3-μm thick (Strazny and Perry, 1984; P. Seifert, unpublished data) and an approximately 0.2-μm thick epidermic (hypodermic) layer facing

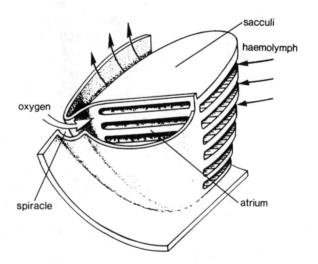

**Figure 3** Structure of the lower part of a book lung. (Adapted from Foelix, 1982).

the hemolymph (Strazny and Perry, 1984). Contraction of a retractor muscle, inserted at the posterior wall of the atrium, results in a parallel expansion of atrium and spiracle. Antagonistic action is most probably caused by hemolymph pressure. Details on structure and morphometric data are given by Kästner (1929), Moore (1976), Anderson and Prestwich (1980), Hexter (1982), and Strazny and Perry (1984; 1987).

After passing the sacculi, hemolymph is collected in lung veins and transferred to the pericardium (see Fig. 2) and, after that, to the heart, a tubelike structure suspended by ligaments. It enters the heart lumen through several pairs of ostia and (during systole) is distributed to the prosoma through the anterior aorta, and to the opisthosoma through the posterior aorta and various lateral arteries. At the ends of the heart, reflux of hemolymph is prohibited by valves. In the prosoma, the anterior aorta ramifies into a series of smaller arteries (Petrunkevitch, 1910; Millot, 1949; Crome, 1953), in which the degree of branching (Fig. 4) probably reflects the oxygen requirement of the tissues.

There is a relatively small degree of ramification in the extremity muscles (Bihlmayer et al., 1989). The terminal diameter of the arterioles is probably about 50–100 $\mu$m. Arachnids do not have a widely ramified capillary network in their locomotor muscles, and the considerable increase in exchange surface found in mammals, for example, does not exist. The oxygen supply to those muscles seems to be maintained from the open hemolymph system. This means that, frequently, rather long diffusion distances must be overcome and, therefore, a high flux of $O_2$ into those tissues seems impossible. This assumption is supported by measurements of muscular oxygen partial pressures, which revealed levels far below venous values, indicating long diffusion distances (Angersbach, 1975). Although mitochondria are scarce within many regions of prosomal locomotor muscles (Linzen and Gallowitz, 1975; Foelix, 1982; Werner et al., 1989), organs and tissues with a high oxygen demand and a high density of mitochondria show special adaptations.

In the heart, which is rich in mitochondria (Foelix, 1982; Werner et al., 1989), the exchange surface with the hemolymph is high owing to a pronounced folding of the inner wall, and the wall, itself, is not very thick (100–200 $\mu$m; cf. Angersbach, 1975). Within the open system, hemolymph drains into sinuses and lacunae and flows along the pressure gradient toward the opisthosomal lung sinus before, once again, it passes the sacculi to recharge with oxygen and give off carbon dioxide.

## III. Book Lung Function

There was a long-standing controversy about the ventilation of book lungs. Willem (1917) observed in *Pholcus phalangioides* a motion of the sacculi synchronized with the heart and also movements of the posterior atrium wall and

**Figure 4**  Prosomal arterial system of *E. californicum,* drawn from a casting-resin preparation. The main arteries are shaded: a, anterior aorta; b, leg artery; c, arteria crassa; d, arteria cephalica; e, trunci peristomacales. (Preparation from S. Zahler, drawing from C. Killi).

he, therefore, postulated various mechanisms of ventilation. By studying *Lyssomanes viridis,* Hill (1977) verified Willem's studies, and found that dorsomedial areas of the sacculus wall were not fixed to the internal cuticular pillars. He suggested a ventilation of the sacculi by suction, forced by hemolymph being driven past these parts of the walls with every heartbeat—the "hemolymph bellows" hypothesis. Anderson and Prestwich (1980) listed morphometric features of the sacculi to support this hypothesis. Despite possible ventilation movements, other scientists, for example, Kästner (1929) or Krogh (1941), thought that the main mechanism of gas exchange within the respiratory tracts of book lungs is diffusion.

   To clarify this question experimentally, a micromanometric method was designed that, similar to spirographic measurements, made possible simultaneous recording of fluctuations in lung volume (ventilation) and oxygen consumption on single book lungs (Paul et al., 1987). In the tarantula, *Eurypelma californicum,* lung volume changes were detected as pressure alterations in the combined long–manometer system. Expired carbon dioxide was absorbed by KOH; hence, oxygen consumption was registered as a continuous, slow pressure drop within the system (Fig. 5). Different types of more rapid pressure changes ("ventilation") were found. Some were synchronized with heartbeat, and some were not, but they all were caused by alterations of the atrial volume. The possibility of

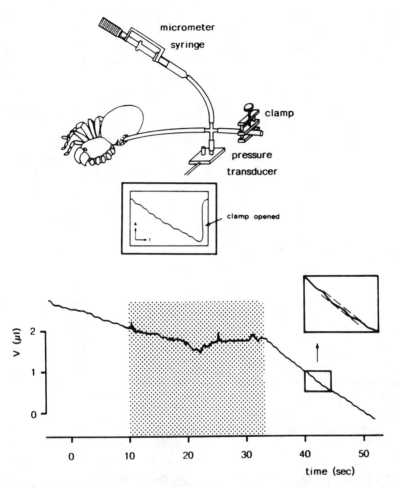

**Figure 5** Top: Measurement of "ventilatory" lung volume changes and oxygen consumption on individual book lungs of *E. californicum* by a micromanometric method (see Paul et al., 1987 for details). Bottom: Registration of a simultaneous measurement of both variables at rest (left), activity (shaded) and recovery (right) by the micromanometric method. (Ordinate is volume change (μl), which refers to ventilatory volume changes, but also to volume units of oxygen consumed.) Small heart-synchronous volume changes (inset) are superimposed on the steady signal decrease from oxygen consumption. Oxygen consumption increases during recovery, but not during activity. (Modified from Paul et al., 1987).

ventilation of the sacculi was eliminated by separate examinations and calculations (Paul et al., 1987). Although volume changes were detectable, comparison of the "ventilated" gas volume per time unit and of the corresponding oxygen consumption rate shows that this ventilation is far too small to enhance gas exchange to any degree. In an average 20-g mammal the ventilation volume/oxygen consumption ratio is about 33 (Stahl, 1967); in an *Eurypelma* of 20 g, it is between 0.1 and 0.3 (Paul et al., 1987). In an effectively ventilated gas exchange organ, the ventilated gas volume per time unit exceeds the volume of consumed oxygen by far (this is also valid for invertebrates such as land crabs; see, e.g., Burggren and McMahon, 1988, Table 8.2). In the tarantula, the ratio between both variables is reversed, which is inconsistent with an effective ventilation of book lungs. Summing up, slight volume changes of the atrial lung region are detectable, probably caused by pulse beats as well as by action of the retractor muscle. But the essential process of gas exchange within the respiratory tract is diffusion; therefore, these book lungs may be characterized as diffusion lungs. The same is valid for the emperor scorpion, *Pandinus imperator*, on which similar experiments were performed.

In an analysis based on morphometric data of the book lungs in *E. californicum*, diffusion actually was sufficient for the oxygen consumption rates measured (Paul et al., 1987). Oxygen has to diffuse across the spiracle, atrium, and sacculi into the hemolymph. In a resting spider, the actual opening of the spiracles is rather small (calculated to be about 0.23 mm$^2$ in all four lungs of a 15-g animal; unpublished data). During an early phase of recovery following locomotion, the openings increase to a total of about 6 mm$^2$ (Fincke and Paul, 1989), accompanied by an intense elevation of oxygen consumption. Obviously, the gas exchange rate is controlled by modification of the spiracle entrance area (combined with parallel movements of the posterior atrium wall). After having passed the atrium (about 1 mm in distance; Paul et al., 1987), oxygen enters the sacculi. It is remarkable that the total entrance area of the sacculi (ca. 5.1 mm$^2$ for all four lungs; Paul et al., 1987) resembles that of the spiracles (6 mm$^2$), which means that, during the early stage of recovery at high oxygen consumption rates [ca. 80 μl $O_2$ · min$^{-1}$ (STPD); Paul et al., 1989b], gas flux in the respiratory tracts of the book lungs is about the same as in a tube of 5.1–6 mm$^2$ in cross-sectional area, and about 4 mm in length (the average diffusion distance in the sacculi being about 3 mm; Paul et al., 1987). Krogh (1920) figured out that diffusion alone accounts for the total gas exchange in the tracheal system of larvae in the genus *Cossus;* the tracheal mean cross-section being 6.7 mm$^2$ and mean length 6 mm. Krogh also found that, with an oxygen consumption of 18 μl $O_2$ · min$^{-1}$ at rest, a difference in partial pressure of 11 torr was necessary for diffusion. From book lung morphometry (see foregoing), the partial pressure difference within the respiratory tract may be calculated, from Fick's law of diffusion, to be about 38 torr for periods of high oxygen consumption (see foregoing) in *Eurypelma*.

Oxygen enters the hemolymph spaces through the sacculus walls. In an *Eurypelma* weighing 15 g, the pulmonary respiratory surface measures about 50 $cm^2$. The chitinous layer, which is mainly responsible for the diffusive resistance, is about 0.2-$\mu$m thick (P. Seifert, unpublished data). To overcome this barrier, a partial pressure difference of approximately 18 torr is needed for periods of high oxygen consumption (unpublished calculation). Maximal $CO_2$ release, which for technical reasons is easier to determine (Paul et al., 1989b), comes to about 75 $\mu$l $CO_2 \cdot min^{-1}$ (STPD) (15-g animal) in *Eurypelma*. From this, a maximal flux rate of about 1.6 $\mu$l $CO_2 \cdot min^{-1} \cdot cm^{-2}$ (STPD) of respiratory surface may be computed (Paul and Fincke, 1989). In the similar-sized emperor scorpion, *Pandinus imperator* (eight book lungs!), the corresponding value is approximately 2.1 $\mu$l $CO_2 \cdot min^{-1} \cdot cm^{-2}$ (STPD). Calculation of $CO_2$ flux rates across the spiracle entrance areas results in maximally 13.5 $\mu$l $CO_2$ $min^{-1} \cdot mm^{-2}$ (STPD) for *Eurypelma* and 19.2 $\mu$l $CO_2 \cdot min^{-1} \cdot mm^{-2}$ (STPD) in *Pandinus* (Fincke and Paul, 1989). The ratios for $CO_2$ flux rates per unit of area past the spiracle as well as through the sacculus walls of *Eurypelma* and *Pandinus* are very similar (1:1.4), which suggests a fixed relationship in size between the respiratory surface and the profile of the respiratory tract.

As may be calculated (see foregoing), a total partial pressure difference of approximately 56 torr (38 + 18 torr) is needed for an oxygen supply by diffusion at high consumption rates. Determination of arterial oxygen partial pressures in the hemolymph ($Pa_{O_2}$) of *Eurypelma* (Angersbach, 1978) led to values of 28 torr, in resting animals, and to about 74 torr during postactive recovery. Thus, for high $O_2$ consumption rates, a surplus of at least 20 torr ($PB_{O_2}$ − 56 torr − 74 torr; $PB_{O_2}$ = 150 torr) seems to exist. In resting individuals at a low $O_2$ consumption rate, this surplus reaches at least 109 torr (unpublished calculation).

Comparison with $CO_2$ partial pressures in resting animals [$Pa_{CO_2}$ = ca. 11 torr (Loewe and Brauer de Eggert, 1979) to 14.8 torr (Paul et al., 1991)] reveals an unsolved problem in book lung physiology. Although at least 122 torr of $O_2$ partial pressure difference ($PB_{O_2}$ − $Pa_{O_2}$) are needed in resting individuals to obtain an oxygen uptake rate of approximately 4.2 $\mu$l $O_2 \cdot min^{-1}$ (STPD) (15- g *Eurypelma*), only about 14.8 torr of $CO_2$ partial pressure difference is required to transfer 3 $\mu$l $CO_2 \cdot min^{-1}$ (STPD) from hemolymph to the atmosphere. Distinct differences in Krogh's constant of diffusion for $O_2$ and $CO_2$ in chitin are not known; in air both constants are in the same order of magnitude (see Dejours, 1981). The epidermic layer is much to thin to account for these differences. As possible explanations, gas exchange/perfusion ratio inequalities in the book lungs or the effects of venous–arterial "blood shunts" may be mentioned (cf. West, 1985). A third possibility would be diffusion of the respiratory gases ($O_2$, $CO_2$) through a distinct additional water layer. As Krogh's constant of diffusion for $O_2$ in water is much lower than that for $CO_2$ (see Dejours, 1981), a much higher $O_2$ partial pressure difference is necessary to achieve adequate gas fluxes [4.2 vs 3 $\mu l \cdot min^{-1}$ (STPD)]. If the sacculi were covered and partly filled with a water layer, as in the terminal tracheoles of insects (Wigglesworth, 1930; 1932; 1953), unequal partial pressure differences might arise.

Computations using Fick's first law of diffusion and morphometric data on the book lungs of *Eurypelma* confirm that diffusion is sufficient for the measured gas exchange rates. The validity of Fick's law in these gas exchange processes implies a proportional relation between gas exchange rates and the spiracle entrance area. This deduction was tested experimentally (Fincke and Paul, 1989). In *E. californicum,* in the labidognathic ctenid spider, *Cupiennius salei,* and in *P. imperator,* the size of the spiracle entrance area and $CO_2$ release (as a parameter of gas exchange) were measured simultaneously on single book lungs. Both variables underwent alterations very slowly and always in parallel. Not only were nonlinear actions indicating ventilation, such as increased $CO_2$ release after fast motions of the spiracle, never observed, but a linear correlation between $CO_2$ release and the corresponding spiracle entrance area was shown (Fig. 6). Only for very high $CO_2$ release rates did deviation from this linearity occur. With a maximally opened spiracle, an increase in release of $CO_2$ must result from a rise in the partial pressure difference across the respiratory tract.

## IV. Gas Exchange in the Tarantula *Eurypelma californicum* in Relation to Energy Metabolism

Many spiders exhibit high locomotor activity for a short period, but rapidly become exhausted (Bristowe and Millot, 1933); usually, they display very little activity. Sometimes a slow "walk" may occur spontaneously, but the seizing of prey (or slight mechanical stimulation in experiments) arouses very fast, burstlike sprints. In contrast, scorpions tend more toward a slower and more constant pace of locomotion. The generally low activity in arachnids goes along with the ability to stay without food for an extended time. There are reports of spiders that did not feed for almost a year (Kaston, 1970). Evidently, these animals follow a strategy of saving energy, and they develop high locomotor activity only to catch prey or while defending themselves.

### A. Metabolism at Rest

Metabolism at rest (Table 1) is characterized by very low oxygen consumption rates (Fig. 7). Similar low rates have been found in other arachnids (e.g., Anderson, 1970; Anderson and Prestwich, 1982). *Eurypelma* and *Pandinus* never

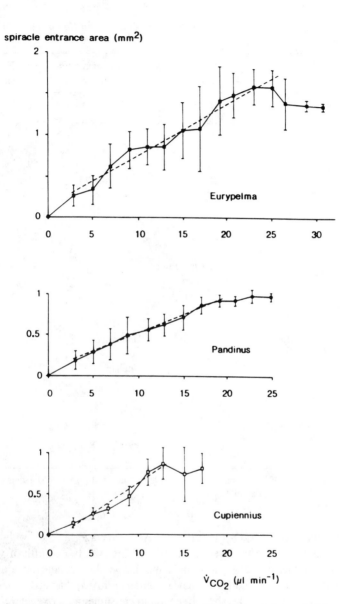

**Figure 6**  Spiracle entrance area plotted versus $CO_2$ release ($\mu$l STPD). Mean values ($\pm$ SD) from all measurements on individual book lungs in (top) *E. californicum*, (center) *P. imperator*, and (bottom) *C. salei*. (From Fincke and Paul, 1989).

**Table 1** Parameters of Gas Exchange and Gas Transport in *Eurypelma californicum* (T = 20–24°C; body mass: 15 g)

| | At rest | During maximum activity | During recovery |
|---|---|---|---|
| *Respiration* | | | |
| $\dot{V}_{O_2}$ (in $\mu l$ $O_2 \cdot min^{-1}$ (STPD)) | 4.2[a] (basal value) | Decrease with subsequent increase[a] | 81[a] |
| $\dot{V}_{CO_2}$ (in $\mu l$ $CO_2 \cdot min^{-1}$ (STPD)) | 3[a] (basal value) | Decrease with subsequent increase[a,b] | 50[a] |
| RQ | 0.71[a] | | 0.73[a] |
| *Circulation* | | | |
| Heart frequency (in beats $\cdot$ min$^{-1}$) | 6[d] (basal value) | Increase[c] | 75[a] |
| | 21[c] (mean value in slightly alert individuals) | | 90[c] (max value) |
| *Hemolymph values* | | | |
| Arterial | | | |
| $P_{O_2}$ (in mm Hg) | 28[e] | Unchanged[e] | 74.2[e] |
| $P_{CO_2}$ (in mm Hg) | 14.8[f] | | |
| pH | 7.49[e] | Unchanged[e] | 7.23[e] (min value) |
| Mixed venous | | | |
| $P_{O_2}$ (in mm Hg) | 16[e] | Decrease[e] | 24.8[e] |
| $P_{CO_2}$ (in mm Hg) | 16.4[f] | | |
| pH | 7.45[e] | Unchanged[e] | 6.95[e] (min value) |

*Sources:* [a]Paul et al., 1989b; [b]Paul and Fincke, 1989; [c]Paul et al., 1989a; [d]Unpublished value; [e]Angersbach, 1978; [f]Paul et al., 1991.

consume more than 1 ml $O_2 \cdot hr^{-1}$ (STPD). As an average, animals weighing 15 g use 0.2–0.3 ml $O_2 \cdot hr^{-1}$ (STPD) (at 20°C). This is only one-fifth of what an average poikilothermic vertebrate of the same size would consume (Hemmingsen, 1960) and only a hundredth of what a homeotherm would need. Even other invertebrates, such as land crabs, often tend to consume more oxygen (cf. Burggren and McMahon, 1988, Table 8.2). Measurements of the respiratory quotient (RQ) in *Eurypelma* resulted in a value of 0.71. This means the very low metabolism is mainly fueled from fat stores, which, in this spider, are located within the midgut gland (180 mg/g gland mass, corresponding to Triolein standards; Werner et al., 1989).

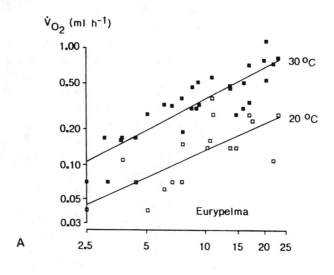

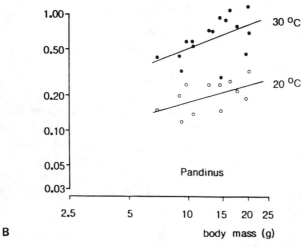

**Figure 7** Basal oxygen consumption rates (ml STPD) at 20° and 30°C plotted versus body mass in *E. californicum* (A) and *P. imperator* (B). (From Paul et al., 1989b).

## B. Metabolism During Activity

Metabolism of *Eurypelma* at rest is primarily aerobic and uses fat. During locomotion (see Table 1), especially if burstlike sprints occur, anaerobic pathways play a vital role (see Prestwich, 1983a,b; Prestwich, 1988b), and phosphagens (arginine-phosphate; Prestwich, 1988b) as well as carbohydrate stores (glycogen; Werner et al., 1989) are drawn upon. As an end product D-lactate accumulates in muscle tissue in concentrations up to 18 $\mu$M/g, and, mainly following lo-comotion, washes out into the hemolymph, where it reaches concentrations of up to 13 $\mu$M/ml (Paul and Storz, 1987; Werner et al., 1989). Connected with this is a drop in pH. Values down to pH 6.9 have been measured in venous hemolymph (Angersbach, 1978). This metabolic acidosis is what most likely causes the rapid exhaustion of the spiders. A postactive rise in hemolymph potassium ion concentration (from 2.5 to 6 $\mu$M/ml; Paul and Storz, 1987) might be caused by an inhibition of the $Na^+$, $K^+$-ATPase in muscle tissue by the decrease in pH, which induces a release of $K^+$ from the muscles (see Stegemann, 1984). In *Pandinus,* a similar increase in D-lactate concentration in the hemo-lymph was found (ca. 15 $\mu$M/ml; Paul and Storz, 1987). Predominance of anaerobic pathways during activity might result from the lack of capillarization of the muscles (see foregoing; Bihlmayer et al., 1989). Histochemical investi-gations show a storage of glycogen in the muscle region, whereas the midgut gland stores glycogen and fat (Werner et al., 1989). This strong dependence of locomotor processes on anaerobic pathways is certainly not disadvantageous to the animals because, as mentioned earlier, activities of this type are very sporadic, and the following recovery periods are long enough to compensate for an oxygen debt. It might be possible that a reduction in mitochondrial density allows more myofibrils to pack into the extremities and more muscle power for a quick, but short, activity pattern to be gained.

With the onset of maximal activity, gas exchange is not instantly intensified; actually, in *Eurypelma* (and in *Cupiennius,* but not in *Pandinus*), at the beginning (26–40 sec) of an activity phase, there is even a decrease in gas exchange rate (Paul and Fincke, 1989). This might be because of a closing of the spiracles, induced by a higher "hydraulic" hemolymph pressure in the opisthosoma (dis-cussed later). In all three species, maximal values of $O_2$ consumption and of $Co_2$ release are reached no earlier than in the period of recovery. In *Eurypelma,* the heart rate increases during locomotion, but its maximum also occurs in recovery.

### C. Metabolism During Recovery

Following strenuous locomotion, a long period of recovery is indicated by the increased respiration and heart rate (Fig. 8; see Table 1). Spiracles are at their maximum width, and both gas exchange in the book lungs and gas transport in the hemolymph reach their highest values.

The time courses of $O_2$ and $CO_2$ exchange differ. Oxygen consumption comes to a maximum fairly rapidly and, after that, diminishes faster than $CO_2$

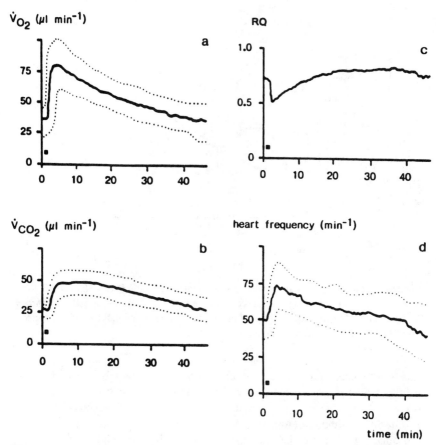

**Figure 8** Time-courses of $O_2$ uptake (a, $\mu$l STPD); $CO_2$ release (b, $\mu$l STPD); respiratory quotient RQ (c); and heart frequency (d) in *E. californicum* during recovery from 1 min of maximum locomotor activity (black bars), obtained from simultaneous measurements. (Mean curves; dotted lines indicate standard deviation). (From Paul et al., 1989b.)

release, which also reaches its maximum later. As a result, the (apparent) RQ is subjected to fluctuations (see Fig. 8). In an early state of recovery, it is lowered, then an elevation follows, before finally it drops back to its original level. Nevertheless, the mean RQ during recovery stays at 0.73, once again indicating decomposition of lipids. The faster time course of $O_2$ uptake might, at least to some degree, be due to the presence of hemocyanin in the hemolymph. In *Eurypelma* at rest, hemocyanin is incompletely oxygenated at the lungs (Angersbach, 1978). If the spiracles open after intense locomotor activity, diffusive resistance declines within spiracle and atrium, which leads to an improved $O_2$

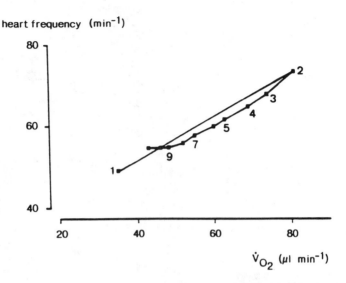

**Figure 9**   Plot of heart frequency versus $O_2$ uptake ($\mu$l STPD) in *E. californicum*. (Data as in Fig. 8). Numbers designate subsequent time intervals from resting state (1); through the maximum of heart frequency just after activity (2); and through the period of recovery (3–9) (Time between successive points: 3.3 min).

flux and, hence, to an increase in arterial $P_{O_2}$. Consequently, the hemocyanin is fully oxygenated and, accordingly, the $O_2$-transport capacity of the hemolymph ($Ca_{O_2} - Cv_{O_2}$) is more fully used. A decrease in mixed-venous hemolymph $P_{O_2}$ during locomotion (Angersbach, 1978), presumably caused by diminished prosomal perfusion (see later discussion), results in a still higher $Ca_{O_2} - Cv_{O_2}$ during the initial phases of recovery.

If we look at $CO_2$ released during recovery, part of it arises from buffering an anaerobically produced pH depression, the rest is from the accelerated aerobic metabolism. The time lag to the accelerated $O_2$ uptake is clear, as transport times within the circulation system must be taken into account. A faster increase in $O_2$ consumption, compared with $CO_2$ release, at the onset of physical work has also been observed in humans (e.g., Hughson and Inman, 1985). As storage capacity in tissues is much higher for $CO_2$ than it is for $O_2$ (Farhi and Rahn, 1955), a delayed elevation of mixed-venous $P_{CO_2}$ (and $CO_2$ release) by buffering action of the tissues has been proposed (Edwards et al., 1972). This might be similar in *Eurypelma*.

During recovery, the heart rate time course almost parallels that of $O_2$ consumption (Fig. 9), whereas the $CO_2$ release time course resembles that of changes in spiracle entrance area, which determines gas exchange in the lung (see Fig. 6). This is similar to the response in humans when the work load increases: $O_2$ input and heart rate (e.g., Heinrich et al., 1968) as well as $CO_2$ output and ventilation, which determine gas exchange in the lung (e.g., Whipp and Ward, 1982; 1985), are closely related. Here, the connection between $O_2$ uptake and heart frequency is explained by the presence of special receptors in the muscles, which send information on the actual metabolic activity in the muscle to the circulation control center (Schmidt-Thews, 1980). Synchronizing ventilation and $CO_2$ release enhances acid–base regulation in the blood, probably in connection with central chemoreceptors (e.g., Whipp and Ward, 1985). This analogy raises the possibility of a similar mechanism in *Eurypelma*.

As mentioned earlier, the period of recovery is long (from more than one to almost two hr, depending on duration of activity). Elevated gas exchange and transport rates are necessary to oxidize D-lactate, or to resynthesize it into carbohydrate by gluconeogenesis. Phosphagen and glycogen stores in muscle tissue have to be refilled, and primary conditions of ion distribution in the body fluids must be reestablished. Supposedly, a kind of Cori cycle exist in *Eurypelma* (Werner et al., 1989): D-lactate, produced in prosomal muscle tissues, is transferred to the opisthosoma by hemolymph. The heart or the midgut gland, or both, might be the locations of oxidation or glucose synthesis. It appears that glycogen in the muscles is restored from glycogen reserves in the midgut gland by glucose transport in the hemolymph. During recovery, a rise in glucose concentration in the body fluid from 0.25 $\mu$M/ml to maximally 2 M/ml (Paul and Storz, 1987) could be interpreted as support of this suggestion. Energy for all these processes should be derived from oxidation of lipid reserves at the midgut gland.

In summary, locomotor activity in *Eurypelma* and in *Pandinus* is supported by anaerobic energy metabolism (also see Anderson and Prestwich, 1985), which implies long postactive periods of recovery. This does not create problems with the animals: having expeditiously seized prey there should be enough time to recover.

## V. Gas Exchange in *Eurypelma* and *Pandinus:* Relations to Acid–Base Balance and Respiratory Control

In contrast with rest, during recovery $CO_2$ release is completely different in similar-sized (mean body mass: ca. 15 g) *Eurypelma* and *Pandinus* (Paul and Fincke, 1989). Independently of activity duration, maximal release is about twice as high in *Pandinus,* and time of recovery (for technical reasons usually given as time of half-recovery; Paul and Fincke, 1989) is about twice as long in *Eurypelma.* Nevertheless, the total amount of $CO_2$ release (above resting level) is almost the same in both arachnids (Fig. 10). In comparison, the rapid reduction in $CO_2$ release after it had reached its maximum becomes conspicuous in the

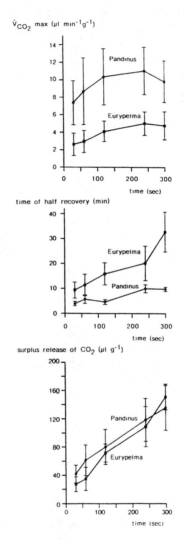

**Figure 10** Comparison of parameters of $CO_2$ release during recovery in *E. californicum* and *P. imperator*. (Top) maximum $CO_2$ release ($\mu$l STPD) plotted versus activity duration, (center) time of half-recovery plotted versus activity duration, and (bottom) total additional $CO_2$ release above resting level plotted versus activity duration (mean values $\pm$ SD). (From Paul and Fincke, 1989.)

scorpion, whereas, in the spider, it only slowly converges with the basal value. Similar relations have been found comparing the ctenid spider *Cupiennius salei* and the scorpion *Leiurus quinquestriatus,* both smaller at a similar mean body mass of about 3 g.

This may be interpreted in two different ways. First, the higher maximum in *Pandinus* is correlated with a larger total respiratory surface (factor 1.7; Paul and Fincke, 1989) in a greater number of book lungs. Increased gas exchange rates are derived from additional book lungs and not from the extension of single respiratory organs. (In *Pandinus* a higher partial pressure difference across the sacculus walls may also contribute.) Second, in a resting scorpion, the $CO_2$-carrying capacity in the hemolymph at a certain partial pressure is about twice that in a tarantula (Paul et al., 1991). In an early phase of recovery, the quantity of dissolved $CO_2$ is reduced by accumulation of anaerobic metabolites. This reduction again is about twice as high in *Pandinus*. Because $CO_2$-binding curves slope only at small angles, partial pressure does not play an important role in the following considerations. For total hemolymph volume (ca. 20% of body mass; Stewart and Martin, 1970), the reduction in dissolved $CO_2$ contributes to the total amount of $CO_2$ release (above resting level) during recovery (see Fig. 10C) by approximately 34% in the tarantula and 61% in the scorpion. This means that, at the beginning of recovery, the animals release $CO_2$ to buffer pH reduction from anaerobic metabolism. Because the accumulation of D-lactate in the hemolymph as well as the surplus of $CO_2$ release during recovery (see Fig. 10C; seen as an index for the $O_2$ debt from activity) are of the same order of magnitude, the rate of anaerobic metabolism during activity should be very similar in both species. Obviously, the action of bicarbonate buffer is distinctly stronger in *Pandinus* than in *Eurypelma*. Therefore, the differences in $CO_2$ release during the first period of recovery (different maxima and times of half-recovery) in spiders and scorpions may be brought about by a different need to use bicarbonate buffering and to expire $CO_2$ to stabilize pH.

The close correlation between acid–base balance and respiration in the arachnids examined may also explain the parallelism of $CO_2$ release and spiracle entrance area during recovery (see Fig. 6). Experiments on respiration control in *Eurypelma* during which partial pressures of $O_2$ and $CO_2$ were changed in a spiracle's environment and, accordingly, also in the hemolymph (Fincke and Paul, 1989), actually demonstrated characteristic correlations between spiracle entrance area and specific ambient gas pressures (Fig. 11). These results strongly suggest the presence of specific chemoreceptors. Spiracles widened with lower $Po_2$ and increased $Pco_2$. The former infers an adaptation of oxygen diffusion resistance in the book lungs to the actual oxygen demand of the tissues. For $CO_2$, the correlation probably implies chemoreceptor functions in connection with acid–base regulation, as discussed earlier. It is remarkable that, once again, there are similarities in human respiration physiology. With reduced alveolar

spiracle entrance area (%)

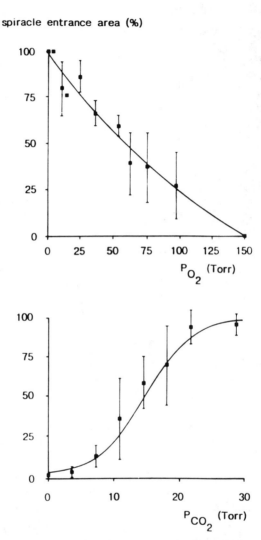

**Figure 11** Relationships between ambient $P_{O_2}$ (top) or $P_{CO_2}$ (bottom) and spiracle entrance area (in relative units), measured on individual book lungs (mean values $\pm$ SD). (From Fincke and Paul, 1989.)

$P_{O_2}$, there is an exponential rise in ventilation (Loeschke and Gertz, 1958), with a rise in alveolar $P_{CO_2}$ it is slightly sigmoidal (Nielsen and Smith,1951).

At rest, the spiracle is almost closed. This was interpreted as a process to reduce respiratory water loss (Angersbach, 1978). Experimental determination of respiratory (Paul et al., 1989b) and total water loss (Paul and Fincke, 1989) in *Eurypelma* and *Pandinus* revealed two aspects: In *Eurypelma*, respiratory water loss is only about 20% of total loss, and the two species do not show a significant difference in total water loss. Since the animals live in completely different habitats, *Eurypelma* in arid zones of North America and *Pandinus* in humid ranches of West Africa, a special adaptation to reduce water loss is not implied. Therefore, avoidance of a deficit in $CO_2$ in the hemolymph might be the better guess to explain the small opening of the spiracle at rest. In other words, spiracle entrance area seems to be adjusted to a level that will keep the bicarbonate buffer system and pH stable. In addition, the mean quantity of dissolved gases in the hemolymph of arachnids may demonstrate the importance of $CO_2$ as a buffer. Hemolymph can carry up to 0.7 $\mu M/ml$ $O_2$ in *Eurypelma* (most of it bound to hemocyanin), but dissolved $CO_2$ at a $P_{CO_2}$ of 15 torr may be as much as 14 $\mu M/ml$; in *Pandinus* even 24 $\mu M/ml$ may be dissolved at the same partial pressure.

To summarize in one sentence: Acid–base balance in arachnids strongly depends on high quantities (in comparison with $O_2$) of dissolved $CO_2$ in the hemolymph and on increased $CO_2$ release from the book lungs during early recovery.

## VI. Circulation in the Tarantula *Eurypelma californicum*

### A. Circulatory System

The physiology of circulation in arachnids is a subject, only known in outlines so far. (Information on anatomy and physiology of the spider heart is found, for example, in Foelix, 1982; Carrel, 1987.) Heart rate in *Eurypelma* ranges from a lowest value of 6 to maximally 90 beats/min (at room temperature). The tubelike organ in the opisthosoma is controlled neurogenically by a dorsal ganglion. In addition, the CNS influences the pulse, which slightly elevates heart rate in spiders that have been disturbed (e.g., by optical sensation) to a mean value of about 20 beats/min (Paul et al., 1989a) in inactive, but, to some degree alert, individuals. Intense fluctuations are noticeable even in resting animals, which might be the cause for similar fluctuations occurring in gas exchange rates (Paul et al., 1989a; Paul and Fincke, 1989).

Perfusion pressure within the closed and open hemolymph spaces of the tarantula *Dugesiella hentzi* is between 12 and 8 torr (systolic and diastolic pressure in the heart; Stewart and Martin, 1974). During locomotor activity, these pressures increase (systolic pressure becomes maximally 55 torr) owing to increased "hydraulic" pressures in the opisthosoma (contraction of opisthosomal muscles). At the same time, pressure in the prosomal hemolymph may rise as far as 480 torr by contraction of the musculi laterales (see foregoing).

Estimation of cardiac output in *Eurypelma* from Fick's principle results in values between 0.7 (at rest) and 4.3 ml/min (maximum during recovery; Paul, 1986). If total hemolymph volume is about 20% of body mass (Stewart and Martin, 1970), circulation time would then be between 4.3 and 0.7 min. Considering heart frequency at rest and while recovering (see Table 1) stroke volume may be estimated to be roughly 50 µl hemolymph per beat (Paul, 1986). Total heart volume is about 100 µl, as revealed by corrosion casts of the heart (S. Zahler, unpublished value).

There is evidence that the direction of cardiac flux is subject to changes in *Eurypelma*, where the main flux may be either forward toward the prosoma or backward into the opisthosoma (Paul et al., 1989a). This has also been reported in the labidognathic spider *Dysdera erythrina* (Bromhall, 1987) and the desert scorpion *Paruroctonus mesaensis* (Farley, 1987). Maybe arachnids complete or substitute a regulation of the supply of different organs through modification of peripheral resistance, by controlling hemolymph flux into the aorta and the various arteries leaving the heart. In the four-lunged *Eurypelma* it seems as if there is a functional separation between anterior and posterior branches of circulation. Probably hemolymph from the prosoma is arterialized in the frontal pair of book lungs, whereas hemolymph from the opisthosoma passes through the second pair (Paul et al., 1989a).

### B. Interactions Between Circulation and the Hydraulic Locomotory System in *Eurypelma californicum*

The hydraulic locomotory system is (in the phylum Arthropoda) a special feature of spider anatomy and physiology. Most probably it does not exist in scorpions (see Manton, 1958). Hemolymph in spiders, therefore, must serve two purposes: on the one hand, it is a medium of transport (blood gases, metabolites) and, on the other hand, it is hydraulic fluid for locomotion.

Two questions arise: First, do high prosomal pressures during locomotion obstruct regular circulation and, thereby, disturb oxygen supply of the anterior part of the body? In other words, is the opithosomal heart able to compete with these prosomal pressures? And second, does the distinct pressure difference between front and rear cause a loss of hydraulic fluid into the opisthosoma, as postulated by Wilson and Bollock (1973) to be the reason for the frequently observed rapid exhaustion in spiders?

The first question was addressed by a thermodilution method in *Eurypelma* (Fig. 12). Hemolymph in an animal was periodically heated by a few degrees in the region of the heart, and allowed to cool intermittently. Simultaneously, temperature was monitored with fine thermocouples in the region of the prosomal aorta and at the posterior main artery. If there is no activity, at both points a

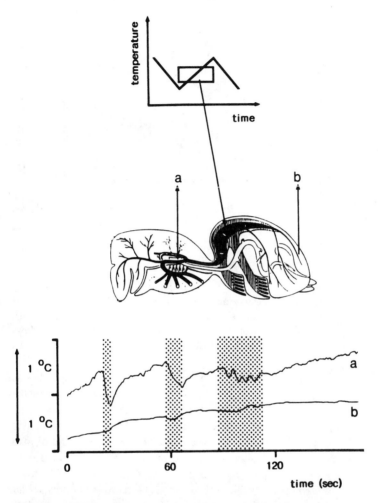

**Figure 12** Top: Measurement of hemolymph flow from the heart to the prosomal aorta (a) and to the opisthosomal main artery (b), as revealed by a thermodilution technique (see Paul et al., 1989a, for details). Bottom: At rest, an increase of temperature at both recording sites demonstrates unimpaired hemolymph flow. During locomotor activity (shaded area), a drop in temperature indicates reduced prosomal perfusion. (From Paul et al., 1989a.)

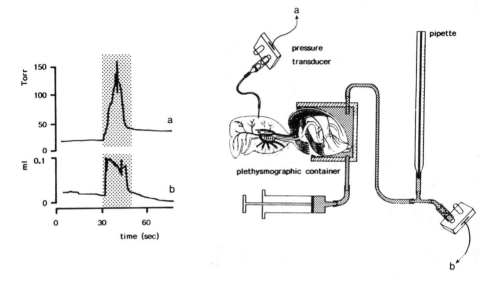

**Figure 13** Simultaneous measurement of prosomal hemolymph pressures (a) and opisthosomal volume changes (b) using a plethysmographic technique (see Paul et al., 1989a, for details). During locomotor activity only 0.1 ml of hemolymph flows from prosoma to opisthosoma. (From Paul et at., 1989a.)

slight rise in temperature occurs from shifted "warm" hemolymph. In contrast, during locomotion, temperature at the prosoma declines, whereas distinctly more heat is observed in the rear of the opisthosoma. This reflects a reduction or complete stop of hemolymph transfer to the front and is seen during rapid motion and often during a slow walk. Just when an increased $O_2$ demand of extremity muscles is expected, perfusion is impeded or blocked. This should induce an ischaemic anoxia in the prosoma and, actually, Angersbach (1978) found that activity in *Eurypelma* causes diminished venous $O_2$ partial pressures, which may fall to almost zero. A restriction of prosomal circulation during locomotion by the hydraulic system actually does not seem to obstruct the muscles in the spider. Their strong dependence on anaerobic glycolysis (discussed earlier) probably enables the development of the dual hemolymph function as a transport and a hydraulic medium in the first place.

To answer the second question (concerning a possible loss of hemolymph), a plethysmographic method was employed (Fig. 13). A closed chamber, filled with water and connected to a standpipe with an integrated pressure sensor, was used to detect any opisthosomal volume changes. And, indeed, the opisthosoma enlarges during locomotor activity, but this increase accounts for only about 3% of the total hemolymph volume. A pronounced loss from the prosoma thus does not take place. Because nothing resembling a valve could be found at the pedicel (Wilson, 1965), other mechanisms must ensure this limitation of hemolymph shunt. A partition between the two pairs of lungs, also found by thermodilution (Paul et al., 1989a), might serve this purpose by limiting hemolymph loss to the frontal pair of lungs and, perhaps, the pericardium. On the other hand, the prosomal pressure pattern is very dynamic (reaching maximal values only in peaks, the basic level being much lower). For higher frequencies (> 8 Hz) prosomal pressure fluctuations cause only minimal opisthosomal volume changes (Paul et al., 1989a). Pedicel, book lungs, and attached structures seem to create a lowpass function for pressure changes. In any event, absence of a marked hemolymph loss from the prosoma leads to the conclusion that other processes must be the reason for the rapid exhaustability, such as anatomical (lack of capillaries) and biochemical (anaerobiosis) features of the muscle region (see also Prestwich, 1988a).

## VII. Summary

Experiments and diverse calculations suggest that the book lungs of the species examined essentially are diffusion lungs. Gas exchange is controlled by variation of the spiracle entrance area. Two modes of aerobic metabolism (mainly based on lipids) may be distinguished: One operates at a very low level at rest, and the other operates during postactive recovery when gas exchange and transport are elevated. Locomotor activity is supported mainly by anaerobic pathways. Acid–base balance and respiration are closely correlated in these arachnids. This hypothesis, among others, is confirmed by experiments on respiratory control. In the spiders, there are distinct influences of the hydraulic locomotory system on circulation.

### Acknowledgments

These studies were supported by the Deutsche Forschungsgemeinschaft (Pa 308/1-1, 1-2, 1-3). Translation of the manuscript into English was done by J. Ritter; the figures were drawn by Mrs. H. Storz.

### References

Anderson, J. F. (1970). Metabolic rates of spiders. *Comp. Biochem. Physiol.*, **33**:51–72.

Anderson, J. F., and Prestwich, K. N. (1975). The fluid pressure pumps of spiders (Chelicerata, Araneae). *Z. Morphol. Tiere*, **81**:257–277.

Anderson, J. F., and Prestwich, K. N. (1980). Scaling of subunit structures in book lungs of spiders (Araneae). *J. Morphol.* **165**:167–174.

Anderson, J. F., and Prestwich, K. N. (1982). Respiratory gas exchange in spiders. *Physiol. Zool.,* **55**:72–90.

Anderson, J. F., and Prestwich, K. N. (1985). The physiology of exercise at and above maximal aerobic capacity in a theraphosid (tarantula) spiders, *Branchypelma smithi* (F. O. Pickard-Cambridge). *J. Comp. Physiol. B,* **155**:529–539.

Angersbach, D. (1975). Oxygen pressures in haemolymph and various tissues of the tarantula, *Eurypelma helluo. J. Comp. Physiol.,* **98**:133–145.

Angersbach, D. (1978). Oxygen transport in the blood of the tarantula *Eurypelma californicum:* Po$_2$ and pH during rest, activity and recovery. *J. Comp. Physiol.,* **123**:113–125.

Bihlmayer, S., Zahler, S., and Paul, R. (1989). Aspects of structure and function of the circulatory system of the tarantula *Eurypelma californicum. Verh. Dtsch. Zool. Ges.,* **82**:223.

Bristowe, W. S., and Millot, J. (1933). The Liphistiid spiders. *Proc. Zool. Soc. Lond.,* **103**:1015.

Bromhall, C. (1987). Spider heart-rates and locomotion. *J. Comp. Physiol B,* **157**:451–460.

Burggren, W. W., and McMahon, B. R. (1988). *Biology of Land Crabs.* Cambridge, Cambridge University Press.

Carrel, J. E. (1987). Heart rate and physiological ecology. In *Ecophysiology of Spiders.* Edited by W. Nentwig. Berlin, Springer-Verlag, pp. 95–110.

Crome, W. (1953). Die Respirations- und Circulationsorgane der *Argyroneta aquatica* Cl. (Araneae). *Wiss. Z. Humboldt-Univ. Berl. Math. Naturwiss. Reihe,* **3/4**:53.

Dejours, P. (1981). *Principles of Comparative Respiratory Physiology.* Amsterdam, Elsevier/North-Holland Biomedical Press.

Edwards, R. H. T., Denison, D. M., Jones, G., Davies, C. T. M., and Campbell, E. J. M. (1972). Changes in mixed venous gas tensions at start of exercise in man. *J. Appl. Physiol.* **32**:165–169.

Ellis, C. H. (1944). The mechanism of extension in the legs of spiders. *Biol. Bull.,* **86**:41–50.

Farhi, L. E., and Rahn, H. (1955). Gas stores of the body and the unsteady state. *J. Appl. Physiol.,* **7**:472–484.

Farley, R. G. (1987). Postsynaptic potentials and contraction pattern in the heart of the desert scorpion, *Paruroctonus mesaensis. Comp. Biochem. Physiol. 86A,* **1**:121–131.

Fincke, T., and Paul, R. (1989). Book lung function in arachnids III: The function and control of the spiracles. *J. Comp. Physiol. B,* **159**:433–441.

Foelix, R. F. (1982). *Biology of Spiders.* Cambridge, Harvard University Press.

Heinrich, K. W., Ulmer, H. V., and Stegemann, J. (1968). Sauerstoffaufnahme, Pulsfrequenz und Ventilation bei Variationen von Tretgeschwindigkeit und Tretkraft bei aerober Ergometerarbeit. *Arch. Ges. Physiol.,* **298**:191–199.

Hemmingsen, A. M. (1960). Energy metabolism as related to body size and respiratory surfaces, and its evolution. *Rep. Steno. Hosp.,* **9**(2):1–110.

Hexter, S. H. (1982). Lungbook microstructure in *Tegenaria* sp. *Bull. Br. Arachnol. Soc.,* **5**:323–326.

Hill, D. E. (1977). Some observations on the physiology of living *Lyssomanes viridis* which should apply to the Araneae in general. *Peckhamia,* **1**:41–44.

Hughson, R. L. and Inman, M. D. (1985). Gas exchange analysis of immediate $CO_2$ storage at onset of exercise. *Respir. Physiol.,* **59**:265–278.

Kästner, A. (1929). Bau und Funktion der Fächertracheen einiger Spinnen. *Z. Morphol. Ökol. Tiere,* **13**:463–558.

Kaston, B. J. (1970). Comparative biology of American black widow spiders. *Trans. San Diego Soc. Natl. Hist.,* **16**:33.

Kjellesvig-Waering, E. N. (1986). *Paleontogr. Am.* **55**:1–287.

Krogh, A. (1920). Studien über Tracheenrespiration 2: Über Gasdiffusion in den Tracheen. *Pflügers Arch.,* **179**:95–112.

Krogh, A. (1941). *The Comparative Physiology of Respiratory Mechanisms.* Philadelphia, University of Pennsylvania Press.

Kükenthal, W., and Renner, M. (1980). *Leitfaden für das Zoologische Praktikum.* Stuttgart, Gustav Fischer Verlag.

Legendre, R. (1968). Sur la presence d'un nerf cardiaque chez les araignees orthognathes. *C. R. Acad. Sci. Paris,* **267**:84.

Levi, H. W. (1967). Adaptations of respiratory systems of spiders. *Evolution,* **21**:571.

Linzen, B., and Gallowitz, P. (1975). Enzyme activity patterns in muscles of the lycosid spider, *Cupiennius salei. J. Comp. Physiol.,* **96**:101–109.

Loeschke, H. H., and Gertz, K. H. (1958). Einfluß des $O_2$-Druckes in der Einatmungsluft auf die Atemtätigkeit des Menschen, geprüft unter Konstanthaltung des alveolaren $CO_2$-Druckes. *Pflügers Arch. Ges. Physiol.,* **267**:460.

Loewe, R., and Brauer de Eggert, H. (1979). Blood gas analysis and acid–base status in the hemolymph of a spider (*Eurypelma californicum*)—influence of temperature. *J. Comp. Physiol.,* **134**:331–338.

Manton, S. W. (1958). Hydrostatic pressure and leg extension in arthropods with special reference to arachnids. *Ann. Mag. Natl. Hist. (Ser. 13)* **1**:161–182.

Millot, J. (1949). Ordre des Araneides (Araneae). In *Traite de Zoologie,* Vol. 4. Edited by P. P. Grasse. Paris, Masson, p. 589.

Moore, S. J. (1976). Some spider organs as seen by the scanning electron microscope, with special reference to the book lung. *Bull. Br. Arachnol. Soc.,* **3**:177–187.

Müller, A. H. (1981). *Lehrbuch der Paläozoologie,* Vol. 2, *Invertebraten.* Jena, Gustav Fischer Verlag.

Nielsen, M., and Smith, H. (1951). Studies on the regulation of respiration in acute hypoxia. *Acta Physiol. Scand.,* **24**:293.

Parry, D. A., and Brown, R. H. J. (1959). The hydraulic mechanism of the spider leg. *J. Exp. Biol.,* **36**:423–433.

Paul, R. (1986). Gas exchange and gas transport in the tarantula *Eurypelma californicum*— an overview. In *Invertebrate Oxygen Carriers.* Edited by B. Linzen. Berlin, Springer-Verlag, pp. 321–326.

Paul, R., and Fincke, T. (1989). Book lung function in arachnids II: Carbon dioxide release and its relations to respiratory surface, water loss and heart frequency. *J. Comp. Physiol. B,* **159**:419–432.

Paul, R., Fincke, T., and Linzen, B. (1987). Respiration in the tarantula *Eurypelma californicum:* Evidence for diffusion lungs. *J. Comp. Physiol. B,* **157:**209–217.

Paul, R., and Storz, H. (1987). On the physiology of the hemolymph of arachnids. *Verh. Dtsch. Zool. Ges.,* **80:**221.

Paul, R., Fincke, T., and Linzen, B. (1989b). Book lung function in arachnids I: Oxygen uptake and respiratory quotient during rest, activity and recovery—relations to gas transport in the haemolymph. *J. Comp. Physiol. B,* **159:**409–418.

Paul, R., Pfeffer, A., Efinger, R., and Storz, H. (1991). Gas transport properties of the haemolymph of arachnids (*Eurypelma californicum, Pandinus imperator, Cupiennius salei*), revealed by a novel methodical approach. *J. Comp. Physiol. B,* (in preparation).

Paul, R., Tiling, K., Focke, P., and Linzen, B. (1989a). Heart and circulatory functions in a spider (*Eurypelma californicum*): The effects of hydraulic force generation. *J. Comp. Physiol. B,* **158:**673–687.

Petrunkevitch, A. (1909). Contributions to our knowledge of the anatomy and relationships of spiders. *Ann. Entomol. Soc. Am.,* **2:**11.

Petrunkevitch, A. (1910). Über die Circulationsorgane von Lycosa carolinensis. *Zool. Jahrb. Anat.,* **31:**161–169.

Prestwich, K. N. (1983a). Anaerobic metabolism in spiders. *Physiol. Zool.,* **56:**112–121.

Prestwich, K. N. (1983b). The roles of aerobic and anaerobic metabolism in active spiders. *Physiol. Zool.,* **56:**122–132.

Prestwich, K. N. (1988a). The constraints on maximal activity in spiders I. Evidence against fluid insufficiency hypothesis. *J. Comp. Physiol. B,* **158:**437–447.

Prestwich, K. N. (1988b). The constraints on maximal activity in spiders II. Limitations imposed by phosphagen depletion and anaerobic metabolism. *J. Comp. Physiol. B,* **158:**449–456.

Schmidt, R. F., and Thews, G. (1980). *Physiologie des Menschen.* Berlin, Springer-Verlag.

Sherman, R. G., Bursey, C. R., Fourtner, C. R., and Pax, R. A. (1969). Cardiac ganglia in spiders (Arachnida, Araneae). *Experientia,* **25:**438.

Stahl, W. R. (1967). Scaling of respiratory variables in mammals. *J. Appl. Physiol.,* **22:**453–460.

Stegemann, J. (1984). *Leistungsphysiologie.* Stuttgart Georg Thieme Verlag.

Stewart, D. M., and Martin, A. W. (1970). Blood and fluid balance of the common tarantula, *Dugesiella hentzi. Z. Vergl. Physiol.,* **70:**223–246.

Stewart, D. M., and Martin, A. W. (1974). Blood pressure in the tarantula, *Dugesiella hentzi. J. Comp. Physiol.,* **88:**141–172.

Strazny, F., and Perry, S. F. (1984). Morphometric diffusing capacity and functional anatomy of the book lungs in the spider *Tegenaria* sp. (Agelenidae). *J. Morphol.,* **182:**339–354.

Strazny, F., and Perry, S. F. (1987). Respiratory system: structure and function. In *Ecophysiology of spiders.* Edited by W. Nentwig. Berlin, Springer-Verlag, pp. 78–94.

Ude, J., and Richter, K. (1974). The submicroscopic morphology of the heart ganglion of the spider *Tegenaria atrica* (C. L. Koch) and its neuroendocrine relations to the myocard. *Comp. Biochem. Physiol.,* **48A**:301.

Werner, R., Storz, H., and Paul, R. (1989). Energy metabolism in the tarantula *Eurypelma californicum. Verh. Dtsch. Zool. Ges.,* **82**:236.

West, J. B. (1985). *Respiratory Physioloy.* Baltimore, Williams & Wilkins.

Whipp, B. J., and Ward, S. A. (1982). Cardiopulmonary coupling during exercise. *J. Exp. Biol.,* **100**:175–193.

Whipp, B. J., and Ward, S. A. (1985). Cardiopulmonary system responses to muscular exercise in man. In *Circulation, Respiration and Metabolism.* Edited by R. Gilles. Berlin, Springer-Verlag.

Wigglesworth, V. B. (1930). A theory of tracheal respiration in insects. *Proc. R. Soc. B,* **106**:229–250.

Wigglesworth, V. B. (1932). The extent of air in the tracheoles of some terrestrial insects. *Proc. R. Soc. B,* **109**:354–359.

Wigglesworth, V. B. (1953). Surface forces in the tracheal system of insects. *Q. J. Microsc. Sci.,* **94**:507–522.

Willem, V. (1917). Observations sur la circulation sanguine et la respiration pulmonaire chez les araignees. *Arch. Neerl. Physiol. Homme* **1**:226–256.

Wilson, R. S. (1965). The pedicel of the spider *Heteropoda venatoria. J. Zool.,* **147**:38–45.

Wilson, R. S. (1967). The heartbeat of the spider *Heteropoda venatoria. J. Insect Physiol.,* **13**:1309–1326.

Wilson, R. S. (1970). Some comments on the hydrostatic system of spiders (Chelicerata, Araneae). *Z. Morphol. Tiere,* **68**:308–322.

Wilson, R. S., and Bullock, J. (1973). The hydraulic interaction between prosoma and opisthosoma in *Amaurobius ferox* (Chelicerata, Araneae). *Z. Morphol. Tiere,* **74**:221–230.

# Part Three

**CIRCULATION**
ENVIRONMENT, ONTOGENY, AND EXERCISE

# 10

## A Conundrum with Reciprocal Cardiorespiratory Variables

Illustration by Differential Baroreflex Control of Heart Period and Heart Rate in Selected Vertebrates

**DEAN F. RIGEL and RONALD W. MILLARD**

University of Cincinnati College of Medicine
Cincinnati, Ohio

## I. Introduction

Many cardiopulmonary variables may be expressed in a reciprocal fashion; for example, lung compliance may be reported as stiffness; airway or pulmonary vascular resistance may be reported as conductance; and respiratory frequency may be reported as inspiratory, expiratory, or total respiratory times. Although one variable is often preferentially selected over the other on the basis of tradition (e.g., compliance and resistance), in other cases either variable is used arbitrarily (e.g., respiratory frequency versus time), depending on the experimental conditions. In any event, it is generally accepted that either reciprocal variable is an equally appropriate means of expressing the same data. It is also usually assumed that utilization of either variable will yield the same experimental conclusion. This is sometimes true, but, under certain conditions, widely disparate conclusions will result, simply from a choice of the reciprocal variable.

We encountered such a problem in the cardiovascular arena when evaluating chronotropic baroreflex data across and within various species (turtle, giraffe, human, dog, pig, fetal lamb, duck, and chicken). When our chronotropic data are expressed in terms of the reciprocal variables heart period versus heart rate, different relative rankings of baroreflex chronotropic sensitivities result.

Similar discrepancies are likely to be associated with cardiopulmonary studies by others, in which data are arbitrarily presented in terms of only one reciprocal variable. In this chapter, we present these data, discuss the conditions under which these interpretational problems arise, and introduce several plausible solutions.

## II.  Illustration of Problem

### A.  Methodology

Baroreflex function is often evaluated in humans and animals by administering a vasoactive agent and observing the degree of cardiac slowing in response to the ensuing arterial pressure rise (Smyth et al., 1969). With this method, baroreflex sensitivity is estimated as the slope of the line relating the beat-by-beat pulse interval (i.e., heart period; HP) to the systolic arterial pressure (SP). The HP is generally selected as the chronotropic variable primarily because of the empirically determined linear relationship between HP and SP (Bristow et al., 1971a,b; Smyth et al., 1969). However, our present analyses indicate that beat-by-beat heart rate (HR) is also linearly related to SP and, therefore, is an equally appropriate chronotropic variable for expression of baroreflex sensitivity.

Our data were collected on the following seven species: red-eared turtle (n = 1; *Pseudemys scripta elegans*), domestic duck (n = 3; *Anas boscas*), domestic chicken (n = 2; *Gallus domesticus*), mongrel dog (n = 6; *Canis familiaris*), giraffe (n = 4; *Giraffa camelopardalis*), pig (n = 2; *Sus scrofa*), and fetal lamb (n = 2; *Ovis aries*). In addition, data on humans (n = 3) were extracted from results published by others (see Fig. 2 of Bristow et al., 1971a; Table 1 and Fig. 1 and 2 of Smyth et al., 1969).

An arterial catheter, or a micromanometer probe, and a venous catheter were implanted under aseptic conditions, with an appropriate short-acting anesthetic. Studies in all species, except giraffe, were conducted in the conscious state at least 24 hr after the surgery; giraffes were sedated with detomidine. Beat-by-beat chronotropic data were derived from the phasic arterial pressure signal or from a surface electrocardiogram. Arterial pressure was acutely elevated by intravenous injection of a vasoconstricting drug (e.g., phenylephrine, methoxamine, angiotensin) that was devoid of direct chronotropic action.

Results were analyzed using the method described in detail by Smyth et al. (1969). Data pairs consisting of beat-by-beat systolic pressure (SP) and the subsequent R-R interval (heart period, HP) were measured 1) at baseline, and 2) during the subsequent elevation of arterial pressure above baseline with the vasoconstrictive agent. Beat-by-beat heart rate (HR) was calculated from each HP (in ms) as 60,000/HP. Slopes, intercepts and correlation coefficients were computed by applying least-squares linear regression analysis to the HP/SP and HR/SP data pairs from the rising pressure stimuli.

## B. Results

Figure 1 displays the SP/HP and SP/HR relationships for each of the eight species. These line segments were generated by averaging the slope and intercept parameters derived from the individual linear regression analyses of the raw SP/HP or SP/HR data. The abscissa (i.e., SP) endpoints of each line reflect the average baseline SP and the peak SP after administering the vasoactive agent. The ordinate endpoints (i.e., HP or HR) were computed from the corresponding SP endpoints and the average linear regression parameters (i.e., slope and intercept) for each species.

It is clear from Figure 1 that the variability in the SP/chronotropic relationships between species is considerable. For example, baseline SPs vary from lows of 21 and 63 in the turtle and lamb, respectively, to highs of approximately 150–160 in the dog, chicken, and duck. It is also clear that there is no correspondence between the baseline SPs and the baseline HP/HR. This disparity is exemplified by the lamb and turtle, which each exhibit low baseline SP but considerably different baseline HR (turtle = 34 beats/min; lamb = 133 beats/min).

Figure 1A also indicates a variability in the slopes of the SP/HP relationships between species. The slope of this relationship has been defined by others as the baroreflex sensitivity (Smyth et al., 1969). Therefore, it appears that the turtle, giraffe, and dog exhibit a high baroreceptor sensitivity, whereas the opposite appears to be true for the duck, chicken, and pig. Interpretation of the relative baroreceptor sensitivities is complicated by the choice of chronotropic variable. Examination of Figure 1B (SP/HR relationships) suggests that the baroreflex sensitivities of the turtle and giraffe are low, whereas those of the chicken and duck are relatively high when baroreflex sensitivity is expressed in terms of HR.

This seemingly contradictory interpretation of these results is illustrated in Figure 2 by comparing the SP/HP slopes (Fig. 2A) with the SP/HR slopes (Fig. 2B) for each species. The rank order of the data in Figure 2 was arbitrarily chosen from the lowest baseline HR (highest HP) to the highest baseline HR (lowest HP). These baseline chronotropic values are portrayed above each column graph for the corresponding species. On the basis of HP, the baroreceptor sensitivities encompass a wide range between species from a high of 99 ms/mm Hg in the turtle, to a low of 1 ms/mm Hg in the chicken. In contrast, there is less variability between species in the baroreflex sensitivities when expressed in terms of HR (Fig. 2B). Thus, the HR sensitivities (negative slopes) vary from lows of 0.4 and 0.5 beats/(min · mm Hg) in the giraffe and pig, respectively, to a high of 3.6 beats/(min · mm Hg) in the duck.

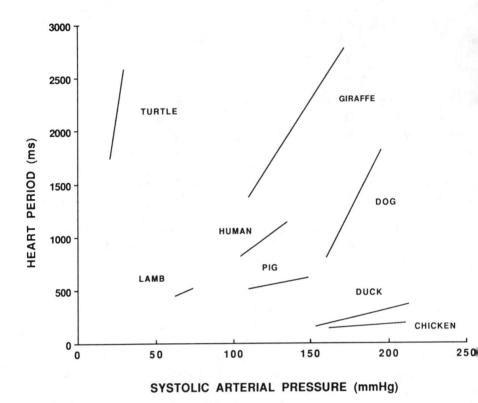

**Figure 1** Systolic pressure/heart period (A) and systolic pressure/heart rate (B) relationships for each of the eight species. Line segments were generated from the average linear regression parameters over the range of systolic pressures (i.e., from baseline to peak pressure after administering the vasoconstrictor agent).

Clearly, the conclusion about which species exhibit high or low relative baroreflex sensitivities is highly dependent upon the choice of chronotropic variable. In terms of HP, species such as the turtle, giraffe, and dog exhibit a high baroreflex sensitivity, compared with species such as the chicken and duck. In other words, for a given rise in arterial pressure, HP was augmented to a much greater degree in the former species than in the latter species. In contrast, a given arterial pressure rise produced a comparable decrease in HR in the turtle, dog, and chicken. Thus, we are led to the discrepant conclusions that the $\Delta HP/\Delta SP$ baroreflex sensitivity in the turtle is 100 times greater than that in the chicken, but that the $\Delta HR/\Delta SP$ sensitivity is slightly less in the turtle than in the chicken. Only the pig exhibited a relatively low sensitivity in terms of either variable,

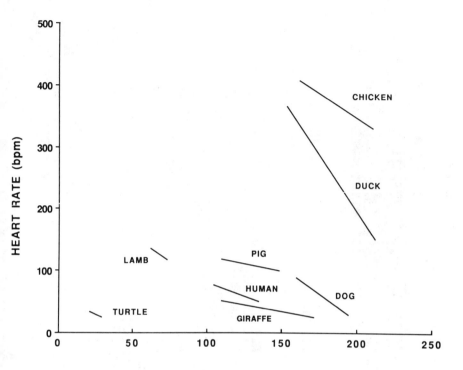

**SYSTOLIC ARTERIAL PRESSURE (mmHg)**

**(B)**

**Figure 1** Continued

whereas the dog exhibited relatively high HP and HR sensitivity. This inconsistency in conclusions is further illustrated by the lack of significant correlation ($r = 0.20$) between the HP/SP slopes and the corresponding HR/SP slopes for the eight species.

### C. Basis of Results

The reason for our disparate conclusions lies entirely in the nonlinear, inverse relationship between HR and HP (Fig. 3) combined with the wide range in the chronotropic operating point (i.e., baseline HP or HR) among species. Consider, for example, hypothetical data (see Fig. 3) based on these experimental results. At a baseline HR of 400 beats/min in the duck, increasing arterial pressure causes a 240-beat/min decrement in HR to 160 beats/min. This HR decrease translates

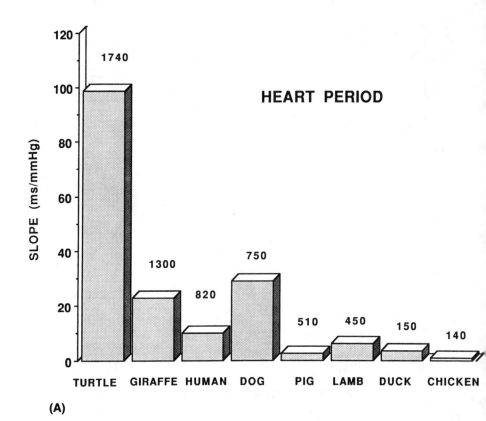

**(A)**

**Figure 2**   Comparison of the systolic pressure/heart period slopes (A) with the systolic pressure/heart rate slopes (B) for each species. Data are displayed in rank order from the lowest baseline heart rates (highest heart periods) to highest heart rates (lowest heart periods). Baseline chronotropic values are portrayed above each column graph for each of the eight species.

into a HP increase of 225 ms from 150 to 375 ms. On the other hand, the baseline HR in the turtle is approximately 34 beats/min, corresponding to a HP of approximately 1740 ms. A small 10-beat/min decrement in HR to 24 beats/min in response to the arterial pressure increase now yields a large HP increase of approximately 750 ms. Hence, data from a particular species with an operating point in the region of the curve with a relatively high ΔHP/ΔHR slope (e.g., turtle) would lead to the disparate conclusions that the baroreflex sensitivity is large when evaluated in terms of HP, but is small when HR was the response variable.

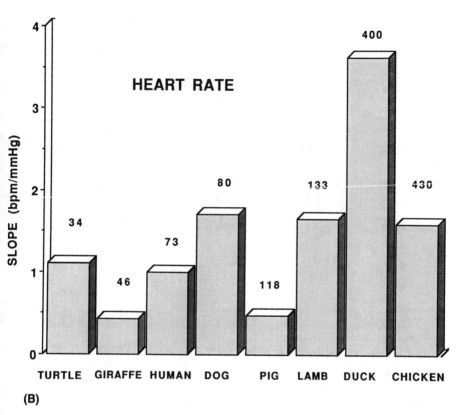

**Figure 2** Continued

### D. Additional Problems

These interpretational problems are not limited to only chronotropic data, but apply to any additional variables that may be expressed in a reciprocal fashion. Examples in the cardiopulmonary sciences include conductance versus resistance, compliance versus stiffness, and nerve or cardiac conduction time versus conduction velocity. Analogous to the chronotropic situation, if the baseline of these variables changes owing to the experimental intervention, discrepant conclusions may result, depending on the choice of variables.

Additional problems may arise with the analysis of reciprocal variables, even if the baselines remain constant. This will be illustrated with the two cases of defining additivity (i.e., simple, facilitative, or occlusive summation) and equivalence of responses. Again, we will use cardiac chronotropic examples, but these examples may be extended to any reciprocal variable. For additivity,

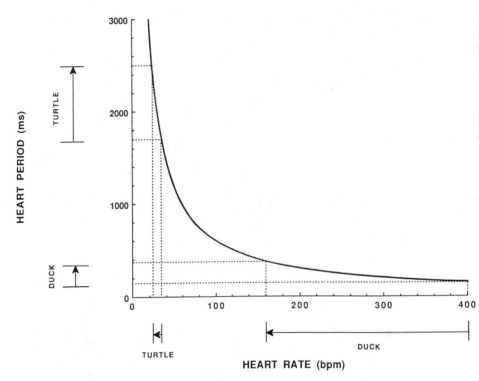

**Figure 3**   Mathematical relationship between heart rate (HR) and heart period (HP) [i.e., HP (ms/beat) = 60,000 (ms/min)/HR (beats/min)].

let us assume that left and right vagal nerve stimulation each decrease HR from 150 to 100 beats/min when applied independently and from 150 to 50 beats/min when applied simultaneously. One would naturally conclude that the two responses combine with simple summation since 2(150 − 100) = (150 − 50). Conversely, the same stimuli increase HP from 400 to 600 ms when applied independently, but from 400 to 1200 ms when applied simultaneously. Since the simultaneous response (800 ms) is now twice the sum of the individual responses (200 + 200 ms) one would quite differently conclude that the same two HP responses add facilitatively. Similar problems may develop when confronted with defining equal, but directionally opposite, chronotropic responses. For example, a given vagal stimulus decreases HR from 150 to 100 beats/min, whereas a sympathetic stimulus increases HR from 150 to 200 beats/min. Are the two stimuli physiologically "equivalent" because they both equally alter HR by 50 beats/min? Again, the answer is moot, since vagal stimulation increases baseline HP by twice as much (400 to 600 = 200 ms) as sympathetic stimulation decreases HP (400 to 300 = 100 ms).

## III. Resolution of Problem

### A. Physiological Approach

Regulation of arterial pressure occurs on a beat-by-beat basis in response to afferent signals arising from specialized pressure receptors located in the cardiopulmonary system. These "baroreceptors" participate in a negative-feedback loop or "barostat" to maintain arterial pressure near a "desired" level by altering systemic vascular resistance and cardiac output. Cardiac output, in turn, is adjusted both by changing the volume of blood ejected per beat and the frequency of beats.

Since arterial pressure is the controlled variable, proper assessment of baroreflex sensitivity requires isolation of the baroreceptor(s) from the vasculature, or an "open-loop" condition. Unfortunately, opening the baroreflex feedback loop is either difficult or nearly impossible in most species. Thus, the technique illustrated in this chapter was developed to assess baroreflex function during "closed-loop" conditions. Because this method evaluates only one arm of the reflex (i.e., cardiac frequency), the derived index is only an indirect indicator of baroreflex sensitivity. Ideally, we would assess baroreflex function in terms of arterial pressure, thereby avoiding the problems associated with chronotropic variables.

In our illustration, a methodological shortcoming forced us to use a reciprocal variable. However, in many instances in cardiopulmonary physiology, reciprocal variables are the desired dependent variables. Therefore, we are left with the problems inherent to these analyses. As in our example, these problems may sometimes be precluded by avoiding baseline shifts. But this is often not possible, such as in our species example or in cases for which the experimental protocol itself necessitates baseline shifts. Furthermore, as we illustrated in Section II.D, interpretational problems may still arise independently of baseline shifts. We should, therefore, seek plausible mathematical approaches to reconcile this problem.

### B. Mathematical Approach

*Relative Change*

One possible approach is to scale the data in terms of relative changes from baseline. Although this method may sometimes tend to normalize the data (Stephenson et al., 1981), more often it will not.

For the sake of simplicity we will illustrate this by focusing on three

**Table 1**  Hypothetical SP, HP, and HR Data for Illustrating Analyses of Data with Relative and Logarithmic Transformations

| Variable | Case number | | |
|---|---|---|---|
| | 1 | 2 | 3 |
| SP | 1 | 1 | 1 |
| | 2 | 2 | 2 |
| | 3 | 3 | 3 |
| | 4 | 4 | 4 |
| HP | 1 | 2 | 3 |
| | 2 | 3 | 4 |
| | 3 | 4 | 5 |
| | 4 | 5 | 6 |
| HR | 1 | 0.5 | 0.33 |
| | 0.5 | 0.33 | 0.25 |
| | 0.33 | 0.25 | 0.20 |
| | 0.25 | 0.20 | 0.16 |
| %Δ HP | 0 | 0 | 0 |
| | 100 | 50 | 33 |
| | 200 | 100 | 67 |
| | 300 | 150 | 100 |
| %Δ HR | 0 | 0 | 0 |
| | −50 | −33 | −25 |
| | −67 | −50 | −40 |
| | −75 | −60 | −50 |
| $Log_{10}$ HP | 0 | 0.30 | 0.48 |
| | 0.30 | 0.48 | 0.60 |
| | 0.48 | 0.60 | 0.70 |
| | 0.60 | 0.70 | 0.78 |
| $Log_{10}$ HR | 0 | −0.30 | −0.48 |
| | −0.30 | −0.48 | −0.60 |
| | −0.48 | −0.60 | −0.70 |
| | −0.60 | −0.70 | −0.78 |

examples of hypothetical data presented in Table 1. In this example, SP and chronotropic data are in arbitrary units. The HR and HP are simple mathematical inverses of each other. We arbitrarily selected the HP data to give the same ΔHP/ΔSP slopes (linear regression; Table 2), but increasing HP baselines. As expected from the HP data and the HP/HR relationship depicted in Figure 3, the HR/SP slopes (see Table 2) decrease considerably as the baseline HR decreases (case 1 to case 3).

Table 2 also shows the data expressed as percentage change from baseline

**Table 2**  Slopes (i.e., $\Delta HP/\Delta SP$, $\Delta\%HP/\Delta SP$, $\Delta Log_{10} HP/\Delta SP$) Derived from Linear Regression of Data in Table 1

| Variable | Case number | | |
|---|---|---|---|
| | 1 | 2 | 3 |
| HP | 1 | 1 | 1 |
| HR | $-0.24$ | $-0.10$ | $-0.06$ |
| $\%\Delta$ HP | 100 | 50 | 33.3 |
| $\%\Delta$ HR | $-24.2$ | $-19.7$ | $-16.5$ |
| $Log_{10}$ HP | 0.20 | 0.13 | 0.10 |
| $Log_{10}$ HR | $-0.20$ | $-0.13$ | $-0.10$ |

HP or baseline HR. Now the slopes derived from the HP data are no longer constant, but decrease. This is expected, since the divisor (baseline) for computing the percentage change increases. On the other hand, HR slopes, expressed in terms of percentage change from baseline, decrease only slightly, compared with those expressed in terms of absolute HR, since the HR baseline decreases from case 1 to case 3. Thus, in this example, the HP slopes are identical, the HR slopes vary by fourfold, the %HP slopes vary by threefold, and the %HR slopes vary only slightly among the three cases. Additional hypothetical data could be derived in which the slopes calculated from the relative HP and HR data differ qualitatively from each other and from the corresponding slopes calculated from the absolute data. It is clear from this hypothetical illustration that scaling data in terms of baseline magnitude will not necessarily result in consistent conclusions with each reciprocal variable. Furthermore, in our species data, the baroreflex sensitivities (i.e., slopes) likewise could be scaled by the baseline SP to further normalize for the species variability in arterial pressure. This computation would likely lead to even different conclusions concerning relative chronotropic baroreflex sensitivities.

### Logarithmic Transformation

Another possible means of reconciling the discrepancies between HR and HP is by the use of logarithmic transformation (Wallick et al., 1979). A given change in the logarithm of HP is identical in magnitude with the corresponding change in the logarithm of HR, independently of the HR or HP operating point. This is true because the logarithm of HP equals the negative logarithm of HR owing to the reciprocal relationship between the two variables. Table 1 also depicts the hypothetical SP/chronotropic data following logarithmic transformation of HP and HR. As expected, the absolute values of the log(HP) and log(HR) data are identical and, consequently, the magnitude of the resulting slopes in terms of HP and HR are likewise identical (see Table 2). Given these logarithmic data, the Δlog(HP)/ΔSP [or Δlog(HR)/SP] slopes now vary by twofold from case 1 to case 3. Although this transformation reconciles the discrepancies between HP and HR, one may question the physiological significance of these slopes.

## IV. Summary

Many variables in cardiopulmonary physiology may be expressed in a reciprocal fashion. It is not commonly recognized that the choice of reciprocal variable may yield widely disparate conclusions. We illustrate this problem with chronotropic (heart rate versus heart period) baroreflex sensitivity data from various species. Two plausible "solutions" (relative scaling and logarithmic transformation) utilized in the literature are evaluated with hypothetical data. Our analyses indicate that the two reciprocal variables may result not only in quantitative differences, but also in qualitatively disparate conclusions. Furthermore, although the two plausible solutions may reconcile the discrepancies between the reciprocal variables, the resulting conclusions may differ from those obtained with the absolute data and with each other. The upshot of our analysis is that when dealing unavoidably with reciprocal variables, the investigator should not arbitrarily select one variable or analysis technique at the exclusion of the others. Only when results with all variables or techniques agree may an unequivocal conclusion be attained.

## References

Bristow, J. D., Brown, E. B., Cunningham, D. J. C., Goode, R. C., Howson, M. G., and Sleight, P. (1971a). The effects of hypercapnia, hypoxia and ventilation on the baroreflex regulation of the pulse interval. *J. Physiol.*, **216**:281–302.

Bristow, J. D., Brown, E. B., Cunningham, D. J. C., Howson, M. G., Petersen, E. S., Pickering, T. G., and Sleight, P. (1971b). Effect of bicycling on the baroreflex regulation of pulse interval. *Circulation*, **28**:582–592.

Smyth, H. S., Sleight, P., and Pickering, G. W. (1969). Reflex regulation of arterial pressure during sleep in man. A quantitative method of assessing baroreflex sensitivity. *Circ. Res.*, **24**:109–121.

Stephenson, R. B., Smith, O. A., and Scher, A. M. (1981). Baroreceptor regulation of heart rate in baboons during different behavioral states. *Am. J. Physiol.*, **241**:R277–R285.

Wallick, D. W., Levy, M. N., Felder, D. S., and Zieske, H. (1979). Effects of repetitive bursts of vagal activity on atrioventricular junctional rate in dogs. *Am. J. Physiol.*, **237**:H275–H281.

# 11

## Developmental Adaptations to Gravity

**ALAN R. HARGENS**

NASA–Ames Research Center
Moffett Field, California

## I. Introduction

Life on Earth has evolved under the constant force of 1 normal gravity (1 $g$). The importance of this gravitational field as an environmental factor is supported by the extent and diversity of physiological adaptations to pressure gradients in living systems. When the force of gravity is removed, some physiological systems are greatly affected (Lenfant and Chiang, 1982). Various organs and organ systems exhibit unique mechanisms of adaptation to gravity to accommodate stresses caused by their columns of fluid and forces of movement (Hargens, 1986). Tissues of particular interest in this chapter include the intervertebral disk, the meniscus, and those of the cardiovascular system. The developing giraffe has served as an important experimental model to provide information about tissue adaptations for increased load bearing with growth. Implications of the results of these studies will be extended to the microgravity environment of space.

## II. Swelling Pressures of the Intervertebral Disk

The intervertebral disk is an important weight-bearing tissue. Each disk consists of a negatively charged nucleus pulposus (primarily proteoglycan macromole-

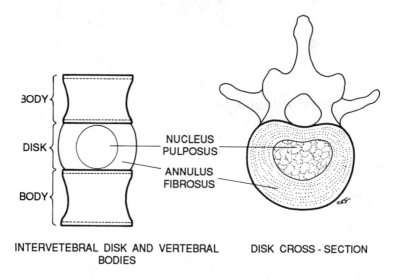

BODY

DISK

BODY

NUCLEUS
PULPOSUS

ANNULUS
FIBROSUS

INTERVETEBRAL DISK AND VERTEBRAL          DISK CROSS - SECTION
BODIES

**Figure 1**   Each intervertebral disk consists of a central, gelatinous nucleus pulposus
that is confined by an annulus fibrosis and two vertebral bodies.

cules) confined by a collagenous annulus (Fig. 1). The disk absorbs shocks and
allows flexibility of the spine during various activities and postures. Increased
loading on the spine during spinal muscle contraction or weight-bearing causes
fluid loss from the disk, whereas decreased loading (e.g., during sleep) allows
fluid influx into the disk. The disk is implicated in the etiology of back pain and
the increased height of astronauts during microgravity. However, little information is available about swelling pressures within the disk, because of methodological problems of measuring these pressures, which typically range between
1 and 3 atm. These swelling pressures are a function of the fixed-charge density
of the proteoglycans, with a small contribution from their osmotic and excluded-
volume effects (Maroudas et al., 1985).

     Cavitation (air-bubble formation) on the side of the membrane opposite
the sample of nucleus pulposus usually occurs when its swelling pressure is
measured in a standard osmometer. With this in mind, we used a modification
of the compression technique developed by Hammel and Scholander (1976) and
Scholander and co-workers (1965) to approach thermodynamic equilibrium. We
employed a compression-type osmometer (Fig. 2) to investigate swelling pressures of intervertebral disks of various animals as related to development and
gravitational stress (e.g., terrestrial versus aquatic environment).

     Fresh samples of the central, gelatinous nucleus pulposus were obtained

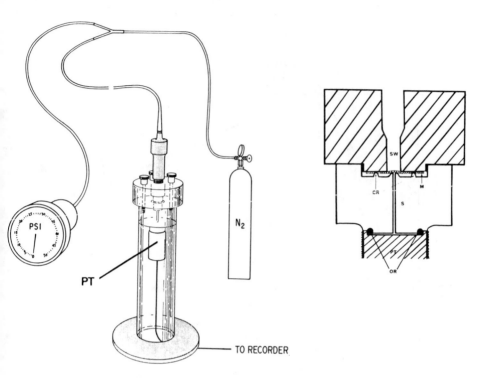

**Figure 2** Compression-type osmometer for measuring swelling pressure of nucleus pulposus: (Left) Plexiglas osmometer mounted on stand with nitrogen gas inlet at top. The osmometer is connected to a nitrogen gas source, precision pressure gauge, and pressure transducer (PT). Trans-membrane pressure gradients are continuously monitored by a strip-chart recorder. (Right) Cross-section of osmometer with sealing of membrane by crimp rings (CR) on the screw-down Plexiglas plate. Nucleus pulposus is placed in the sample well (SW) on top of the membrane (M). Pressure gradients across the membrane are transmitted by the saline fluid column (S) and monitored by the pressure transducer (PT), fitted tightly to the bottom of the osmometer using an O-ring seal (OR). (From Glover et al., 1991.)

from intervertebral disks of rats, rabbits, pigs, humans, and various aquatic species. In rabbits, swelling pressure increased from 1.20 ± 0.20 atm at 3 months to a maximum of 5.05 ± 0.85 atm at 1 year of age (Fig. 3). Disks of older rabbits had lower swelling pressures, as was previously documented in older humans (Urban and McMullin, 1985). Swelling pressures of mammalian disks were highest in the lumbar region. Swelling pressures of disks of aquatic

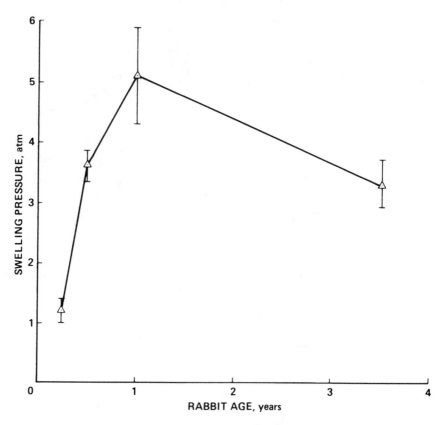

**Figure 3**   Swelling pressures of rabbit disks as related to age.

species (frogs and various fishes) were essentially zero, correlating with the relatively low gravitational stress in their environment (Fig. 4). In mammals, however, swelling pressures did not always correlate directly with degree of weight bearing (weight of the animal, or quadrupedal versus bipedal stature), although the highest pressures yet measured were in the giraffe (Fig. 5).

In summary, aging has a great effect on swelling pressure of the intervertebral disk. Disk herniation in humans seems to correlate with middle-age, when swelling pressure of the nucleus pulposus is maximal. Aquatic species have the lowest swelling pressures, correlating with the relatively low gravitational stress in their environment. In mammals, however, this correlation does not always exist and better age or developmentally matched studies are needed to resolve this issue. The effects of microgravity on intradiskal swelling pressures are currently under study in the Space Physiology Laboratory at Ames Research Center.

## III. Cellularity and Nutrition of the Meniscus as Modified by Age

The meniscus, an important load-bearing structure of the knee, is prone to degenerative midsubstance tears during middle-age. It has been postulated that the central core of the meniscus is less well nourished than the periphery, and that with aging a further nutritional loss induces a degenerative process that produces horizontal cleavage tears (Peters and Smillie, 1972).

In these studies, development of the rabbit meniscus was investigated as a function of growth (increased body weight) and age. We have compared cell density, sulfate uptake, and the effects of a reproducible form of exercise—continuous passive motion (CPM) versus immobilization (IMMOB)—in menisci of young and old rabbits (Hargens et al., 1988). Forth-two New Zealand white rabbits were used, of which 24 were young (0.5 year, approx. 3 kg) and 24 were old (3.5–6.0 year, approx. 5 kg). Each rabbit was sacrificed by anesthetic overdose intravenously, after which [35 S] sodium sulfate (100 $\mu$Ci in 0.1 ml saline) was injected into both knees. Moving each leg three times through its range of motion distributed the isotope throughout each knee. One limb was placed on a CPM device (Fig. 6) for 4 hr (flexion range 40°– 130° at 6 cycles/min), while the contralateral limb remained immobile. Medial and lateral menisci were then removed, given four 1-hr washings in 10% buffered formalin, sectioned, and processed for emulsion autoradiography. Serial sections were cut from the anterior, middle, and posterior meniscal thirds. The amount and location of sulfate uptake were determined by counting the number of labeled cells and the total number of cells in a counting grid placed over five distinct areas (Fig. 7): regions 1, 3, and 4 represented the superficial margins, and regions 2 and 5 represented the central core. Differences between means were examined statistically by ANOVA and paired $t$-tests with significance set at $p < 0.05$.

The total cell density of right and left knees combined was significantly lower for the old rabbits than that for the young rabbits in both medial menisci and lateral menisci for every region (Fig. 8). In the old rabbits, there was no significant regional variation in cell density, whereas in the young rabbits, the superficial regions 1, 3, and 4 had higher cell density than the central core regions 2 and 5. Young rabbits had significantly more labeled cells in superficial regions than in deep regions, but old rabbits had uniformly low numbers of labeled cells in all regions (Fig. 9). Continuous passive motion significantly increased the

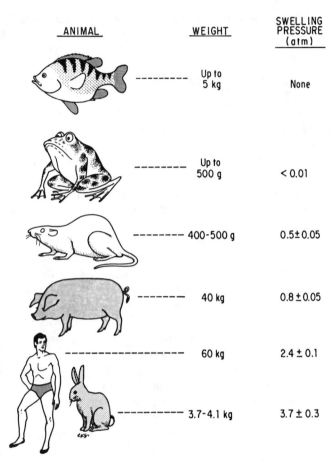

| ANIMAL | WEIGHT | SWELLING PRESSURE (atm) |
|---|---|---|
| | Up to 5 kg | None |
| | Up to 500 g | < 0.01 |
| | 400-500 g | 0.5 ± 0.05 |
| | 40 kg | 0.8 ± 0.05 |
| | 60 kg | 2.4 ± 0.1 |
| | 3.7-4.1 kg | 3.7 ± 0.3 |

**Figure 4**   Swelling pressures of disks compared with species' weight.

uptake of [$^{35}$S]sulfate in most of the superficial and deep regions of menisci of young rabbits, but had no effect on [$^{35}$S]sulfate uptake in the old rabbits. Similar results were obtained for the anterior, middle, and posterior thirds of both medial and lateral menisci.

These results suggest that CPM, a mild form of passive exercise or mechanical stress, may be more beneficial to young than to old menisci, increasing cellular activity or convective transport in avascular regions. Also, our results may provide insight into the etiology and healing capacity of degenerative midsubstance tears in menisci of young compared with old patients.

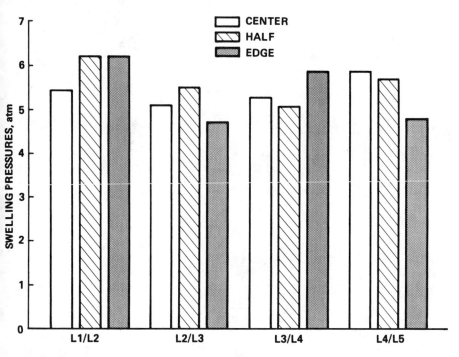

**Figure 5** Disk swelling pressures within the giraffe lumbar spine. Region within the specific disk is indicated.

## IV. The Giraffe as a Model of Tissue-Morphology Adaptations to Gravitational Stress

### A. Cardiovascular Responses

When compared with our knowledge of the effects of microgravity on bone and muscle, relatively little is known about its effects on other load-bearing structures such as connective tissues. Furthermore, more studies of developmental biology are needed to elucidate mechanisms by which various tissues adapt to bearing increasing weight on Earth. Such investigations may provide important information concerning readaptation of space travelers to Earth's gravity after prolonged microgravity. With this knowledge, countermeasures against atrophy or degeneration of load-bearing tissues may be developed more easily.

The giraffe, *Giraffa camelopardalis,* is an important mammalian model for developmental studies of tissue adaptation to bearing increasing weight. Whereas giraffes develop in a quasiweightless milieu as fetuses, after birth they

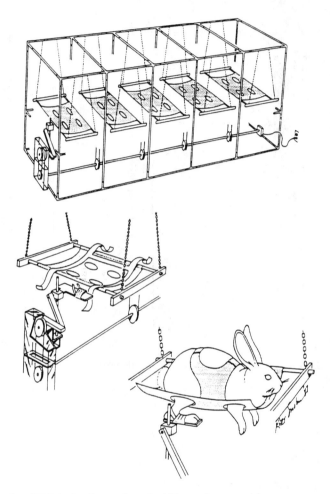

**Figure 6** CPM device for studies of rabbit meniscus nutrition.

must contend with increasing load bearing in their dependent tissues as they grow to heights of over 5 m and weights of over 1000 kg.

We have obtained preliminary data concerning developmental alterations in load-bearing tissues of newborn and adult giraffes (Hargens et al., 1988). In this chapter, emphasis is placed on vascular wall thickness in relation to local blood pressure and on meniscal adaptations to increased load bearing in the developing giraffe. Tissue samples were collected from four 5- to 6-year-old, 3.5- to 4-m, male and female giraffes during the 1985 Giraffe Physiology Expedition to Africa, and from three newborn and two 5-m adult giraffes (age 25

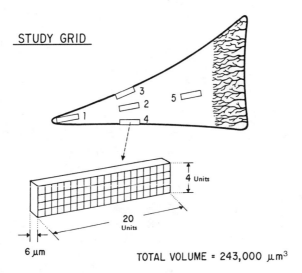

**Figure 7** Cross-section of meniscus with regions of study depicted. Total volume of tissue studied in each block was 243,000 μm³.

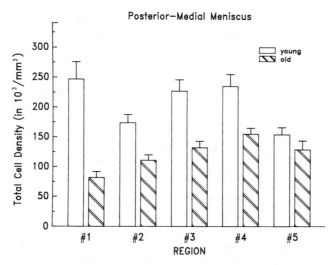

**Figure 8** Cell densities in menisci of old rabbits compared to those of young rabbits.

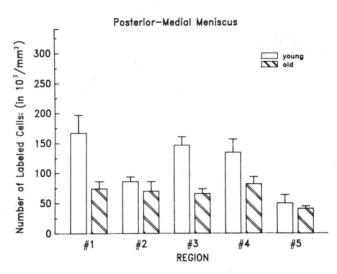

**Figure 9**   Metabolic activity of meniscal cells of old rabbits compared to those of young rabbits.

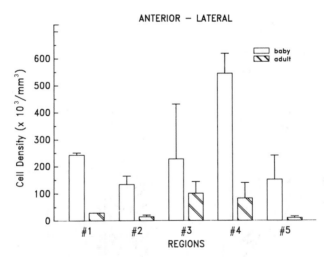

**Figure 10**   Meniscocyte density in anterior portion of lateral menisci from newborn versus adult giraffes. Cell densities were lower in adult menisci than in baby menisci. Similar trends to lower vascular density were observed in menisci of newborns, when compared with adults. Also, note that central regions 2 and 5 have fewer cells than superficial regions 1, 3, and 4, as found in the rabbit.

and 35) from the Cincinnati and Cheyenne Mountain Zoos. Arteries were obtained from the neck (carotid) and forelimbs (digital) and fixed in 10% buffered formalin before processing. Arterioles and other microcirculatory vessels were sampled from skin and muscle of the head, neck, thorax, legs, and feet. Medial and lateral menisci were collected from the hindlimbs of two newborn and two aged giraffes (25- and 35-year-old females). Cell and vascular densities were measured in 6-μm-thick cross sections of each meniscal region. The results indicate that cell densities are significantly higher, in most regions studied, in the menisci of newborn giraffes than in those of adult giraffes (Fig. 10).

Arteries of the feet are sometimes exposed to blood pressures higher than 400 mm Hg in adult giraffes (Hargens et al., 1987b). These vessels have developed pronounced smooth-muscle hypertrophy and narrowed lumens in response to their extraordinary blood pressures. Our previous finding of a less-than-normal arterial pressure gradient from heart to foot in the upright, stationary giraffe (Hargens et al., 1987a) suggests that the reduction in lumen cross-sectional area plays some role in blood pressure reduction in dependent tissues. The arterial wall hypertrophy was apparently confined to dependent vessels with diameters of over 400 μm in adults and was not observed in newborn giraffes or in vessels near the head in adult giraffes. Although this chapter presents results from studies of the arterial system and menisci of giraffes, other load-bearing tissues, such as bone, muscle, intervertebral disk, cartilage, ligament, tendon, fascia, and veins, await investigation.

Although we did not have the opportunity to measure blood pressures in newborn giraffes, studies of humans (Guyton, 1977) and other species support the hypothesis that arterial pressures of baby giraffes are significantly lower at heart level and in dependent tissues than those in adult giraffes. It was apparent that dependent arteries in adults had much thicker walls than did those in newborn giraffes (Fig. 11). This arterial wall hypertrophy correlated directly with the degree of tissue dependency (Table 1); wall-thickness/lumen-size ratios of large arteries increase from head to foot. In the tissues that we examined, arterial wall hypertrophy was restricted to vessels with outer diameters larger than 400 μm.

### B. Meniscal Responses

The lower cell and vascular densities observed in adult giraffe menisci may be related to increased load bearing and occlusion of the microcirculation during ambulation in the growing giraffe. In adult humans, blood perfusion of the meniscus is confined to its peripheral 10-25% (Danzig et al., 1983), and human menisci lose vascularity during development from fetus to adult (Clark and Ogden, 1983). Regions of the rat meniscus adapt differently, both morphologically and biochemically, to prolonged load-bearing exercise (Vailas et al., 1986). Other changes observed during meniscal development in cell culture include differentiation of cell types and proteoglycan-producing capacity in rabbits (Web-

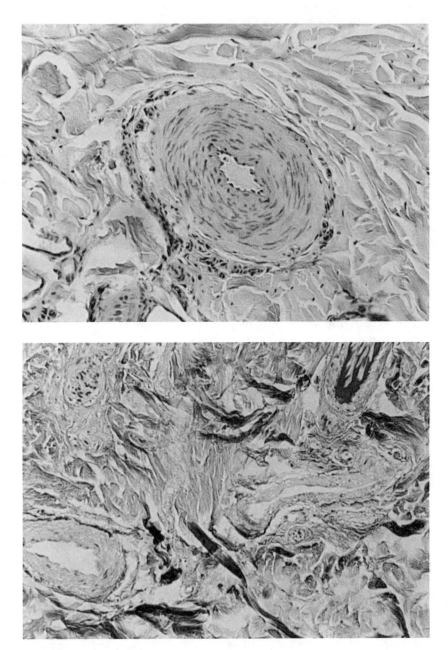

**Figure 11** (Top) 400-μm diameter arteries from foot skin of adult compared with newborn (bottom left) giraffe. (From Hargens et al., 1988.)

**Table 1** Smooth-Muscle Wall Thickness/Lumen Ratios (w/r) for Arteries from the Neck to the Feet of Adult Giraffes

| Artery | w/r | Outer diameter (mm) |
|--------|------|---------------------|
| Carotid | 0.15–0.20 | 9.5–1.0 |
| Brachial | 0.33–0.43 | 5.5–7.5 |
| Femoral | 0.65–0.68 | 4.0–4.2 |
| Ulnar | 0.70 | 7.2 |
| Radial | 0.70 | 5.4 |
| Metatarsal | 0.51–0.81 | 3.1–4.8 |
| Digital | 0.56 | 4.0 |

*Source:* Modified from Hargens et al., 1988.

ber et al., 1986). The lower cell density that we observed in adult giraffe specimens may represent an adaptation to decreased vascular density and poorer nutrition of central regions 2 and 5, as previously postulated by Smillie (1978). As reported earlier for the rat (Vailas et al., 1985), we observed calcium deposits in menisci of aged giraffes.

More studies of the developmental biology of giraffes are needed to elucidate mechanisms by which tissues adapt to aging and increased weight bearing. Such knowledge may provide useful information for understanding the effects of microgravity on load-bearing tissues and for developing countermeasures to aid readaptation of these tissues to normal gravity after prolonged space flight.

## V. Cardiovascular Adaptations to Gravity in the Giraffe

This section reviews our results (Hargens et al., 1987a,b) concerning hemodynamics and fluid balance in the giraffe as they pertain to gravitational physiology. By virtue of its stature, the giraffe provides a sensitive animal model for investigating adaptive mechanisms to high blood pressure in a normal gravitational field. Compared with other mammals, adult giraffes are unique because they grow to a height of 5–6 m and walk around most of the day and night in an upright posture. Previous physiological studies of the giraffe have focused upon arterial blood pressures at levels of the head and neck (Goetz et al., 1960; Patterson et al., 1975; Van Citters et al., 1968; Warren, 1974). Briefly, these investigations demonstrated that arterial pressure near the giraffe heart is about twice that in humans, so that sufficient blood pressure and perfusion can be provided to the brain. However, another important question about gravitational adaptations of tall animals is how they avoid pooling of blood and other fluid in dependent tissues. Assuming that a 5.5-m giraffe has a mean arterial pressure of 200 mm Hg at heart level, one may roughly calculate that the mean arterial pressure in the foot may exceed 400 mm Hg. As reported by Warren (1974),

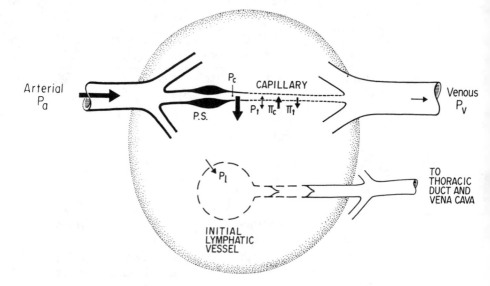

**Figure 12** Starling pressures that govern fluid exchange across the capillary membrane are filtration pressures (capillary blood pressure Pc and interstitial fluid colloid osmotic pressure $\pi_t$) and resorptive pressure (blood colloid osmotic pressure $\pi_c$). Interstitial fluid pressure Pt is sometimes positive (favoring resorption) and sometimes negative (favoring filtration). Usually, fluid is filtered across the capillary membrane into the interstitium and drained by the initial lymphatic system. (From Hargens, 1987.)

the famous Danish physiologist August Krogh speculated that colloid osmotic pressure must be very high in the blood in giraffes' feet to prevent edema formation. However, before our expedition in 1985, no one had measured colloid osmotic or hydrostatic pressures in blood or tissue of giraffe feet.

The forces that regulate transcapillary fluid balance were first identified by the pioneering British physiologist Ernest Starling (1896). These fluid pressures are commonly called "Starling pressures" and are represented by Pc, Pt, $\pi_c$, and $\pi_t$ (Fig. 12) in the following formulation of transcapillary fluid flow $J_c$:

$$J_c = LpA[(Pc - Pt) - \sigma_p (\pi_c - \pi_t)] \tag{1}$$

where Lp is fluid conductivity, A is the capillary membrane surface area, and $\sigma_p$ is the protein reflection coefficient for the capillary membrane (Hargens, 1987).

During the 1985 Giraffe Physiology Expedition to South Africa, eight 3- to 4-m male and female giraffes were studied with respect to their Starling pressures, regional blood flow, and histomorphology. (As part of a culling program unique to South Africa, two of the eight giraffes were killed by a local butcher, who allowed harvesting of multiple tissue samples from various regions of the giraffes' bodies.) Separately, arterial and venous blood pressures were determined by saline-filled, polyethylene tubing connected to pressure transducers kept level with each catheter tip. This method also permitted periodic sampling of arterial and venous blood for determination of colloid osmotic pressure by the technique of Aukland and Johnson (1974). Concurrently, interstitial fluid pressure (Pt) was measured by the wick catheter technique (Hargens et al., 1981), still maintaining the pressure transducer level with the catheter tip. Empty wick catheters were used to collect 5-$\mu$l samples of interstitial fluid for determination of colloid osmotic pressure. Jugular vein pressures were measured, with the Millar Mikrotip transducer, as a function of hydrostatic height in three giraffes. These venous pressures (Pv) were determined without a saline-filled catheter because the pressure-sensing surface was at the catheter's tip. Pv measurements were correlated with the results of studies of venous valve spacing in dissected veins. Local blood flow in neck and leg tissues were measured by the [133]Xe-washout procedure (Henrikson, 1977). Our initial studies were done with the giraffes in a stationary upright posture. The giraffes were sedated with a mixture of detomidine and azaparone during all catheterizations and blood flow measurements. Subsequently, a radiotelemetry system was mounted in a backpack at the base of each giraffe's neck. This enabled continuous monitoring of blood and interstitial fluid pressures while the giraffe moved about during normal day and night activities.

Mean values for arterial and venous pressures qualitatively matched the expected gravitation pressure gradients, with the heart used as a reference for fluid discontinuity between the head and foot (Fig. 13). Although Pc was not measured directly in the giraffe, it is probably near Pv (150 mm Hg) in the feet and 10–20 mm Hg at the top of the neck (Hargens et al., 1987b). Surprisingly, $\pi_c$ was identical in the giraffe and the human, thus $\pi_c$ in the giraffe foot offers no unusual resorptive pressure for preventing dependent edema. Although some Pt measurements in the neck were negative, average body Pt ranged between 1 and 6 mm Hg, except under the tight skin and fascia of the extremities, at which mean Pt was 44 mm Hg. This relatively high Pt is indicative of a "natural antigravity suit" in the giraffe leg. Interestingly, $\pi_t$ was very low (1 mm Hg) except in foot samples, which were contaminated by blood. This finding provides evidence that giraffe capillaries are highly impermeable to plasma proteins and that $\sigma p$ approximates unity. This conclusion was supported by studies of peripheral lymph that indicated only trace amounts of protein were present and $\pi_{lymph}$ equalled zero.

Blood flows in skeletal muscle of the neck and the leg at rest both averaged 4 ml $\cdot$ min$^{-1}$ $\cdot$ 100 g$^{-1}$. Therefore, it is apparent that arteriolar smooth muscle is effective in normalizing blood flow in the leg, despite significantly higher

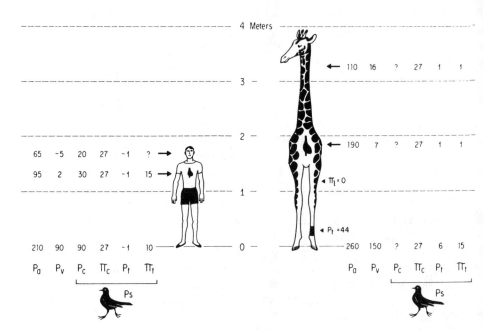

MEAN BLOOD AND TISSUE FLUID PRESSURES ( mmHg )
DURING UPRIGHT, STANDING POSTURE

**Figure 13**  Mean arterial Pa, venous Pv and Starling pressures (Pc, $\pi_c$, Pt, and $\pi_t$) in giraffe (right) as compared with human (left) at hydrostatic levels between the head and feet. Lymph samples obtained from the leg had only trace amounts of protein and $\pi_t = 0$. Foot samples for $\pi_t$ were often contaminated by blood and, therefore, were less reliable. It is noteworthy that Pt beneath the tight skin and fascia of the legs ranged between 40 and 50 mm Hg, indicating the presence of a "natural anti-g-suit" in the giraffe. Data for human pressures are obtained from several sources besides our previous studies. (From Hargens et al., 1987b.)

arterial perfusion pressures. The presence of precapillary sphincters combined with pronounced arterial and arteriolar wall hypertrophy in dependent tissues, were prominent features of our giraffe histomorphometric studies.

Inserting our values for the Starling pressures into Eq. (1) yields a net resorptive pressure of − 7 mm Hg in the giraffe neck and net filtration pressures of + 88 to + 152 mm Hg in tissues of the leg. These calculations suggest that giraffes in an upright, stationary posture are susceptible to dependent edema. However, our radiotelemetry data for the giraffe foot indicate that Pa (ranging from 70 to 380 mm Hg), Pv (− 250 to + 240 mm Hg) and Pt (− 120 to + 180 mm Hg) are highly variable during normal ambulation. Consequently, it appears that there is an effective pumping mechanism in the vascular and interstitial spaces for moving blood and interstitial fluid against gravity. The tight skin and fascial layers of the giraffe leg provide a functional "antigravity suit" to prevent pooling of blood and interstitial fluid in dependent tissues.

For adaptation to high gravitational pressures in its cardiovascular system, the giraffe is certainly unique. The edema-preventing mechanisms detected in giraffe legs include (1) variable and sometimes negative Pv and Pt; (2) impermeable capillary membranes to retain intravascular proteins; (3) arterial wall hypertrophy and vasoconstriction to reduce dependent blood flow (Nilsson et al., 1988); (4) a prominent lymphatic system; and (5) skin and fascial antigravity suit combined with one-way valves in the veins and lymphatics to reduce venous capacitance and to propel blood and peripheral lymph upward against a gravitational pressure gradient. This study demonstrates that intravascular and interstitial fluid pressures are highly variable during normal exercise and that studies of recumbent and upright, stationary animals may give misleading information about transcapillary fluid balance. For example, it is generally known by zoo veterinarians that sick giraffes die soon after assuming the recumbent position. Also, static, upright measurements provide an incomplete picture. Normal exercise activities with concomitant pumping of interstitial fluids, venous blood, and peripheral lymph (both of the latter containing one-way valves) are important for edema prevention in dependent tissues. In this context, it is noteworthy that taller mammals (e.g., giraffes and humans) have tight fascial layers around their lower extremities, whereas shorter mammals (e.g., rats and rabbits) do not. Apparently the cyclical compression and decompression associated with muscular activity and tight fascial enclosure (Sejersted et al., 1984) explain the highly variable Pa, Pv, and Pt that were observed.

The existence of impermeable capillaries in the giraffe tends to raise $\pi_c$ and lower $\pi_t$, but also, this relative impermeability may importantly reduce fluid conductivity, Lp, through the capillary membrane, thereby permitting the lymphatic system to carry away any excess interstitial fluid that forms. In addition, from our [133]Xe-washout results it is apparent that precapillary vasoconstriction normalizes blood flow and reduces the capillary filtration area, A, in dependent tissues.

Some anatomical adaptations of the giraffe and humans obviously represent developmental adjustments to high and variable gravitational pressures. For example, the important work of Williamson and colleagues (1971) documents that capillary basement membrane thickness increases twofold from neck muscle to leg muscle of adult giraffes and humans. On the other hand, such membranes in the human fetus are uniform and considerably thinner than those in children and adult humans. A thicker capillary membrane in dependent tissues of the adult provides anatomical evidence for lower permeability to plasma ultrafiltration across the capillary. In this context, it would be interesting and valuable to investigate alterations of edema-preventing parameters in human legs during long-term exposure to microgravity and subsequent readjustment to Earth's 1 *g* to hypergravity conditions on a larger planet. It is possible that the smooth-muscle tone of precapillary arterioles and lymphatic vessels in dependent tissues is lost during long-term space flight in the absence of appropriate countermeasures. Long-term bed rest studies of edema-preventing mechanisms in humans may elucidate the time course of this postulated vascular deconditioning. The effect of long-term microgravity of fascia and other connective tissue structures needs careful assessment as well. Such studies should provide knowledge about mechanisms and rates of deconditioning and reconditioning in space travelers, as well as in patients exposed to long-term bed rest.

The pressure gradient down the jugular vein was about one-tenth that expected for a continuous column of blood (Fig. 14). The nonhydrostatic pressure gradient down the giraffe's jugular vein indicates that blood flows down from the head in a discontinuous column, and that circulation above heart level does not depend upon a siphonlike principle (Seymour and Johansen, 1987), as recently proposed (Badeer, 1986; 1988; Hicks and Badeer, 1989). Moreover, if the siphoning mechanism was important, giraffes wouldn't need such high arterial pressures as those measured at heart level. The abundance of valves in the head and distal neck; compared to their sparseness in the proximal neck; indicates their importance for preventing retrograde venous flow, for example, during the short periods when the giraffe's head is lowered below heart level during drinking.

The results obtained in these studies of the giraffe suggest avenues of future gravitational physiology research in giraffes and in other animals, including humans. For example, adaptations to head-down drinking in the giraffe require further study to determine whether intracranial hypertension is a problem in this posture. Cerebrospinal fluid pressures should be measured in various positions and activities. Lymphatic flow and pressures warrant detailed studies in upright giraffes and in patients exposed to long-term bed rest. More complete histomorphometric studies would provide information about the anatomical basis of the physiological mechanisms involved in edema prevention. Sleep patterns and neck muscle tone in the giraffe should be studied because of the lack of recumbency. Fascia and skin compliance should be studied in legs of various animals. Studies of other gravity-sensitive animals [e.g., snakes (Lillywhite, 1985) and tall birds such as ostriches and flamingoes] are indicated. Finally, better and more complete studies of venous pressures from the head into the thoracic cavity and the right ventricle are needed.

### Acknowledgments

My giraffe study colleagues (Ron Millard, Knut Pettersson, David Gershuni) and I fondly recall our studies with the late Kjell Johansen whom we miss, and

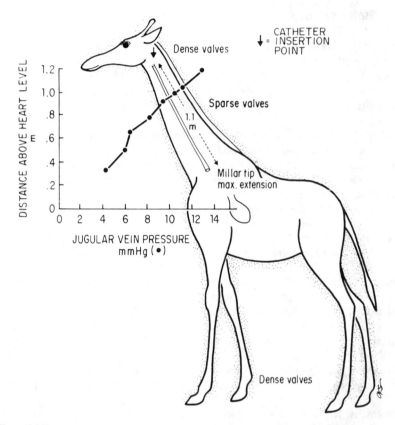

**Figure 14** Blood pressure as a function of hydrostatic height in the jugular vein and intervalve distances in the giraffe neck and leg. In one giraffe the jugular vein pressure gradient was approximately 0.14 cm $H_2O$/cm of vertical distance. Intervalve distances were short in the head, distal neck, and proximal legs, but long in the proximal neck. (From Hargens et al., 1987a.)

in whose honor this satellite symposium of the IUPS Congress is dedicated. These studies were supported by grants from the National Science Foundation (DCB-8409253), the National Institutes of Health (HL-32703), the National Geographic Society (3072-85), the Veterans Administration, and NASA. Professor Wouter van Hover and the Department of Zoology, University of Pretoria, provided giraffes and facilities for our 1985 Giraffe Physiology Expedition. Dr. D. G. A. Meltzer and Roodeplaat Research Labs, Dr. Richard Burroughs and the National Zoological Gardens in Pretoria, and Dr. Frik J. Stegmann and the University of Pretoria Veterinary School at Onderstepoort contributed excellent veterinary support for our giraffe studies. Dr. Paul Calle, the Cheyenne Mountain Zoo, and the Cincinnati Zoo provided giraffe specimens.

## References

Aukland, K., and Johnson, H. M. (1974). A colloid osmometer for small fluid samples. *Acta Physiol. Scand.,* **90:**485–490.

Badeer, H. S. (1986). Does gravitational pressure of blood hinder flow to the brain of the giraffe? *Comp. Biochem. Physiol.,* **83A:**207–211.

Badeer, H. S. (1988). Haemodynamics of the jugular vein in the giraffe. *Nature,* **332:**788–789.

Clark, C. R., and Ogden, J. A. (1983). Development of the menisci of the human knee joint. *J. Bone Joint Surgery,* **65A:**538–547.

Danzig, L., Gonsalves, M. R., Resnick, D., and Akeson, W. H. (1983). Blood supply to the normal and abnormal menisci of human knee. *Clin. Orthop.,* **172:**271–276.

Glover, M. G., Hargens, A. R., Mahmood, M. M., Gott, S., Brown, M. D., and Garfin, S. R. (1991). A new technique for the in vitro measurement of nucleus pulposus swelling pressure. *J. Orthop. Res.,* **9:**61–67.

Goetz, R. H., Warren, J. V., Gauer, O. H., Patterson, J. L., Jr., Doyle, J. T., Keen, E. N., and McGregor, M. (1960). Circulation of the giraffe. *Circ. Res.,* **8:**1049–1058.

Guyton, A. C. (1977). *Basic Human Physiology: Normal Function and Mechanisms of Disease.* Philadelphia, W.B. Saunders, pp. 202–203, 887.

Hammel, H. T., and Scholander, P. F. (1976). *Osmosis and Tensile Solvent.* Berlin, Springer-Verlag, 133 pp.

Hargens, A. R. (1986). *Tissue Nutrition and Viability.* New York, Springer-Verlag, 312 pp.

Hargens, A. R. (1987). Interstitial fluid pressure and lymph flow. In *Handbook of Bioengineering.* Edited by R. Skalak and S. Chien. New York, McGraw-Hill, pp. 19.1–19.25.

Hargens, A. R., Cologne, J. B., Menninger, F. J., Hogan, J. S., Tucker, B. J., and Peters, R. M. (1981). Normal transcapillary pressures in human skeletal muscle and subcutaneous tissues. *Microvasc. Res.,* **22:**177–189.

Hargens, A. R., Gershuni, D. H., Danzig, L. A., Millard, R. W., and Pettersson, K. (1988). Tissue adaptations to gravitational stress: Newborn versus adult giraffes. *Physiologist,* **31:**S110–S113.

Hargens, A. R., Millard, R. W., Pettersson, K., and Johansen, K. (1987a). Gravitational haemodynamics and oedema prevention in the giraffe. *Nature,* **329:**59–60.

Hargens, A. R., Millard, R. W., Pettersson, K., van Hoven, W., Gershuni, D. H., and Johansen, K. (1987b). Transcapillary fluid balance in the giraffe. In *Interstitial–Lymphatic Liquid and Solute Movement, Advances in Microcirculation,* Vol. 13. Edited by N. C. Staub, J. C. Hogg, and A. R. Hargens. Basel, S. Karger, pp. 195–202.

Henriksen, O. (1977). Local sympathetic reflex mechanisms in regulation of blood flow in human subcutaneous adipose tissue. *Acta Physiol. Scand. Suppl.,* **450:**1–48.

Hicks, J. W., and Badeer, H. S. (1989). Siphon mechanism in collapsible tubes: application to circulation of the giraffe head. *Am. J. Physiol.,* **256:**R567–R571.

Lenfant, C., and Chiang, S.-T. (1982). Weightlessness: From Galileo to Apollo. In *A*

*Companion to Animal Physiology*. Edited by C. R. Taylor, K. Johansen, and L. Bolis. Cambridge, Cambridge University Press, pp. 339–348.

Lillywhite, H. B. (1985). Postural edema and blood pooling in snakes. *Physiol. Zool.,* **58**:759–766.

Maroudas, A., Ziv, I., Weisman, N., and Venn, M. (1985). Studies of hydration and swelling pressure in normal and osteoarthritic cartilage. *Biorheology,* **22**:159–169.

Nilsson, O., Booj, S., Dahlstrom, A., Hargens, A. R., Millard, R. W., and Pettersson, K. S. (1988). Sympathetic innervation of the cardiovascular system in the giraffe. *Blood Vessels,* **25**:299–307.

Patterson, J. L., Jr., Goetz, R. H., Doyle, J. T., Warren, J. V., Gauer, O. H., Detweiler, D. K., Said, S. I., Hoernicke, H., McGregor, M., Keen, E. N., Smith, M. H., Jr., Hardie, E. L., Reynolds, M., Flatt, W. P., and Waldo, D. R. (1975). Cardiorespiratory dynamics in the ox and giraffe, with comparative observations on man and other mammals. *Ann. N.Y. Acad. Sci.,* **127**:393–413.

Peters, T. J., and Smillie, I. S. (1972). Studies on the chemical composition of the menisci of the knee joint with special reference to the horizontal cleavage lesion. *Clin. Orthop.,* **86**:245–252.

Scholander, P. F., Hammel, H. T., Bradstreet, E. D., and Hemmingsen, E. A. (1965). Sap pressure in vascular plants. *Science,* **148**:339–346.

Sejersted, O. M., Hargens, A. R., Kardel, K. R., Blom, P., Jensen, O., and Hermansen, L. (1984). Intramuscular fluid pressure during isometric contraction of human skeletal muscle. *J. Appl. Physiol. Respir. Environ. Exer. Physiol.,* **56**:287–295.

Seymour, R. S., and Johansen, K. (1987). Blood flow uphill and downhill: Does a siphon facilitate circulation above the heart? *Comp. Biochem. Physiol.,* **88A**:167–170.

Smillie, I. S. (1978). *Injuries of the Knee Joint*. Edinburgh, Churchill–Livingstone.

Starling, E. H. (1896). On the absorption of fluids from connective-tissue spaces. *J. Physiol. Lond.,* **19**:312–326.

Urban, J. P. G., and McMullin, J. (1985). Swelling pressure of the intervertebral disc. *Biorheology,* **22**:145–157.

Vailas, A. C., Zernicke, R. F., Matsuda, J., Curwin, S., and Durivage, J. (1986). Adaptation of rat knee meniscus to prolonged exercise. *J. Appl. Physiol.,* **60**:1031–1034.

Vailas, A. C., Zernicke, R. F., Matsuda, J., and Peller, D. (1985). Regional biochemical and morphological characteristics of rat knee meniscus. *Comp. Biochem. Physiol.,* **82B**:283–285.

Van Citters, R. L., Kemper, S., and Franklin, D. L. (1968). Blood flow and pressure in the giraffe carotid artery. *Comp. Biochem. Physiol.,* **24**:1035–1042.

Warren, J. V. (1974). The physiology of the giraffe. *Sci. Am.,* **231**(5):96–105.

Webber, R. J., Zitaglio, T., and Hough, A. J., Jr. (1986). In vitro cell proliferation and proteoglycan synthesis of rabbit meniscal fibrochondrocytes as a function of age and sex. *Arthritis Rheum.,* **29**:1010–1016.

Williamson, J. R., Vogler, N. J., and Kilo, C. (1971). Regional variations in the width of the basement membrane of muscle capillaries in man and giraffe. *Am. J. Pathol.,* **63**:359–370.

# 12

## The Importance of an Ontogenetic Perspective in Physiological Studies
### Amphibian Cardiology as a Case Study

**WARREN W. BURGGREN***

University of Massachusetts
Amherst, Massachusetts

## I. Introduction

Undeniably, anatomical complexity increases with ontogeny. From the first union of sperm and egg, cell numbers increase astronomically, and the differentiation into various cell types allows the formation of many types of specialized tissues. A widespread, general perception of anatomical development (especially by comparative physiologists) is that development progression equals increasing anatomical complexity, and that the most complex forms of a species are also the sexually mature, adult forms. (This perception persists even though the larval forms of many lower vertebrates show unique and anatomically complex specializations for feeding and behavior, to mention just a few examples; see Seymour, 1984, for review). A corollary of the view that development continually leads to increasing anatomical complexity is that development of increasing anatomical complexity also leads to increasing physiological complexity. Thus, a common attitude in comparative physiology seems to be that the adults of a given species will show the most complex physiological processes.

Perhaps as a consequence of these biases, the vast majority of studies in comparative physiology are directed exclusively to investigation of the mature, adult form of the species. Yet, the physiology of adult animals is not more

*Present affiliation:* University of Nevada at Las Vegas, Las Vegas, Nevada.

"interesting" compared with immature developmental stages, nor are physiological processes in adults more important in adaptation to environmental change or to extreme environments. Indeed, ontogenetic studies have considerable merit when the goal is to study evolution of physiological adaptation, and this essay will take two approaches to argue this point. First, the theoretical case for performing developmentally oriented physiological studies will be advanced. Second, data from developmental studies of cardiac physiology in amphibians will be presented and discussed as a case study to demonstrate that cardiac physiology of the adult is not necessarily representative of the species over its entire life cycle.

## II.  The Arguments for Developmental Studies of Physiology

Developmental studies of physiological traits (processes) should be included wherever possible in studies of physiological adaptation. This statement is valid for several reasons, as will now be discussed.

### A.  Natural Selection and Development

When comparative physiologists study "adaptation to the environment," they implicitly, if not explicitly, study evolution (see Burggren and Bemis, 1990). A vital mechanism in the evolutionary process is *natural selection,* which is simply the differential survival and successful reproduction of individuals with different heritable traits. Selection pressures, such as low oxygen or extremes in temperature or salinity, result in increased mortality in those individuals that, relative to the survivors in a population, do not have the combination of physiological, anatomical, and behavioral traits that ensure survival and reproduction by an individual.

Almost invariably, studies in comparative physiology that investigate "physiological adaptation" to a particular environmental condition or set of conditions are limited to examination of adult, sexually mature specimens. Certainly, understanding the mechanisms that allow differential survival during environmental challenge in adults is important—the survival of immature developmental stages is immaterial if the adults are unable to survive and reproduce successfully. Yet, it is important to emphasize that *natural selection acts on all developmental stages, not just adults.* Figure 1 is an "ontogeny–phylogeny" diagram, showing the hypothetical evolution of three closely related species. A conventional view of comparative physiology is that the evolution from species A to B to C is epitomized by the change in heritable traits characterized by the transition in adults. If species A, B, and C all differ for a particular trait, then that trait is assumed to have been altered through natural selection and is in some way linked to the survival of the animal in challenging environmental conditions. If, how-

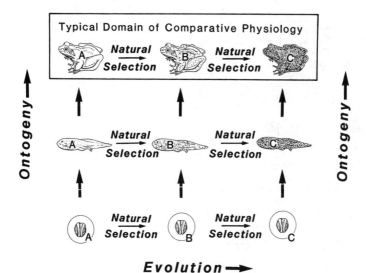

**Figure 1** Evolution of species A, to B, to C occurs as a result of natural selection by environmental or other factors. Importantly, natural selection can act at any or all levels of development, not just on adults. Typically, comparative physiological studies investigate adaptations in adults and fail to consider important adaptations that could occur in larvae and eggs.

ever, a trait is the same in adults A, B, and C, then it is usually assumed that evolutionary changes in that trait have been unimportant for the adaptation of the species to a particular environmental condition.

Unfortunately, this approach ignores the effects of natural selection on the immature developmental stages and, in the most extreme case, even on the eggs and sperm. For example, three species of fishes showing varying degrees of ability to withstand low-oxygen conditions may, as adults, all have exactly the same blood respiratory properties. Does this mean that blood oxygen affinity plays no role in terms of adaptation of that species to the environment? In fact, a high blood oxygen affinity of the larvae may be a major factor contributing to the survival of that developmental stage (and thus to the survival of the species). In adults, however, other factors (increased gill surface area, reduced blood–water diffusion distance, reduced branchial blood shunts, increased oxygen extraction by tissues, aerial gas exchange, to name but a few) may be the primary adaptations favoring survival in hypoxic water. To state categorically that blood respiratory properties play no role in the evolutionary process by which one species is better adapted to hypoxia than another species is to ignore the effects of natural selection on immature stages.

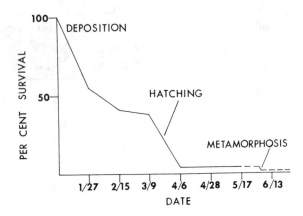

**Figure 2** Survivorship curve for the tiger salamander, *Ambystoma tigrinum*. Data were collected during the first 6–7 months of 1969. (From Anderson et al., 1971.)

Differential rates of mortality accompany different developmental stages and the transitions between these stages. This is graphically demonstrated in Figure 2, which presents a survivorship curve for the tiger salamander, *Ambystoma tigrinum*. High rates of mortality are associated with egg deposition, hatching, and metamorphosis, whereas embryonic and larval development are relatively "safe." This can result not only from variation in the ability of different developmental stages to survive a fixed environmental challenge, but also because the importance of a given environmental factor (oxygen, temperature, salinity, acidity) can vary with developmental stage. To continue with the example of aquatic hypoxia, newly fertilized eggs of aquatic and amphibious vertebrates are notoriously resistant to hypoxia, compared with later developmental stages (Detwiler and Copenhaver, 1940; Gregg, 1962; Rose et al., 1971; Weigmann and Altig, 1975; Adolph, 1979). In the adults of air-breathing fishes and many amphibians, aquatic hypoxia can be "escaped" once the developmental changes allowing air breathing have occurred (see reviews by Johansen, 1970; Burggren, 1984). Thus, aquatic hypoxia may be a major selection pressure affecting survival primarily in the intermediate, rather than very early or adult, developmental stages of air-breathing fishes and amphibians. This does not mean that the effects of environmental hypoxia on adults have been unimportant to the evolution of these species, but it does mean that to understand the full impact of oxygen as a selection pressure requires that the physiological and anatomical responses to oxygen be investigated in the context of a developmental series within species. To summarize, the adult is *not* more informative than any other single developmental stage when attempting to understand the physiological adaptation of the species as a whole.

## B.  Allometry and Development

Although the physiological consequences of interspecific allometry (scaling) have been extremely well analyzed (Peters, 1983; Schmidt-Nielsen, 1984; Calder, 1984), there are very few *intraspecific* studies of the allometry of physiology (e.g., Burggren et al., 1987; Hou and Burggren, 1989). To state that "this is how species X (more truthfully, almost always the *adult* of species X) is adapted to environment Y" downplays the fact that adult individuals of a species are almost always larger than immature individuals. At the risk of stating a truism, small animals differ physiologically from large animals. Smaller individuals of any stage exhibit, for example, higher mass-specific metabolic rate, higher heart rate, and higher cardiac output than larger individuals. As a consequence, small, immature individuals may respond to an environmental challenge quite differently from the larger adults simply by virtue of their size difference and the physiological demands and constraints this difference imposes. To give a hypothetical example, environmental oxygen could be a more potent selection factor in smaller, immature individuals of a species than in the larger mature forms, since the latter will have a higher rate of aerobic metabolism. In extreme cases, a physiological trait (or lack of trait) that might be of adaptive advantage from the perspective of a large adult could actually be of no benefit or even maladaptive in smaller, immature stages. The point is that putative physiological adaptations are best interpreted in the context of a wide range of developmental stages and body sizes.

## C.  Size-Independent Developmental Changes

Developmental studies in adaptational physiology are important also because of changes owing to development, per se. Although immature individuals of a species are often smaller than mature individuals and differ in predictable ways, as described by allometric relationships, there are also "pure" developmental differences that are due to tissue differentiation and organogenesis, rather than to changes in body mass. These differences may be either *quantitative,* involving differences in the magnitude of physiological or anatomical traits common to all developmental stages, or they may be *qualitative,* involving processes or structures found only in either the immature form or the adult. The importance of these two distinct types of differences between immature forms and adults of a species can be indicated by a few examples.

### Quantitative

Generally, within vertebrate species, larger individuals have a larger heart. In the specific example of heart mass (and stroke volume, which is usually very closely correlated with heart mass), a general finding among vertebrates is that

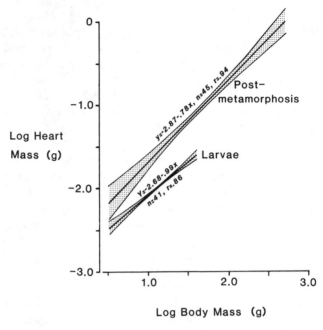

**Figure 3** Relationship between log heart mass and log body mass in larval (Taylor–Kollros stage IV–XX) and adult bullfrogs, *Rana catesbeiana*. Linear regressions and the 95% confidence intervals are shown for the broad developmental groups. Also shown is the line equation, number of individuals, and correlation coefficient.

heart mass is directly proportional to body mass. That is, heart mass scales to body mass with the exponent equal to 1 or, if expressed as mass-specific values, the slope of the line relating the two variables is zero (Peters, 1983). Armed with this information, a cardiovascular physiologist might tend to overlook measurements in smaller individuals of the species because, presumably, this information could be calculated from body mass. Yet, *quantitative differences* in the allometric relationship between heart mass and body mass can be associated with developmental change. Figure 3 illustrates the relationship between log heart mass and log body mass in larval and postmetamorphic bullfrogs (*Rana catesbeiana*), including data from very small adults and very large larvae that fall within the same body mass range. Note, that although log heart mass increases linearly with log body mass and at approximately similar rates both before and after metamorphosis, over their entire body mass range, larvae have a smaller heart mass as a proportion of total body mass than do adults. Larvae with their smaller hearts could potentially have higher heart rates to produce the same mass-specific cardiac output as an adult, although such measurements have not been made. Alternatively, larvae may have a lower cardiac output. In either event, there is no single set of values for cardiac variables that can adequately describe the species *R. catesbeiana* through all its developmental stages.

A second example is drawn from our investigations of development, allometry, and heart function in the domestic mouse, *Mus musculus* (Hou and Burggren, 1989). Before weaning (1 g up to about 10 g), heart rate increases with increasing body mass, counter to the trend that would be predicted solely on the basis of interspecific scaling. Yet, after weaning, heart rate begins to decline with increasing body mass at the rate predicted from allometric relationships. Clearly, a rather marked change in development of heart rate is associated with the transition to maturity in *M. musculus*. Measurement of heart rate over a narrow body mass representing a particular developmental stage does not allow informed conclusions about cardiac physiology and its possible role in adaptation to a particular environment.

The important point emerging from both of these studies is that quantitative changes in important physiological or anatomical traits can be associated with development, completely independently of changes that might be induced by natural selection by environmental factors.

### Qualitative

Immature individuals may possess completely different physiological mechanisms compared with those in adults (e.g., branchial versus pulmonary oxygen uptake in some amphibians). By studying only the adult form, we risk missing altogether important mechanisms for surviving environmental challenge. For example, in early larvae of the teleost *Monopterus albus,* the pectoral fins generate a flow of water over the body surface from head to tail, whereas the direction of capillary blood flow in the skin is in the opposite direction (Liem, 1981; Fig. 4). As Liem (1981) states, ". . . The larva as a whole is a functional analogue of a fish gill lamella." The cutaneous gas exchange organ (the major gas exchange organ in this developmental stage) thus operates as a countercurrent exchanger, reaping the increased efficiency of gas exchange inherent in this configuration of blood and water flow (see Chap. 5). Presumably, this physiological arrangement helps larval *Monopterus* to survive aquatic hypoxia, common in its natural habitat. Adult *Monopterus* show no similar arrangement of water and blood flow, this pattern having been lost during further development. The adults develop the ability to breathe air, however, and circumvent the effects of aquatic hypoxia in a manner completely different from the larvae. Obviously, neither a single description of countercurrent cutaneous exchange in the larvae or of air breathing in the adult will adequately describe the physiological adaptation to hypoxia in this species.

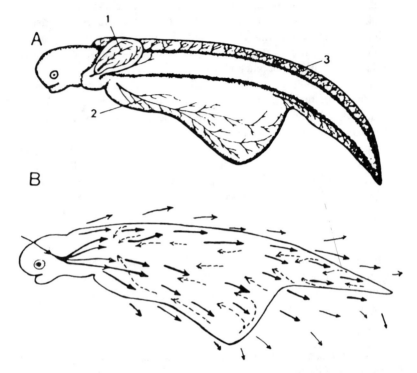

**Figure 4**  Countercurrent gas exchange in the larva of the air-breathing teleost *Monopterus albus:* (A) Diagram showing the large vascular pectoral fins (1), the well-developed respiratory capillaries on the yolk sac (2), and the unpaired median fins (3). (B) The direction of water flow (heavy arrows) and blood flow (dashed arrows) evident when the oxygen level in water falls below 40% air equilibrium. (From Liem, 1981.)

## III. Ontogeny of Cardiac Physiology in Amphibians: A Case Study

The preceding theoretical points emphasizing the importance of an ontogenetic perspective can be amply illustrated using the case study of the development of amphibian cardiac physiology. The ontogeny of the cardiac anatomy of lower vertebrates has been investigated for literally hundreds of years, and it forms a significant part of a classic (and immense) literature on embryological development. Unfortunately, our knowledge of how *physiology* changes with heart development lags far behind our understanding of how *anatomy* changes, and is rudimentary and fragmented at best. Important observations certainly have been made (e.g., Millard, 1945; Adolph and Ferrari, 1968; Heath, 1980; Feder,

1985; Malvin and Heisler, 1988), but infrequently is the cardiac physiology of a particular species examined in the context of a complete (for even partial) range of developmental stages of a particular species; nor is the anatomical literature of great use. Although many critical insights into function can be gained from the study of structure, inferring physiology from anatomy is quite dubious for the cardiovascular system, especially in lower vertebrates in which intracardiac shunts and multiple systemic arches can generate extremely complex physiological conditions (see Johansen and Burggren, 1985). Thus, the comparatively large amount of anatomical information on cardiac development is of limited use in interpreting physiological function. Consequently, we still know surprisingly little about the physiological development of the heart in lower vertebrates (Burggren and Pinder, 1991).

As indicated in the foregoing, natural selection acts on all developmental stages (although not necessarily equally), and selection pressures leading to the evolution of complex physiological traits are not any more or less likely to occur in adults, compared with the less-developed stages. Nowhere is this more evident than in a study of the cardiac physiology of anuran amphibians, for which the data that will now be discussed indicate that the larval forms possess physiological regulatory mechanisms of equal, if not greater, "complexity" than in the adult forms.

## A. Cardiac Frequency and Development

Studies focusing on ontogenetic changes in heart rate ($f_H$) have been completed for two species of anuran amphibians, the bullfrog, *Rana catesbeiana,* and the coqui, *Eleutherodactylus coqui. R. catesbeiana* is a temperate frog that lays aquatic eggs, and leaves water only for brief periods to bask. *Eleutherodactylus coqui* is a neotropical anuran from Puerto Rico. It has a most interesting life history in that the female lays large, terrestrial eggs that are guarded by the male until hatching. Importantly, the coqui is a direct-developing anuran that hatches as a miniature adult (Townsend and Stewart, 1985). As for almost all vertebrates, changes in development and body mass are almost inextricably entwined in both *R. catesbeiana* and *E. coqui* (see foregoing), and it is beyond the scope of this essay to interpret in full the observed changes in $f_H$. However, comparison of developmental changes in heart rate of these two species (Fig. 5) makes two obvious points:

1. Changes in heart rate during development in a single species are complex and not intuitively obvious from patterns of organogenesis or from an ecological or energetic perspective.
2. Changes in heart rate during development differ greatly between species—there is no "anuran" pattern. (If one insists on using the misleading term "representative" to describe any anuran, then surely *E.*

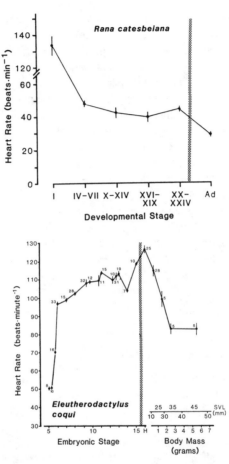

**Figure 5**   Resting heart rate (23–25°C) in the bullfrog *Rana catesbeiana* (upper panel) and the Puerto Rican anuran *Eleutherodactylus coqui* (lower panel), as a function of development. Mean values ± 1 SE are indicated for both species. For each species, heart rate data begin with the developmental stage in which the heart first begins. The vertical hatched bar indicates the point of development of the air-breathing adult morph. Townsend–Stewart stages were used for *E. coqui*, with Taylor–Kollros stages used for *R. catesbeiana*. Combined data are shown for mature adult bullfrogs (70–400 g), whereas data for adult *E. coqui* of several sizes are indicated. (Data for *R. catesbeiana*, modified from Burggren and Doyle, 1986a; for *E. coqui* from Burggren et al., 1990.)

*coqui* is far more representative of anurans than is any ranid frog. *Eleutherodactylus* is one of the largest vertebrate genera, with over 400 named species.)

If one is attempting to examine physiological adaptations to a particular set of environmental conditions, and if those studies include consideration of cardiovascular physiology, then, clearly, one might come to quite different conclusions, depending upon which developmental stages are considered. In *E. coqui*, for example, heart rate (and cardiac output?) falls dramatically with a relatively modest increase in adult size. Conclusions about the ability of the cardiovascular system to transport oxygen or about blood circulation times, for example, might be quite different if one were using a base heart rate of 130 versus 80 beats · min⁻¹.

## B. Ontogeny of Cardiac Regulation

### Extrinsic and Intrinsic Regulation

In spite of considerable information on extrinsic (i.e., neural and hormonal) regulation of cardiac function in adult amphibians (Shelton and Boutilier, 1982; West and Burggren, 1984; Bagshaw, 1985; Van Vliet and West, 1987), the ontogeny of extrinsic cardiac regulation in amphibians has received little attention. This is somewhat surprising, given the prominent role that studies of the amphibian nervous and endocrine systems have played in the general field of vertebrate development (Gilbert and Frieden, 1981; see Fox, 1984).

Studies, to date, have focused on the bullfrog, *R. catesbeiana*, and have concentrated almost exclusively on the regulation of heart rate. Newly hatched larvae show very little spontaneous change in heart rate (<3–5% change), and neither voluntary nor forced activity produce any change in heart rate (Burggren and Doyle, 1986b). These data indicate that the heart of a newly hatched larva is not neurally or hormonally regulated, and that the heart comes under control by these systems only after further larval development.

The results of experiments designed to determine the extent of sympathetic and parasympathetic (vagal) tone in resting animals are indicated in the upper panel of Figure 6. Blockade of β-receptors by propranolol causes no increase in resting $f_H$ in any developmental stage, indicating that there is no sympathetic tone at rest. Blockade of muscarinic cholinergic receptors with atropine has no effect in early larval stages, but in later larval stages, heart rate ($f_H$) increases following cholinergic blockade, indicating that resting heart rate reflects a vagal tone in these later larval stages. The vagal tone at rest thus appears midway through larval development.

Following on the theme developed earlier in this section, however, the onset of vagal tone midway through larval life does not set the stage for the

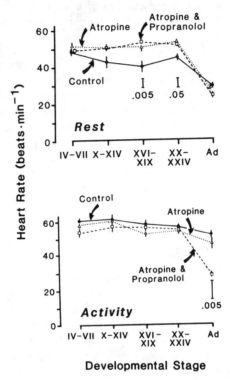

**Figure 6**  Heart rate at rest (upper panel) and following induced activity (lower panel) in *Rana catesbeiana* as a function of Taylor–Kollros developmental stage. Mean values ± 1 SE are shown for control conditions and after cholinergic and β-adrenergic blockade by atropine and propranolol, respectively. The significance level for ANOVAs between treatment effects within a developmental stage are shown if $p < 0.05$. The vertical bars represent the minimum significant difference (MSD) for unplanned multiple comparisons, which is the amount by which any two mean values for a developmental stage must differ for the difference to be significant. (Modified from Burggren and Doyle, 1986a.)

appearance of new and "better" cardiac regulatory mechanisms with further development. Indeed, injection of atropine had no effect on $f_H$ in resting adult bullfrogs, indicating that the vagal tone present at rest in larvae disappears again after metamorphosis. This, of course, does not mean that the ability to slow the heart through vagal braking disappears in adults (this is the mechanism behind diving bradycardia in adults; Lillo, 1979). Rather, it suggests that the ability to regulate heart rate through vagal braking occurs well before metamorphosis, and is retained during the developmental events leading to the adult morph.

When stimulated to show locomotor activity, all developmental stages of *R. catesbeiana,* with the sole exception of newly hatched larvae, show significant increases in $f_H$. Injections of cholinergic and β-adrenergic blockers were used to asseses the mechanism underlying these heart rate changes. In larvae, neither atropine nor propranolol blocks the activity tachycardia. Experiments involving altering the preload of the heart indicate that, even in cholinergically and β-adrenergically blocked hearts, increased venous return resulted in accelerated heart rate, presumably by the direct effect of stretching on the cardiac pacemaker. In adults, however, an activity tachycardia can result from β-adrenergic stimulation, since this response is completely eliminated by propranolol.

The observation that preload alters heart rate naturally leads to a discussion of the ontogeny of the Frank–Starling relationship in amphibian hearts. Although the ontogeny of intrinsic regulation of cardiac output has been investigated in chick embryos (Wagman and Clark, 1985), to my knowledge this has not been studied in any lower vertebrate. Unpublished observations in our laboratory (P. Kimmel and W. Burggren), however, provide circumstantial evidence that a Frank–Starling relationship does exist in larval *R. catesbeiana*. Figure 7 shows recordings of blood velocity in the central arterial vessels of stage III–V bullfrog larvae exhibiting spontaneously lengthened diastolic periods as well as spontaneous changes in heart rate. In both cases, longer diastolic periods and, presumably, the greater heart filling that results, produced a greater injection velocity in the next heart beat, a finding consistent with the occurrence of a Frank–Starling relationship. A systematic study of the ontogeny of intrinsic heart regulation would be very informative, particularly if measurements could be made in the earliest developmental stages in which the embryonic heart tube begins to undergo S-folding.

### Pharmacology of Heart Muscle

Recent studies in our laboratory have focused on the pharmacology of atrial and ventricular muscle, both in pithed animals with exposed, but otherwise intact, hearts, and in in vitro muscle strip preparations. Dose–response curves were constructed for the chronotropic effects of acetylcholine (ACh) applied directly to the exposed, but intact, heart of larval and adult bullfrogs, *R. catesbeiana* (Burggren and Doyle, 1986b). All animals used in this study were of similar body mass (10–20 g) and had very similar heart sizes, ensuring that the effective dose supplied by an aliquot of a particular drug applied externally to the heart was the same in each instance. Acetylcholine slows heart rate or stops the heart, depending upon dose, in larvae as well as in adults (Fig. 8A). The dose–response curve for this effect is shown in Figure 8B. At any given dose, the chronotropic response of the heart increases as larval development increases. After metamorphosis, however, the heart of adults is the *least sensitive to ACh* of any stage

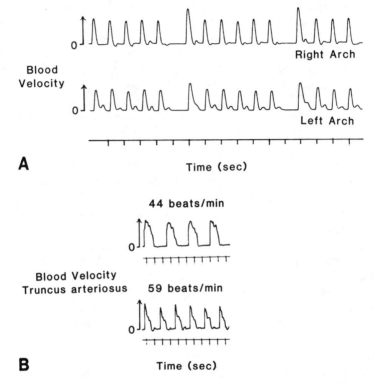

**Figure 7** The correlation between length of time for diastolic filling and blood velocity in central arterial arches in Taylor–Kollros stage III–IV larvae of the bullfrog, *Rana catesbeiana*. Panel A illustrates how a spontaneous lengthening of the diastolic period results in enhanced blood ejection in the next systole. Panel B shows the effect on blood velocity associated with a spontaneous increase in heart rate. The two recordings in panel B were taken 30-sec apart. (From P. Kimmel and W. Burggren, unpublished.)

examined. In fact, after metamorphosis, a 100-fold higher concentration of ACh is required to produce the same degree of slowing, compared with a larva immediately before metamorphosis.

A study of the inotropic responses of isolated ventricular strips from *R. catesbeiana* (S. Petrou, I. Wahlqvist, and W. Burggren, unpublished) has similarly shown that one should not assume, a priori, that adults will show the greatest sensitivity to pharmacological agents. The upper panel of Figure 9 shows the dose–response curves of ventricular strips to ACh. The inotropic pattern of change for the ventricular response to ACh is opposite that for the chronotropic

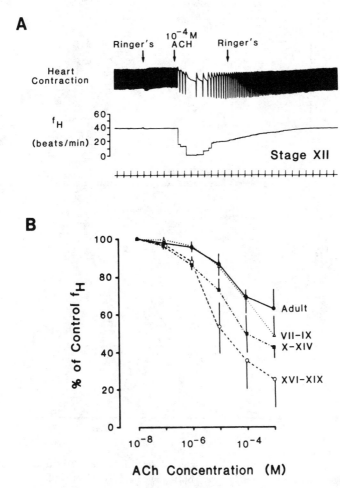

**Figure 8** Chronotropic responses to exogenously applied acetylcholine in the in situ heart of *Rana catesbeiana:* (A) Heart contraction and heart rate in a 11.8-g Taylor–Kollros stage XII larva. (B) Dose–response curves for the effect of acetylcholine upon heart rate in three larval groups and recently postmetamorphic adults. Mean values ± 1 SE are presented. (From Burggren and Doyle, 1986b.)

response. As larval development proceeds, increasingly large doses of ACh are required to decrease the strength of heart contraction. After metamorphosis, however, the heart muscle is far more sensitive to the inotropic effects of ACh than just before metamorphosis.

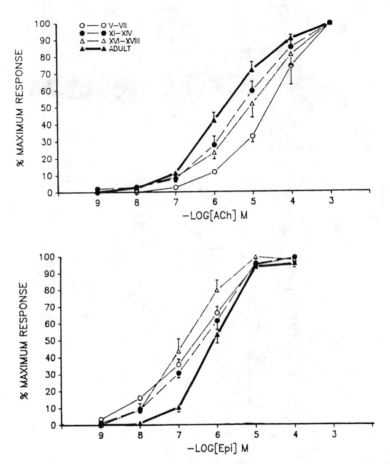

**Figure 9**  Inotropic responses of ventricular strips of *Rana catesbeiana* to acetylcholine (ACh) (upper panel) and epinephrine (Epi) (lower panel). Mean values ± 1 SD are presented. The data for adults are connected by the heavy line. (S. Petrou, I. Wahlqvist, W. Burggren, unpublished.)

Adding complexity to interpretation of developmental changes in cardiac pharmacology, the inotropic responses of the ventricular muscle of *R. cates-beiana* to epinephrine show developmental changes in sensitivity that are the opposite of those for ACh (see Fig. 9, lower panel). Whereas the inotropic responses to ACh were most sensitive in adults, the adult ventricle showed the lowest sensitivity of any stage to epinephrine, such that after metamorphosis, far higher doses of epinephrine are required to produce comparable inotropic effects. Thus, developmental changes in cardiac pharmacology are highly drug-specific.

In summary, the developmental changes in cardiac pharmacology of the heart of *R. catesbeiana* are extremely complex, with a relatively high degree of independence between 1) ontogenetic inotropic and chronotropic responses to a single drug, and 2) between inotropic responses to different drugs.

## IV. Conclusion

Providing an ontogenetic perspective to studies of physiological adaptation is important for several reasons. When we restrict our studies to adults, whether for convenience or lack of interest in immature forms, we are learning about only one segment (and often a specialized, nonrepresentative segment) of a species' existence. Natural selection acts on all developmental stages, and the most important physiological adaptations may occur in immature, rather than mature, stages. Thus, physiological studies restricted to adults may give false impressions of how a species survives environmental challenges. In fact, it is simplistic to assume that we can ever identify single physiological adaptations manifest only in adults that ensure the survival of a species. Rather, a series of adaptations, each effective at a particular developmental stage, may be responsible for the perpetuation of the species. Studies performed in isolation solely on larvae, or solely on fertilized eggs, are no more or less informative than studies solely on adults—the most useful and informative studies of physiological adaptation to the environment are performed in the context of a developmental continuum.

Amphibian cardiovascular physiology provides a useful case study with which to illustrate these points. The patterns of developmental change in heart rate are complex and show marked variation between species. Neural mechanisms regulate heart rate, at least during rest in anuran larvae—these mechanisms are in no way "inferior" to those of the adult. Moreover, intrinsic regulation (i.e., Frank–Starling mechanism) appears early in larval heart development and, thus, operates throughout development, rather than just in adults. Pharmacological studies of heart muscle indicate that the chronotropic and inotropic responses to cholinergic inhibition and adrenergic excitation change in complex ways with development, and the larval cardiac tissue, in many instances, shows greater pharmacological sensitivity to exogenously applied drugs.

In summary, both theoretical arguments based on evolutionary theory, as well as case studies of physiological development, indicate that a thorough understanding of the physiology of a species requires that the "complete species" be investigated, rather than the currently typical approach of focusing on a single stage or limited range of developmental stages.

## Acknowledgments

W. Bemis and P. Kimmel provided many valuable comments on the first draft of this manuscript. The author was supported by NSF operating grant DCB8916938.

## References

Adolph, E. F. (1979). Development of dependence on oxygen in embryo salamanders. *Am. J. Physiol.*, **236**:R282–R291.

Adolph, E. F., and Ferrari, J. M. (1968). Adaptation to temperature in heart rates of salamander larvae before cardiac innervation. *Am. J. Physiol.*, **215**:124–126.

Anderson, J. D., Hassinger, D. D., and Dalrymple, G. H. (1971). Natural mortality of eggs and larvae of *Ambystoma t. tigrinum*. *Ecology*, **52**:1107–1112.

Bagshaw, R. J. (1985). Evolution of cardiovascular baroreceptor control. *Physiol. Rev.*, **60**:121–162.

Burggren, W. W. (1984). Transition of respiratory processes during amphibian metamorphosis: From egg to adult. In *Respiration in Embryonic Vertebrates*. Edited by R. Seymour. The Hague, Junk, pp. 31–53.

Burggren, W. W., and Bemis, W. E. (1990). Studying physiological evolution: Paradigms and pitfalls. In *Evolutionary Innovations: Patterns and Processes*. Edited by M. Nitecki and D. Nitecki. Oxford, Oxford University Press.

Burggren, W. W., and Doyle, M. (1986a). Ontogeny of heart rate regulation in the bullfrog, *Rana catesbeiana*. *Am. J. Physiol.*, **251**:R231–R239.

Burggren, W. W., and Doyle, M. (1986b). The action of acetylcholine upon heart rate changes markedly with development in bullfrogs. *J. Exp. Zool.*, **240**:137–140.

Burggren, W. W., Dupre, R. K., and Wood, S. C. (1987). Allometry of red cell oxygen binding and hematology in larvae of the tiger salamander, *Ambystoma tigrinum*. *Respir. Physiol.*, **70**:73–84.

Burggren, W. W., Infantino, R. L., Jr., and Townsend, D. S. (1990). Developmental changes in cardiac and metabolic physiology of the direct-developing tropical frog *Eleutherodactylus coqui*. *J. Exp. Biol.* **152**:129–147.

Burggren, W., and Pinder, A. (1991). Ontogeny of cardiovascular and respiratory physiology in lower vertebrates. *Annu. Rev. Physiol.* **53**:107–135.

Calder, W. A. III (1984). *Size, Function and Life History*. Cambridge, Mass., Harvard University Press.

Detwiler, S. R., and Copenhaver, W. M. (1940). The developmental behaviour of *Ambystoma* eggs subjected to atmospheres of low oxygen and high carbon dioxide. *Am. J. Anat.*, **66**:393–410.

Feder, M. E. (1985). Effect of developmental stage and body size on oxygen consumption of anuran larvae: A reappraisal. *J. Exp. Zool.*, **220**:33–42.

Fox, H. (1984). *Amphibian Morphogenesis*. Clifton, N. J., Humana Press.

Gilbert, L. I., and Frieden, E., eds. (1981). *Metamorphosis—A Problem in Developmental Biology*. New York, Plenum Press.

Gregg, J. R. (1962). Anaerobic glycolysis in amphibian development. *Biol. Bull.*, **123**:555–561.

Heath, A. G. (1980). Cardiac responses of larval and adult tiger salamanders to submergence and emergence. *Comp. Biochem. Physiol.*, **65A**:439–444.

Hou, P.-C. L., and Burggren, W. W. (1989). Differential contributions of development and body mass changes to heart rate and hematology in the mouse *Mus musculus*. *Respir. Physiol.*, **78**:265–280.

Johansen, K. (1970). Air breathing in fishes. In *Fish Physiology*, Vol. 4. Edited by W. S. Hoar and D. J. Randall. New York, Academic Press.

Johansen, K., and Burggren, W., eds. (1985). *Cardiovascular Shunts: Phylogenetic, Ontogenetic and Clinical Aspects*. Copenhagen, Munksgaard.

Liem, K. F. (1981). Larvae of air-breathing fishes as countercurrent flow devices in hypoxic environments. *Science*, **211**:1177–1179.

Lillo, R. S. (1979). Autonomic cardiovascular control during submergence and emergence in bullfrogs. *Am. J. Physiol.*, **237**:R210–R216.

Malvin, G. M., and Heisler, N. (1988). Blood flow patterns in the salamander, *Ambystoma tigrinum*, before, during and after metamorphosis. *J. Exp. Biol.*, **137**:53–74.

Millard, N. (1945). The development of the arterial system of *Xenopus laevis*, including experiments on the destruction of larval aortic arches. *Trans. R. Soc. S. Afr.*, **30**:217–234.

Peters, R. H. (1983). *The Ecological Implications of Body Size*. Cambridge, Cambridge University Press.

Rose, F. L., Armentrout, D., and Roper, P. (1971). Physiological responses of paedogenic *Ambystoma tigrinium* to acute anoxia. *Herpetologica*, **27**:101–107.

Schmidt-Nielsen, K. (1984). *Scaling: Why is Animal Size So Important?* Cambridge, Cambridge University Press.

Seymour, R. S., ed. (1984). *Respiration and Metabolism of Embryonic Vertebrates*. The Hague, Junk.

Shelton, G., and Boutilier, R. G. (1982). Apnoea in amphibians and reptiles. *J. Exp. Biol.*, **100**:245–273.

Townsend, D. S., and Stewart, M. M. (1985). Direct development in *Eleutherodactylus coqui* (Anura: Leptodactylidae): A staging table. *Copeia*, **1985**:423–436.

Van Vliet, B. N., and West, N. H. (1987). Response characteristics of pulmocutaneous arterial baroreceptors in the toad *Bufo marinus*. *J. Physiol.*, **338**:55–70.

Wagman, A., and Clark, E. B. (1985). Frank–Starling relationship in the developing cardiovascular system. In *Cardiac Morphogenesis*. Edited by V. Ferresn, G. Rosenquist, and C. Weinstein. New York, Elsevier. pp. 245–252.

Weigmann, D. L., and Altig, R. (1975). Anaerobic glycolysis in two larval amphibians. *J. Herpetol.*, **9**:355–357.

West, N. H., and Burggren, W. W. (1984). Factors influencing pulmonary and cutaneous arterial blood flow in the toad, *Bufo marinus*. *Am. J. Physiol.*, **247**:R884–R894.

# Part Four

## BLOOD GAS TRANSPORT

# 13

## Molecular Strategies in the Adaptation of Vertebrate Hemoglobin Function

ROY E. WEBER

Institute of Zoology and Zoophysiology
University of Aarhus
Aarhus, Denmark

## I. Introduction

Although the uptake and internal transport of $O_2$ in animals is supported by a wide range of organismic, organ, and cellular functions (ventilation of the gas exchange surfaces, blood circulation, and erythrocytic metabolism and ion transport), tissue $O_2$ delivery ultimately depends on the properties of the hemoglobin (Hb) molecules, and the physicochemical conditions under which they operate in life.

Hemoglobin is exquisitely engineered to bridge wide and independent variations in $O_2$ tensions between the sites of $O_2$ loading and unloading. Knowledge of the molecular mechanisms basic to its function and adaptive variation in vertebrates have increased greatly following the pioneering x-ray diffraction studies of Perutz and co-workers at Cambridge, and significant new advances may be expected with the increasing use of molecular engineering as a tool to probe intramolecular stereochemical reactions.

This essay focuses on the genetically determined basis for differences in Hb function (i.e., the structural constraints that determine intrinsic $O_2$ affinity, and its sensitivity to modulating cofactors), with particular reference to the Hb systems of fish living in hypoxic water, birds that tolerate extreme altitudes, and embryonic and fetal mammals, that lack direct access to atmospheric $O_2$. In addition to being adaptive to decreases in ambient $O_2$ availability, species-specific differences in Hb structure and function may form preadaptations to *internal* hypoxia resulting from such (patho)physiological perturbations as impaired gas exchange at the respiratory surfaces, excessive metabolic demand for $O_2$, extreme unevenness in the relationship between ventilation and perfusion of the respiratory organ, excessive shunting of venous blood bypassing the respiratory exchange surfaces, and reductions in the amount of functional circulating Hb (cf. Hughes, 1973). A guiding principle in interspecific functional–structural correlations is the observation that most amino acid substitutions are functionally neutral; that is, that macromolecular adaptations to new stimuli involve only a few exchanges at key positions in the protein moiety (cf. Kimura, 1979; Perutz, 1983). The short-term, intraspecific adaptations in Hb function (which primary involve changes in red cell pH or in the abundance or type of erythrocytic cofactors that modulate Hb–$O_2$ affinity), have been dealt with in other recent studies (cf. Powers, 1980; Wood, 1980; Weber, 1982; Nikinmaa, 1986; Weber and Jensen, 1988; Wells et al., 1989).

## II.  Physicochemical Basis for Molecular Adaptations

### A.  Quaternary Structure

Vertebrate Hbs are tetramers consisting of two $\alpha$- and two $\beta$-polypeptide chains, which in human Hb A consist of 141 and 146 amino acid residues, respectively. The $\alpha$- and $\beta$-chains are composed, respectively, of seven and eight helical segments (labeled A to H) that are interrupted by nonhelical segments (AB, BC, etc.) and preceded and followed by two others (NA and HC), which form the corners and cause the characteristic tertiary folding of the chains. For simplicity, the amino acid residues associated with specific functions will be identified by their position in the chain (counting from the $NH_2$-terminus), rather than their helical notation (see Fig. 1), although this might appear to give inconsistencies because of interspecific variation in the number of residues. Thus, HC1, is labeled $\beta$143 in humans and $\beta$144 in carp in which the $\beta$-chains have 147 amino acids.

The molecule may be viewed as a system of interacting dimers $\alpha_1\beta_1$ and $\alpha_2\beta_2$ (cf. Ackers and Smith, 1985), each of which forms a tightly cohering unit owing to numerous hydrogen bonds (between *N* and *O* atoms, through an intermediate *H* atom), whereas the dimer pairs are loosely connected by salt bridges (between positively charged nitrogen and negatively charged oxygen atoms). Oxygen binding is associated with small changes in the tertiary structure near the hemes that break or weaken interchain connections and cause a large shift in quaternary structure (from the "tense" to the "relaxed" states) as one dimer rotates relative to the other. This T→R conformational change is associated largely with changes at three intersubunit interfaces: $\alpha^1\beta^2$, $\alpha^2\beta^1$, and $\alpha^1\alpha^2$ (since $\alpha^1\beta^1$ and $\alpha^2\beta^2$ dimers cohere relatively tightly and the two $\beta$-chains do not touch). The T structure has low affinity for $O_2$ and a high one for protons, $Cl^-$, organic phosphates, and $CO_2$, whereas these affinities are reversed in the R state.

## B. Intramolecular Interactions

Physiological $O_2$ binding by Hb is a function of 1) its "intrinsic $O_2$ affinity" (that measured in vitro in the isolated protein under standardized physicochemical conditions), and 2) its sensitivity to modulating cofactors. Oxygen binding is controlled by two key intramolecular mechanisms: homo- and heterotropic interactions.

Homotropic interactions occurring between the $O_2$-binding hemes are basic to the sigmoid nature of the $O_2$ equilibrium curve, and increase tissue $O_2$ delivery by raising the $O_2$ capacitance (Ca − Cv)/(Pa − Pv); that is the arteriovenous (a–v) $O_2$ content difference for a given a–v $Po_2$ difference. Expressing cooperativity, the sigmoid shape of the curve is a direct manifestation of the differences in Gibbs free energies for the successive oxygenation steps of the tetrameric Hb molecule (cf. Ackers and Smith, 1985).

Heterotropic interactions occurring between different ligand-binding sites are generally antagonistic. The best-known example is the Bohr effect (inverse relationship between proton and $O_2$ binding), which enhances $O_2$ unloading from the blood in the acid tissues and is mediated by oxygenation-induced changes in the protein conformation that modulate the pK values of acid groups, resulting in proton dissociation. The reducing effects of anionic organic phosphates on Hb–$O_2$ affinity in vertebrate red cells depend on homologous reciprocating interactions between the hemes and cationic phosphate-binding sites. As reviewed (cf. Bartlett, 1980; Weber and Wells, 1989), the major phosphate cofactors are 2,3-diphosphoglycerate (DPG) in mammals, inositol pentaphosphate (Ins-$P_5$) in birds, and adenosine triphosphate (ATP) in ectothermic vertebrates, whereas some fish species additionally exhibit high erythrocytic levels of other nucleoside triphosphates (NTP), chiefly guanosine triphosphate (GTP).

## C. Ligand Binding Sites

In human Hb A, which forms a convenient basis for comparative studies, only a few amino acids are involved in binding allosteric ligands (Perutz, 1983; Figs. 1 and 2). The *DPG* binds to seven positively charged amino acid residues that face the cavity between the two $\beta$-chains, namely, Val-1, His-2, and His-143 of both $\beta$-chains and Lys-82 of one $\beta$-chain. *Chloride*, which similarly depresses $O_2$ affinity binds at $\alpha$1 Val (also interacting with $\alpha$131 Ser) and at $\beta$82 Lys (also interacting with $\beta$1 Val; cf. Riggs, 1988). *Protons* bind mainly at the $NH_2$-terminal valines (-$NH_2$ groups) of the $\alpha$-chains, and the COOH-terminal histidine

**α-CHAINS**

```
                          C H Cl^a
                          \ | /
Human Hb A          Val - Leu - Ser --------- Ser - Lys - Tyr - Arg     Braunitzer, Rudloff and Hilschmann (1963)
Numerical position   1     2     3            138   139   140   141
Helical site        NA1   NA2   A1             H1   HC1   HC2   HC3

carp              Ac-Ser - Leu - Ser --------- Glu - Lys - Tyr - Arg    Takeshita et al. (1984)
                                               140   141   142   143
                                                H1
```

**β-CHAINS**

```
                  C D^2 H^&     D^2 H^&           D H Cl^b          D^2 H^&*                  H
                   \ | /         \ | /             \ | /             \ | /
Human Hb A          Val - His - Leu -------- Lys ----- Cys ------- His - Lys - Tyr - His    Braunitzer, Rudloff and Hilschmann (1963)
Numerical position   1     2     3            82       93           143   144   145   146
Helical site        NA1   NA2   A1            EF6      F9           H21   HC1   HC2   HC3
```

**anodal fish Hbs**

```
                  A G^2   A G                                      R            A G
                   \ /     \ /                                                   \ /
Carp                Val - Glu - Trp -- Lys --- Ser ------- Arg - Gln - Tyr - His   Grujic-Injac et al. (1980)
                                                           144   145   146   147

trout Hb IV         Val - Asp - Trp --- Lys ---- Ser ------- Arg - Gln - Tyr - His   Petruzelli et al. (1984)

eel 'fast' Hb       Val - Glu - Thr ------------------------------- His   Amano, Hashimoto and Matsuura (1972a, b)
```

**cathodal fish Hbs**

```
trout Hb I          Val - Glu - Trp -- Lys ---- Ala ------- Ser - Arg - Tyr - Phe   Barra et al. (1983)
                                                            143   144   145   146

eel 'slow' Hb       Val - Gln - Ser ----------------------------- Arg   Amano, Hashimoto and Matsuura (1972a, b)
```

**bird Hb A**

```
                    I^2   I^2         I^2      I^2   I^2        I^2
                     |     |           |        |     |          |
chicken             Val - His - Trp -- Lys -- Arg - His ---- Arg - Lys - Tyr - His   cf. Kleinschmidt and Sgouros (1987)
                     1     2     3     82    135   139        143   144   145   146

Ostrich             Val - Gln - Trp -- Arg -- His -- Arg ---- Arg - Lys - Tyr - His   cf. Kleinschmidt and Sgouros (1987)
```

**Figure 1** Major sites for binding DPG (D), Bohr protons (H), $CO_2$ (C), and chloride ions (Cl) in the α- and β-chains of human Hb A, and corresponding amino acid residues in fish and bird Hbs, indicating binding sites for ATP (A) and GTP (G) in carp Hb and for Ins-P$_5$ (I) in chicken Hb. [&]Proton binding in the presence of DPG, [*]contributes to the acid Bohr effect in the absence of DPG, [2]phosphate binding to both β-chains, [a]also interacts with α131-serine, [b]also interacts with β1-valine. [R]bonding associated with the Root effect

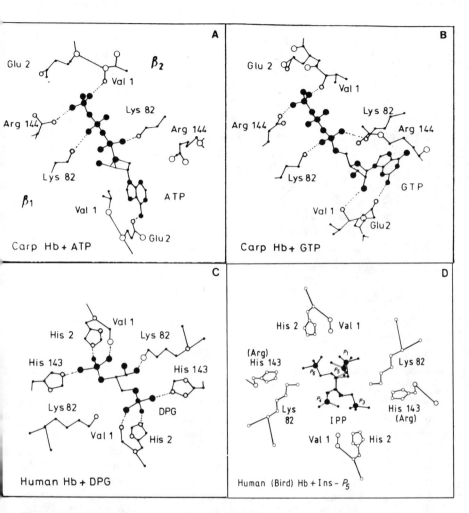

**Figure 2** Binding sites of (A) ATP and (B) GTP to carp hemoglobin, and (C) DPG and (D) Ins-P₅ to human Hb A. Moreover, (D) shows the amino acid substitutions in chicken Hb (in parenthesis), in which Ins-P₅ faces the eight basic amino acid residues shown, in addition to four from Arg-135 and His-139 (not shown). [Modified after Gronenborn et al., 1984 (A and B); Arnone, 1972 (C); Arnone and Perutz, 1974 (D). C and D printed by permission from Nature, **249**, p. 34, Copyright © 1974, Macmillan Magazines Ltd.]

residues (imidazole groups) of the β-chains (accounting for about 30 and 50%, respectively, of the Bohr effect at alkaline pH), although other of the 22 surface histidines of the tetramer may make minor contributions to the Bohr effect, depending on the ionic environment (Riggs, 1988). *Carbon dioxide* binding (as carbamino compounds) occurs at the $NH_2$-terminal valines of both chains.

Binding of different ligands to the same residues results in various interacting effects. As expected, anion binding at cationic sites increases with decreasing pH and, thus, raises the measured Bohr effect (insofar as the ligand decreases $O_2$ affinity). Because it is involved in $Cl^-$ and DPG binding, β82 Lys makes a $Cl^-$-dependent contribution to the Bohr effect in the absence of DPG (Perutz et al., 1980). In the presence of DPG, Bohr protons also bind at β2 His and β143 His, and at pH below approximately 6.5, proton binding at β143 His contributes to the reversed, acid Bohr effect.

Obviously, amino acid substitutions at interchain contacts and ligand-binding sites are of particular interest in tracing the molecular mechanisms of species-specific Hb adaptation.

### D. Multiplicity

Although Hb A forms more than 92% of Hb in adult humans (cf. Imai, 1982), most other vertebrates have multiple genes coding for several different globin types. This results in different "isohemoglobin" components (encountered in the same individuals) or "allohemoglobins" (occurring in different subspecific taxa of the same species). The number and proportions of isoHbs may vary with developmental stage (as exemplified by the successive preponderance of embryonic, fetal, and adult Hbs in mammals) and acclimation history, whereby changes in the relative abundance of Hb components form a potential mechanism for intraspecific adaptation.

It should, however, be borne in mind that multiple tetrameric components occurring in in vivo mixtures (the same subcellular compartments) may form hybrid molecules (as observed in bullfrog hemoglobins; Tamm and Riggs, 1984) that may not be evident in separatory procedures. These and other biological implications of Hb multiplicity are reviewed separately (Weber, 1990).

### III. Molecular Adaptations to Hypoxia

### A. Fish

Fish Hbs exhibit large variations in intrinsic $O_2$ affinities and cofactor sensitivities, both interspecifically and among multiple Hbs, which now will be related to structural differences. Whereas relatively little is known about the molecular basis for variations in intrinsic $O_2$ affinities, plausible explanations exist for differences in ligand sensitivities.

### Allosteric Effects

The use of ATP as allosteric modulator in fish (compared with DPG in humans) correlates with β-chain substitutions at NA2 (β2 His→Glu/Asp, which denotes the substitution of the second amino acid of the β-chains, which is histidine in humans, by glutamic or aspartic acids in fish) and HC1 (β143 His→β144 Arg). Making these exchanges in models of human deoxyHb produces a constellation of charged groups that are stereochemically complementary to strain-free ATP (Perutz and Brunori, 1982). The fact that GTP depresses the $O_2$ affinity of carp and eel Hb about 1.7–2.0 times as much as ATP, reflects additional hydrogen bonding between GTP and Hb (Weber et al., 1975; Weber and Lykkeboe, 1978) that increases the free energy contributed to the stability of the T structure by 1.2–1.6 kcal (calculated as RT 2.303ΔlogL, where Δlog L = 4Δlog $P_{50}$, and L is the allosteric constant; cf. Gronenborn et al., 1984). This value is consistent with modeling that shows five hydrogen bonds between ATP and carp deoxyHb (at $β^21$ Val, $β^12$ Glu, and $β^1144$ Arg and with $β^{1+2}82$ Lys), and an unique additional bond formed with GTP (at $β_11$ Val) when rotated 180° about its long axis, compared with bound ATP (Gronenborn et al., 1984; see Fig. 2).

As with human Hb A, increases in phosphate/Hb ratio and protein concentration decrease $O_2$ affinity of fish Hb by increasing the allosteric constant L (the ratio between molecules in the T and R states) and reducing $K_T$ (the association equilibrium constant of the deoxygenated T state), without significantly affecting the affinity constant of the R state, $K_R$ (Fig. 3; Weber et al., 1987a). At high ligand concentrations NTP and protons also decrease $K_R$ in tench Hb. Consistent with its greater hydrogen bonding, GTP exerts a greater effect than ATP on $O_2$ affinity of both the T and R states (Weber et al., 1987a).

Given that key criteria for the Root effect (a reduction in $O_2$-carrying capacity of acidified blood that promotes the secretion of $O_2$ into the swim bladder and eyes of fish; Ingerman and Terwilliger, 1982) are loss of cooperativity and suppression of the T→R transition at low pH, the decreases in $K_R$ observed at high proton, ATP, and GTP concentrations (see Fig. 3) provides a control mechanism for NTP enhancement of the Root effect, and the greater effect of GTP than ATP (Weber and De Wilde, 1975; Vaccaro Torracca et al., 1977; Pelster and Weber, 1990).

### Functional Heterogeneity

Teleost isoHbs exhibit either 1) similar affinities and ligand sensitivities, as in carp, plaice, and flounder, for which all Hbs are electrophoretically anodic (Gillen and Riggs, 1972; Weber and De Wilde, 1976); or 2) pronounced functional

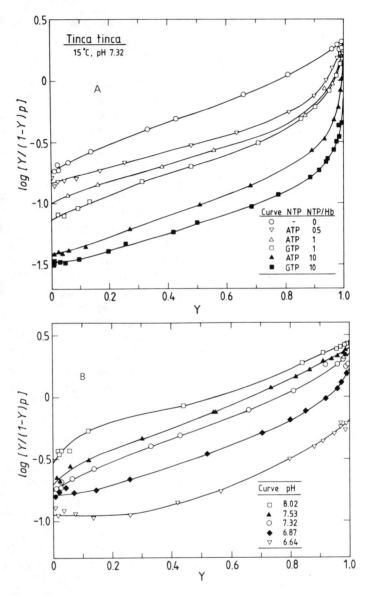

**Figure 3**   Modified Scatchard plots (on which Y = fractional $O_2$ saturation, P = $O_2$ tension) depicting the effects of (A) different molar ratios of ATP/Hb and GTP/Hb, and (B) pH, on $O_2$ equilibria of solutions of tench Hb at 15°C. The intercepts with the left and right ordinates reflect $O_2$ affinities of the deoxygenated and oxygenated Hbs, respectively; the difference is a measure of the free energy of oxygenation (cf. Imai, 1982). For further explanation see text. (After Weber et al., 1987a).

differences, with cathodic components having small or reversed Bohr effects and anodic ones exhibiting normal pH sensitivity, as found in salmon, trout, and eels (cf. Hashimoto et al., 1960; Binotti et al., 1971; Weber et al., 1975). The physiological significance of functional differentiation may be that the high-affinity cathodic components form a (circulating) $O_2$ reservoir, or that they function as an emergency $O_2$ transporter under ambient hypoxia (cf. Hashimoto et al., 1960) or under activity-induced acidosis (Powers, 1972) when $O_2$ binding to the pH-sensitive anodic components is inhibited by the Bohr and Root effects. Fish isoHbs also differ in NTP effects. In trout, the cathodic component Hb I is insensitive to ATP (Brunori et al., 1975; Weber et al., 1976), whereas in eel it shows greater ATP and GTP sensitivity than the anodic components (Weber et al., 1975; Fig. 4).

The pH insensitivity of the cathodic Hbs is attributable to acetylation of the $NH_2$-terminal α-chain residue and substitution of the COOH-terminal His→Phe residue (β146 His→Phe) which are the main sites for proton binding in humans (cf. Powers 1980; see also Fig. 1). Analogously, presence of the Bohr effect in the anodic Hbs is explained by the retention of the β-chain COOH-terminal histidines.

The insensitivity of trout Hb I to organic phosphates appears to be due to substitution of only one NTP-binding site, namely β143 His→Ser, the others (Val-1, Glu-2, and Lys-82) being retained as in carp Hb (see Fig. 1). Interestingly, the greater NTP effect in cathodic eel Hb (Weber et al., 1975), correlates with the replacement of β2 Glu (in anodic eel and carp Hbs) by glutamine (Amano, 1972a,b), suggesting greater oxygenation-linked phosphate binding to latter residue.

### The Root Effect

Differences in the expression of the Root effect in different Hbs can be similarly related to primary structures. The pH dependence of the Root effect obviously suggests involvement of the proton-binding histidine residues. Indeed, removal of the (COOH-terminal) β147 His reduces the Bohr and Root effects of carp Hb (Parkhurst et al., 1983). Perutz and Brunori (1982) proposed that the Root effect can be linked to a single replacement of β93 Cys by serine, which forms hydrogen bonds that stabilize the T structure, with COO⁻ and —NH groups of β147 His (see Fig. 1). This is compounded by the fact that a salt bridge between the COOH-terminal histidine and β144 Lys, which increases affinity by stabilizing the R structure in mammalian Hbs, cannot form in fish Root-effect Hbs owing to the β144 Lys→(145)Gln substitution (see Fig. 1). Moreover, at low pH, a salt bridge may be formed between β147 His and β94 Glu that decreases $O_2$ affinity in the R as well as the T state (Perutz and Brunori, 1982), which is consistent with the depressant effect of low pH on $K_R$ in fish Hbs (Chien and Mayo, 1980; Weber et al.,

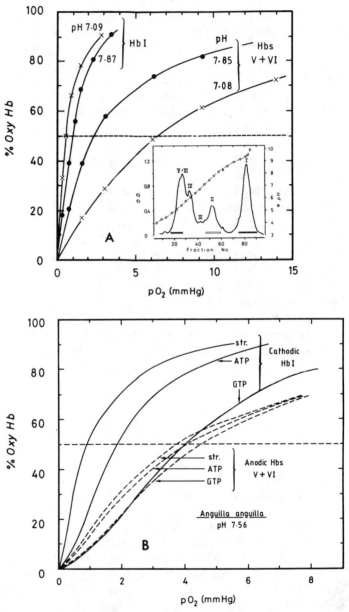

**Figure 4** Effects of pH (A) and saturating concentrations of ATP and GTP (B) on $O_2$ equilibria of anodic (Hb I) and cathodic (Hb V + VI) Hb components from the eel *Anquilla anguilla* (separated by isoelectric focusing as shown in inset). Temperature, 20°C; ATP/Hb and GTP/Hb ratio, 1.8. (Modified from Weber et al., 1975.)

1987a). That other as yet unknown mechanisms, perhaps related to the specific tertiary and quaternary structural characteristics of teleost Hbs (Riggs, 1988), may be implicated follows from the fact that a mutant human Hb with β93 Cys→Ser substitution synthesized in *Escherichia coli,* has an essentially unchanged normal Bohr effect (Nagai et al., 1985), and that Hb of the South American lungfish *Lepidosiren* lacks a Root effect, despite having β-chains with Ser-93, Glu-94, and COOH-terminal histidine (Perutz and Brunori, 1982). However, a Root effect is expressed in hybrid Hb molecules composed of human α-chains and *Xenopus* β-chains—which do have β93 Ser (Brunori et al., 1989).

In contrast with the anodic Hbs, the cathodic components of trout and eel lack a Root effect (Itada et al., 1970; Binotti et al., 1971; Vaccaro Torracca et al., 1977; Pelster and Weber, 1990). This correlates with the presence of a COOH-terminal histidine and β93 Ser in anodic trout Hb, and in carp and goldfish Hbs (Petruzelli et al., 1984; Grujic-Injac et al., 1980; Rodewald and Braunitzer, 1984), and the replacement of these residues in trout Hb I by phenylalanine and alanine, respectively (Barra et al., 1983).

## B. Mammals

As has been well established (Bunn, 1971; Perutz, 1983), mammalian Hbs, functionally speaking, broadly fall into two groups: one with intrinsically high $O_2$ affinities that are lowered in vivo by DPG as in humans, and another with intrinsically low affinities and low sensitivities to DPG, as in ungulates and cats. Human and bovine Hbs exhibit the same $K_R$ values, but bovine Hb exhibits a lower $K_T$ value, revealing stronger constraints in the deoxy state as cause of its lower affinity.

In bovine Hb (as in other ungulates such as deer, elk, goat, sheep, and yak; see Kleinschmidt and Sgouros, 1987), decreased DPG sensitivity results from deletion of the $NH_2$-terminal residue of the β-chains, and replacement of the adjacent one (cationic β2 His in humans) by neutral methionine. Being hydrophobic, methionine avoids the solvent, and points to the interior of the β-chain, locking it in the deoxy T structure (Perutz and Imai, 1980), permanently mimicking the action of DPG. A similar effect is achieved by phenylalanine and leucine found at β2 in, respectively, cat and lemur Hbs.

Molecular structural adaptations contributing to high-altitude tolerance is illustrated in camelids. Although llama Hb exhibits low intrinsic Hb–$O_2$ affinity, its blood has a higher affinity than other, similar-sized mammals, owing to a lower DPG binding, which is explained simply by the substitution of β2 His by asparagine that has a shorter side chain that is at a greater distance from the organic phosphate (Perutz, 1983). This substitution also is expressed in the vicuna (cf. Kleinschmidt and Sgouros, 1987), which has the highest blood $O_2$ affinity of mammals thus far investigated ($P_{50}$ = 18 mm Hg; Jürgens et al., 1988).

A recent study of adult and fetal yak Hbs (Weber et al., 1988) elucidates altitudinal adaptations, which in the fetal stages, is compounded by the lack of direct access to atmospheric $O_2$. Yaks commonly have two types of α-chains ($α^I$ and $α^{II}$) that, in combination with adult and fetal β-type chains, form two fetal and two adult Hbs: $A_2$ ($α^{II}_2 β^{II}_2$), $A_1$ ($α^I_2β^{II}_2$), $F_2$ ($α^{II}_2γ_2$) and $F_1$ ($α^I_2γ_2$). Coexisting in newly born individuals, these Hbs show a cascade of $O_2$ affinities increasing from $A_2$ to $F_1$, which reflects the sequence in which the components will be deoxygenated under decreasing $Po_2$. The fetal components, moreover, exhibit lower n values, implying higher affinities than the adult components at low $Po_2$ values (as expected in the fetal circulation). The overlapping occurrence of different components in fetuses and calves predictably extends the range of $Po_2$ and pH conditions under which the blood transports $O_2$ at various altitudes.

Elaborate molecular adaptations to embryonic life are illustrated in the pig (Weber et al., 1987b), which lacks fetal Hbs, but expresses two globin genes of the α-type (α and ζ) and three of the β-type (β, ε, and γ) that combine, giving four embryonic components [Gower I (GI), Heide I (HI), Gower II (GII), and Heide II (HII)] and adult Hb A (Fig. 5). These Hbs exhibit a cascade of $O_2$-binding affinities—those with embryonic α- and β-type chains (HI and GI) showing the highest affinities, and the lowest Bohr factors and cooperativity coefficients, whereas Hb A has lowest affinity and highest Bohr and cooperativity coefficients, and Hbs HII and GII exhibit intermediate properties (see Fig. 5). Importantly, HI and GI dominate quantitatively when the embryos are 20-mm or less (crown–rump length), compensating for large diffusion distances between the maternal and fetal circulations in early embryonic development, when placental development is incomplete and their high affinities and low Bohr and cooperativity coefficients will favor maternal–embryonic $O_2$ transfer under acidotic and hypoxic conditions. The available data indicate qualitatively similar adaptations in the multiple embryonic Hbs of mouse and rabbit (Purdie et al., 1973; Jelkmann and Bauer, 1978; Wells, 1979).

How are these properties explained by molecular structure? As in human embryonic Hb (and fish Hb; see foregoing), the lower Bohr factor in the embryonic Hbs is attributable to acetylation of the α-amino groups of the ζ-chains (Weber et al., 1987b). Given that GI and GII (and HI and HII) have identical β-type chains, their markedly different $O_2$ affinities must be attributable to amino acid differences in the α-like chains (ζ and α). A prominent candidate is the α130 Ala→Thr substitution seen in the ζ-chains, which similarly is considered responsible for the high intrinsic affinity in the vicuna Hb by introducing a polar group that reduces $Cl^-$ binding at the adjacent α131-residue (Kleinschmidt et al., 1986).

## C. Birds

Birds commonly display two Hb components, a major component Hb A comprising 60–90% of the total Hb and a minor one Hb D, although some species

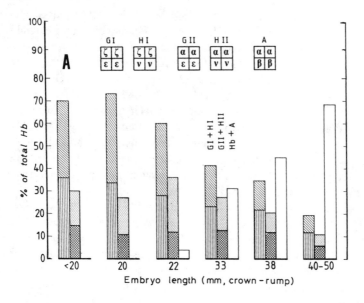

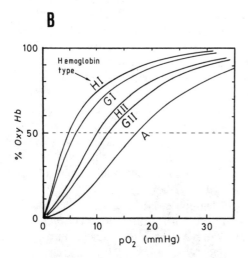

**Figure 5** (A) Chain composition and relative abundances of pig embryonic Hbs (Gower I and II and Heide I and II) and adult Hb A, as a function of body length. (B) $O_2$ equilibrium curves of Hbs GI, HI, GII, HII, and A, isolated from embryonic pigs, measured at 37°C, and pH 7.4 in the presence of excess DPG. (Modified after Weber et al., 1987b.)

only have Hb A (cf. Schnek et al., 1984). These Hbs share the same β-chain and, thereby, the same phosphate-binding site. Bearing distinct structural resemblance to avian embryonic α-type chains, the $α^D$-chains may represent persistent expression of the embryonic gene (Oberthür, et al., 1986).

Chicken and goose Hbs exhibit 12 contact points with IHP (Arnone and Perutz, 1974; see Fig. 2) [i.e., β1 Val, β2 His, β82 Lys, and β143 Arg of both β-chains (the same positions at which DPG binds in human Hb)], and two further basic residues facing the cavity between the β-chains: Arg-135 and His-139 (which substitute alanine and asparagin, respectively, in human Hb A). The introduction of four arginines at the phosphate-binding site increases the free energy for phosphate binding at high pH, reducing the pH dependence of the Bohr effect (Brygier et al., 1975).

Ostriches have a higher blood $O_2$ affinity than other birds ($P_{50}$ = 24.5 mm Hg at 37°C; Isaacks et al., 1977), which is consistent with a lower weight-specific $O_2$ demand and reduced $O_2$ unloading in tissues of large (Lutz et al., 1974) and inactive animals. The higher affinity correlates with the fact that the major erythrocytic phosphate is inositol tetraphosphate (Ins-$P_4$), which has a smaller depressant effect on Hb-$O_2$ affinity than Ins-$P_5$ (Isaacks et al., 1977). The use of Ins-$P_4$ tallies with the replacement of β2 His (a DPG- and Ins-$P_5$-binding residue in mammalian and other avian Hbs) by glutamine in ostrich and rhea (cf. Kleinschmidt and Sgouros, 1987), another large flightless bird. This replacement, however, has also been recorded in starling, tree sparrow, blackbird, and swift, predicting higher affinities in these Hbs (Nothum et al., 1989).

A beautiful example of molecular–functional differentiation is provided by the barheaded goose (*Anser indicus,* which flies at altitudes of 8800 m in migrations over Mount Everest (Swan, 1970; Hiebl et al., 1986) and the greylag goose (*A. anser*), which colonizes lower plains (although ringing experiments indicate that it also may be able to cross the Himalayas; McClure, 1974). The intrinsic $O_2$ affinity of stripped (cofactor-free) Hb is slightly higher in the former, the difference being amplified approximately tenfold in whole blood, or by Ins-$P_4$ addition (Petschow et al., 1977).

Compared with the greylag goose, Hb A of the barheaded goose reveals only four exchanges: α18 Gly→Ser, α63 Ala→Val, α119 Pro→Ala and β125 Glu→Asp, of which α119 Pro→Ala is unique among birds and mammals (Kleinschmidt and Sgouros, 1987; Wrightstone, 1988), suggesting that it explains the higher $O_2$ affinity by destabilizing the $α^1$(119)/$β^1$(55) interface.

This hypothesis was collaboratively investigated by Dr. T. Jessen and the late Professor G. Braunitzer (Max-Planck-Institute for Biochemistry, Munich), Drs. G. Fermi and J. Tame (Laboratory of Molecular Biology, Cambridge) and myself, by site-directed mutagenesis to form a mutated (α119 Pro→Ala) human Hb (expressing the mutated gene for the α-chain in *E. coli* and reconstituting the harvested α-chains with native β-chains) and functional characterization of

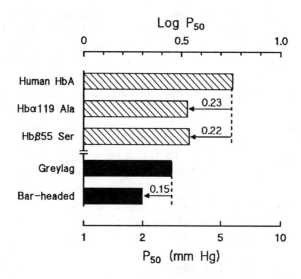

**Figure 6** Differences in intrinsic $O_2$ affinities between human native and mutant Hbs (HbA, $\alpha119$ Pro→Ala and $\beta55$ Met→Ser, respectively; hatched histograms), and between greylag and barheaded goose Hbs ($\alpha119$ Pro and Ala, respectively; solid histograms), illustrating the effect of amino acid exchanges at the $\alpha^1119$-$\beta^155$ contact. $P_{50}$ values refer to pH 7.2, 25°C and 0.1 M Cl⁻. (Data from Jessen et al., 1991 and Weber et al., unpublished.)

the recombinant tetramers. Analogously, a $\beta55$ Met→Ser mutant was created, mimicking the substitution in Hb of the South American Andean goose (*Chloephaga melanoptera*), which similarly lives at high altitudes and exhibits high $O_2$ affinities. Measured under the same conditions, log $P_{50}$ of the recombinant Hbs exceeded that of Hb A by the same ratio as observed in barheaded and greylag goose Hbs, indicating that changes at a single interchain contact ($\alpha^1119/\beta^155$) play a significant role in altitude adaptation in the barheaded and Andean geese (Jessen et al., 1991; Fig. 6). This supports recent evidence for the importance of $\alpha^1\beta^1$ contacts in determining $O_2$ affinity.

The record-holder for altitudinal tolerance is Rüppel's griffon, which has caused aircraft engine shutdown at an altitude of 11.3 km (Laybourne, 1974), where the ambient $Po_2$ is only about 36 mm Hg! Unprecedented among birds, it has four Hb components (Hbs A, A', D, and D'), all sharing the same β-chain (Hiebl et al., 1988). These isoHbs exhibit cascaded intrinsic $O_2$ affinity differences, which are amplified in the presence of IHP, and may provide an automatic division of labor in maintaining $O_2$ loading and unloading under changing altitudinal hypoxia (Weber et al., 1988).

The molecular mechanisms can similarly be traced to interchain constraints, but contacts other than in the geese appear to be implicated. The lower affinity in Hb A than in the other components is consistent with $\alpha 34$ Ile$\rightarrow$Thr which allows formation of an $\alpha^1 34$ Thr/B$^1 125$ Asp H-bond that stabilizes the T structure (depressing $O_2$ affinity). Analogously, the higher affinities in Hbs D and D' correlate with $\alpha^1 38$ Pro$\rightarrow$Gln, whereby H bonds ($\alpha^1 38$ Gln/$\beta^2 97$ His and $\alpha^1 38$ Gln/$\beta^2 99$ Asp), which stabilize the R structure and, thereby, increase affinity, can be formed (Hiebl et al., 1988). The importance of this $\alpha^1/\beta^2$ contact, which may be "the" switch between the T and R structures (Perutz, 1983), is, moreover, illustrated by the higher affinity of Hb D than Hb A in the chicken (Huisman et al., 1964), correlating with $\alpha 38$ Pro(Hb A)$\rightarrow$Gln(Hb D) exchange (cf. Kleinschmidt and Sgouros, 1987). The series formed by the Andean goose, bar-headed goose, and Rüppell's vulture illustrate how deletions of specific hydrogen bonds that constrain the Hb moiety in the deoxy state may be associated with successive 2000- to 3000-m increases in altitude tolerance (cf. Hiebl, 1987).

## IV. Concluding Remarks

Although variations in the abundance of allosteric effectors, such as protons and other ions, play an important role in tuning Hb functions to exogenous and endogenous stimuli, species-specific molecular structures set the framework within which function can be expressed. The fact that very few (of the 574 or so) amino acid residues found in vertebrate Hbs bind chemical modulators or are involved in intra- or interchain contacts is consistent with the concept that, at the molecular level, most evolutionary change and intraspecific variability are caused by random drift of mutant genes that are selectively equivalent, rather than by selection (Kimura, 1979). Moreover, this limitation of the number of functionally important sites limits the number of molecular strategies available for adaptive variation, thus explaining the convergence in molecular strategies (e.g., acetylation of the $\alpha$-chain NH$_2$-terminal residues, which is the major site for binding of Bohr protons, to reduce the Bohr effect) in phylogenetically diverse species. The conservatism is illustrated by identity of most of the residues implicated in phosphate binding in Hbs from different classes of vertebrates, despite the use of different phosphate cofactors. Also, as pointed out by Perutz (1983), despite their phylogenetic distance and some 140 amino acid exchanges per dimer, the Hbs of carp and man show only five substitutions of the 32 $\alpha^1/\beta^2$ contact points listed by Perutz and Fermi (1981).

Obviously, the molecular and functional properties of Hbs here discussed are tuned by cellular mechanisms, which include changes in erythrocytic organic phosphate levels, which modify $O_2$ affinity both by direct allosteric interaction and by changes in cellular pH (cf. Wood and Johansen, 1973; Weber and Jensen, 1988), and which are manifested even in species from stable $O_2$-rich environments (Wells et al., 1989). These molecular and cellular mechanisms are integrated with organismic functions (e.g., blood circulation and ventilation of respiratory surfaces) to secure mitochondrial $O_2$ supply and aerobic metabolism under various exogenous and endogenous stresses.

## Acknowledgment

Supported by grants from the Danish Natural Science Research Council (no. 11-7764) and NATO.

## References

Ackers, G. K., and Smith, F. R. (1985). Effects of site-specific amino acid modification on protein interactions and biological function. *Ann. Rev. Biochem.,* **54**:597–629.

Amano, H., Hashimoto, K., and Matsuura, F. (1972a). Studies on the N-terminal sequence of eel hemoglobin-I. Valyl polypeptide chain. *Bull. Jpn. Soc. Sci. Fish.,* **38**:345–350.

Amano, H., Hashimoto, K., and Matsuura, F. (1972b). Studies on the C-terminal amino acid of eel hemoglobin. *Bull. Jpn. Soc. Sci. Fish.,* **38**:351–357.

Arnone, A (1972). X-ray diffraction study of binding of 2,3-diphosphoglycerate to human deoxyhaemoglobin. *Nature,* **237**:146–149.

Arnone, A., and Perutz, M. F. (1974). Structure of inositol hexaphosphate–human deoxyhaemoglobin complex. *Nature,* **249**:34–36.

Barra, D., Petruzelli, R., Bossa, F., and Brunori, M. (1983). Primary structure of hemoglobin from trout (*Salmo irideus*). Amino acid sequence of the β chain of trout Hb I. *Biochim. Biophys. Acta,* **742**:72–77.

Bartlett, G. R. (1980). Phosphate compounds in vertebrate red blood cells. *Am. Zool.,* **20**:103–129.

Binotti, I., Giovenco, S., Giardina, B., Antonini, E., Brunori, M., and Wyman, J. (1971). Studies on the functional properties of fish hemoglobins-II. The oxygen equilibrium of isolated hemoglobin components from trout blood. *Arch. Biochem. Biophys.,* **142**:274–280.

Braunitzer, G., Rudloff, V., and Hilschmann, N. (1963). Die Analyse der α- und β-Ketten des adulten normalen Humanhämoglobins aus seinen tryptischen Spaltprodukten. *Hoppe-Seyler's Z. Physiol. Chem.,* **331**:1–32.

Brunori, M., Falcioni, G., Fortuna, G., and Giardina, B. (1975). Effect of anions on the oxygen binding properties of the hemoglobin components from trout (*Salmo irideus*). *Arch. Biochem. Biophys.,* **168**:512–519.

Brunori, M., Bellelli, A., Condo, S., Falcioni, G., and Giardia, B. (1989). Molecular aspects of the Root effect in different hemoglobins. *Soc. Exp. Biol. Edinb. Meet. Abstr.* April 1989, 91.

Brygier, J., de Bruin, S. H., van Hoof, P. M. K. B., and Rollema, H. S. (1975). The interaction of organic phosphates with human and chicken hemoglobin. *Eur. J. Biochem.,* **60**:379–383.

Bunn, H. F. (1971). Differences in the interaction of 2,3-diphosphoglycerate with certain mammalian haemoglobins. *Science,* **172:**1049–1052.

Chien, C. J. W., and Mayo, K. H. (1980). Carp hemoglobin. I. Precise oxygen equilibrium and analysis according to the models of Adair and Monod, Wyman and Changeux. *J. Biol. Chem.,* **255:**9790–9799.

Gillen R. G., and Riggs, A. (1972). Structure and function of the hemoglobins of the carp, *Cyprinus carpio. J. Biol. Chem.,* **247:**6039–6046.

Gronenborn, A. G., Clore, G. M., Brunori, M., Giardina, B., Falcioni, G., and Perutz, M. F. (1984). Stereochemistry of ATP and GTP bound to fish hemoglobins. *J. Mol. Biol.,* **178:**731–742.

Grujic-Injac, B., Braunitzer, G., and Stangl, A. (1980). Hämoglobine XXXV. Die Sequenz der $\beta_A$- und $\beta_B$-Ketten der Hämoglobine des Karpfens (*Cyprinus carpio* L.). *Hoppe-Seyler's Z. Physiol. Chem.,* **361:**1629–1639.

Hashimoto, K., Yamaguchi, Y., and Matsuura, F. (1960). Comparative studies on two hemoglobins of salmon. IV. Oxygen dissociation curve. *Bull. Jpn. Soc. Sci. Fish.,* **26:**827–834.

Hiebl, I. E. (1987). Molekulare Grundlagen der Höhenatmung der Andengans und des Sperbergeiers. Ph. D. thesis, Ludwig-Maximilians-Universität, Munich. pp. 1–93.

Hiebl, I., Schneeganss, D., and Braunitzer, G. (1986). The primary structures of the $\alpha^D$-chains of the bar-headed goose (*Anser indicus*), the greylag goose (*Anser anser*) and the Canada goose (*Branta canadensis*). *Biol. Chem. Hoppe-Seyler,* **367:**591–599.

Hiebl, I., Weber, R. E., Schneeganss, D., Kösters, J., and Braunitzer, G. (1988). Structural adaptations in the major and minor hemoglobin components of adult Rüppell's griffon (*Gyps ruepellii,* Aegypiinae): A new molecular pattern for hypoxic tolerance. *Biol. Chem. Hoppe-Seyler,* **369:**217–232.

Hughes, G. M. (1973). Respiratory responses to hypoxia in fish. *Am. Zool.,* **13:**475–489.

Huisman, T. H. J., Schillhorn van Veen, J. M., Dozy, A. M., and Nechtman, C. M. (1964). Studies on animal hemoglobins. II. Influence of inorganic phosphate on the physico-chemical and physiological properties of the hemoglobin of the adult chicken. *Biochim. Biophys. Acta,* **88:**352–366.

Imai, K. (1982). *Allosteric Effects in Hemoglobin.* Cambridge, Cambridge University Press, pp. xvi;1–275.

Ingerman, R. I., and Terwilliger, R. C. (1982). Presence and possible functional significance of Root effect hemoglobins in fishes lacking functional swim bladders. *J. Exp. Zool.,* **220:**171–177.

Isaacks, R., Harkness, D., Sampsell, R., Adler, J., Roth, S., Kim, C., and Goldman, P. (1977). Studies on avian erythrocyte metabolism. Inositol tetrakisphosphate: The major phosphate compound in the erythrocytes of the ostrich (*Struthio camelus camelus*). *Eur. J. Biochem.,* **77:**567–574.

Itada, I., Turitzen, S., and Steen, J. B. (1970). Root shift in eel hemoglobin. *Respir. Physiol.,* **8:**276–279.

Jelkmann, W., and Bauer, C. (1978). Embryonic hemoglobins: Dependence of functional characteristics on tetramer composition. *Pflügers Arch.,* **377:**75–80.

Jessen, T.-H., Weber, R. E., Fermi, G., Tame, J., and Braunitzer, G. Adaptation of bird hemoglobins to high altitudes: Demonstration of molecular mechanism by protein engineering. *Proc. Natl. Acad. Sci. USA*, **88**:(in press).

Jürgens, K. D., Pietschmann, M., Yamaguchi, K., and Kleinschmidt, T. (1988). Oxygen binding properties, capillary densities and heart weights in high altitude camelids. *J. Comp. Physiol. B*, **158**:469–477.

Kimura, M. (1979). The neutral theory of molecular evolution. *Sci. Am.*, **241**(5):94–104.

Kleinschmidt, T., and Sgouros, J. G. (1987). Hemoglobin sequences. *Biol. Chem. Hoppe-Seyler*, **368**:579–615.

Kleinschmidt, T., März, J., Jürgens, K. D., and Braunitzer, G. (1986). Interaction of allosteric effectors with α-globin chains and high altitude respiration in mammals. The primary structure of two Tylopoda hemoglobins with high oxygen affinity: Vicuna (*Lama vicugna*) and alpaca (*Lama pacos*). *Biol. Chem. Hoppe-Seyler*, **367**:153–160.

Laybourne, R. C. (1974). Collision between a vulture and an aircraft at an altitude of 37,000 feet. *Wilson Bull.*, **86**:461–463.

Lutz, P. L., Longmuir, I. S., and Schmidt-Nielsen, K. (1974). Oxygen affinity of bird blood. *Respir. Physiol.*, **20**:325–330.

McClure, H. E. (1974). Migration and survival of the birds of Asia. US Army Medical Component, SEATO Medical Project, Bangkok, Thailand.

Nagai, K., Perutz, M. F., Poyart, C. (1985). Oxygen binding properties of human mutant hemoglobins synthesized in *Escherichia coli*. *Proc. Natl. Acad. Sci. USA*, **82**:7252–7255.

Nikinmaa, M. (1986). Control of red cell pH in teleost fishes. *Ann. Zool. Fenn.*, **23**:223–235.

Nothum, R., Weber, R. E., Kösters, J., Schneeganss, D., and Braunitzer, G. (1989). Amino acid sequences and functional differentiation of hemoglobins A and D from swift (*Apus apus*, Apodiformes). *Biol. Chem. Hoppe-Seyler*, **370**:1197–1207.

Oberthür, W., Godovac-Zimmermann, J., and Braunitzer, G. (1986). The expression of $\alpha^D$-chains in the hemoglobin of adult ostrich (*Struthio camelus*) and American rhea (*Rhea americanus*). The different evolution of adult bird $\alpha^A$-, $\alpha^D$- and β-chains. *Biol. Chem. Hoppe-Seyler*, **367**:507–514.

Parkhurst, L. J., Goss, D. J., and Perutz, M. F. (1983). Kinetic and equilibrium studies on the role of β-147 histidine in the Root effect and cooperativity in carp hemoglobin. *Biochemistry*, **22**:5401–5409.

Pelster, B., and Weber, R. E. (1990). Influence of organic phosphates on the Root effect of multiple fish hemoglobins. *J. Exp. Biol.* **149**:425–437.

Perutz, M. F. (1983). Species adaptation in a protein molecule. *Mol. Biol. Evol.*, **1**:1–28.

Perutz, M. F., and Brunori, M. (1982). Stereochemistry of cooperative effects in fish and amphibian haemoglobins. *Nature*, **299**:421–426.

Perutz, M. F., and Fermi, G. (1981). *Hemoglobin and Myoglobin*, Vol. 2. Atlas of Molecular Structures in Biology. Oxford, Claredon Press, pp. vi; 1–104.

Perutz, M. F., and Imai, K. (1980). Regulation of oxygen affinity of mammalian haemoglobins. *J. Mol. Biol.*, **136**:183–191.

Perutz, M. F., Kilmartin, J. V., Nishikura, N., Fogg, J. H., and Butler, P. J. G. (1980). Identification of residues contributing to the Bohr effect of human haemoglobin. *J. Mol. Biol.*, **138**:649–670.

Petruzelli, R., Barra, D., Goffredo, B. M., Bossa, F., Coletta, M., and Brunori, M. (1984). Amino-acid sequence of β-chain of hemoglobin IV from trout (*Salmo irideus*). *Biochim. Biophys. Acta*, **789**:69–73.

Petschow, D., Würdinger, I., Baumann, R., Duhm, J., Braunitzer, G., and Bauer, C. (1977). Causes of high blood $O_2$ affinity of animals living at high altitude. *J. Appl. Physiol. Respir. Environ. Exerc. Physiol.*, **42**:139–143.

Powers, D. A. (1972). Hemoglobin adaptation for fast and slow water habitats in sympatric catastomid fishes. *Sci. N.Y.*, **177**:360–362.

Powers, D. A. (1980). Molecular ecology of teleost fish hemoglobins. Strategies for adapting to changing environments. *Am. Zool.*, **20**:139–162.

Purdie, A., Wells, R. M. G., and Brittain, T. (1973). Molecular aspects of embryonic mouse hemoglobin ontogeny. *Biochem. J.*, **215**:377–383.

Riggs, A. (1988). The Bohr effect. *Annu. Rev. Physiol.*, **50**:181–204.

Rodewald, K., and Braunitzer, G. (1984). Die Primärstruktur des Hämoglobins vom Goldfisch (*Carassius auratus*). *Hoppe-Seyler's Z. Physiol. Chem.*, **365**:95–104.

Schnek, A. G., Paul, C., and Leonis, J. (1984). Evolution and adaptation of avian and crocodilian hemoglobins. In *Respiratory Pigments in Animals. Relation Structure–Function*. Edited by J. Lamy, J.-P. Truchot, and R. Gilles. Heidelberg, Springer-Verlag, pp. 141–158.

Swan, L. A. (1970). Goose of the Himalayas. *Natl. Hist.*, **79**:68–75.

Takeshita, S., Aoki, T., Fukumaki, Y., and Takagi, Y. (1984). Cloning and sequence analysis of a cDNA for the α-globin mRNA of carp, *Cyprinus carpio*. *Biochim. Biophys. Acta*, **783**:265–271.

Tamm, L. T., and Riggs, A. F. (1984). Oxygen binding and aggregation of bullfrog hemoglobin. *J. Biol. Chem.*, **259**:2610–2616.

Vaccaro Torracca, A. M., Raschetti, R., Salvioli, R., Ricciardi, G., and Winterhalter, K. H. (1977). Modulation of the Root effect in goldfish by ATP and GTP. *Biochim. Biophys. Acta.*, **496**:367–373.

Weber, R. E. (1982). Intraspecific adaptation of hemoglobin function in fish to environmental oxygen availability. In *Exogenous and Endogenous Influences on Metabolic and Neural Control*, Vol. 1. Edited by A. D. F. Addink and N. Spronk. Oxford, Pergamon Press, pp. 87–102.

Weber, R. E. (1990). Functional significance and structural basis of multiple hemoglobins with special reference to ectothermic vertebrates. In *Animal Nutrition and Transport Processes, Vol. 2*. Transport, Respiration and Excretion: Comparative and Environmental Aspects. Edited by J.-P. Truchot and B. Lahlou. *Comp. Physiol.* Basel, Karger, pp. 58–75.

Weber, R. E., and De Wilde, J. (1975). Oxygenational properties of hemoglobins from the flatfish plaice (*Pleuronectes platessa*) and flounder (*Platichthys flesus*). *J. Comp. Physiol.*, **101**:99–110.

Weber, R. E., and De Wilde J. (1976). Multiple haemoglobins in plaice and flounder and their functional properties. *Comp. Biochem. Physiol.*, **54B**:433–437.

Weber, R. E., and Jensen, F. B. (1988). Functional adaptations in hemoglobins from ectothermic vertebrates. *Annu. Rev. Physiol.*, **50**:161–179.

Weber, R. E., and Lykkeboe, G. (1978). Respiratory adaptations in carp blood: Influences of hypoxia, red cell organic phosphates, divalent cations and $CO_2$ on hemogloboin–oxygen affinity. *J. Comp. Physiol.*, **128**:127–137.

Weber, R. E., and Wells, R. M. G. (1989). Hemoglobin structure and function. In *Comparative Pulmonary Physiology, Current Concepts*. Edited by S. C. Wood. (*Lung Biology in Health and Disease*, Vol 39. Edited by C. Lenfant.) New York, Marcel Dekker, pp. 279–310.

Weber, R. E., Hiebl, I., and Braunitzer, G. (1988). High altitude and hemoglobin function in the vultures *Gups rueppellii* and *Aegypius monachus*. *Biol. Chem. Hoppe-Seyler*, **369**:233–240.

Weber, R. E., Jensen, F. B., and Cox, R. P. (1987a). Analysis of teleost hemoglobins by Adair and Monod-Wyman-Changeux models. *J. Comp. Physiol.*, **157B**:145–152.

Weber, R. E., Kleinschmidt, T., and Braunitzer, G. (1987b). Embryonic pig hemoglobins Gower I ($\zeta_2\varepsilon_2$), Gower II ($\alpha_2\varepsilon_2$), Heide I ($\zeta_2\vartheta_2$) and Heide II ($\alpha_2\vartheta_2$): Oxygen binding functions related to structure and embryonic oxygen supply. *Respir. Physiol.*, **69**:347–357.

Weber, R. E., Lalthantluanga, R., and Braunitzer, G. (1988). Functional characterization of fetal and adult yak hemoglobins: An oxygen binding cascade and its molecular basis. *Arch. Biochem. Biophys.*, **263**:199–203.

Weber, R. E., Lykkeboe, G., and Johansen, K. (1975). Biochemical aspects of the adaptation of hemoglobin–oxygen affinity in eels to hypoxia. *Life Sci.*, **17**:1345–1350.

Weber, R. E., Wood, S. C., and Lomholt, J. P. (1976). Temperature acclimation and oxygen binding properties of blood and multiple haemoglobins of rainbow trout. *J. Exp. Biol.*, **65**:333–345.

Wells, R. M. G. (1979). Haemoglobin–oxygen affinity in developing embryonic erythroid cells of the mouse. *J. Comp. Physiol.*, **129**:333–338.

Wells, R. M. G., Grigg, G. C., Beard, L. A., and Summers, G. (1989). Hypoxic responses in a fish from a stable environment: Blood oxygen transport in the Antarctic fish *Pagothenia borchgrevinki*. *J. Exp. Biol.*, **141**:97–111.

Wood, S. C. (1980). Adaptation of red blood cell function to hypoxia and temperature in ectothermic vertebrates. *Am. Zool.*, **20**:163–172.

Wood, S. C., and Johansen, K. (1973). Organic phosphate metabolism in nucleate red cells. Influence of hypoxia on eel $HbO_2$ affinity. *Neth. J. Sea Res.*, **7**:328–338.

Wrightstone, R. N. (1988). Policies of the International Hemoglobin Information Center (IHIC) Comprehensive Sickle Cell Center. Hemoglobin, **12**:207–308.

# 14

## Physiological Adaptation of Crustacean Hemocyanins

### An Extended Investigation of the Blue Crab, *Callinectes sapidus*

**CHARLOTTE P. MANGUM**

College of William and Mary
Williamsburg, Virginia

## I. Introduction

Because of the essentially impermeable exoskeleton, the blood of a crab generally carries more than 90% of the $O_2$ consumed by the tissues. When the blood fails to supply enough $O_2$ to support a resting level of aerobic metabolism, many species are unable either to turn down metabolism or to survive anaerobiosis for more than a few hours. Consequently, the functioning of the $O_2$-transport system is far more important to these stenoxic animals than to many others; and yet, the effective functioning of the system often is perturbed by imperfect regulatory responses to environmental variables such as salinity, oxygen, and temperature (Mangum, 1980; 1983c).

In 1970, Kjell Johansen, together with Claude Lenfant and Tony Mecklenberg, made a major contribution to understanding crustacean $O_2$-transport systems under environmentally optimal conditions. They showed that, contrary to notions prevailing at the time, the hemocyanin (Hc) of the dungeness crab *Cancer magister* does become fully oxygenated at the gill and that it maintains a large venous reserve that is exploited, in part, during locomotor activity.

With the qualification that the venous reserve is smaller in species found in warmer water, this pattern is now known to be generally true of many crabs.

Species found in quite different environments arrive at much the same end by utilizing carrier molecules with different functional properties, each adapted to its own set of operating conditions (Mangum, 1982; 1983a).

In the past decade or so investigations of crustacean $O_2$ transport have focused upon suboptimal conditions (i.e., mechanisms of intraspecific adaptation to environmental change). The following discussion centers upon a single euryhaline, aquatic species, in part because it has been the subject of much of my own work for the past 15 years; but, in addition, the available information (albeit limited) suggests that the Hcs of terrestrial species are curiously unadaptable in the adult stage, often completely so (e.g., Morris and Bridges, 1986).

## II. Adaptation of Hemocyanin–Oxygen Transport to Environmental Change

### A. Salinity

*The Problem*

Crustacean hemocyanins are highly sensitive to the inorganic ions in the blood, much more than mammalian hemoglobins (Hbs). And yet, when environmental salinity decreases, no euryhaline, subtidal crab of which I am aware has the ability to maintain a truly homeostatic condition of blood ions. In the blue crab, *Callinectes sapidus*, a highly euryhaline species found in waters ranging from hypersaline lagoons to fresh water, total blood salts change by a factor of almost 3 (Colvocoresses et al., 1974). Since hypersaline waters are rare in nature (and perhaps more to the point, since respiratory adaptation to them has never been studied), a more meaningful quantity might be the blood salt difference between normal seaside and brackish or fresh water, which is about 35–40% (Mangum and Towle, 1977). When the blood is dialyzed against physiological salines, representing the two ends of this salinity gradient, $O_2$ affinity differs by about 40% in the physiological pH range (Mason et al., 1983).

It has been known for many years that hemocyanins contain a cation-binding site, linked to the $O_2$-binding site, for which divalent cations and $H^+$ compete. In the presence of relatively high levels of $H^+$, crustacean Hcs are stabilized in the low $O_2$-affinity conformation (i.e., they have a normal Bohr shift) and, in the absence of high levels of $H^+$, the site is occupied by divalent cations, which stabilize the Hc in the high-affinity conformation (Pickett et al., 1966; Morimoto and Kegeles, 1971; Chantler et al., 1973; Arisaka and Van Holde, 1979). An exhaustive ion substitution study revealed that the salinity effect on *C. sapidus* Hc is, essentially in toto, due to relatively small changes in blood $Ca^{+2}$ (Mason et al., 1983), a conclusion reached earlier for a closely related Hc (Truchot, 1975). Thus, until recently, $Ca^{+2}$ has been regarded as an allosteric perturber of Hc–$O_2$ binding, rather than a modulator, which implies an adaptive compensation (but see later discussion).

## The Adaptations

### Systemic Level

The crustacean cardiovascular and ventilatory systems are capable of only limited compensatory responses. In the blue crab, there is no significant rise in blood $P_{O_2}$ at low salinity (Weiland and Mangum, 1975).

### Exogenous Molecular Effectors

For many years we have also known that there is no significant difference between the $O_2$ affinity of blue crab Hc in animals freshly caught in seaside or in brackish waters. Originally, we suggested that the opposite effects of $Ca^{+2}$ and $H^+$ were responsible (Mangum and Towle, 1977). If a pH increase accompanied a $Ca^{+2}$ loss at low salinity, which it does (Truchot, 1973; Weiland and Mangum, 1975), then the two changes might be counterbalancing, and the imperfect regulation of each might be considered a nonhomeostatic or enantiostatic form of adaptation. Although this concept remains valid, we now know that additional mechanisms are involved. At the time, the quantitative effects of $Ca^{+2}$ and $H^+$ had not been described in detail in this species, at least not under physiological conditions. Moreover, we were unaware of organic modulators, such as L-lactate and urate, which, like $Ca^{+2}$, raise the $O_2$ affinity of many crustacean Hcs (discussed later). Because much of the estuary is a chronically hypoxic as well as low-salinity environment, it is quite possible that lactate or urate, or both, had been present in our original low salinity sample. When all four effects are figured in, the $O_2$ affinity did not approximate the observed value. Even if the exogenous effectors do not act fully cumulatively (Morris et al., 1987), the discrepancy was too great. The $O_2$ affinity of low-salinity, high-pH, high-lactate and urate blood should have been much higher than that of high-salinity, low-pH, and lactate- and urate-free blood (Mangum, 1986).

### Intrinsic Molecular Change

The first evidence that an intrinsic molecular change might be responsible emerged when we compared the purified Hcs of low- and high-salinity animals under common conditions of inorganic ions and pH (Fig. 1). The Hc of low-salinity animals had a lower $O_2$ affinity than that of high-salinity animals, regardless of total ionic strength.

It is truly amazing that migratory habits of this commercially valuable species are so poorly known, despite almost a century of study of other aspects of their biology. But the populations we studied are believed to interbreed freely, and the few data available on protein polymorphisms provide no reason to suppose otherwise (T. Coles, personal communication; see also following). Moreover,

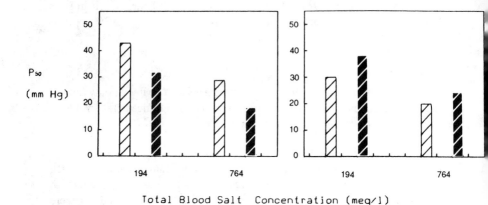

**Figure 1**   Oxygen affinity of Hcs of (light bar) seaside and (dark bar) brackish water *Callinectes sapidus* dialyzed against each of two physiological salines. Left panel shows results for freshly caught crabs and right panel shows results for same individuals 8 days after transfer to the alternative salinity; 25°C, pH 7.53. (Data from Mason et al., 1983.)

when we transferred the same individuals from one salinity to another and reexamined their Hcs after a period of acclimation, we found that, in one direction, the difference had disappeared in full and, in the other direction, it had shifted in large part, suggesting a phenotypically labile response (see Fig. 1).

We also found that, following the acclimation period, Hc concentration rose in the animals transferred from high to low salinity and dropped in those transferred from low to high salinity (Mason et al., 1983). We suspect that the molecular adaptation may be expedited by Hc metabolism. We also suspect that the elevated Hc levels at low salinity result from relaxation of an inhibition that exists at high salinity (relative both to their terrestrial counterparts and to most other animal groups that contain blood $O_2$ carriers, aquatic crabs are notorious for their low blood $O_2$-carrying capacities). Blue crabs are almost always hyperosmotic to their ambient medium and, accordingly, the driving osmotic gradient is inward. They must maintain an excess of blood hydrostatic over colloid osmotic pressure to form primary urine, the major mechanism of water balance (Mangum, 1986). In high-salinity habitats the margin is very small. When heart rate and blood hydrostatic pressure increase at low salinity, Hc concentration and thus colloid osmotic pressure can increase.

These findings, although very exciting, were also very unexpected, and we did not have enough material to maintain the paired observations design for further investigation. To examine the subunit composition of the Hc we were forced to pool what was left.

### Quaternary Structure of the Arthropod Hemocyanins

All arthropod Hcs are built of monomeric subunits of a similar molecular mass (65–80 kd), loosely linked to one another. In crustaceans the number of different polypeptide chains constituting the native polymers, however, is quite diverse, ranging from only one to as many as eight (Mangum, 1983a). Both protein biochemists and physiologists have recently asked why crabs often have Hc polymers with so many different polypeptide chains. One answer, certainly largely true, is that one kind of chain forms the basic building block of the polymer, another links them together, and still others may stabilize the aggregate (Markl, 1986).

Despite the underlying homology at the monomeric level, in the different arthropod subtaxa, the native polymers are often distinctive (Mangum, 1983a). Isopod Hc is made of only one kind of chain assembled to a hexamer, the smallest multiple that possesses the necessary respiratory properties in an arthropod, such as cooperativity. Crab hemocyanins usually assemble to a dodecamer, which requires a second kind of chain to bridge together a pair of hexamers. Other arthropods possess 24-, 36-, or 48-mers. This is a physiologically important process, not because it necessarily continues to enhance cooperativity, which it does not. The Hc of the horseshoe crab, *Limulus polyphemus*, a chelicerate more closely related to the spiders and scorpions than to the blue crab, is a 48-mer, but only somewhat cooperative (n < 2). *Polymerization is important because it minimizes the colloid osmotic pressure of the blood without influencing its $O_2$-carrying capacity* (Snyder and Mangum, 1982).

### Molecular Adaptation of Blue Crab Hemocyanins Salinity Change

The monomeric subunits of arthropod Hcs can be dissociated in the native conformation and separated electrophoretically by charge, a procedure that is quite sensitive.

When we examined the Hcs in the two pools from low- and high-salinity animals before transfer, we found that the native low-salinity Hc was composed of six different subunits. We refer to them as bands 1 through 6, proceeding from cathode to anode. Native high-salinity Hc, with its intrinsically higher $O_2$ affinity, was composed of only five subunits, and one of those was present in low concentration (Mason et al., 1983). Specifically, subunit 3 was absent and 5 was scarce (Fig. 2). Unfortunately, no material from the transfer from high to low salinity remained for subunit analysis. But the sample from the low- to high-salinity transfer, which had exhibited an incomplete, but highly significant, shift in $O_2$ affinity, also exhibited an intermediate subunit composition, with subunits 3 and 5 present in intermediate concentrations (Mason et al., 1983).

We then took a much larger sample from each of the two bodies of water and described the frequency of the phenotypes. Somewhat miraculously, of 51

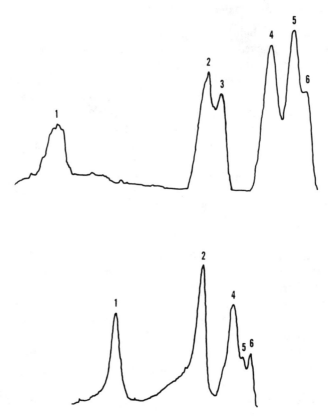

**Figure 2**   Densitometer scans of polyacrylamide gels showing electrophoretic separation of monomeric subunits of *C. sapidus* Hcs. Top panel shows representative phenotype of seaside animals and bottom panel shows representative phenotype of brackish water animals. (From Mangum and Rainer 1988.)

animals in each sample, 45 had the phenotype associated with that salinity in the transfer experiment, 3 had the phenotype associated with the alternative salinity, and 3 had the intermediate phenotype. The minorities may represent recent migrations of animals that had not had time to acclimate in full to their new environment. In these larger samples, we found that a third subunit, number 6, is also variable, but the frequency was about the same in both populations (C. P. Mangum and G. Godette, unpublished observations).

On numerous subsequent occasions, we tried to repeat the transfer experiment while maintaining the paired-observations design throughout both $O_2$-binding measurements and subunit electrophoresis, without success. The failures were probably exacerbated by the need to perform it in mid-summer, since that was the time of the original experiment, and we know that intrinsic molecular change also occurs with season (discussed later). Blue crabs are notoriously fragile in the middle of the summer. When we took enough blood before the transfer to perform both analyses, the crabs died before the end of the acclimation period. When we took smaller volumes, insufficient material was available for electrophoresis. When we tried using much shorter acclimation periods, there was little or no change. We did succeed in confirming the original difference in $HcO_2$ binding between the native seaside and estuarine populations (Mangum and Rainer, 1988).

We then decided to adopt an alternative approach to learning whether the observed variation in subunit composition could quantitatively account for the observed shifts in $O_2$ binding. We had continued to sample natural populations and, by this time, it was clear that each of the three variable subunits varies independently of the others. Since each can be present in one of two conditions (high or low concentration), then $2 \times 2 \times 2 = 8$ combinations are possible. At present, our cumulative sample totals more than 800 individuals and all eight combinations have been recovered. Although some are so rare that $n = 1$, others are frequent enough that additional samples of 50 or so individuals should contain at least some of them.

Therefore, we took a sample of about that number, bled the animals without concern for survival, quickly performed the electrophoresis, and identified five of the eight phenotypes. *All of these individuals were taken from the same salinity within a few meters of one another and hundreds of kilometers from the alternative salinity.* We then dialyzed the five Hcs against the same physiological saline and performed $O_2$-binding measurements under common conditions.

The results, once again, showed that the Hc with low levels of subunits 3 and 5 has an $O_2$ affinity about 35–40% higher than the Hc with high levels of all six (Fig. 3). They also showed no difference between a Hc with low levels of band 3 alone and one with low levels of bands 3 and 5. So the condition of band 5 may not influence $O_2$ binding, although we have never measured the $O_2$ binding of a molecule with low levels of only band 5. Finally, these results showed that a decrease in concentration of band 6 (the salinity-independent variable) alone significantly raises $O_2$ affinity, although not as much as a change in subunit 3, perhaps because, on this occasion, the change in subunit 6 was not very large. We concluded that the change in only subunit 3 can fully explain the difference between the two natural populations (Mangum and Rainer, 1988).

Blue crab blood contains a mixture of hexamers and dodecamers, the ratio reported to be as high as 1:1 (Herskovits et al., 1981) and as low as 1:4 (Johnson et al., 1981). Since it is subunit 3 that forms dodecamers from hexamers, our results did not enable us to decide between two alternative molecular hypotheses: 1) Subunit 3 has a much lower $O_2$ affinity than 1, 2, 4, and 5 and, hence, its impoverishment or enrichment directly and simply biases the average. 2) Subunits

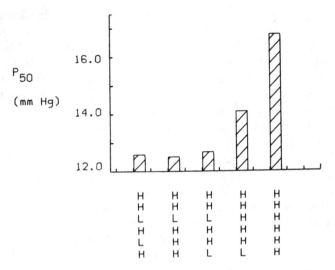

**Figure 3** $O_2$ affinity of different phenotypes of *C. sapidus* Hcs dialyzed against the same physiological saline. Letters on abscissa show concentration (H for high, L for low) of subunits 1 through 6 in descending order. 25°C, pH 7.60.

1–5 have the same $O_2$ affinity, but hexamers and dodecamers differ, so the variability of subunit 3 indirectly influences the net result by its polymer-forming properties.

At this writing I am presently performing an experiment designed to decide the question. However, even more recent results on the response to hypoxia may make it moot.

### B. Hypoxia

*The Problem*

Because of both human abuse and natural hydrographic factors, the waters of large and well-formed estuaries are typically characterized by large areas of hypoxia, ranging in levels from severe to moderate and in chronology from tidal to permanent (reviewed by deFur et al., 1990). Although severe hypoxia is simply lethal to a blue crab, survival is good at levels in which anaerobic end products do not accumulate appreciably. However, blood $P_{O_2}$ declines sharply and $O_2$ uptake at the gill becomes a problem (deFur et al., 1988).

*The Adaptations*

Systemic Level

In a number of crustaceans, moderate hypoxia is accompanied by hyperventilation, which raises blood $P_{O_2}$ above acutely hypoxic levels and blood pH above normoxic levels (reviewed by deFur et al., 1990). Because of the normal Bohr shift, blood $O_2$ affinity rises and $O_2$ uptake is strongly regulated. For reasons that are somewhat unclear, this response does not always occur in blue crabs. Moreover, oxyregulation fails at an ambient $Po_2$ above the incipient lethal level (Laird and Haefner, 1976). Blood flow has never been estimated, but the decrease in heart rate is so great (deFur and Mangum, 1979) that it seems unlikely to be fully compensated by a rise in stroke volume.

## Exogenous Modulators of Hemocyanin–Oxygen Binding

In crabs, the accumulation of L-lactate in the blood during exercise hypoxia is highly adaptive. It allosterically raises $HcO_2$ affinity (Truchot, 1980) and, by so doing, opposes the effect of acidosis, in spite of the large normal Bohr shift; $O_2$ affinity is restored to the normoxic value either in part (Booth et al., 1982) or in full (Graham et al., 1983). The only puzzle is that the problem arises from the large normal Bohr shift, which is not a necessary feature of the Hcs, and that a reversed Bohr shift seems to be a more adaptive feature (Johanson and Petersen, 1975; Mangum, 1983c; Mangum and Ricci, 1989). Lactate does not, however, accumulate to a physiologically important level during sublethal environmental hypoxia (ambient $Po_2$ 40–50 mm Hg) in either the blue crab (deFur et al., 1988) or its relative *Carcinus maenas* (Lallier et al., 1987). Morris and associates (1985; 1986) have recently shown that urate also allosterically raises $O_2$ affinity of a crayfish Hc, and that it accumulates in the blood during environmental hypoxia, probably as a result of purine catabolism (Dykens and Shick, 1988). Urate can also be important in crabs during environmental hypoxia (Lallier et al., 1987). However, even though urate has the same action on blue crab Hc, it does not accumulate during sublethal hypoxia (deFur et al., 1988), possibly because this species cannot carry on anaerobic metabolism and survive for very long.

It has become clear recently that $Ca^{+2}$ is an important modulator during environmental hypoxia (but not during exercise; C. E. Booth, personal communication) in all species examined (Mangum, 1985; Lallier et al., 1987; deFur et al., 1988). Within 24 hr of hypoxia, blood $Ca^{+2}$ levels rise, often by large factors, probably owing to mobilization from the skeleton. As indicated in the foregoing, $Ca^{+2}$ raises $O_2$ affinity of crustacean Hcs. Moreover, all known Hcs are sensitive to $Ca^{+2}$, although not to the organic modulators (Mangum, 1983; Morris et al., 1985).

Nonetheless, it has also become clear that prolonged environmental hypoxia induces an intermolecular adaptation of the same magnitude as a salinity change.

## Shift in Subunit Composition

After 7 days at $Pi_{O_2}$ of 50–55 mm Hg, blue crab Hc exhibits a small, but significant, increase in $O_2$ affinity when purified and compared with that of normoxic animals under the same experimental conditions (Mangum et al., 1988;

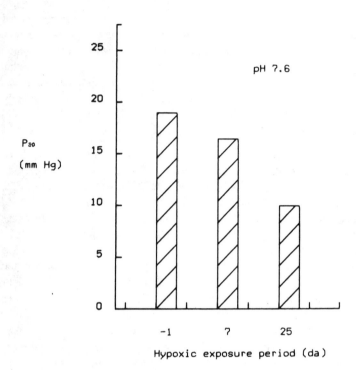

**Figure 4**   Oxygen affinity of *C. sapidus* Hcs dialyzed against the same physiological saline, before and after exposure to water $Po_2$ 50–55 mm Hg; 25°C, pH 7.60. (Data from Mangum et al., 1988.)

deFur et al., 1990). The increase is accompanied by a clear change in subunit composition. Here subunit 6 decreases in concentration as well as subunits 3 and 5. After 25 days, the change in both $HcO_2$ affinity (Fig. 4) and subunit composition (deFur et al., 1990) is far more dramatic, and Hc concentration has risen by 50% again suggesting a metabolic component of the adaptation.

The change in subunit 3 is smaller than that induced by the salinity transfer, but the change in subunit 6 (which is salinity-insensitive) is greater than described in Figure 3. We still have no evidence to suggest that the variability of subunit 5 is physiologically important, but it occurs during adaptation to hypoxia, as well as to salinity. This experiment suggests that the variation in subunit 6 is also phenotypically labile, which was not clear from our observations on natural populations. Because subunit 6 does not play a role in dodecamer formation, this experiment also suggests that its intrinsic $O_2$-binding properties are responsible for its influence on net $O_2$ affinity.

## Natural Populations

By this point, we had almost completed a far more detailed examination of natural populations at a dozen locations along a salinity gradient ranging from zero to 33% (Rainer, 1989). And these data clearly implicate a second, confounding variable that influences the concentration of subunits 3 and 5. Although the characteristic estuarine and seaside phenotypes observed in the laboratory and in our initial samples from nature could be found in almost all individuals in a given sample from the respective salinities, the pattern could also be quite anomalous. Samples taken in 2 successive years showed significantly different salinity distributions. This is exactly what one would expect if water $Po_2$ were the confounding variable because, in a natural body of seawater that is measurably diluted by freshwater runoff, salinity and $Po_2$ are not related in a simple fashion. The $Po_2$ often varies quite dramatically from year to year, whereas the salinity regime changes much less (reviewed by deFur et al., 1990), and also vice versa. In nature, water $Po_2$ may be the primary, and salinity the secondary, factor determining the particular Hc phenotype.

### C. Temperature?

#### The Problem

All but a few of the several dozens of Hcs yet examined show a common, conventional pattern of temperature dependence. The $O_2$ affinity rises and cooperativity diminishes as the polypeptide chains assume a more stable conformation at low temperature. Moreover, the magnitude of temperature sensitivity varies inversely with temperature, often disappearing at above about 25°C (Burnett et al., 1987). When the Bohr shift is also normal and large, the intrinsic effect of temperature is aggravated by the extrinsic effect of pH, which also rises at low temperature; $O_2$ affinity increases even more than it would if the carrier were pH-independent or if it had a reversed Bohr shift (Mangum and Ricci, 1989). At some temperature, $O_2$ affinity becomes so great that the Hc cannot unload at tissue $Po_2$, even though the latter is quite low (Mauro and Mangum, 1982). The animal becomes entirely dependent on the free $O_2$ in its blood and, not surprisingly, $O_2$-uptake drops precipitously, and locomotor and feeding activities cease.

#### The Adaptations

##### Systemic Level

Although cardiovascular activity decreases as expected with temperature, there is some ventilatory compensation at temperatures transitional between the summer and winter plateaus (Mauro and Mangum, 1982). Below about 10°C, however, the ventilatory system also becomes minimally active. When the crab is cooled below that threshold, all locomotor and feeding activity cease abruptly within minutes and, in the following weeks, a negative metabolic acclimation ensues. In nature, the crab gives up for the winter, crawls into the bottom and awaits spring.

### Extrinsic Effectors

The effects of temperature on allosteric modulation of crustacean Hcs have not been investigated.

### Intrinsic Molecular Change?

The physiological evidence would seem to implicate a molecular adaptation that lowers $O_2$ affinity of crustacean Hcs at low temperature. Truchot's (1975) data show a clear, although small, difference in $O_2$ affinity (measured at the same temperature and pH) of an Hc from warm- and cold-exposed *C. maenas*, even after dialysis against the same saline. Rutledge's (1981) evidence for a crayfish Hc is equally convincing. In the blue crab, during two successive years, we found a lower $O_2$ affinity in the winter than the summer (Mauro and Mangum, 1982); however, we could not reverse the effect by a temperature transfer lasting the same or longer periods than the salinity and oxygen transfers discussed earlier. Moreover, the collection sites of our summer and winter animals, which were purchased from commercial watermen, could have been quite different, especially in $Po_2$ which varies with season far more than salinity.

I recently obtained blue crabs from a single site, the Patuxent River estuary of Maryland, in both July and February. I could find no difference in subunit composition. It is quite possible that the stimulus responsible for the seasonal adaptation in this species is $Po_2$, which would be expected to be lower in the summer than in the winter, even though the factor to which the Hc adapts is temperature. Whether this hypothesis pertains to Truchot's (1975) and Rutledge's (1981) findings is unclear from the original reports and, perhaps, even from the original experiments. In our temperature transfer experiments the animals were held in well-aerated aquaria, and a change in $Po_2$ was not available as a stimulus.

## III. Conclusion

I mentioned at the outset that Kjell Johansen had made a seminal contribution to basic crustacean respiratory physiology. I did not explicitly emphasize his many contributions to numerous other themes discussed within the constraints of my proscribed topic. They include 1) the demonstration that exogenous modulators of $O_2$ transport are important mechanisms of respiratory adaptation to environmental stress such as hypoxia (in his experiments the subject was the teleost hemoglobins, rather than the crustacean Hcs); 2) the demonstration that the reversed Bohr shift of the chelicerate Hcs is a highly adaptive feature that raises blood $O_2$ affinity during the acidosis accompanying hypoxia; and 3) the importance of colloid osmotic pressure as a variable in animal bloods.

He (and his esteemed friend Jorge Petersen) never completed their all-encompassing survey of gas exchange and transport throughout the animal kingdom. Nonetheless, for those of us who ask questions about the several dozen animal phyla, his works made a lasting impact, the magnitude of which even he would be unaware.

## Acknowledgment

Supported by NSF DCB 88-16172 (Physiological Processes).

## References

Arisaka, F., and Van Holde, K. E. (1979). Allosteric properties and the association equilibria of hemocyanin from *Callianassa californiensis*. *J. Mol. Biol.*, **134**:41–73.

Booth, C. E., McMahon, B. R., and Pinder, A. W. (1982). Oxygen uptake and the potentiating effects of increased hemolymph lactate on oxygen transport during exercise in the blue crab. *Callinectes sapidus*. *J. Comp. Physiol.*, **148**:111–121.

Burnett, L. E., Scholnick, D. A., and Mangum, C. P. (1988). Temperature sensitivity of molluscan and arthropod hemocyanins. *Biol. Bull.*, **174**:153–162.

Chantler, E. N., Harris, R. R., and Bannister, W. H. (1973). Oxygenation and aggregation properties of haemocyanin from *Carcinus mediterraneus* and *Potamon edulis*. *Comp. Biochem. Physiol.*, **46A**:333–343.

Colvocoresses, J. A., Lynch, M. P., and Webb, K. L. (1974). Variations in serum constituents of the blue crab, *Callinectes sapidus*: Major cations. *Comp. Biochem. Physiol.*, **49**:787–803.

deFur, P. L., and Mangum, C. P. (1979). The effects of environmental variables on heart rates of invertebrates. *Comp. Biochem. Physiol.*, **63A**:549–554.

deFur, P. L., Mangum, C. P., and Reese, J. E. (1990). Respiratory responses of the blue crab *Callinectes sapidus* to long-term hypoxia. *Biol. Bull.*, **178**:46–54.

deFur, P. L., Mangum, C. P., and Reiber, C. L. (1988). Effects of long term hypoxia on respiration in *Callinectes sapidus*. *Am. Zool.*, **28**:62A.

Dykens, J. A., and Shick, H. M. (1988). Relevance of purine catabolism to hypoxia and recovery in euryoxic and stenoxic marine invertebrates, particularly in bivalve molluscs. *Comp. Biochem. Physiol.*, **91C**:35–42.

Graham, R. A., Mangum, C. P., Terwilliger, R. C., and Terwilliger, N. B. (1983). The effect of organic acids on oxygen binding of hemocyanin from the crab *Cancer magister*. *Comp. Biochem. Physiol.*, **74A**:45–50.

Herskovits, T. T., Erhunmwunsee, L. J., San George, R. L., and Herp, A. (1981). Subunit structure and dissociation of *Callinectes sapidus* hemocyanin. *Biochim. Biophys. Acta*, **667**:44–58.

Johansen, K., Lenfant, C., and Mecklenberg, T. A. (1970). Respiration in the crab, *Cancer magister*. *Z. Vergl. Physiol.*, **70**:1–19.

Johansen, K., and Petersen, J. A. (1975). Respiratory adaptations in *Limulus polyphemus* (L.). in *Physiological Ecology of Estuarine Organisms*. Edited by F. J. Vernberg. Columbia, S. C., University of South Carolina Press, pp. 129–145.

Johnson, B. A., Bonaventura, C., and Bonaventura, J. (1984). Allosteric modulation of *Callinectes sapidus* hemocyanin by binding of L-lactate. *Biochemistry*, **23**:872–878.

Laird, C. M., and Haefner, P. A. (1976). The effects of intrinsic and environmental factors on oxygen consumption of the blue crab, *Callinectes sapidus* Rathbun. *J. Exp. Mar. Biol. Ecol.*, **22**:171–178.

Lallier, F., Boitel, F., and Truchot, J. P. (1987). The effect of ambient oxygen and temperature on haemolymph L-lactate and urate concentrations in the shore crab *Carcinus maenas*. *Comp. Biochem. Physiol.*, **86A**:255–260.

Mangum, C. P. (1980). Respiratory function of the hemocyanins. *Am. Zool.*, **20**:19–38.

Mangum, C. P. (1982). On the relationship between $P_{50}$ and the mode of gas exchange in tropical crustaceans. *Pac. Sci.*, **36**:403–410.

Mangum, C. P. (1983a). Oxygen transport in the blood. In *Biology of the Crustacea*, Vol. 5. Edited by L. H. Mantel. New York, Academic Press, pp. 373–429.

Mangum, C. P. (1983b). On the distribution of lactate sensitivity among the hemocyanins. *Mar. Biol. Lett.*, **4**:139–149.

Mangum, C. P. (1983c). Adaptability and inadaptability among $HcO_2$ transport systems: An apparent paradox. *Life Chem. Rept. Suppl.*, **1**:335–352.

Mangum, C. P. (1985). Oxygen transport in the invertebrates. *Amer. J. Physiol.*, **248**: R505–R514.

Mangum, C. P. (1986). Osmoregulation in marine and estuarine animals: The view of a respiratory physiologist. *Boll. Zool.*, **53**:1–7.

Mangum, C. P., and Rainer, J. S. (1988). The relationship between subunit composition and $O_2$ binding of blue crab hemocyanin. *Biol. Bull.*, **174**:77–82.

Mangum, C. P., and Ricci, J. (1989). The influence of temperature on oxygen uptake and transport in the horseshoe crab *Limulus polyphemus*. *J. Exp. Mar. Biol. Ecol.*, **129**:243–250.

Mangum, C. P., and Towle, D. W. (1977). Physiological adaptation to unstable environments. *Am. Sci.*, **65**:67–75.

Mangum, C. P., deFur, P. L., and Reese, J. E. (1988). Effects of hypoxia on hemocyanin $O_2$ transport in *Callinectes sapidus*. *Am. Zool.*, **28**:62A.

Markl, J. (1986). Evolution and function of structurally diverse subunits in the respiratory protein hemocyanin from arthropods. *Biol. Bull.*, **171**:90–115.

Mason, R. P., Mangum, C. P., and Godette, G. (1983). The influence of inorganic ions and acclimation salinity on hemocyanin–oxygen binding in the blue crab *Callinectes sapidus*. *Biol. Bull.*, **164**:104–123.

Mauro, N. A., and Mangum, C. P. (1982). The role of the blood in the temperature dependence of oxidative metabolism in decapod crustaceans. I. Intraspecific responses to seasonal differences in temperature. *J. Exp. Zool.*, **219**:179–188.

Morimoto, K., and Kegeles, G. (1971). Subunit interactions of lobster hemocyanin. I. Ultracentrifuge studies. *Arch. Biochem. Biophys.*, **142**:247–257.

Morris, S., and Bridges, C. R. (1986). Oxygen binding by the hemocyanin of the terrestrial hermit crab *Coenobita clypeatus* (Herbst)—the effect of physiological parameters in vitro. *Physiol. Zool.*, **59**:606–615.

Morris, S., Bridges, C. R., and Grieshaber, M. K. (1985). A new role for uric acid: Modulator of haemocyanin oxygen affinity in crustaceans. *J. Exp. Zool.*, **235:135–139.**

Morris, S., Bridges, C. R, and Grieshaber, N. K. (1986). The potentiating effect of purine bases and some of their derivatives on the oxygen affinity of haemocyanin from the crayfish *Austropotamobius pallipes*. *J. Comp. Physiol.*, **156**:431–440.

Morris, S., Bridges, C. R., and Grieshaber, M. K. (1987). The regulation of haemocyanin oxygen affinity during emersion of the crayfish *Austropotamobius pallipes*. III. The dependence of $Ca^{2+}$–haemocyanin binding on the concentration of L-lactate. *J. Exp. Biol.*, **133**:339–352.

Pickett, S. H., Riggs, A. F., and Larimer, J. L. (1966). Lobster hemocyanin: Properties of the minimum functional subunit and of aggregates. *Science*, **151**:1005–1007.

Rainer, J. S. (1989). Distribution of the heterogeneous hemocyanin subunits of *Callinectes sapidus* Rathbun along a salinity gradient. M. A. Thesis, College of William and Mary, Williamsburg, Va., 62 pp.

Rutledge, P. S. (1981). Effects of temperature acclimation on crayfish hemocyanin oxygen binding. *Am. J. Physiol.*, **240**:R93–98.

Snyder, G. K., and Mangum, C. P. (1982). The relationship between the size and shape of an extracellular oxygen carrier and the capacity for oxygen transport. In *Physiology and Biology of Horseshoe Crabs*. Edited by J. Bonaventura, C. Bonaventura, and S. Tesh. New York, Allan R. Liss, pp. 173–188.

Truchot, J. P. (1973). Fixation et transport de l'oxygène par le sang de *Carcinus maenas*: variations en rapport avec diverses conditions de température et de salinité. *Neth. J. Sea Res.* **7**:482–495.

Truchot, J. P. (1975). Factors controlling the in vitro and in vivo oxygen affinity of the hemocyanin in the crab *Carcinus maenas* (L.). *Respir. Physiol.*, **24**:173–189.

Truchot, J. P. (1980). Lactate increases the oxygen affinity of crab hemocyanin. *J. Exp. Zool.*, **214**:205–208.

Weiland, A. L., and Mangum, C. P. (1975). The influence of environmental salinity on hemocyanin function in the blue crab *Callinectes sapidus*. *J. Exp. Zool.*, **193**:265–274.

# 15

## Behavioral Hypothermia
An Adaptive Stress Response

**STEPHEN C. WOOD and GARY M. MALVIN**

Lovelace Medical Foundation
Albuquerque, New Mexico

## I. Introduction

All vertebrates have a center in the anterior hypothalamus that is specialized for thermoregulation. The sensory and integrative circuits are similar (Crawshaw and Hammel, 1973), and the outputs, behavioral and physiological, provide feedback control of body temperature ($T_b$).

Ectotherms depend mainly on behavioral mechanisms for $T_b$ control. The only physiological mechanisms available to ectotherms are panting (some lizards), color changes, and control of cutaneous blood flow. The latter provides transient control of heat flux. Endotherms also employ behavior to find or create a thermoneutral environment. They also use a variety of physiological mechanisms unavailable to ectotherms (shivering and nonshivering thermogenesis, sweating, panting, and such) to control their $T_b$.

Most ectotherms display a $T_b$ preference in a heterothermal environment. A variety of factors can modify the $T_b$ selected by ectotherms. Selection of a higher than normal $T_b$ in response to pyrogen injection was first demonstrated by Kluger and co-workers in lizards (Kluger et al., 1975). This proved to be an adaptive response to infection (i.e., it enhanced survival). Behavioral fever was later described for amphibians and fishes (Reynolds and Casterlin, 1982). Fever enhances survival by increased production of T cells and increased effectiveness of interferon, an antiviral agent.

The focus of this chapter is not fever, but the opposite behavioral response of ectotherms (i.e., behavioral hypothermia).* Behavioral hypothermia occurs in a variety of ectothermic species and some mammals. Diverse factors elicit behavioral hypothermia (e.g., hypoxia, hypercapnia, anemia, dehydration, ethanol, and toxic chemicals). Behavioral hypothermia in response to these factors should be adaptive by reducing oxygen demand, water loss, and chemical toxicity. The following sections review the mechanisms and importance of behavioral hypothermia as a stress response.

## II. Hypoxia-Induced Hypothermia

A changing $T_b$ has a marked effect on metabolic rate ($\dot{V}O_2$) of resting animals (Krogh, 1914). If the temperature coefficient of metabolism ($Q_{10}$) is 2.5, the resting $\dot{V}O_2$ changes about 10% for each 1°C change in $T_b$. Consequently, if there is a limited $O_2$ supply or $O_2$-transport capacity, fever or hyperthermia will aggravate hypoxemia. Conversely, a moderate degree of hypothermia could be beneficial, particularly to heart and brain, in several ways: 1) by reducing $O_2$ demand, 2) by increasing hemoglobin–oxygen affinity and arterial saturation, and 3) by avoiding the costly processes of increasing cardiac output and ventilation.

The effect of hypoxia on physiological thermoregulation in small mammals is well known. Hypoxia induces hypothermia, particularly in neonates, owing to decreased heat production and increased heat loss (Lintzel, 1931; Gellhorn and Janus, 1936; Adolph, 1957; Miller and Miller, 1966; Lister, 1984; Dupré et al., 1988).

The effect of hypoxia on behavioral thermoregulation in ectotherms is a newer area of research. A model of $O_2$ transport in animals with shunts led to the hypothesis that hypoxia would elicit behavioral hypothermia (Wood, 1984). This was tested and confirmed in lizards by Hicks and Wood (1985). The threshold for a behavioral response as inspired $[O_2]$ decreased was at $\approx$ 10%. Other species from various taxa also show behavioral hypothermia in response to hypoxia (Table 1). Many of these display a nongraded response, with a threshold at $\approx$ 10% $[O_2]$. The import of the 10% $O_2$ threshold probably relates to the shape of the $O_2$ dissociation curve. As inspired $[O_2]$ is reduced from 21%, arterial

---

*Behavioral hypothermia is a poor term, since there is evidence that $T_b$ is *regulating* at a lower value. Hypothermia, like hyperthermia, is an unregulated change in $T_b$. A better term would be one analogous to "fever" (i.e., one that describes a regulated change in $T_b$). The term *anapyrexia* has been suggested for pathological conditions that lower the set-point (Cabanac, 1987).

**Table 1** Effect of Hypoxia on Body Temperature

| Inspired $O_2$ | $n$ | $T_b$, °C 21% | $T_b$, °C 5–10% | Ref. |
|---|---|---|---|---|
| Insects | | | | |
| Tenebrid beetle | 36 | 17.3 | 20.2 | Wood et al., 1987 |
| Arachnids | | | | |
| *Aphoropelura chalcodes* | 3 | 31.3 | 32.1 | Wood et al., unpublished |
| Crustaceans | | | | |
| *Procambarus simulans* | 6 | 22.1 | 17.6* | Dupré and Wood, 1988 |
| Fish | | | | |
| *Carasius auratus* | 3 | 23.0 | 20.9 | Wood et al., 1985 |
| *Salmo gairdneri* | 9 | 16.6 | 15.7* | Schurmann and Steffenson, 1989 |
| Amphibians | | | | |
| *Ambystoma tigrinum* | 5 | 18.8 | 16.2* | Dupré and Wood, 1988 |
| *Bufo marinus* | 9 | 25.6 | 18.2* | Riedel and Wood, 1988 |
| Reptiles | | | | |
| *Iguana iguana* | 4 | 35.4 | 28.1* | Hicks and Wood, 1985 |
| *Ctenosaurus pectinata* | 6 | 35.5 | 30.6* | Hicks and Wood, 1985 |
| *Varanus varius* | 1 | 35.6 | 30.6 | Hicks and Wood, 1985 |
| *V. exanthematicus* | 8 | 34.9 | 29.2* | Hicks and Wood, 1985 |
| Birds | | | | |
| *Melopsittacus un.* | 6 | 39.5 | 35.8* | Wood et al., 1985 |
| Mammals | | | | |
| *Rattus norvegicus* | 22 | 37 | 34.5* | Riedel and Wood, 1988 |
| *Spermophilus lateralis* | 6 | 37.2 | 36.2 (10%) 32.4* (5%) | Wood et al., 1985 |
| *Mus musculus* | 5 | 36.3 | 35.8* (9.3%) 29.3* (5.5%) | Gordon and Fogelson, 1991 |
| *Mesocricetus auratus* | 6 | 37.1 | 36.2* (10%) 34.0* (5.8%) | Gordon and Fogelson, 1991 |

* $p < 0.05$.

saturation is initially preserved along the flat upper portion of the dissociation curve, whereas 10% inspired $[O_2]$ produces marked desaturation. Among the invertebrates tested, crayfish show a behavioral hypothermia, but tenebrid beetles and tarantula spiders do not. Tarantulas have a preferred $T_b$ of 31°C, and this is not altered by inspired $[O_2]$ as low as 3%.

Exposure of fish to hypoxia elicits behavioral hypothermia (see Table 1), and exposure to anoxia affects later $T_b$ selection in a normoxic thermal gradient. Goldfish exposed to anoxia for 5 hr select a $T_b \approx 5$°C lower than the corresponding normoxic controls (Crawshaw et al., 1989). Ethanol may mediate this

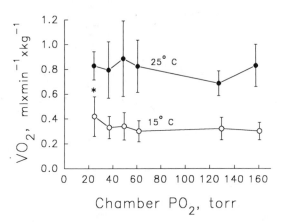

**Figure 1** Oxygen uptake of *B. marinus* at 25° and 15°C during graded hypoxia. There was no significant effect of hypoxia except at 4% inspired $O_2$ at 15°C. The effect of temperature was significant at each level of inspired $O_2$. (Data from Wood and Malvin, 1991.)

response because it is a by-product of anaerobic metabolism in goldfish, and ethanol injected into the hypothalamic thermoregulatory center elicits an immediate behavioral hypothermia of ≈ 8°C.

Hypoxia alters behavioral thermoregulation in rats (Dupré and Owen, 1989) and mice (Gordon and Fogelson, 1991). Mice show a close parallel to the amphibian and reptilian responses. Mice select a lower-than-normal ambient temperature at an $O_2$ threshold of ≈ 10%. This is also the threshold at which core temperature starts to drop, probably facilitated by the reduction of ambient temperature.

Biochemical depression of metabolism at a constant $T_b$ is also an effective adaptation to hypoxia. This has been documented in some species as a mechanism to survive low $O_2$ or other harsh conditions (Hochachka, 1988; Storey, 1988). Little is known about possible interaction between the $Q_{10}$ effect and biochemical depression of metabolism in hypoxic animals. This can readily be done by comparing the $Q_{10}$ of normoxic and hypoxic animals; that is, ectotherms exposed to combined events of hypoxia exposure and temperature drop would have a larger $Q_{10}$ than animals exposed solely to a temperature drop. We recently tested this possibility in toads, *Bufo marinus*, by measuring $\dot{V}O_2$ during graded hypoxia at 25° and 15°C. There was no evidence for depressed aerobic metabolism at either temperature as inspired $[O_2]$ was reduced from 26 to 4% (Fig. 1). In fact, at 15°C, each animal showed an elevated $\dot{V}O_2$ at 4% inspired $O_2$, a finding also reported for hypoxic *B. marinus* at 22°C (Pörtner et al., 1990). The potential interaction between metabolic and cold depression of metabolism needs further study in other species.

## III. Importance of Behavioral Hypothermia During Hypoxia

The potential benefits of hypothermia in hypoxic animals are summarized in the following

### A. Survival

A decrease in $T_b$ is a normal response of mammals to hypoxia. Neonatal mammals (Miller and Miller, 1966) and anemic rabbits (Gollan and Aono, 1973) show increased survival when they are hypothermic. Asphyxiated neonates treated by hypothermia have a mortality of 11.5% compared with 48% in 288 cases not using hypothermia (Dunn and Miller, 1969). Lizards allowed to cool during hypoxia show 100% survival versus 100% mortality of animals kept at the normoxic preferred temperature (Hicks and Wood, 1985).

### B. Central Nervous System

A common cause of CNS damage in childhood is perinatal hypoxia. The consequences include motor disturbances, behavioral abnormalities, and learning disabilities (Kreussler and Volpe, 1984). The hypoxic–ischemic neural degeneration is apparently mediated by endogenous excitatory amino acids, glutamate and aspartate (Rothman and Olney, 1986). Busto et al. (1987) measured the effects of brain temperature during brain ischemia in rats. They found that brain temperature decreased spontaneously from 36° to 30–31°C during ischemia. Furthermore, this cooling of the brain prevented cell damage, whereas animals in which the brain temperature was maintained by heat lamps showed significant histopathology in the hippocampus following ischemia.

### C. Tissue Metabolism

The resting metabolic rate is reduced by $\approx$ 11%/°C reduction in $T_b$ (for a $Q_{10}$ = 2.5). In addition, critical $Po_2$ may be reduced. Critical $Po_2$ is the $Po_2$ below which normal resting $\dot{V}o_2$ can no longer be maintained. There are theoretical and experimental data showing that critical $Po_2$ in some ectothermic species is decreased with decreased $T_b$ (Hicks and Wood, 1989).

### D. Ventilation

In reptiles and amphibians, lowering $T_b$ reduces the ventilatory response to hypoxia (Glass et al., 1983; Kruhøffer et al., 1987; Dupré et al., 1989). Glass et al. (1983) showed that the arterial $Po_2$ needed to elicit a ventilatory response of turtles became progressively less as $T_b$ was lowered. They pointed out that, in spite of varying arterial $Po_2$ values at the hypoxic threshold, the arterial $[O_2]$ was relatively constant owing to the effect of temperature on the position of the $O_2$ dissociation curve of blood. In any event, the reduction of selected $T_b$ during hypoxia will reduce or abolish the ventilatory response and further conserve energy.

### E. Oxygen Transport

The effect of hypothermia on $\dot{V}o_2$ is predictable ($Q_{10}$ effect), but not, a priori, for systemic $O_2$ transport (SOT), the product of cardiac output ($\dot{Q}$) × arterial $O_2$ content ($Ca_{O_2}$). Cardiac output may or may not decrease, depending on sympathetic reflexes or possible alterations in contractility. The $Ca_{O_2}$ may or may not change depending on degree of hypoxia and left shift of the oxyhemoglobin dissociation curve (Lister, 1984). Both of the foregoing will depend on changes in acid–base status from metabolic, respiratory, or temperature effects.

### F. Potential Disadvantages of Hypothermia

Despite the potential advantages of hypothermia during hypoxic and other stresses, there are also possible disadvantages and uncertain advantages. For example, prolonged hypothermia may decelerate brain development (Schain and Watanabe, 1971) and interfere with the normal immune response. Ventricular fibrillation may occur in hypothermic mammals during hypothermia unless the blood pH is allowed to rise following the "buffalo curve" (Kroncke et al., 1986). Furthermore, although the effect of $T_b$ on $\dot{V}o_2$ is predictable for standard metabolic rate ($Q_{10}$ effect), during hypoxia the effects of alertness, activity, or catecholamines may intervene.

Also, the effect of hypothermia on systemic $O_2$ transport is not readily predictable. The $Ca_{O_2}$ may or may not change depending on the degree of hypoxia, the degree of intracardiac shunt, and the left shift of the oxyhemoglobin dissociation curve (Lister, 1984). These factors will depend on changes in hemodynamics and acid–base status caused by metabolic, respiratory, or temperature effects. For SOT, potential advantages can be related to the Fick principal; that is, $\dot{V}o_2 = \dot{Q} \times (Ca_{O_2} - C\bar{v}_{O_2})$. By definition, $SOT = \dot{Q} \times Ca_{O_2}$, and oxygen extraction ($Eo_2$) = $(Ca_{O_2} - C\bar{v}_{O_2})/Ca_{O_2}$. Combining these equations gives the relationship, $\dot{V}o_2 = SOT \times Eo_2$. There are three possible outcomes of the measurements of $\dot{V}o_2$ and SOT in animals during hypothermia and hypoxia. First, if hypothermia reduces basal metabolic rate more than SOT, then $Eo_2$ will decrease. This could be beneficial by increasing venous and tissue $Po_2$. Second, SOT and $\dot{V}o_2$ could decrease by the same amount (same $Q_{10}$), with no net effect on $EO_2$. Third, SOT might decrease more than $\dot{V}O_2$, with a potentially deleterious increase in $EO_2$.

## G. Data Versus Theory

We tested the hypotheses that hypoxic *B. marinus* will select a lower-than-normal $T_b$ and that this behavior hypothermia will reduce the stress of hypoxia (Wood and Malvin, 1991). The stress of hypoxia and physiological significance of behavioral hypothermia were determined for metabolic rate, $Sa_{O_2}$, acid–base balance, and ventilation. We found that *B. marinus* selected a $T_b$ of 24.2°C ± 3.6°(SD) under normoxic conditions, but as inspired $O_2$ was reduced to 10%, the selected $T_b$ became 15°C ± 2.4°. In addition to lowering the $O_2$ demand (see Fig. 1), reducing $T_b$ to 15°C under hypoxic conditions caused a significant increase in arterial saturation and a substantial reduction in the ventilatory response to hypoxia. Therefore, in this species, behavioral hypothermia is a highly beneficial response.

## IV. Anemia-Induced Hypothermia

Whatever an animal's preferred $T_b$, it must have the $O_2$-transport capacity to satisfy the resting $\dot{V}O_2$ for that temperature. This argument led to the hypothesis that ectothermic animals, faced with a reduced $O_2$-transport capacity (e.g., hematocrit reduction), would select a lower-than-normal $T_b$.

Hicks and Wood (1985) measured the thermal behavior of lizards in response to hematocrit reduction. In the four species studied, there was a rapid behavioral hypothermia of ≈ 8°C in response to hematocrit reduction, and a return to normal $T_b$ selection after spontaneous recovery of the hematocrit.

Recent studies in the toad, *B. marinus,* extended the study of hematocrit effects on $T_b$ control to include cross-sectional and longitudinal analyses (Wood, 1990). In cross-sectional analysis, there was no correlation between selected $T_b$ and hematocrit of toads. However, when hematocrit was lowered by removal of blood, toads selected a significantly lower temperature. The magnitude of change in selected temperature ($\Delta T_b$) was related to the magnitude of the fall in hematocrit. Linear regression analysis for the anemia experiments gave a regression of $\Delta T_b = 0.42 + 0.45 \, \Delta\%Hct$ (n = 7; r = 0.86; p < 0.013). For example, a fall in Hct from 35 to 25% would elicit the selection of a 4.9°C cooler $T_b$. This would result in a reduction of $\dot{V}O_2$ of ≈ 51%, assuming a $Q_{10}$ of ≈ 2.5.

Hematocrits are lower and more variable in ectotherms than in homeotherms (Atland, 1971). The relatively imprecise regulation of hematocrit of ectotherms probably reflects lower rates of aerobic metabolism and higher tolerance of anaerobic metabolism. For example, bullfrogs can survive with hematocrits of 0% following injection of phenylhydrazine (Flores and Frieden, 1968). Therefore, the lack of a correlation, in cross-sectional analyses, between selected $T_b$ and hematocrit is not surprising. Even if there were a correlation, it would not suggest a cause-and-effect relationship. However, when the hematocrit of individual lizards or toads is reduced, selected $T_b$ is reduced. For *B. marinus*, the amount of $T_b$ reduction is closely correlated with the degree of hematocrit reduction, as if $T_b$ selection is "tracking" hematocrit. Once again, it is conjecture to infer cause and effect from this correlation.

## V.  Hypercapnia-Induced Hypothermia

Physiological thermoregulation of endotherms becomes impaired during hypercapnia. In humans, hypercapnia reduces heat production and increases heat loss by augmenting sweating and inhibiting shivering (Schaefer et al., 1975). Little is known about behavioral thermoregulation of ectotherms in response to hypercapnia. Exposure of *B. marinus* to 10% $CO_2$ elicits a significant behavioral reduction of selected $T_b$. This severe hypercapnia is well outside the range of normally encountered $CO_2$ levels (in burrows). Exposure to 5% $CO_2$, a level that is encountered in burrows, has no effect on $T_b$ selection (Riedel and Wood, 1988). More studies are needed to determine if a hypothermic response to hypercapnia is ecologically relevant or, rather, a manifestation of a generalized stress response, possibly mediated by release of arginine vasotocin (see later discussion).

## VI.  Hypothermia Induced by Dry Environments

Because water has a high heat of vaporization, evaporation of water from body surfaces is very effective in lowering $T_b$. Many animals take advantage of this to regulate $T_b$ by sweating or panting. Water's high heat of vaporization also causes the vapor pressure of water to be very sensitive to changes in temperature (e.g., at 38°C the vapor pressure of water (50 torr) is twice as high as at 25°C (24 torr). As a result, altering $T_b$ can be a very effective method of regulating evaporative water loss.

To restrict evaporative water loss, most reptiles, birds, and mammals rely primarily on a waterproof skin. Additional mechanisms exist in some animals for reducing evaporation, such as a countercurrent exchange of water during ventilation in the respiratory passages to reduce respiratory water loss (Schmidt-Nielsen, 1969). Amphibians are different. In most species, the skin is highly permeable to water, allowing evaporation rates several hundred times those of other terrestrial vertebrates (Shoemaker and Nagy, 1977). To prevent rapid dehydration, many amphibians stay close to water their entire lives. However, hundreds of amphibian species are terrestrial. For these animals, survival on

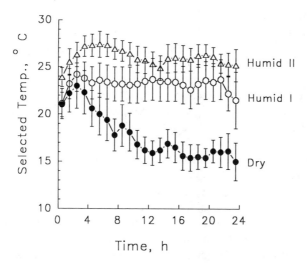

**Figure 2** Behavioral thermoregulation of *B. marinus* under humid and dry conditions. Values are means ± SEM; n = 9. The dotted line indicates a significant difference (p < 0.05) between the dry period and the second humid period. The solid line indicates a significant difference between the dry period and the initial humid period. (Data from Malvin and Wood, 1991.)

land depends on several special adaptations. These include the ability to withstand large amounts of water loss (up to 60% of body water), the ability to reabsorb water from the bladder and, in some species, uricotelism.

An additional adaptation occurs in toads (i.e., behavioral hypothermia in response to dry environmental conditions; Malvin and Wood, 1991). The effect of humidity on behavioral thermal regulation of *B. marinus* was examined in a thermal gradient for 3 days. On days 1 and 3, water dishes were available, and humid air was circulated through the chamber. On day 2, water dishes were removed, and dry air circulated through the gradient chamber. Toads selected a 8.6°C lower $T_b$ within the gradient during the dry conditions (5–7% relative humidity) than during the humid periods (67–90% relative humidity) (Fig. 2).

This drop in $T_b$ will have a large effect on the driving gradient for evaporative water loss. For example, a reduction in $T_b$ from 24° to 15.5°C will lower the vapor pressure of the blood by 41%. If the vapor pressure of air is zero, this change will reduce the driving gradient for water loss between the blood and air by 41%.

Temperature affects factors besides the driving gradient for evaporative water loss. In additional experiments on *B. marinus,* water loss and the driving gradient for evaporative water flux between blood and air were measured at two different temperatures ($T_b$s of 17.7° and 12.3°C). From these measurements, the conductance of the animal for evaporative water flux ($G_{H_2O}$—the mass of water evaporating per time per unit difference in water vapor pressure between the blood and air) was calculated. If temperature influences evaporative water loss only by affecting the driving gradient for that process, then $G_{H_2O}$ should be insensitive to temperature. However, the 5.4°C fall in $T_b$ caused a 27.7% reduction in $G_{H_2O}$. A fall in $G_{H_2O}$ combined with a decrease in the driving gradient for evaporative water loss will be additive in conserving water. The factors responsible for the change in $G_{H_2O}$ with temperature are not known. One possibility is a reduction in pulmonary ventilation that occurs with a decrease in temperature (Kruhøffer et al., 1987). However, this should have only a very small effect on total water loss because pulmonary water loss is only a small percentage of cutaneous loss in amphibians (Bentley and Yorio, 1979). Water loss is also affected by posture (i.e., the amount of skin surface exposed to air). Posture may also affect the pattern of airflow around the animal, another important factor affecting evaporation rate (Machin, 1964). However, there is no evidence to evaluate these possibilities. Cutaneous blood flow and the water permeability of the skin are not factors regulating evaporative water loss because the skin presents little or no barrier to evaporative water loss in toads (Shoemaker and Nagy, 1977).

Hypothermia to reduce water loss is not unique to *B. marinus*. This response also occurs in animals with less permeable skins. The reptiles, *Sceloporus undulatus* (Crowley, 1987) and *Anniella pulchra* (Bury and Balgooyen, 1976), reduce $T_b$ behaviorally when dehydrated, but the desert iguana does not (Dupré and Crawford, 1985). Two unusual tree frogs, *Chiromantis xerampelina* and *Phyllomedusa sauvagei,* have skin that is only slightly permeable to water. They decrease selected $T_b$ when dehydrated (Shoemaker et al., 1989). The effect of a decrease in $T_b$ in these animals will be similar to that in toads; a decrease in evaporative water loss, but the impact on total water economy should not be as dramatic.

## VII. Toxin and Drug-Induced Hypothermia

Numerous substances and environmental conditions are known to elicit behavioral and physiological hypothermia (e.g., ethanol, urine, vasopressin, morphine, prostaglandins, histamine, hypoxia, dry air, anemia, pesticides, food deprivation, and toxic chemicals; Gordon, 1988a,b). Other drugs and toxins elicit hyperthermia in mammals (Olson and Benowitz, 1984), so the response is not uniform. Laboratory mammals select lower temperatures when exposed to toxic substances and regulate $T_b$ at a lower value. For example, nickel chloride affects both behavioral and autonomic control of $T_b$ in rats (Gordon and Watkinson, 1989).

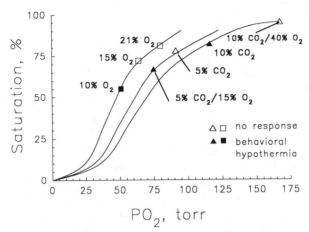

**Figure 3** Arterial blood gases of *B. marinus* under normoxic, hypoxic, and combined hypoxic–hypercapnic conditions. (Data from Reidel and Wood, 1988.)

The resulting hypothermia reduces the toxicity of most xenobiotic compounds (Gordon, 1988; Gordon et al., 1988).

## VIII. Potential Mediators of Behavioral Hypothermia

The physiological pathways involved in behavioral thermoregulation are largely unknown. Consequently, it is difficult to identify the mediators of the hypothermic response. However, it is possible to rule out some factors and to focus on others as potential mediators.

An initial question about behavioral hypothermia under conditions of hypoxia, anemia, or hypercapnia was, "what triggers the behavior?" The initial focus was on $O_2$, either $PO_2$ (hypoxia), $O_2$ saturation (hypoxia), or $O_2$ content (anemia). Exposure to 10% $CO_2$ was expected to reduce $O_2$ saturation (by shifting the $O_2$ dissociation curve to the right), to have unpredictable effects on $PO_2$ (at a constant saturation, $PO_2$ would increase as the dissociation curve shifts to the right, but decreasing saturation would offset or negate this affinity effect), and to decrease pH. However, behavioral hypothermia was elicited under conditions of increasing, rather than decreasing, $O_2$ saturation and $PO_2$ (Fig. 3). These experiments argue against $O_2$ or pH as the eliciting stimulus, per se.

Three potential mediators that could be common to the varied stimuli of behavioral hypothermia are arginine vasopressin (AVP), histamine, and adenosine. Arginine vasotocin (AVT) is a peptide hormone closely related to AVP and functions as a transmitter in amphibians, reptiles, and birds. Several lines of evidence suggest that AVT is involved as a mediator of both physiological and behavioral hypothermia.

1. Hypoxia stimulates the release of AVP in rats (Walker, 1986), in fetal sheep (Stegner et al., 1984), and in human infants born after hypoxic distress (Ruth et al., 1988). In hypoxic dogs, reducing arterial $[O_2]$ to 8 vol%, causes a 250% increase in blood flow to the neurohypophysis and a concurrent rise in plasma AVP from 8 to 52 pg/ml (Wilson et al., 1987). Carotid and aortic chemoreceptor denervation abolishes both the blood flow response and AVP response.

2. Arginine vasopressin is an endogenous antipyretic peptide in mammals. Centrally administered AVP elicits thermoregulatory actions that are both neuroanatomically and functionally specific (Naylor et al., 1986). There is also evidence that AVP is released centrally in response to hypoxia, hypercapnia, dehydration, and such (Wang et al., 1984). It is a central neurotransmitter that coordinates autonomic and endocrine responses to homeostatic perturbations (Riphagen and Pittman, 1986). Arginine vasotocin is known to be involved in thermoregulation of birds (Robinzon et al., 1988) and a vasotocin neurosecretory system has been identified in lizards (Bons, 1983).

3. There is enhanced AVP release in response to hypercapnic acidosis in rats (Walker, 1987). Hypercapnia induces behavioral hypothermia in toads (Riedel and Wood, 1988).

4. Dehydration increases AVP release in mammals (Wade et al., 1983) and increases AVT release in amphibians (Shoemaker and Nagy, 1977).

Histamine is another potential mediator of altered thermoregulation during hypoxia. It is involved in mammalian thermoregulation (e.g., Bligh et al., 1980), and its release has been implicated in radiation-induced hypothermia in rats (Kandasamy et al., 1988). Histamine infusion into either the lateral ventricle or fourth ventricle of rats induces hypothermia (Dey and Mukhopadhaya, 1986). It is also involved in behavioral thermoregulation of fish (Green and Lomax, 1976) and salamanders (Hutchison and Spriestersbach, 1986). The behavioral response of salamanders was blocked with $H_1$- and $H_2$-blocking agents (pyrilamine and cimetidine). Although histamine does not readily pass the blood–brain barrier in mammals, it apparently can in ectotherms (Green and Lomax, 1976).

Another potential mediator is adenosine. The adenosine agonist 5'-$N$-ethylcarboxamidoadenosine produces a 10°C drop of $T_b$ in rats that can be blocked by caffeine, an adenosine receptor antagonist (Seale et al., 1988). Adenosine is a normal product of ATP catabolism and increases during hypoxia. Thus, both histamine and adenosine provide reasonable alternative hypotheses to AVP for the mediation of hypoxia-induced hypothermia.

**Table 2** Stressors That Elicit Behavioral Hypothermia and the Physiological Significance of Reduced Body Temperature. Feedback Control System for Each is Illustrated in Figure 4.

| Stress | Importance of Hypothermia |
|--------|---------------------------|
| Hypoxia | Left shift of the oxyhemoglobin dissociation curve ( $\downarrow$ $P_{50}$) with the resulting improvement of $O_2$ loading in the lungs |
| Hypoxia, anemia | Decreased $\dot{V}O_2$ according to the $Q_{10}$ effect (e.g., $\dot{V}O_2$ would decrease $\approx$ 11%/°C |
| Hypoxia, anemia | Energetically costly processes (e.g., increased cardiac output and ventilation are reduced or avoided) reduced "critical $PO_2$" |
| Hypoxia, anemia | Prevention or reduction or neurological damage and learning disturbances |
| Hypercapnia | Ventilatory response is reduced, $\dot{V}O_2$ is reduced |
| Dry air, dehydration | Evaporative water loss is reduced |
| Toxins | The $LD_{50}$ is increased (toxicity is reduced) |
| Food deprivation | Metabolic rate is reduced |

## IX. Summary

Amphibians and reptiles share a feature that dominates their lives; a body temperature that is controllable primarily by behavior. This feature restricts their distribution to certain habitats, latitudes, and altitudes. It is also an important aspect of control mechanisms for blood pH, ventilation, circulation, and metabolism.

At their preferred body temperature, amphibians and reptiles are potentially more susceptible to hypoxia than are endotherms because their blood has a relatively lower $O_2$ affinity. By having shunts and a right-shifted $O_2$ dissociation curve, most species do not have the hypoxic reserve of the upper plateau of the $O_2$ dissociation curve that allows mammals and birds to tolerate moderate hypoxia with minimum arterial desaturation. Amphibians and reptiles cope with this problem in many ways, including a high capacity and tolerance for anaerobic metabolism. Amphibians and reptiles can also cope with hypoxic stress by taking advantage of their ectothermy to utilize behavioral hypothermia and, thereby, reduce $O_2$ demand.

Table 2 summarizes the stresses that are ameliorated by behavioral hypothermia. No doubt, this list will increase as future studies examine the link between thermoregulation and stress response.

Ectothermic animals are often depicted as being metabolically and functionally impaired when they are kept at a temperature lower than their "preferred" $T_b$. Studies of lizards have shown that all kinds of functions, including endurance,

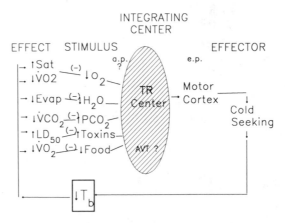

**Figure 4**  Negative-feedback control of body temperature induced by various stressful stimuli; a.p. and e.p. refer to afferent and efferent pathways.

burst speed, digestion, and hearing, are impaired at temperatures below the preferred $T_b$ (Huey, 1982). A common theme is that the evolution of increased locomotor and exercise capacity was linked to the evolution of endothermy and that "warmer is better" (Bennett, 1987).

However, the preferred $T_b$ is affected by many ecological and physiological factors. Under a variety of stressful conditions, it seems that "cooler is better." What has yet to be determined is the mechanism of the behavioral hypothermia; that is, what triggers and mediates behavioral hypothermia under these various stresses? Whatever this proves to be—AVT or something else—ectotherms can take advantage of their ectothermy, by using behavioral hypothermia to reduce the rates of energy consumption and water loss when supplies are limited. Figure 4 summarizes the feedback control of $T_b$ by behavioral means that results in a reduction of the various stressful stimuli.

### Acknowledgments

Research of the authors was supported by grants from the Flinn Foundation, Phoenix, Arizona and NIH (HL40537) (S. W.) and by the NIH (HL38942) (G. M.). Inspiration of the authors to explore biology came from Kjell Johansen, who taught us by example.

### References

Adolph, E. F. (1957). Ontogeny of physiological regulations in the rat. *Q. Rev. Biol.*, **32**:89–137.

Atland, P. D. (1971). Erythrocyte and hemoglobin values: Vertebrates other than man. In *Respiration and Circulation*. Edited by P. L. Altman and D. S. Dittmer. Bethesda, Md., Federation of Societies for Experimental Biology, pp. 151–153.

Bennett, A. F. (1987). Evolution of the control of body temperature: Is warmer better? In *Fidia Research Series*, Vol. 9. Edited by P. Dejours, L. Bolis, C. R. Taylor, and E. R. Wiebel. Padova, Liviana Press, pp. 421–431.

Bentley, P. J., and Yorio, T. (1979). Evaporative water loss in anuran amphibia: A comparative study. *Comp. Biochem. Physiol.*, **62A**:1005–1009.

Bligh, J., Silver, A., and Smith, C. A. (1980). The effects of thermoregulatory mechanisms produced by intracerebroventricular injections of histamine in the sheep. *J. Therm. Biol.*, **5**:41–51.

Bons, N. (1983). Immunocytochemical identification of the mesotocin and vasotocin-producing systems in the brain of temperate and desert lizard species and their modifications by cold exposure. *Gen. Comp. Endocrinol.*, **52**:56–66.

Bury, R. B., and Balgooyen, T. G. (1976). Temperature selectivity in the legless lizard, *Anniella pulchra*. *Copeia*, **1976**:152–155.

Busto, R., Dalton, W., Dietrich, T., Globus, M., Valdés, I., Scheinberg, P., and Ginsberg, M. (1987). Small differences in intraischemic brain temperature critically determine the extent of ischemic neuronal injury. *J. Cereb. Blood Flow Metab.*, **7**:729–738.

Cabanac, M. (1987). The pathology of human temperature regulation: Thermiatrics. *Experientia*, **43**:19–27.

Crawshaw, L. I., Wollmuth, L. P., and O'Conner, C. S. (1989). Intracranial ethanol and ambient anoxia elicit selection of cooler water by goldfish. *Am. J. Physiol.*, **256**:R133–R137.

Crawshaw, L. I., and Hammel, H. T. (1973). Behavioral temperature regulation in the California horn shark, *Heterodontus francisci*. *Brain Behav. Evol.*, **7**:447–452.

Crowley, S. R. (1987). The effect of dessication upon the preferred body temperature and activity level of the lizard, *Sceloporus undulatus*. *Copeia* **1987**:25–32.

Dey, P. K., and Mukhopadhaya, N. (1986). Involvement of histamine receptors in mediation of histamine induced thermoregulatory response in rats. *Indian J. Physiol. Pharmacol.*, **30**:300–306.

Dunn, J. M., and Miller, J. A., Jr. (1969). Hypothermia combined with positive pressure ventilation in resuscitation of the asphyxiated neonate. *Am. J. Obstet. Gynecol.*, **104**:58.

Dupré, R. K., and Owen, T. L. (1989). Behavioral thermoregulation in hypoxic rats. *Fed. Proc.*, **3**:A838.

Dupré, R. K., and Crawford, E. C., Jr. (1985). Behavioral thermoregulation during dehydration and osmotic loading of the desert iguana. *Physiol. Zool.*, **58**:357–363.

Dupré, R. K., and Wood, S. C. (1988). Behavioral temperature regulation by aquatic ectotherms during hypoxia. *Can. J. Zool.*, **66**:2649–2652.

Dupré, R. K., Hicks, J. W., and Wood, S. C. (1989). Effect of temperature on chemical control of ventilation in Mexican black iguanas. *Am. J. Physiol.*, **257**:R1258–1263.

Dupré, R. K., Romero, A. M., and Wood, S. C. (1988). Thermoregulation and metabolism in hypoxic animals, In *Oxygen Transfer from Environment to Tissues*. Edited by R. Fedde and N. Gonzalez. New York, Plenum Press, pp. 347–351.

Flores, G., and Frieden, E. (1968). Induction and survival of hemoglobin-less and erythrocyte-less tadpoles and young bullfrogs. *Science,* **159**:101–103.

Gellhorn, E., and Janus, A. (1936). The influence of partial pressures of $O_2$ on body temperature. *Am. J. Physiol.,* **116**:327–329.

Glass, M. L., and Wood, S. C. (1983). Gas exchange and control of breathing in reptiles. *Physiol. Rev.,* **63**:232–259.

Glass, M. L., Boutelier, R. G., and Heisler, N. (1983). Ventilatory control of arterial $Po_2$ in the turtle, *Chrysemys picta bellii:* Effects of temperature and hypoxia. *J. Comp. Physiol.,* **151**:145–153.

Gollan, F., and Aono, M. (1973). The effect of temperature on sanguinous rabbits. *Cryobiology,* **10**:321–327.

Gordon, C. J. (1988). Effect of nickel chloride on body temperature and behavioral thermoregulation in rats. *Neurotoxicol. Teratol.,* **11**:317–320.

Gordon, C. J., and Fogelson, L. (1991). Comparative effects of hypoxia on behavioral thermoregulation in the rat, hamster, and mouse. *Am. J. Physiol.,* **260**:R120–R125.

Gordon, C. J., Mohler, F. S., Watkinson, W. P., and Rezvani, A. H. (1988). Temperature regulation in laboratory mammals following acute toxic insult. *Toxicology,* **53**:161–178.

Green, M. D., and Lomax, P. (1976). Behavioral thermoregulation and neuroamines in fish (*Chromus chromus*). *J. Therm. Biol.,* **1**:237–240.

Hicks, J. W., and Wood, S. C. (1985). Temperature regulation in lizards: Effects of hypoxia. *Am. J. Physiol.,* **248**:R595–R600.

Hicks, J. W., and Wood, S. C. (1989). Oxygen homeostasis. In *Comparative Respiratory Physiology*. Edited by S. C. Wood. (Biology of the Lung in Health and Disease, Vol. 39. Edited by C. Lemfant). New York, Marcel Dekker, pp. 311–42.

Hochachka, P. W. (1988). Metabolic suppression and $O_2$ availability. *Can. J. Zool.,* **66**:152–158.

Huey, R. B. (1982). Temperature, physiology, and ecology of reptiles. In *Biology of the Reptilia*, Vol. 12. Edited by C. Gans and F. H. Pough. New York, Academic Press, pp. 25–92.

Hutchison, V. H., and Spriesterbach, K. K. (1986). Histamine and histamine receptors: Behavioral thermoregulation in the salamander, *Necturus maculosus*. *Comp. Biol. Physiol.,* **85**:199–206.

Kandasamy, S. B., Hunt, W. A., and Mickley, G. A. (1988). Implication of prostaglandin and histamine $H_1$ and $H_2$ receptors in radiation-induced temperature responses of rats. *Radiat. Res.,* **114**:42–53.

Kluger, M., Ringler, D. H., and Anver, M. R. (1975). Fever and survival. *Science,* **188**:166–168.

Kreussler, K. L., and Volpe, J. J. (1984). The neurological outcome of perinatal asphyxia. *Early Brain Damage,* **1**:151–167.

Krogh, A. (1914). The quantitative relation between temperature and standard metabolism in animals. *Int. Z. Phys. Chem. Biol.*, **1**:491–508.

Kroncke, G. M., Nichols, R. D., Mendenshall, J. T., Myerowitz, P. D., and Starling, J. R. (1986). Ectothermic philosophy of acid base balance to prevent fibrillation during hypoxia. *Arch. Surg.*, **121**:303–304.

Kruhøffer, M., Glass, M. L., Abe, A. S., and Johansen, K. (1987). Control of breathing in an amphibian, *Bufo paracnemius:* Effects of temperature and hypoxia. *Respir. Physiol.*, **69**:267–275.

Lintzel, W. (1931). Uber die Wirkung der Luftverdunnung auf Tiere. V. Mitteilung Gaswechsel weisser Ratten. *Pfügers Arch. Ges. Physiol.*, **227**:673–708.

Lister, G. (1984). Oxygen transport in the intact hypoxic newborn lamb: Acute effects of increasing $P_{50}$. *Pediatr. Res.*, **18**:172–177.

Machin, J. (1964). The evaporation of water from *Helix aspera*. II. Measurement of air flow and the diffusion of water vapor. *J. Exp. Biol.*, **41**:771–781.

Malvin, G. M., and Wood, S. C. (1991). Behavioral thermoregulation of the toad, *Bufo marinus:* Effects of ambient humidity. *J. Exp. Zool.*, (in press).

Miller, J. A., and Miller, F. S. (1966). Interactions between hypothermia and hypoxia–hypercapnia in neonates. *Fed. Proc.*, **25**:1338–1341.

Naylor, A. M., Ruwe, W. D., and Veale, W. L. (1986). Thermoregulatory actions of centrally administered vasopressin in the rat. *Neuropharmacology*, **25**:787–794.

Olson, K. R., and Benowitz, N. L. (1984). Environmental and drug induced hyperthermia. *Emerg. Med. Clin. North Am.*, **2**:459–474.

Pörtner, H. O., MacLatchy, L. M., and Toews, D. P. (1991). Metabolic responses of the toad, *Bufo marinus*, to environmental hypoxia: An analysis of the critical $P_{O_2}$. *Physiol. Zool.*, (in press).

Reynolds, W. W., and Casterlin, M. E. (1982). The pyrogenic responses of non-mammalian vertebrates. In *Pyretics and Antipyretics*. Edited by A. S. Milton. Berlin, Springer-Verlag, pp. 649–668.

Riedel, C., and Wood, S. C. (1988). Effects of hypercapnia and hypoxia on temperature selection of the toad, *Bufo marinus*. *Fed. Proc.*, **2**:A500.

Riphagen, C. L., and Pittman, Q. J. (1986). Arginine vasopressin as a central neurotransmitter. *Fed. Proc.*, **45**:2318–2322.

Robinzon, B., Koike, T. I., Neldon, H. L., Kinzler, S. L., Hendry, I. R., and el-Halawani, M. E. (1988). Physiological effects of arginine vasotocin and mesotocin in cockerels. *Br. Poultry Sci.*, **29**:639–652.

Rothman, S. M., and Olney, J. W. (1986). Glutamate and the pathophysiology of hypoxic–ischemic brain damage. *Ann. Neurol.*, **19**:105–111.

Ruth, V., Fyhrquist, F., Clemons, G., and Raivio, K. O. (1988). Cord plasma vasopressin, erythropoietin, and hypoxanthine as indices of asphyxia at birth. *Pediatr. Res.*, **24**:490–494.

Schaefer, K., Messier, A. A., Morgan, C., and Baker, G. T. III. (1975). Effect of chronic hypercapnia on body temperature regulation. *J. Appl. Physiol.*, **38**:900–906.

Schain, R. J., and Watanabe, K. (1971). Postnatal changes in protein metabolism of brain. II. Effects of alteration of ambient temperature and gaseous composition of inspired air. *Pediatr. Res.*, **5**:173–180.

Schmidt-Nielsen, K. (1969). The neglected interface: The biology of water as a liquid–gas system. *Q. Rev. Biophys.*, **2**:283–304.

Schurmann, H., and Steffensen, J. F. (1989). Temperature preference of rainbow trout at various oxygen tensions. *Proc. Kjell Johansen Symp.* (abstr.).

Seale, T. W., Abla, K. A., Shamim, M. T., Carney, J. M., and Daly, J. W. (1988). 3,7-Dimethyl-1-proparglyxanthine: A potent and selective in vivo antagonist of adenosine analogs. *Life Sci.*, **43**:1671–1684.

Shoemaker, V. H., and Nagy, K. A. (1977). Osmoregulation in amphibians and reptiles. *Annu. Rev. Physiol.*, **39**:449–71.

Shoemaker, V. H., Baker, M. A., and Loveridge, J. P. (1989). Effect of water balance on thermoregulation in waterproof frogs (*Chiromantis* and *Phyllomedusa*). *Physiol. Zool.*, **62**:133–146.

Stegner, H., Leake, R. D., Palmer, S. M., Oakes, G., and Fisher, D. A. (1984). The effect of hypoxia on neurohypophyseal hormone release in fetal and maternal sheep. *Pediatr. Res.*, **18**:188–191.

Storey, K. B. (1988). Suspended animation: The molecular basis of metabolic depression. *Can. J. Zool.*, **66**:124–132.

Wade, C. E., Keil, L. C., and Ramsey, D. J. (1983). Role of volume and osmolality in the control of plasma vasopressin in dehydrated dogs. *Neuroendocrinology*, **37**:349–353.

Walker, B. A. (1986). Role of vasopressin in the cardiovascular response to hypoxia in the conscious rat. *Am. J. Physiol.*, **251**:H1316–H1323.

Walker, B. A. (1987). Cardiovascular effects of Vlf vasopressinergic blockade during acute hypercapnia in conscious rats. *Am. J. Physiol.*, **252**:R127–R133.

Wang, B. C., Sundet, W. D., and Goetz, K. L. (1984). Vasopressin in plasma and cerebrospinal fluid of dogs during hypoxia or acidosis. *Am. J. Physiol.*, **247**:E449–455.

Wilson, D. A., Hanley, D. F., Feldman, M. A., and Traystman, R. J. (1987). Influence of chemoreceptors on neurohypophyseal blood flow during hypoxic hypoxia. *Circ. Res.*, **61**:94–101.

Wood, S. C. (1990). Effect of hematocrit on behavioral temperature regulation of the toad, *Bufo marinus. Am. J. Physiol.*, **258**:R848–851.

Wood, S. C. (1984). Cardiovascular shunts and oxygen transport in lower vertebrates. *Am. J. Physiol.*, **247**:R3–R14.

Wood, S. C., and Malvin, G. M. (1991). Physiological significance of behavioral hypothermia in hypoxic toads, *Bufo marinus. J. Exp. Biol.*, (in press).

Wood, S. C., Hicks, J. W., and Dupré, R. K. (1987). Hypoxic reptiles: Blood gases, body temperature, and control of breathing. *Am. Zool.*, **27**:21–29.

# Part Five

**CIRCULATION**
COMPARATIVE STUDIES

# 16

## Circulation in the Giant Earthworm, *Glossoscolex giganteus*
Blood and Extracellular Fluid Volumes

**ARTHUR W. MARTIN**

University of Washington
Seattle, Washington

**KJELL JOHANSEN†**

University of São Paulo
São Paulo, Brazil

## I. Introduction

Like the vertebrates, oligochaetes have a closed circulatory system. This is true of most annelids, but the polychaetes tend to have important local circulations limited to each segment. There are many propulsive small vessels so that the forward and rearward pumping of the dorsal and ventral vessels, respectively, serves more to mix blood from many segments than to provide the major force for the capillary circulation. How much segmental circulation is present in oligochaetes is still under debate, and this will be commented on later, but the high pressures and valve locations in oligochaetes indicate that capillary circuits derive their pressure from the ventral vessel. This, again, results in a situation similar to that in vertebrates with, first, a necessity for controlled tone in many parallel vessel circuits and, second, the necessity for a sufficient blood volume. The pressure in the major vessels of *Glossoscolex giganteus* has been described (Johansen and Martin, 1965), with some of the respiratory parameters (1966). The present paper now adds another step to the analysis by reporting the blood

---

†Deceased

and extracellular fluid volumes of this same species and indicating the adequacy for filtration and reabsorption of the forces in balance around the capillaries.

To make the pressure measurements, and to allow sampling from the vascular system, it was possible to cannulate the dorsal and ventral vessels of this large worm and, consequently, to make the volume measurements by modern methods. Toulmond (1971) measured the volume of coelomic fluid (35% of wet body weight) in the polychaete *Arenicola marina* by draining the fluid into a graduated cylinder. He obtained the blood volume (2.8–7.3%) by extracting all the pigment and comparing its concentration, corrected for dilution, with a sample of normal blood. We have found no measurements of blood volume in an oligochaete. We have been unable to free these large worms of their contained soil and so report the composition by weight of various parts to allow comparison with other values in the literature.

## II. Materials and Methods

The experiments to be described were done in Sao Paulo, Brazil. The methods used in obtaining, keeping, and operating upon the animals have been described (Johansen and Martin, 1965). Early on the day of an experiment, an animal was weighed, anesthetized, a major blood vessel cannulated, and the animal allowed to recover, then reweighed. Intravascular pressures were usually recorded for some time, but several animals were used at once for blood volume measurements to make sure that nearly normal volumes were being studied.

Blood volume was determined by the dilution of known amounts of T 1824 (Evans blue); extracellular fluid volume was determined with inulin or sucrose (Kruhoffer, 1946). A sample of normal blood was drawn for the preparation of standards, and replaced by blood from another animal, used to wash in the reagent solution. Dye was first mixed with blood from another animal to bind the dye to protein. Tissues of the body did not appear stained after the injection of this material, and the dye remained in the blood for more than 2 days. Dye concentrations were compared with standards with a Zeiss spectrophotometer at 600 nm. Comparison gives the volume directly, since there were relatively few blood cells. Blood concentrations were followed for 2 hr because, although T 1824 equilibrated in 45 min, the inulin or sucrose required about 1.5 hr for complete equilibration.

For analyses in which the blood required deproteinization, the reagents of Somogyi (1930) were used. Normal blood was added to each standard, and the mixture was deproteinized simultaneously with the experimental samples. Sucrose concentration was measured with diphenylamine after the method of Harrison (1942). Inulin was determined by the same method after acid hydrolysis. Blood proteins were heat precipitated, filtered, and washed on asbestos fibers in tared Gooch crucibles, then dried to constant weight.

**Table 1** Soil and Water Content of Specimens of *G. giganteus*

| Worm no.[a] | Initial weight (g) | Dry weight (g) | Water (%) | Soil wet weight (g) | Soil dry weight (g) | Water (g) | Body without soil; wet (g) | Body without soil; dry (g) | Water in body without soil (%) |
|---|---|---|---|---|---|---|---|---|---|
| 1 | 117 | 14.3 | 87.8 | 13.3 | 4.3 | 67.7 | | 10.0 | |
| 2 | 140 | | | | | | | | |
| 3[b] | 160 | 28.9 | 81.9 | 45.4 | 9.6 | 78.8 | 114.6 | 19.4 | 83.1 |
| 4 | 180 | 41.1 | 77.2 | 46.0 | 21.0 | 54.4 | 134.0 | 20.1 | 85.0 |
| 5 | 190 | 38.9 | 79.5 | 37.5 | 14.9 | 60.3 | 152.5 | 24.0 | 84.3 |
| 6 | 195 | 36.2 | 81.4 | | 19.2 | | | 17.0 | |
| 7[b] | 215 | | | | | | 141.8 | 29.0 | 79.6 |
| 8 | 220 | 54.7 | 75.1 | 54.9 | 26.2 | 52.3 | 165.1 | 28.6 | 82.7 |
| 9[b] | 245 | 46.0 | 81.2 | 66.0 | 15.1 | 77.1 | 179.0 | 30.9 | 82.9 |
| n | 9 | 7 | 7 | 6 | 7 | 6 | 6 | 8 | 6 |
| Means | 184.7 | 37.2 | 80.6 | 43.9 | 15.8 | 65.1 | 147.8 | 22.4 | 82.9 |
| SE | 13.5 | 4.9 | 1.5 | 7.3 | 2.8 | 4.6 | 9.4 | 2.5 | 0.8 |

[a]Worms 3, 4, 5, 8, and 9 were frozen before dissection.
[b]Worm 3 had autotomized 33 g; worm 7, 55 g; worm 9, 40 g.

It did not prove possible to clear the intestines of soil by feeding bran or cellulose, and the first dissection to remove soil was unsatisfactory. A few, more careful, dissections were made, but not until the worms were frozen overnight, and the soil dissected out of the frozen worms, were satisfactory measurements made.

The worms lost weight in known amounts (up to 10% of body weight) during the experiments and the dissections. It was assumed that water lost during the experiments was entirely from the body; water lost during the dissection was apportioned to the soil and to the body in proportion to their respective weights. In this way the wet body and wet soil weights were made to equal the total initial weight. The dry weights were not corrected.

## III. Results

If the gut of *G. giganteus* is never empty of soil after the first feedings, it may prove of interest to know the fluid volumes as percentages both of the whole weight and the soil-free weight. Note that not every measurement was made on every worm; therefore, each worm has the same identifying number in Tables 1 and 2. The mean composition of the bodies of several worms is reported in Table 1. It may be calculated from the values in this table that the gut contents represented a substantial part of the wet body weight, at a mean of 22.3 ± 2.4%. The water content of the soil averaged 65.1 ± 4.6%, considerably lower than the water content of the worm body tissues at 82.9 ± 0.8%. The water content of the whole worm was intermediate at 80.6 ± 1.5%.

Individual results of the measurement of blood and extracellular fluid volumes are given in Table 2. Blood volume, expressed as percentage body weight in the soil-free animal, averaged 7.7 ± 0.6%; as percentage total body weight, 6.0 ± 0.3%. Total extracellular fluid was 23.6 ± 1.4% and 31.5 ± 2.3% soil-free and total body weight, respectively. If blood volume is subtracted, the remainder of the extracellular fluid totaled 23.3 ± 1.8% of the soil-free weight. It was not possible in this species to collect sufficient pure coelomic fluid to allow differentiation of the tissue fluid space from the coelomic fluid space.

One may use the values for five of the worms in the two tables to estimate the cellular water. The wet weight of the body without soil is corrected by subtracting the volume of extracellular fluid. The dry weight of the body without soil is corrected by subtracting the weight of blood protein, estimated at 15%, and by subtracting the salt of the extracellular fluid, estimated at 0.8%. From these corrected values, one obtains a mean cellular water of 77 ± 1.4%. Worm number 7, the only one of the five that was dissected without freezing, was quite low at 72%. If this worm is omitted the mean for the other four worms is 78.3 ± 0.8%.

Many annelids are able to autotomize portions of the body. This happened several times in the laboratory during the induction of anesthesia. It has been assumed that the vigorous contraction of the posterior part of the body expressed blood from the autotomized segments into the body proper. We have no statistically valid evidence on this point, but can report that three of the worms, numbers 3, 7, and 9 in Tables 1 and 2, autotomized segments weighing 33, 55, and 40 g, respectively. The blood volumes of these three animals, after autotomy, were slightly higher than the average of all worms. At least, there was no significant blood loss. Examination of Table 2 shows that the extracellular fluid volumes measured in these three animals were also slightly higher than the mean for all experiments, suggesting that fluid had not been transferred to the blood compartment.

The question may be raised, however, of how quickly blood volume can be restored in this species. Two experiments were done to answer this question. An earthworm had been cannulated and experimented upon, including loss of about 5 ml of blood. It appeared to be in excellent condition the next day, so blood was drawn and the protein content determined. The bleeding was repeated at intervals and the results are set forth in Figure 1. It may be seen that the blood volume had been restored in the intervals between samples.

These observations warranted the use of a worm specifically for this type

**Table 2** Blood and Extracellular Fluid Volume[a] in *G. giganteus*

| Worm no.[a] | Initial weight (g) | Blood volume (ml) | Percentage body weight | Percentage body less soil | Extra-cellular fluid (ml) | Percentage body weight | Percentage body less soil | Extracellular fluid minus blood as % of body less soil |
|---|---|---|---|---|---|---|---|---|
| 1 | 117 | 6.0 | 5.1 | 5.8 | | | | |
| 2 | 140 | | | | 37.0 | 26.4 | | |
| 3[b] | 160 | 10.0 | 6.3 | 9.4 | 41.5 | 25.9 | 36.0 | 27.5 |
| 4 | 180 | | | | | | | |
| 5 | 190 | 12.5 | 6.6 | 8.2 | 47.6 | 25.0 | 31.0 | 23.0 |
| 6 | 195 | 12.5 | 6.4 | | 46.5 | 23.8 | | |
| 7[b] | 215 | 14.3 | 6.7 | | 48.8 | 22.7 | 34.4 | 24.3 |
| 8 | 220 | 11.0 | 5.0 | 6.7 | 38.2 | 17.4 | 23.1 | 16.5 |
| 9[b] | 245 | 14.8 | 6.0 | 8.3 | 59.1 | 24.1 | 33.0 | 24.8 |
| n | 9 | 7 | 7 | 5 | 7 | 7 | 5 | 5 |
| Mean | 184.7 | 11.6 | 6.0 | 7.7 | 45.5 | 23.6 | 31.5 | 23.2 |
| SE | 13.5 | 1.1 | 0.3 | 0.6 | 2.9 | 1.4 | 2.3 | 1.8 |

[a]All blood volumes were done with T 1824; extracellular fluid volumes of worms 5, 6, and 7 were done with sucrose, all others with inulin.
[b]Worms 3, 7, and 9 autotomized.

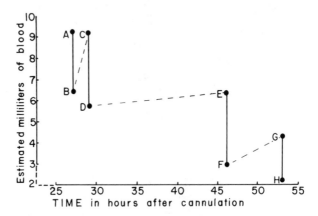

**Figure 1**   A worm of 162-g body weight had been experimented upon for 8 hr on July 21, with a loss of about 5 ml of blood. Kept in the refrigerator overnight it was in good condition on the 22nd. A blood sample of 2.8 ml was drawn (line A to B), protein concentration = 13.6%. On the assumption that this worm had an initial blood volume of 5.7% of body weight (9.23 ml) the initial blood protein would amount to 1.26 g. After bleeding protein content was reduced to 0.87 g, assuming no mobilization from tissue stores. A second blood sample, of 3.5 ml was taken 2 hr later (line C to D), the protein concentration was 9.5%, indicating that the blood volume at time C had been restored to 9.2 ml, with a total protein content of 0.54 g. A third blood sample, of 3.4 ml was taken the next day (line E to F), and had a protein concentration of 6.5%, indicating a blood volume at time E of 6.3 ml. This loss of 0.22 g of protein would leave 0.33 g. A fourth blood sample, of 2.1 ml was taken 5 hr later (line G to H) and had a protein concentration of 5.9%, indicating a blood volume at time G of 4.3 ml. At this point, the remaining protein was calculated as 0.13 g and the experiment was terminated.

of experiment. The sequence of events is set forth in Figure 2, showing the response to a large and then to several smaller bleedings. In each case, there was an appreciable and rapid restoration of blood volume.

## IV.   Discussion

The advantage of a closed circulatory system has been thought to be the efficient circulation of a small quantity of blood having a high capacity for oxygen transport. Polychaetes conform, in part, to this idea, but the fluid compartments are large, and the oxygen transporting pigment is dilute. In *Glossoscolex* we have the nearest approach to the vertebrate system, with hemoglobin, a pigment of high oxygen-carrying capacity, and pressures close to those of vertebrates. Since the circulation is organized like the vertebrate system we infer the same

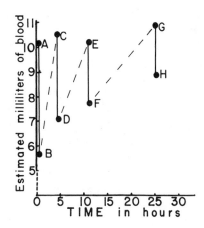

**Figure 2** A worm of 203-g body weight was assumed to have a blood volume of 5% of body weight (10.15 ml) at time A. After vessel cannulation, 4.5 ml of blood was drawn (line A to B); the blood protein level was 17.05%, or 1.73 g of protein was present initially in the blood. About 4 hr later a second sample of 3.5 ml was taken (line C to D) and, at this point, the protein level was down to 9.2%. On the assumption that all protein left in the blood after the first bleeding was still present, a calculation of the blood volume at time C yielded 10.5 ml. Another bleeding of 2.5 ml (line E to F) was made after about 7 hr, yielding a protein content of 6.35%. Calculation shows a restoration of volume at time E to 10.2 ml. Still a fourth bleeding (line G to H) of 2.5 ml was done after 5 hr, yielding a protein concentration of 4.5%. Calculation from the estimated remaining protein shows that the blood volume at time G had been restored to 10.9 ml.

compelling requirements: There must be an adequate capillary pressure; there must be tonus in the blood vessels to produce equitable distribution through many parallel circuits; and the blood volume must be maintained.

In *G. giganteus* there are adequate blood pressures (Johansen and Martin, 1965). The pressure at the venous end of capillaries is not known, and at first glance might be considered to be high, since the blood is entering a dorsal blood vessel where the low pressures are 5–40 cm $H_2O$. It is suggested, however, that the situation is more likely to be like that in the veins of an octopus (Smith, 1962), in which the pressure in peripheral veins is low and increases centrally because of active peristaltic pumping of the veins. The pressure at the venous ends probably approaches zero. It is accepted that there are propulsive peristaltic waves on the veins of polychaete worms (for review see Federighi, 1928; confirmed by Nicoll, 1954). It has even been argued that the segmental circulations are more vigorous than the anteroposterior one, which serves merely to mix the blood. In oligochaetes, the situation is not clear. Johnston and Johnson (1902) argue from the efficient valves in the segmental vessels of *Lumbricus* that there cannot be a segmental circulation, and the flow from the ventral vessel must supply all the subsidiary circuits. There may, however, be species differences. Cineroentgen pictures taken in living *G. giganteus* (Johansen and Martin, 1965) suggested that in each segment the contrast medium moved away from the dorsal vessel in one set of segmental vessels, but not in the other set. This would result in local circuits assisting the major propulsion carried out by the lateral hearts. In any event, we may assume that the pressures at the venous ends of earthworm capillaries are low enough to permit liquid reabsorption. The other major portion of the balance is provided by the osmotic pressures acting across capillary membranes. The blood vessels are lined with a complete intima (Hanson, 1949), providing the material basis for differential permeability. The reports on the distribution of small ions between blood and coelomic fluid (Bahl, 1945; 1947 not in support, but see Kamemoto et al., 1962; Ramsay, 1949) show that these ions are not responsible for the balance, a view supported by Mangum and Johansen (1975). Several measurements have been made of the hemoglobin levels in oligochaetes, with general agreement that the molecular weights of those examined are so large that they minimize their osmotic effect.

The reports of plasma protein levels (Bahl, 1947; de Jorge et al., 1965) do not discriminate hemoglobin from smaller proteins. For our purposes, some inferences can be drawn from comparisons of results in the present paper with iron analyses done by Johansen and Martin (1966) on blood from the same species of worm. From the iron content, one can calculate the hemoglobin level, the remainder might be low-molecular-weight proteins. Waxman (1971) reported for *Arenicola* that there was one heme for one 26,000 molecular weight protein; therefore, the hemoglobin units of annelids can be approximated to 0.215% iron, quite different from vertebrate hemoglobin in which the iron makes up about 0.34%. The first worm used for blood replacement study had already lost several milliliters of blood and could not be assumed to have had a normal hemoglobin content at the time of measurement. The second worm was quite normal and had an initial total protein of 17.05.% Employing the mean iron content of *G. giganteus* blood as 30 mg% (Johansen and Martin, 1966), the hemoglobin percentage would be 14.95. The remainder of the protein, 3.1% could be low-molecular-weight proteins, which could be important osmotically in the recapturing of fluid for the vascular system. With each successive bleeding, the major portion of the protein loss would be hemoglobin, and the low-molecular-weight fractions might be replaced more rapidly than the hemoglobin. At any rate, the figures suggest that blood volume was restored with great rapidity. A similar, very rapid, fluid replacement rate has been reported by Länne and Lundvall (1989) in mammals after pronounced hypovolemia.

Small earthworms are able to clear the gut of soil, and workers dealing with water balance in these species have commonly cleared their worms by keeping them in water or on moist filter paper for a few days. Ingested food and soil pass through the gut in a relatively short time, depending upon whether they are detritivorous or geophagus (Lee, 1985). Satchell (1967) working with *Lumbricus terrestris,* which consumes both detritus and soil, found them to contain 100 mg of dry soil per gram wet body weight, and the food to pass through the gut in 24 hr. Barley (1959) gave values for *Allolobophora caliginosa* of 200–300 mg dry weight of soil per gram body weight. In comparison, *G. giganteus* specimens, which had been starved for several days and had passed minimal amounts of soil, contained $81.5 \pm 11.8$ mg/g wet body weight. The amounts of soil in these different species appear to be quite comparable.

It would appear from our limited observations that *Glossoscolex* never clears its gut of soil; hence, we may have to consider the soil as a permanent part of the worm, and express its fluid values on the basis of the entire worm. It became obvious on dissecting the frozen worms that there was a steady increase in the size of the soil particles as one passed aborad. We may assume that small particulate matter is swept past the large particles by regular peristalsis, but we may ask how the earthworm, the gut of which is relatively fragile, never voids the large particles that are present. An appealing hypothesis takes advantage of a rather old idea. Giard (1887) was impressed by the widespread phenomenon of autotomy through at least six phyla. He classified the types as reproductive and defensive. Later workers have suggested that autotomy of posterior parts of earthworms might serve to rid the body of many coelomic parasites accumulated there (Keilin, 1925) and to rid the body of necrotic tissue and accumulated waste products that appear to be transported to the posterior end of the body (Dales, 1978). To these functions, we may add as defensive the ridding of the body of the accumulation of very large particles by autotomy, a defense against constipation.

## Acknowledgment

The indispensable assistance of Dr. Paulo Sawaya, Department of General and Animal Physiology, University of São Paulo, is gratefully acknowledged.

## References

Bahl, K. N. (1945). Studies on the structure, development and physiology of the nephridia of oligochaetes. VI. The physiology of excretion and the significance of the enteronephric type of nephridial system in Indian earthworms. *Q. J. Microsc. Sci.,* **85:**343–389.

Bahl, K. N. (1947). Excretion in the Oligochaeta. *Biol. Rev.,* **22:**109–147.

Barley, K. P. (1959). The influence of earthworms on soil fertility. II. Consumption of soil and organic matter by the earthworm *Allolobophora caliginosa*. *Aust. J. Agric. Res.*, **10**:179–185.

Dales, R. P. (1978). Defense mechanisms. In *Physiology of Annelids*. Edited by P. J. Mill. New York, Academic press, pp. 484–485.

Federighi, H. (1928). The blood vessels of annelids. *J. Exp. Zool.*, **50**:257–294.

Giard, A. (1887). L'autotomie dans la serie animale. *Rev. Sci.*, **13**:629–663.

Hanson, J. (1949). The histology of the blood system in oligochaetes and polychaetes. *Biol. Rev.*, **24**:127–173.

Harrison, H. E. (1942). A modification of the diphenylamine method for determination of inulin. *Proc. Soc. Exp. Biol. N. Y.*, **49**:111–114.

Jackson, C. M. (1926). Storage of water in various parts of the earthworm at different stages of exsiccation. *Proc. Soc. Exp. Biol. N. Y.*, **23**:500–504.

Johansen, K., and Martin, A. W. (1965). Circulation in a giant earthworm, *Glossoscolex giganteus*. I. Contractile processes and pressure gradients in the large blood vessels. *J. Exp. Biol.*, **43**:333–347.

Johansen, K., and Martin, A. W. (1966). Circulation in a giant earthworm, *Glossoscolex giganteus*. II. Respiratory properties of the blood and some patterns of gas exchange. *J. Exp. Biol.*, **45**:165–172.

Johnston, J. B., and Johnson, S. W. (1902). The course of blood flow in *Lumbricus*. *Am. Nat.*, **36**:317–328.

de Jorge, F. B., Haeser, P. E., Ditadi, A. S. F., Petersen, J. A., Ulhoa Cintra, A. B., and Sawaya, P. (1965). Biochemical studies on the giant earthworm *Glossoscolex giganteus*. *Comp. Biochem. Physiol.*, **16**:491–496.

Kamemoto, F. I., Spalding, A. E., and Keister, S. M. (1962). Ionic balance in blood and coelomic fluid of earthworms. *Biol. Bull (Woods Hole)*, **122**:228–231.

Keilin, D. (1925). Parasitic autotomy of the host as a mode of liberation of coelomic parasites from the body of the earthworm. *Parasitology*, **17**:170–172.

Kruhoffer, P. (1946). Inulin as an indicator for the extracellular space. *Acta Physiol. Scand.*, **11:16–36.**

Länne, T., and Lundvall, J. (1989). Very rapid net transcapillary fluid absorption from skeletal muscle and skin in man during pronounced hypovolaemic circulatory stress. *Acta Physiol. Scand.*, **136**:1–6.

Lee, K. E. (1985). *Earthworms. Their Ecology and Relationships with Soils and Land Use*. New York, Academic Press, pp. 1–350.

Mangum, C. P., and Johansen, K. (1975). The colloid osmotic pressures of invertebrate body fluids. *J. Exp. Biol.*, **63**:661–671.

Nicoll, P. A. (1954). The anatomy and behavior of the vascular systems in *Nereis virens* and *Nereis limbata*. *Biol. Bull. (Woods Hole)*, **106**:69–82.

Ramsay, J. A. (1949). The osmotic relations of the earthworm. *J. Exp. Biol.*, **26**:46–56.

Satchell, J. E. (1967). Lumbricidae. In *Soil Biology*. Edited by A. Burges and F. Raw. New York, Academic Press, pp. 259–318.

Smith, L. S. (1962). The role of venous peristalsis in the arm circulation of *Octopus dofleini*. *Comp. Biochem. Physiol.*, **7**:269–276.

Somogyi, M. (1930). A method for the preparation of blood sugar filtrates for the determination of sugar. *J. Biol. Chem.*, **86:**655.

Toulmond, A. (1971). Determination du volume des compartiments coelomique et circulatoire chez l'*Arenicola marina* L. *C. R. Acad. Sci. Ser. D*, **272:**257–260.

Waxman, L. (1971). The hemoglobin of *Arenicola cristata*. *J. Biol. Chem.*, **246:**7318–7327.

# 17

## August Krogh and His Work on Capillaries

**BODIL SCHMIDT-NIELSEN**

University of Florida College of Medicine
Gainesville, Florida

In 1986, Kjell Johansen gave the August Krogh lecture at the International Congress of Physiology in Vancouver, British Columbia, Canada, and he was kind enough to send me a copy of his talk. In the lecture he said: "It was never my privilege to meet August Krogh. I was too young for that. Yet I feel that I am a student of his. He is one of the very few who will continue to have students for many generations to come."

Kjell Johansen was indeed a worthy student of August Krogh and a true zoophysiologist. In his capillary work, he has explored, in a variety of animals, problems of capillary flow as it serves in temperature regulation. For this reason, it seems appropriate to speak about Krogh and his work on capillaries in the lecture I present today. Another applicable reason is that I am now writing my father's biography.*

In October 1920, when Krogh was awarded the Nobel Prize in Medicine for his work on the function of the capillaries, he was still unknown to most of the medical faculty at the University of Copenhagen. The reason being that Krogh was not a member of the medical faculty, he was Professor of Zoophys-

---

*The author is the youngest daughter of August Krogh.

iology in the Mathematical–Natural Science Faculty, an appointment he received in 1916. Thus, when journalists arrived at the yearly university festivities to find the recipient of the Nobel Prize in Medicine, they were told: "There is no professor Krogh here." One journalist found where Krogh was sitting with his wife Marie and showed him the telegram, Krogh said: "That cannot be true, why should I get it?" (Rehberg, 1974). Now when a Nobel Prize is awarded, the recipient is already older and well known to people in the field. But in 1920, the committee deliberately awarded the Nobel Prize to a young—46-year-old—scientist, who was imaginative, and intensely productive. Krogh explained to his friend Frances Benedict:

> The award of the Nobel Prize came as a perfect surprise to me and when it was first told me by a journalist I declined to believe it because in my opinion the work on the capillaries was so far only a promising beginning. I have learned later, that was just why. They wanted to give the prize for a definite piece of work before its value should be obvious to everybody. I believe the prize was as great a surprize to everyone here as it was to myself and you will readily understand that during the months of November and December I had a very glorious and very exacting time. Now at least I have approximately returned to my normal existence and I am pushing the work forward as hard as I can to do something to deserve the prize. (Krogh to Benedict, 1/18, 1921).

The work for which the award was given consisted of five papers on capillary function, published by Krogh within the span of a single year: namely, between May 1919 and May 1920. Before publication, Krogh sent some of the papers to his close friend and colleague Joseph Barcroft in Cambridge, saying:

> I am today sending two papers to you and in a few days one more will follow. They are intended for the journal [*J. Physiol.*]. Langley has practically accepted them and why I send them to you is only because you might like to see the results and read part of them before they are printed. The two first are rather dull though— I hope–useful, but I venture to believe that you will find the third one interesting. I at least found it very interesting when doing the work, but of course that may be quite a different matter (1/19, 1919, Krogh to Barcroft).

When we think of the time this took place it cannot have been the easiest time to write the papers. World War I had just ended in November, the Kroghs had a new baby daughter, and the whole family had been ill with the Spanish flu. Krogh actually published as many as 15 papers in the 2-year period from 1919 to 1920, on insect respiration, physiology of work, metabolism in man, gas analysis, and several other topics.

The three papers Krogh sent to Barcroft were published 20 May 1919, in the English *Journal of Physiology*. They were: 1) *The rate of diffusion of gases through animal tissues, with some remarks on the coefficient of invasion*; 2) *The number and distribution of capillaries in muscles with calculations of the oxygen*

**Figure 1** August Krogh in 1915.

*pressure head necessary for supplying the tissue*; and 3) *The supply of oxygen to the tissue and the regulation of the capillary circulation*. (Krogh, 1919a,b,c). On July 12th, followed a "preliminary notice" for the *Proceedings of the Physiological Society*: *The contractility and innervation of capillaries* (Krogh 1919d). On 18 May 1920, another paper was published in the *Journal of Physiology*: *Studies on the capillariomotor mechanism. 1. The reaction to stimuli and the innervation of the blood vessels in the tongue of the frog* (Krogh, 1920).

If the awarding of the Nobel Prize to Krogh was intended to promote research in the field just opened by Krogh, it did just that as witnessed by the explosive increase in knowledge and understanding of capillaries that took place between the publication of the first edition of Krogh's capillary book *The Anatomy and Physiology of Capillaries,* in 1922, and the second edition in 1929. Many of these studies came from Krogh's own laboratory where scientists came to work from all over the world.

Krogh (Fig. 1) formulated his first working hypothesis on the function of the capillaries in 1915, while sitting in the library writing a monograph on "respiratory exchange in animal and man," which he had been invited to write for a series of biochemical monographs to be published in England. He has written:

> The book was to deal with the respiratory metabolism at rest. From the available literature it was concluded that the oxygen tension in tissues and particularly in muscles was probably very low and that the tension might be the limiting factor for the rate of oxidation (Krogh, 1950).

Krogh, together with Johannes Lindhard, had recently completed a series of studies measuring rates of circulation and respiration in man during rest and heavy muscular work. These studies became the foundation of exercise physiology. Krogh and Lindhard had found an enormous increase in metabolic rate and in the total circulation rate induced by muscular work—an increase clearly necessary to supply the oxygen actually used up by the muscles. Now Krogh could not help speculating on how the capillaries carrying the oxygen to the muscles could adequately supply the muscles during work, compared with rest, when the call "for oxygen" by the muscle tissue could increase by a factor of 20.

Then, the generally accepted view of the capillary circulation was that the capillaries are passive, that blood flows continuously through all of them at rates determined by the state of contraction or dilatation of the corresponding *arterioles,* and that the dilatation of an arteriole will cause a rise of pressure in the corresponding capillaries. They will become passively expanded by the increased pressure, to contract again by their own elasticity when the pressure is reduced (Krogh, 1919c). As this model clearly did not agree with the available facts, he arrived at the concept that capillaries can open and close as they respond to the tissue's call for oxygen. Every capillary could be conceived as a tube with walls permeable to oxygen and surrounded by a cylinder of tissue through which oxygen would diffuse toward the periphery, being reduced all the way by the metabolic processes (Fig. 2). He visualized that, to supply the working fibers, formerly closed capillaries would have to open during work.

That evening he discussed his ideas with his wife, Marie (Fig. 3) and writes:

> An idea or an hypothesis is a very insignificant, but very essential part of an investigation. Most ideas are wrong and almost all are faulty: but even so experiments have to be planned so as to give an answer: right or wrong. Most ideas are quite vague. Nothing short of experimentation helps more to clarify them and bring them to the testing stage than discussion with a sympathetic and critical colleague (Krogh, 1950).

The discussion with his sympathetic and critical colleague, Marie Krogh, made him decide that the problem was worth pursuing. He must have gone to

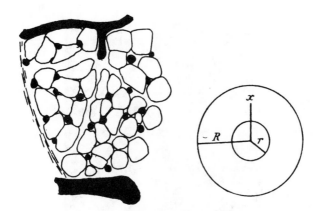

**Figure 2**   (Right) Transverse section of injected muscle from the tongue of a cat. The arterioles are more or less at right angles to the muscle fibers; they branch out into a comparatively large number of capillaries that run parallel to the fibers. On a cross-section vertical to the fibers, the injected capillaries show as stained dots between the fiber cross-sections, and sometimes even running inside a fiber. (Left) Model of the capillary (represented by the circle the radius; r), surrounded by a cylinder of tissue (R) that is supplied with oxygen by the capillary. Oxygen molecules will constantly leave the capillary through the wall, entering the surrounding tissue where they will be used up at a rate determined by the gas exchange [metabolic rate]. The oxygen pressure difference between the capillary wall and a point at the distance x from the center of the capillary must be proportional to the gas exchange and inversely proportional to the diffusion rate. This model was used to establish a mathematical formula for calculating the pressure difference: $(T_0 - T_x) = p/d \, [1/2 \, R^2 \log_{nat} x/r - (x^2 - r^2)/4]$. (From Krogh, 1919b.)

work on it right away, because late in the year of 1915 he needed many frogs, which he got from Barcroft, even though England was at war then (letter from Barcroft to Krogh, 1915).

Krogh first needed to have accurate quantitative measurements of oxygen diffusion rates through various tissues. For the study, he designed four new instruments. One measured the diffusion of gases from air or a fluid through a tissue membrane to blood (Fig. 4). The second measured the thickness of the membrane with great accuracy (Fig. 5), and the third, diffusion from air through tissue to air (Fig. 6). The fourth measured the "invasion coefficient" postulated by Bohr, which turned out to be many times higher than postulated (probably infinite). With his instruments Krogh was able to measure the diffusion constant in a number of tissues with great accuracy.

In his second paper, Krogh described the capillaries in muscles of frogs, cod, and mammals and measured their maximal density. He used a technique of injecting India ink or gelatine stained with Prussian blue through the aorta or

**Figure 3**   Marie Krogh in 1915.

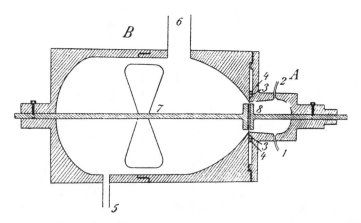

**Figure 4**   The apparatus made by Krogh for measuring diffusion of gases through a membranous tissue. The apparatus was made from brass gilded on the inside. Chamber A had a capacity of 1.5 ml and was filled with a reduced hemoglobin solution. The stretched tissue membrane was held in place between chambers A and B with two brass rings (3 and 4). Chamber B was filled either with a gas flowing continuously through the chamber or with a fluid. In either case it was kept well stirred. (From Krogh 1919a.)

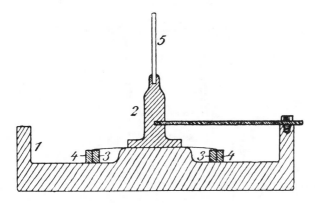

**Figure 5** This apparatus was used to measure the exact thickness of the tissue membrane. Krogh writes:

> The membrane with the rings 3 and 4 was placed in saline in the small circular trough 1 which was mounted on a horizontal microscope. The small weight 2 was placed upon it. This weight carried a glass plate 5 on which a horizontal and a vertical fine line were engraved. The microscope was provided with a screw micrometer eyepiece. The vertical line on the glass plate was made to coincide with the vertical thread in the micrometer and the position of the horizontal line was measured alternately with weight standing directly on its small platform in the trough and with the membrane interposed. Usually a series of at least ten alternate readings were taken. (From Krogh 1919a.)

large vessels. But he found that it was difficult to obtain complete injections, and he writes a statement that surprised me: "I believe that the material to be injected is best left for a day or two after killing the animal before injection is made!" The reason that he had trouble getting the capillary bed injected was that many capillaries were closed, but after the animal was dead, they opened. The values obtained are shown in Table 1. As many as 3000 capillaries were found per square millimeter. In the same study, he presented the mathematical formula (worked out for him by the mathematician Erlang) for calculating the relationship between pressure head (To $- T_R$) and distance for oxygen diffusion (Krogh, 1919b).

In the third paper—the one he himself found "very interesting"—Krogh deals with the discrepancy that his findings had called attention to. Calculated from the number of capillaries that he had actually found in the muscles, the pressure head necessary for supplying the tissue was extremely low, which would mean that *the oxygen pressure everywhere in the organism must be practically equal to that of the capillary blood*. This finding did not agree with the finding

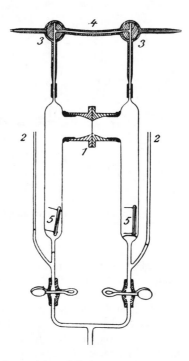

**Figure 6**  Apparatus for studying diffusion through a membrane from pure oxygen to pure nitrogen at different temperatures. The tissue membrane was mounted between the two identical vessels. The lower ends of the vessels were connected with a single mercury reservoir. The vessels are filled with gas through the tubes 2. 5 are stirrers that can be moved up and down by means of a magnet. The apparatus was placed in a constant temperature bath. Krogh found that the diffusion rate in the tissue was proportional to the temperature, owing to the decrease in internal friction in water with increasing temperature. According to Hufner the diffusion rate should have decreased with increasing temperature owing to the decrease in absorption coefficient of the gases in the fluid. (From Krogh 1919a.)

by other authors that the oxygen pressure in tissues is close to zero. In the publication he writes:

> It seemed to me clear that there might be some mechanism regulating the conditions of supply [of oxygen]. With constant conditions the facilities for transport must either be ridiculously out of proportion to the requirements of the muscles during rest or ridiculously inadequate to meet their needs during heavy work.

Krogh and Lindhard had found the oxygen tension of venous blood was only 12 mm during work, compared with 35 mm during rest. Krogh wrote in his paper:

**Table 1** Measurements of Total Capillary Density in Various Animals and Calculations of Oxygen Pressure Head

|  | Weight (kg) | Metabolism (cal/kg/hr) | Number of capillaries mm² of striped muscle | $R$ (μm) | Diameter of red corpuscles $2r$ (μm) | $T_0 - T_R$ (mm Hg) |
|---|---|---|---|---|---|---|
| Cod | 1 | 0.4 | 400 | 28 | 8.5 | 0.4 |
| Frog | 0.04 | 0.4 | 400 | 28 | 15 | 0.25 |
| Horse | 500 | 0.5 | 1400 | 15 | 5.5 | 0.1 |
| Dog | 5 | 3 | 2500 | 11.3 | 7.2 | 0.2 |
| Guinea pig | 0.5 | 6 | 3000 | 10.3 | 7.2 |  |

$R$ = longest distance an oxygen molecule has to travel, which is half the distance between capillaries.
*Source:* Krogh, 1919b.

It cannot therefore be doubted that during work a much increased volume of oxygen diffuses from capillaries into the muscles, while the available pressure appears to be considerably diminished . . . The increase in the rate of blood flow through the capillaries and even a passive distention of them caused by the increased blood pressure would obviously be of no avail to explain the discrepancy, and I was led to the conclusion . . . the only possibility must be an increase in the number of available capillaries. (Krogh, 1919c).

He now began studying the opening and closing of capillaries by direct observations on living tissues, such as the tongue of deeply narcotized frogs and muscles of frogs and guinea pigs, studied by either transmitted or reflected light. He writes:

When the circulation of a muscle is not extremely feeble the open capillaries are generally seen to be arranged at fairly regular intervals (200–500 μ). By electrical stimulation or by gentle massage, an increased circulation can be brought about in any muscle where it was feeble beforehand with the invariable result that the number of visible capillaries is greatly increased, their average distance being diminished to 60–70 μ.

For more accurate measurements of capillary distribution, he studied them in specimens of resting and working muscles injected with India ink, dialyzed for several days against Ringer solution. By using the Erlang equation, he now showed that the pressure head (To − $T_R$) was sufficient to supply the working muscles when many capillaries were open and that in resting muscles when many capillaries are closed oxygen pressure is normally zero in considerable portions of the muscles (Table 2). He calculated that the amount of blood present in the

**Table 2** Measurements of Open Capillaries in Resting and Working Muscles and Calculations of Oxygen Pressure Head

| | $a$<br>$O_2$ consumed per minute vol% of the tissue | $b$<br>Number of capillaries/mm² cross-section | $c$<br>$R$ (μm) | $d$<br>$2r$ (μm) | $e$<br>$T_0 - T_R$ (mm Hg) | $f$<br>Total surface of capillaries in 1 cm³ muscle (cm²) | $g$<br>Total capacity of capillaries vol% of the tissue | $h$<br>Surface of 1 cm³ blood in capillaries (cm²) |
|---|---|---|---|---|---|---|---|---|
| **Frog muscle** | | | | | | | | |
| Rest | 0.03 | 10 | 180 | 4.4 | 10 | 1.4 | 0.015 | 9500 |
| Rest | 0.03 | 90 | 60 | 4.4 | 0.7 | 12 | 0.14 | 8500 |
| Work | 0.3 | 325 | 31 | 6.8 | 1.2 | 70 | 1.2 | 6000 |
| **Guinea-pig muscle** | | | | | | | | |
| Rest | 0.5 | 31 | 100 | 3.0 | 45 | 3 | 0.02 | 15000 |
| Rest | 0.5 | 85 | 61 | 3.0 | 12 | 8 | 0.06 | 13000 |
| Rest | 0.5 | 270 | 34 | 3.8 | 3 | 32 | 0.3 | 10500 |
| Massage | 0.5 | 1400 | 15 | 4.6 | 0.4 | 200 | 2.8 | 7000 |
| Work | 5 | 2500 | 11 | 5.0 | 1.4 | 390 | 5.5 | 7000 |
| **Maximum circulation** | 10 | 3000 | 10 | 8 | 1.2 | 750 | 15 | 5000 |

*Source:* Krogh, 1919c.

working muscle was 750 times the amount present in the muscle at rest (Krogh, 1919c).

The mechanism regulating the capillary circulation was the next problem to be investigated. That the capillaries show independent contractility unrelated to arteriolar pressure was demonstrated by Krogh's own observations, as well as by numerous examples from the literature. Krogh attributed the contractility of the capillaries to the Rouget cells lying outside the capillary wall. In his tape-recorded memoirs, Dr. P. Brandt Rehberg, has told about the time in 1921 when a steady stream of visitors came to Krogh's laboratory. Rehberg often had to interrupt his experiments to demonstrate the capillaries. Then frequently Dr. Vimtrup would point to a place on the capillary and say "there lies a muscle cell outside the capillary wall." Rehberg says:

> Nobody but Vimtrup was able to see it clearly, but when I electrically stimulated the place Vimtrup had pointed to, the cell contracted and the long threads of protoplasm were clearly seen to contract around the capillary. The observers would call out "it gets legs, it gets legs" as the capillary was contracted by the Rouget call (Rehberg, 1975).

Much of the capillary action was recorded on the famous capillary film. Rehberg gave vivid descriptions of the filming at the symposium for Krogh's 100th birthday and in his memoirs (Rehberg 1974; 1975). Krogh knew that Rehberg had previous training in photography and, therefore, asked him to work on the filming of the capillaries with him. They bought a primitive 32-mm movie camera for amateurs. Then Krogh changed it by putting a periscope into the camera, so that he could look at the film directly with a mirror and a magnifying glass. This technique, which has never been used before or after, made it possible for them to create absolutely sharp images. Even today, the film is unique in its clarity. Electrically run movie cameras did not exist in 1921. But instead of rolling the film manually they used a flywheel to get a uniform speed and keep free their hands. The two would film a short sequence, and then Rehberg would rush into the darkroom to develop it. The 16-mm copies do not do justice to the original film. The camera is now set up in the Copenhagen film museum (Rehberg, 1975).

In the years following the publication of the first papers, many aspects of the regulation of capillary contraction and relaxation, and the regulation of capillary flow were published from August Krogh's laboratory.

Fifty years after the publication of Krogh's first capillary papers, an Alfred Benzon Symposium was held in Copenhagen on *The Transfer of Molecules and Ions Between Capillary Blood and Tissue*. At the symposium, no less than six modified versions of Krogh's capillary–tissue cylinder model were presented. I think I can best state the continued importance of Krogh's work by quoting a paragraph from Eugene Landis' tribute to Krogh at the 1969 Alfred Benzon

Symposium (Landis, 1969). Landis, one of Krogh's most valued students, worked with him in 1930–1931, and later became professor at Harvard University. Landis writes:

> Professor Krogh's four papers of 1919 grew into the Silliman lectures in 1922, and into his monograph on capillaries. Very few books yielded as prompt and as widespread stimulation of research as this monograph did when it was read by histologists, physiologists, pathologists, and clinicians. This symposium itself indicates persisting expansion of research on capillaries into many special questions and methods.

Even today, 70-years after Krogh's first publications on capillaries, his work is persistently quoted in the literature as the basis for capillary research.

## References

Krogh, A. (1919a). The rate of diffusion of gases through animal tissues, with some remarks on the coefficient of invasion. *J. Physiol.*, **52**:391–408.

Krogh, A. (1919b). The number and distribution of capillaries in muscles with calculations of the oxygen pressure head necessary for supplying the tissue. *J. Physiol.*, **52**:409–415.

Krogh, A. (1919c). The supply of oxygen to the tissue and the regulation of the capillary circulation. *J. Physiol.*, **52**:457–474.

Krogh, A. (1919d). The contractility and innervation of capillaries. In *Proceedings of the Physiological Society*, July 12, 1919. *J. Physiol.*, **53.**

Krogh, A. (1920). Studies on the capillariomotor mechanism. I. The reaction to stimuli and the innervation of the blood vessels in the tongue of the frog. *J. Physiol.*, **53**:399–419.

Krogh, A. (1922). *The Anatomy and Physiology of Capillaries*, 1st ed. New Haven. Yale University Press, 276 pp.

Krogh, A. (1929). *The Anatomy and Physiology of Capillaries*, 2nd ed. New Haven, Yale University Press, 422 pp.

Krogh, A. (1950) Reminiscences of work on capillary circulation. A lecture to the students in the Harvard Medical School, 1946. *ISIS*, 14–20.

Landis, E. (1969). Professor August Krogh: An appreciation. In *Capillary Permeability. The Transfer of Molecules and Ions Between Capillary Blood and Tissue*, Alfred Benzon Symposium II. Copenhagen, Munksgaard.

Letters quoted are from "The August Krogh archives" in the Royal Library of Denmark (Det Kongelige Bibliotek, Kobenhavn).

Rehberg, P. B. (1974). Lectures given at symposium in honor of August Krogh at his 100th birthday. Lectures are available on tapes at the August Krogh Institute.

Rehberg, P. B. (1975). Memoirs on tape deposited in the Royal Library of Denmark (Det Kongelig Bibliotek, Copenhagen).

# 18

# Central Cardiovascular Anatomy and Function in Crocodilia

**GORDON GRIGG**

The University of Queensland
Queensland, Australia

## I. Introduction

Among the vertebrates, crocodilians have the most complex anatomy of the heart and outflow channels. Their cardiovascular anatomy may also be the most functionally sophisticated, combining as it does the best features of both reptilian and mammalian (and avian) systems.

The puzzlingly complex "plumbing" of crocodilians has fascinated anatomists and physiologists for a very long time, the first paper being that by Panizza (1833). Gradually, with the application of successive techniques of investigation as they became available, its functional significance has become reasonably clear, and the complexity is now revealed as a cardiovascular system of considerable elegance.

In this paper I will review the main anatomical features of the heart and outflow channels, discuss what is known about the way they work, and speculate about the probable functional significance.

## II. Anatomy

The heart lies medially, close to the ventral surface and midway between the origins of the front and hind limbs. In a supine specimen, the beating of the heart is usually visible externally.

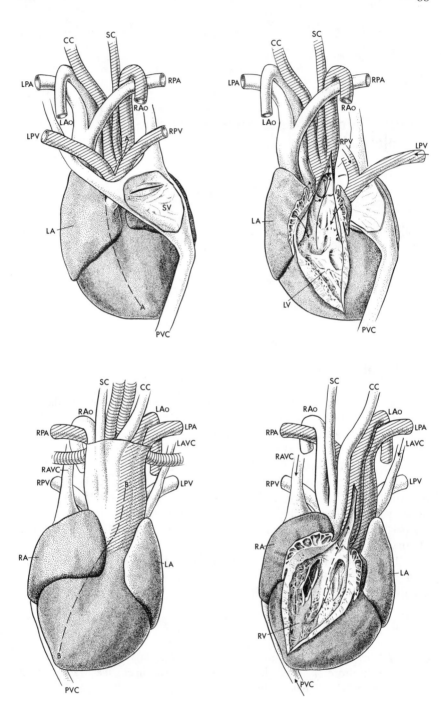

The most recent comprehensive review of the heart anatomy is that by Webb (1979), but there has been a lack of detailed anatomical drawings, until those in Grigg (1989), which are reproduced here (Fig. 1) with dorsal and ventral views represented, both intact and dissected to show internal anatomy. Functional aspects, however, are most easily interpreted with reference to a simplified schematic (Fig. 2).

The significant structural elements that set apart the crocodilian heart and aortic arches from other reptiles are as follows: Left and right ventricles are separate and complete. Both left and right systemic aortas are present, as in most reptiles, but there is a considerable asymmetry (particularly in larger specimens), with the right aorta being the larger. Most strikingly, however, the left aorta comes not from the left, but from the right ventricle, adjacent to the pulmonary artery. Each has a bicuspid valve at the base. Most interestingly, there is a foramen joining the two in their common wall where left and right aortas cross over each other, the foramen of Panizza, about which there has been considerable speculation concerning function. The foramen is located deep down in the valve pockets, its position suggesting that blood could traverse between the two aortas only during diastole when the opening is not obscured by the valve flap (Fig. 3). The origin of the pulmonary aorta has a significant pulmonary stenosis, which is muscular and, in some specimens at least, seems able to be blocked by blocks or lobes of tissue (see later). A further significant departure from the typical reptilian anatomy is the asymmetry of the dorsal confluence where left and right aortas join (see Fig. 2). The two join through only a small vessel, which suggests that most of the blood traversing the left aorta would probably be directed to the gut.

Because anatomical and functional studies on a diversity of crocodilian species have thus far revealed similarities, rather than differences, it seems reasonable to pool results gained on different species.

---

**Figure 1** (Top) dorsal and (bottom) ventral views of the heart of *Crocodylus porosus*. The right-hand panel shows the heart opened dorsally and ventrally, along the lines A–A and B–B, respectively. The location of the foramen of Panizza is indicated in top and bottom right drawings by the black dot at the level of the aortic valves. Top right, solid arrows indicate the direction of blood flow during normal air breathing, from left atrium to left ventricle to right systemic arch and, through the foramen, to the left systemic arch. Bottom right, the solid arrow shows the direction of flow during normal air breathing, from right atrium to right ventricle to pulmonary arch. The dashed arrow, from right ventricle to left systemic arch, indicates the direction of flow when the pulmonary bypass shunt operates. (LA, left atrium; RA, right atrium; LV, left ventricle; RV, right ventricle; PVC, posterior vena cava; RAVC, right anterior vena cava; RPV, right pulmonary vein; LPV, left pulmonary vein; LPA, left pulmonary artery; RPA, right pulmonary artery; RAo, right aorta; LAo, left aorta; CC, common carotid artery; SC, subclavian artery.)

## III. Functioning

### A. Operation During Normal Air Breathing

It was recognized early (e.g., Sabatier 1873) that the opening of the left aorta from the right ventricle afforded the opportunity for a pulmonary bypass shunt through which blood from the pulmonary circuit could cross to the systemic circuit. Nevertheless, this was also seen by some (e.g., Goodrich, 1919) as a counterproductive pathway that would lead to obligate mixing of deoxygenated blood in the systemic circuit.

The test was the measurement of blood oxygen capacity in left and right aortas (White, 1956; Greenfield and Morrow, 1961; Khalil and Zhaki, 1964) and in *Caiman crocodilus, Alligator mississippiensis,* and *Crocodylus niloticus,* respectively, it is clear that both left and right aortas carry well-oxygenated blood during normal air breathing. This has been confirmed in *Crocodylus porosus* and *C. johnstoni* by Grigg and Johansen (1987).

These findings have two important implications. First, the bicuspid valve at the base of the left aorta must remain closed in normal air breathing, presumably because of lower pressure in the right ventricle than the left aorta. Second, the source of oxygenated blood must be the right aorta, through the foramen of Panizza, as suggested by both Panizza (1833) and Sabatier (1873).

Pressure recordings have confirmed lower pressures in the right ventricle than the left aorta throughout the cardiac cycle in crocodilians at rest (White, 1956; Greenfield and Morrow, 1961; van Mierop and Kutsche, 1985; Grigg and Johansen, 1987). A typical example for *Crocodylus porosus* is seen in Figure 4.

The entry of blood from the right aorta to the left through the foramen of Panizza, as proved by close similarity of blood oxygen capacities in both vessels, posed a problem concerning the mechanism. Some authors (e.g., White, 1976) have apparently assumed that blood can flow easily from the right to the left aorta through the foramen, but others (e.g., Sabatier, 1873; Greenfield and Morrow, 1961; Webb, 1979; Grigg and Johansen, 1987) have recognized that the anatomy seems to argue against its easy occurrence (see Fig. 3). Sabatier (1873) and Greenfield and Morrow (1961) accepted that opportunities for blood to flow through the foramen would occur only in diastole, when the pocket valve flaps closed, exposing the foramen deep in the pocket. Indeed, the latter authors reported asynchronous pressure events in left and right aortas of *A. mississippiensis,* showing that their interpretation was correct. Grigg and Johansen (1987) found this to be the normal circumstances in *C. porosus* and *C. johnstoni* also (see Fig. 4). This conflicted, however, with pressure data presented by White (1976), in which pressures in left and right aortas were synchronous. The matter is now partly resolved, because Grigg and Johansen (1987) found that the latter pattern occurred also in *C. porosus,* uncommonly, during low central blood pressures, correlating with either bradycardia in a dive or with low

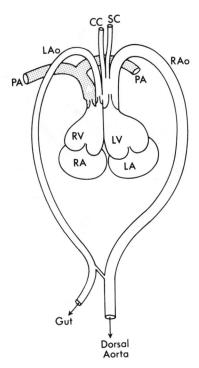

**Figure 2** Schematic diagram of the heart and major arteries of a crocodilian. The heart has been rotated 180° around the long axis of the body to "untwist" the outflow channels, thus clarifying their relationship with the ventricles. Note particularly: complete division between left and right ventricles, left aorta arising from right ventricle (along side pulmonary aorta), the foramen of Panizza (shown as a gap in the common wall between left aorta and right aorta), and left aorta smaller than right aorta, their dorsal connection being made by only a small vessel.

water temperatures (Fig. 5). Interestingly, White's (1956) blood pressure data were lower than those reported by Greenfield and Morrow (1961), strengthening the possibility that this is the explanation for the difference between the two sets of results.

It seems, therefore, that any model to account for the mechanism by which blood flows through the foramen has to accommodate some functional flexibility. Accordingly, Grigg and Johansen (1987) proposed that the foramen may be of variable caliber, opening widely in some situations so that the cusps provide no barrier to flow during systole, particularly when blood pressure is low. (It is worth noting that, whereas the most conservative interpretation may be that blood flow continues to be from right to left aorta, there is an alternative possibility that flow direction

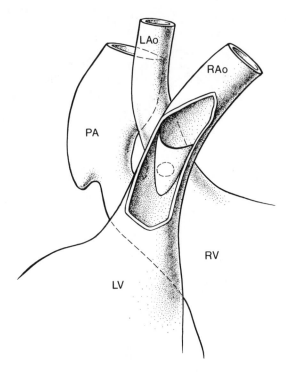

**Figure 3**  Semischematic diagram to show the position of the foramen of Panizza (dotted circle) in the common wall of left and right aortas where they cross over, obscured in the pocket of a semilunar valve.

through the foramen is from left to right during synchronous pressure events. This possibility is discussed later.)

But what could be the mechanism for varying the caliber of the foramen? White (1956) drew attention to the presence of a cartilaginous strut, part of the central cartilage (Fig. 6), which sweeps around the distal margin of the foramen. He interpreted this to be well placed to hold the foramen open. However, it may be of still more importance to enable enlargement of the foramen under muscular action. Whether or not this occurs is now entirely speculative, but warrants further attention.

Most commonly, however, blood flows into the left aorta during ventricular diastole, and recent papers by Axelsson et al. (1989) and Pettersson et al. (reported in Chap. 19) have reported measurements of flow for the first time. Broadly, these results confirm the interpretations of cardiac function that were drawn from pressure recordings, and provide further detail. In particular, the flow pattern in the left aorta is complex, the net flow being small in comparison with that in the right aorta. The

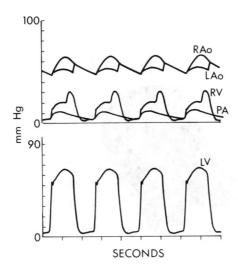

**Figure 4** Typical blood pressures within the heart and major outflow vessels in *Crocodylus porosus* at rest. The main pressure event in the left aorta, the so-called foramen spike occurs just after peak systolic pressure in the right aorta. Note the pressure difference between systemic and pulmonary circuits, a situation more reminiscent of mammals than reptiles.

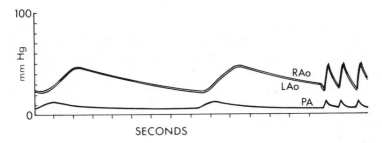

**Figure 5** A less typical pattern of blood pressures, with synchronous pressure events of equal magnitude in left and right aortas. This pattern may be seen at lower temperatures or when systemic blood pressures are low. To account for such observations, the hypothesis has been advanced that the foramen may be able to be opened wide in some circumstances (see text).

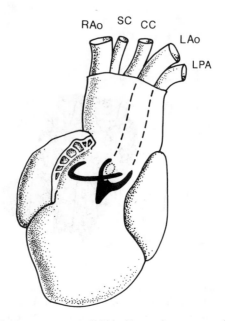

**Figure 6**   Cartilaginous structures (solid black) may have some role in the operation of the foramen of Panizza (dotted circle). (After White, 1958.)

small flow is in agreement with Grigg and Johansen (1987), who argued from theoretical grounds, that the flow in the left aorta would be small in crocodiles at rest, unlikely to exceed 10% of that in the right aorta. The complexity of the pattern was, however, unpredicted. There is a small anterograde flow early in systole, then a reversal, then a second anterograde flow coincident with the foramen spike. This mirrors the pressure events (see Fig. 4), and the first pulse demands an explanation. Grigg and Johansen (1987) agreed with the proposal by Webb (1979) that the initial pressure rise in the left aorta early in systole was transmural, from its close contact with the pulmonary artery and the right aorta, as all three vessels lie within a common connective tissue sheath. This could also explain the early peak of anterograde flow and, after first appearing to favor the idea of a partially open foramen early in systole (Axelsson et al., 1989), these authors, too, now apparently favor the transmural explanation (see Chap. 19).

### B.   Operation of a Pulmonary Bypass Shunt

White (1969) force-dived alligators with fixed cannulation of major vessels and showed that, as bradycardia developed, right ventricular pressure rose until a right–left shunt developed, which he concluded was under vagal control originating in the pulmonary outflow tract. It is clear from his papers that White was thinking in terms of the shunt being significant during dives in which metabolism shifts from oxidative to anaerobic pathways, with the perfusion of certain parts of the systemic vasculature being reduced.

Grigg and Johansen (1987) studied crocodiles that were unrestrained in the experimental tank and that were free to dive or surface at will. Typically, individuals spent long periods resting on the bottom of the tank, surfacing for a few breaths every 5–20 min. Wright (1985) has shown that during such dives *C. porosus* shows a small, but significant, bradycardia; that normal resting rates of oxygen consumption are maintained; that muscle and plasma lactate levels do not increase; and that oxygen reserves are not even nearly exhausted before the animal surfaces for a resupply. In other words, all indications are that these dives are undertaken aerobically.

During such dives in our experiments, it frequently happened that the pressure trace in the left aorta began to show an additional peak, the result of increased right ventricular pressure pushing through the valves into the left aorta (Fig. 7b compared with 7a). This varied in the extent to which it developed, and it often obscured the pressure surge (foramen spike) that is the correlate of pressure surge into the left aorta through the foramen during diastole (see Fig. 7c). Grigg and Johansen (1987) considered that this variable impact of right ventricular pressure onto the left aortic trace indicated the operation of a variable pulmonary bypass shunt. The interpretation was confirmed, in many instances, by the concomitant observation of "mixed" blood in the left aorta.

White (1969) observed similar pressure patterns and made similar interpretations, the difference being that Grigg and Johansen (1987) observed animals diving voluntarily and known to be undertaking dives well within their aerobic capabilities. The operation of the shunt as a correlate of aerobic rather than anaerobic dives puts an entirely new light on the matter because it demands a different answer to questions about the functional import of the shunt pathway.

Before passing to questions of functional significance, Figure 8 provides a useful summary of cardiac outflow pathways under normal air-breathing conditions and when the shunt is in operation.

## IV. Functional Significance

### A. The Best Features of Both Reptilian and Mammalian Circulatory Systems

Crocodilian hearts combine the "best" features of reptilian and mammalian (and avian) hearts. Oxygenated and deoxygenated blood is kept separate within the heart, as in mammals and birds. Also, as in mammals and birds, blood pressures are much higher in the systemic circuit than in the pulmonary circuit (see Fig.

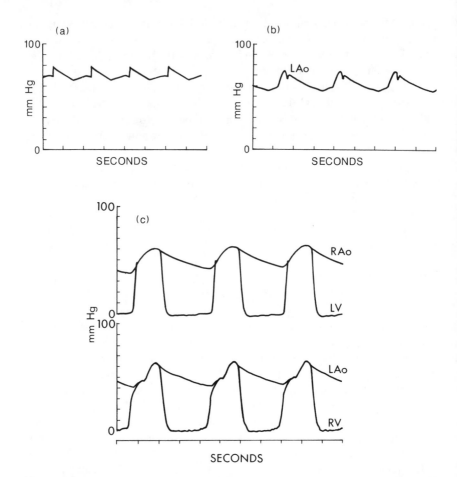

**Figure 7** Left aortic pressure traces from a crocodile at rest (a) and during aerobic dives in which the pulmonary bypass shunt developed (b,c). The main pressure event in trace (a) is the foramen spike that results when blood fills the left arch, through the foramen of Panizza, just after the right aortic semilunar valves close at the end of systole. The main pressure event in (b) is the result of increased right ventricular pressure pushing open the left aortic semilunar valves and injecting less-well-oxygenated blood into the left arch. The foramen spike is still visible. In (c), the main pressure event is, again, of right ventricular origin, to the extent that the foramen spike is completely obscured.

4). Interestingly, typical systemic blood pressures in crocodiles are higher than in most reptiles, whereas pulmonary arterial pressures are lower (see Grigg and Johansen, 1987) so that crocodilian circulatory pressures are not too discrepant from mammalian values. Both the blood pressure differences and the separation

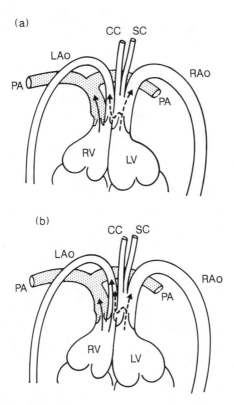

**Figure 8**   Schematic diagram to show the direction of blood flow in a crocodilian during normal air breathing (a), and with the pulmonary bypass shunt in operation (b). Note that oxygenated blood (dashed arrow) reaches the left aorta through the foramen of Panizza. Blood in the right ventricle (low oxygen, solid arrow) exits only to the pulmonary arch during normal air breathing, but some is diverted to the left aorta when the shunt operates, so the left aorta carries mixed blood at those times.

of oxygenated and deoxygenated blood follow from the heart having a complete division of the ventricle. However, unlike mammals and birds, but like all reptiles yet studied, blood from the pulmonary circuit may be diverted to the systemic circuit. In most reptiles, this occurs by the operation of an intracardiac shunt, rather than an extracardiac shunt. In either event, there can be a pulmonary bypass shunt, whereas in mammals blood flow in pulmonary and systemic circuits must remain equal. Thus, crocodiles seem to have evolved a mammalian-style circulatory system relative to pressure gradients and separation of oxygenated blood, while retaining the shunting capability.

## B. The Distinctive Features of the Crocodilian Cardiovascular System All Contribute to a Sophisticated Pulmonary Bypass Shunt

The pulmonary bypass shunt in crocodilians is represented not by direct right–left ventricular flow, but by a separate vessel, the left aorta. Being extracardiac, this shunt pathway has marked advantages. Apart from allowing the complete division of the ventricle, persistence of the left aorta and its origin from the right, rather than the left, ventricle means that low-oxygen blood bypassing the heart when the shunt is in operation need not enter the systemic circuit until downstream of the carotid circuit (see Fig. 2) and, if the relative diameters of vessels seen in dissection is any indication, most of the low-oxygen, shunted blood would go to the gut. Thus, oxygen levels in the cephalic blood and in most of the systemic circuit would seem to be able to be maintained while the shunt operates, a situation quite different from what must occur in most reptiles. Thus, all the significant features of the complex anatomy that typify crocodilians, the persistent left aorta originating from the right ventricle, the characteristically crocodilian foramen of Panizza, and the asymmetry at the dorsal confluence, support the operation of a sophisticated pulmonary bypass shunt.

## C. What Is the Advantage of Having Such a Shunt?

This is obviously the crucial question, and it is of broader significance. Grigg and Johansen (1987) discussed the question at length. We concluded that perfusion matching offers a much more likely explanation than earlier ideas about savings in cardiac energy, and the idea has been discussed more fully in general terms by Burggren (1985, 1987) in a comprehensive review of ideas put forward to account for reptilian intracardiac shunting. According to Grigg and Johansen, the shunt enables crocodilians to match lung perfusion to oxygen requirements as the dive progresses, maintaining oxygen flow because of greater arteriovenous differences at lower partial pressures (because of the shape of the oxygen equilibrium curve), even at reduced heart rates, while sequestering carbon dioxide away from the lungs and, thereby, prolonging efficient oxygen uptake. Wright (1985) has shown that oxygen consumption remains constant during the progress of an aerobic dive, despite falling pulmonary oxygen stores and a slowing heart rate. Consideration of the Fick equation shows that this can be achieved by an increased arteriovenous difference. The shape of the oxygen equilibrium curve (Grigg and Cairncross, 1980) implies that, as the dive progresses and pulmonary and arterial oxygen partial pressures fall, the system begins to operate on the steeper part of the curve, increasing arteriovenous difference. This means that lung perfusion may be matched to oxygen requirements with some independence from systemic flow; an option closed to mammals and birds. As a consequence, $CO_2$ is sequestered in the tissues, facilitating oxygen unloading, whereas $CO_2$

buildup in the lungs is minimized, favoring maximum removal of oxygen from the lungs.

### D. Reverse Flow Through the Foramen of Panizza?

The logical endpoint of a pulmonary bypass shunt would be the diversion of all blood from the pulmonary circuit to the systemic, stopping pulmonary perfusion altogether. One can imagine circumstances in which it may be useful for a crocodilian to be able to stop pulmonary perfusion altogether, enabling it to hold an oxygen store in the lungs, perhaps to allow periodic reoxygenation of the brain, during a period supported otherwise by anaerobic metabolism. Such circumstances could arise during an active, struggling dive associated with prey capture or escape from predation. Dives associated with attempted escape from an investigator have been studied by Seymour and colleagues (1985) who found a significant buildup in blood lactate during exercise. Another circumstance when substantial anaerobic dependence may occur may be during a "fright dive" (Gaunt and Gans, 1969; Wright, 1985) in which there is sudden and severe bradycardia. The suddenness of its onset suggests a rapid switching to anaerobiosis, perhaps conserving oxygen stores in the lung.

If pulmonary perfusion ceased, so would pulmonary venous return. Here, the only route for blood flow to continue in the systemic circuit would be through the left aortic outflow, driven from the right ventricle, fed from systemic venous return, as normal. In this circumstance, blood would be likely to flow through the foramen of Panizza into the right aorta (i.e., in the reverse of normal direction). Such an idea is entirely hypothetical at present, but the anatomical basis for it does exist and, furthermore, four pieces of evidence support the idea. First, in larger crocodiles the left aorta is comparatively much smaller than the right, yet the base of the left aorta remains large (Webb, personal communication). Perhaps the distal part of the left aorta, past the foramen, only needs to be small to cope with a partially developed pulmonary bypass shunt (and supply of oxygenated blood to the gut during normal air breathing), whereas the proximal section must be large to cope with a larger flow to feed the systemic circulation during complete pulmonary shutdown. Obviously, there would be some sort of transition situation between the two states. Second, the presence of intriguing structures at the base of the pulmonary aorta in *C. porosus*, described by Webb (1979), strongly suggests that pulmonary flow can be very severely restricted, if not stopped altogether. Webb described and illustrated "blocks of tissue" in the funnel leading to the pulmonary aorta. He observed that they fit together "like teeth of opposing cogs" and appear to be implicated in the mechanical closure of the pulmonary artery. White (1968; 1969; 1976) discussed the role of active control over the pulmonary outflow tract at its base, whereas Greenfield and Morrow (1961) noted "cartilaginous bars" projecting into the outflow tract in a way that suggested an active role in obstructing the vessel. Increased pulmonary stenosis presumably leads to increased right ventricular pressure that, in turn, initiates the spill of blood through the valves into the left aorta as shunt operation commences. If complete stenosis can occur, as the photograph of Webb (1979) would seem to suggest, then the proposed flow pattern seems a compelling possibility. Third, it cannot be overlooked that the synchronous pressure profiles in left and right aortas (see Fig. 5), which occurred associated with severe bradycardia (and at low temperatures) may be a correlate of such a pattern of "reverse flow." Finally, and most interestingly, reverse flow through the foramen has been demonstrated by Pettersson et al. (see Chap. 19) following the experimental occlusion of the pulmonary arch, although these authors considered that the complete occlusion of the pulmonary arteries is unlikely to occur naturally. If not, then other explanations will have to be sought for the nubbins of tissue surrounding the pulmonary outflow tract and for the longitudinal change in diameter in the left aorta.

It should be emphasized that this is speculation and little more, but it opens up intriguing possibilities that would seem to be worth further investigation. After more than 150 years of thought about the crocodilian cardiovascular system, there are still provocative questions to be answered.

## Acknowledgments

I wish to thank Springer-Verlag and the Australian Physiological and Pharmacological Society for permission to reuse figures from previous publications and to June Jeffery who drew most of them. My interest in crocodile hearts was stimulated in the 1960s by my first vertebrate zoology teacher, Maurice Bleakly. The interest grew during the 1970s because of opportunities for crocodile work provided by Harry Messel, and found expression in experiments during the 1980s, particularly with Kjell Johansen. Sadly, Kjell never saw our crocodile work in print; his death came soon after the acceptance of the revised manuscript. I met him when I was 22 and he came to Australia to study Queensland lungfish. We stayed in contact for the next 22 years. Nobody had a larger influence on the way I think about animal physiology. For that influence and for his friendship I am extremely grateful.

## References

Axelssen, M., Holm, S., and Nilsson, S. (1989). Flow dynamics of the crocodilian heart. *Am. J. Physiol.*, **256**:R875–879.
Burggren, W. W. (1985). Hemodynamics and regulation of central cardiovascular shunts in reptiles. In *Cardiovascular Shunts: Phylogenetic, Ontogenetic and Clinical*

*Aspects*. Alfred Benzon Symposium 21. Edited by K. Johansen and W. W. Burggren. Copenhagen, Munksgaard, pp. 121–142.

Burggren, W. W. (1987). Form and function in reptilian circulations. *Am. Zool.*, **27**:5–20.

Gaunt, A. S., and Gans, C. (1969). Diving bradycardia and withdrawal bradycardia in *Caiman crocodilus*. *Nature*, **223**:207–208.

Goodrich, E. S. (1919). Note on the reptilian heart. *J. Anat.*, **53**:298–304.

Greenfield, L. J., and Morrow, A. G. (1961). The cardiovascular hemodynamics of Crocodilia. *J. Surg. Res.*, **1**:97–103.

Grigg, G. C. (1989). The heart and patterns of cardiac outflow in Crocodilia. *Proc. Aust. Physiol. Pharmacol. Soc.*, **20**:43–57.

Grigg, G. C., and Cairncross, M. (1980) Respiratory properties of the blood of *Crocodylus porosus*. *Respir. Physiol.*, **41**:367–380.

Grigg, G. C., and Johansen, K. (1987). Cardiovascular dynamics in *Crocodylus porosus* breathing air and during voluntary aerobic dives. *J. Comp. Physiol.*, **157**:381–392.

Khalil, F., and Zaki, K. (1964). Distribution of blood in the ventricle and aortic arches in reptilia. *Z. Vergl. Physiol.*, **48**:663–689.

Panizza, B. (1833). Sulla structura del cuore e sulla circolazione del sangue del *Crocodilus lucius*. *Biblioth. Ital.* **87**:87–91.

Sabatier, A. (1873). Etudier sur le coeur et la circulation centrale dans la serie des vertebres. *Ann. Sci. Nat. Zool. Paleontol. Ser.* 5, **18**:1–89.

Seymour, R. S., Bennett, A. F., and Bradford, D. F. (1985). Blood gas tensions and acid–base regulation in the salt-water crocodile *Crocodylus porosus*, at rest and after exhaustive exercise. *J Exp. Biol.*, **118**:143–59.

Van Mierop, L. H. S., and Kutsche, L. M. (1985). Some aspects of comparative anatomy of the heart. In *Cardiovascular Shunts: Phylogenetic, Ontogenetic and Clinical Aspects*. Alfred Benzen Symposium 21. Edited by K. Johansen and W. W. Burggren, Copenhagen, Munksgaard, pp. 38–56.

Webb, G. J. W. (1979). Comparative cardiac anatomy of the Reptilia III. The heart of crocodilians and a hypothesis on the completion of the interventricular septum of crocodilians and birds. *J. Morphol.*, **161**:221–240.

White, F. N. (1956). Circulation in the reptilian heart (*Caiman sclerops*). *Anat. Rec.*, **125**:417–432.

White, F. N. (1968). Functional anatomy of the heart of reptiles. *Am. Zool.*, **8**:211–219.

White, F. N. (1969). Redistribution of cardiac output in the diving alligator. *Copeia*, **1969**:567–570.

White, F. N. (1970). Central vascular shunts and their control in reptiles. *Fed. Proc.* **29**:1149–1153.

White, F. N. (1976). Circulation. In *Biology of the Reptiles*, Vol. 5, Physiology A. Edited by C. Gans. London, Academic Press, pp. 275–334.

Wright, J. (1985). Diving and exercise physiology in the estuarine crocodile, *Crocodylus porosus*. PhD thesis, The University of Sydney, Australia.

# 19

## Shunting of Blood Flow in the Caiman
Blood Flow Patterns in the Right and
Left Aortas and Pulmonary Arteries

**KNUT PETTERSSON**

Cardiovascular Research Laboratories
AB Hässle
Mölndal, Sweden

**MICHAEL AXELSSON
and STEFAN NILSSON**

University of Göteborg
Göteborg, Sweden

## I. Introduction

The cardiovascular system of crocodilians is unique in several aspects. For instance, in addition to the pulmonary artery, the left aorta (LAo) issues from the right ventricle and arcs caudally to the gut. The right aorta (RAo) runs from the left ventricle and forms the main systemic (dorsal) aorta. The two aortae communicate at two points: 1) the foramen of Panizza (foramen Panizzae; Panizza, 1833), a small opening immediately distal to the aortic valves; and 2) an abdominal vascular anastomosis in the anterior part of the abdomen. A detailed anatomical description of the crocodilian cardiovascular system is given in Chapter 18 (see also Webb, 1979; Grigg and Johansen, 1987; Grigg, 1989).

Although the peculiar anatomical arrangement of the cardiovascular system and the amphibious life of crocodilians have raised a number of questions about the regulation of blood flow in the aortas, few studies relating to this have been published. White (1956) demonstrated that the blood in the LAo is well oxygenated, similar to the levels in the RAo, and also that the LAo and RAo blood pressures showed similar patterns. He concluded that the foramen of Panizza was normally open, allowing blood to communicate between the two aortae.

Greenfield and Morrow (1961) reported lack of synchrony between the

LAo and the RAo pressure events, and it was shown by Grigg and Johansen (1987) that the periodic synchrony of pressure events in the two aortas depended upon blood pressure and heart rate.

To obtain direct information about blood flow in the two aortas and the patterns of distribution of blood between them, we studied caimans (*Caiman crocodylus*) with permanently implanted electromagnetic flow probes around the LAo, RAo, and one of the pulmonary arteries. In addition to the flow probes, intravascular cannulas in the same vessels were used to record the pressure events in one of the two animals described here. This chapter describes in detail flow patterns and pressure events in two individuals, for which the signals were stored on tape and subjected to off-line computer-assisted analysis (Axenborg, 1989). The bulk of the study has been reported elsewhere (Axelsson et al., 1989). Implantation of blood flow probes and intravascular cannulas was performed as described by Axelsson et al. (1989).

The surgery was performed in two steps: first the femoral artery and vein were cannulated under cold- and local anesthesia, and several days later the flow probes and, in one of the animals, the intra-aortic cannulas were implanted under sterile conditions. Flow probes were placed around the LAo and RAo just as these emerge from the outflow tract, and the cannulas were inserted into the vessels inside the outflow tract. Cannulas and flow probe leads were tunneled subcutaneously to the dorsal side of the animal.

The results presented here were stored on tape and processed by off-line computer-assisted analysis (Axenborg, 1989). To obtain detailed flow and pressure tracings, four to ten consecutive heart cycles were digitalized and averaged. It is difficult to obtain a true zero flow reference in vivo, and also small errors in the zero calibration will markedly affect the estimations of absolute volume flow. Therefore, the results are presented graphically and the effects of interventions are discussed in qualitative terms.

## II. Blood Flow Patterns in Normally Breathing Caimans

Blood flows and pressures in the central arteries are shown in Figure 1. There was a continuous flow in the pulmonary artery throughout the cardiac cycle, with small variation between diastole and systole. The RAo flow was more distinctly pulsatile, remaining positive also during diastole.

Flow patterns in the LAo were complex, and they varied between animals and also with time in the same animal (cf. Axelsson et al., 1989). The basic pattern comprised two peaks of anterograde flow, one in early systole and the second during diastole. There was a reversal of flow in late systole between the two peaks (see Fig. 1).

Mechanical occlusion of the LAo in an anesthetized, openchest caiman was used by Axelsson et al. (1989) to establish a true zero flow, and it could

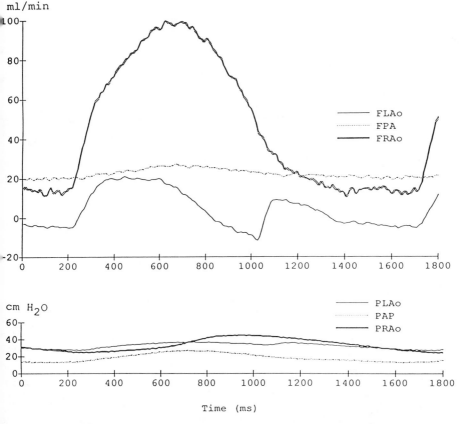

**Figure 1** Blood flows (upper panel) and blood pressures (lower panel) obtained in a normally breathing caiman. Note small pressure peak around 1100 ms (foramen spike) and that PLAo exceeds PRAo during the early part of systole: FLAo, left aortic blood flow; FRAo, right aortic blood flow; FPA, pulmonary arterial flow; PLAo, left aortic blood pressure; PRAo, right aortic blood pressure; PPA, pulmonary arterial pressure.

be demonstrated unequivocally that the LAo blood flow is bidirectional during the cardiac cycle, with a very small net anterograde flow.

Simultaneous recordings of LAo, RAo, and pulmonary arterial blood pressure were useful for the interpretation of the flow patterns. Mean blood pressures in the aortas were similar, but the patterns differed slightly during the cardiac cycle, as previously reported from several studies (Greenfield and Morrow, 1961; Grigg and Johansen, 1987; Axelsson et al., 1989). During the early part of systole, RAo blood pressure did not exceed that in the LAo (Fig. 1, Fig. 2, left

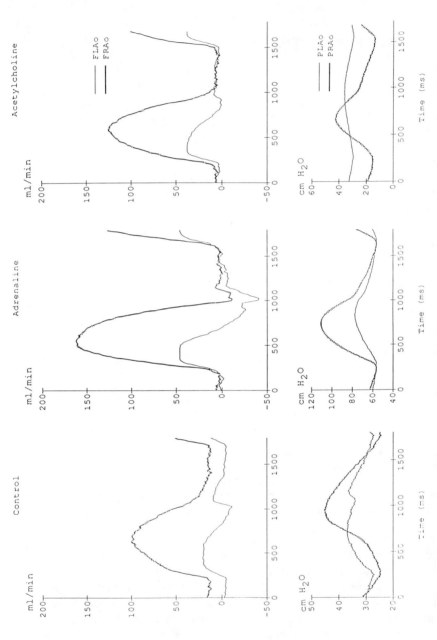

**Figure 2** Effects of epinephrine (adrenaline) and acetylcholine on left and right aortic blood flow (upper panel) and blood pressure (lower panel) (abbreviations as in Fig. 1).

358

panel). If this observation is correct, RAo-to-LAo blood flow through the foramen of Panizza cannot take place during this part of the cardiac cycle. Thus, the first small anterograde flow peak observed cannot be due to flow through the foramen, and other explanations must be sought. A transmural "squeeze" of the LAo lumen within the outflow tract was suggested by Grigg and Johansen (1987) as a possible cause of the pressure pulse observed by them. However, this cannot be the sole cause, since, in our experiments, the tendency would be for the LAo to squeeze the RAo, and not vice versa. The problem clearly warrants further attention.

The second anterograde flow peak that occurs at the end of the systole is associated with a small pressure pulse in the LAo (see Fig. 1, about 1100 ms), the "foramen spike" (Grigg and Johansen, 1987). It is suggested that the foramen is closed during (part of) the systole. Such closure could be the result of the cusps of the RAo valves covering the foramen, an arrangement described by Greenfield and Morrow (1961). When the valves close, the foramen would again be open and a pressure (foramen spike) and flow (second anterograde peak) surge from the RAo into the LAo through the open foramen would result. At this stage, RAo blood pressure exceeds that in the LAo (see Figs. 1 and 2).

The results are compatible with those of White (1956), demonstrating similar oxygenation of the LAo and RAo blood, but not with the view of a perpetually open foramen of Panizza.

## III. Manipulation of the Blood Flow Patterns

The physiological circumstances during which the normal flow patterns are altered remain largely unknown. Normally, voluntary dives in crocodilians appear to be aerobic (see Grigg, 1989; also Chap. 18), but pulmonary bypass may occur during "forced" or "fright" dives (White, 1969). An increase in pulmonary vascular resistance or a decrease of the systemic vascular resistance is prerequisite for such shunting, which requires an opening of the LAo valves. It has been suggested that, during such dives, the cholinergic innervation of the pulmonary vasculature would produce the necessary increase in pulmonary vascular resistance, thereby allowing the right ventricle to generate the pressure needed to open the LAo valves (White, 1969). In addition to the pulmonary vascular bed, a structure at the base of the pulmonary artery may serve to regulate pulmonary blood flow (see Chap. 18).

In this study, vasoactive drugs were used to manipulate the cardiovascular functions. Acetylcholine was used to increase pulmonary vascular resistance, and epinephrine (adrenaline) to increase the systemic vascular resistance.

The effects of the drugs on the RAo and LAo blood flows and pressures are summarized in Figure 2. Epinephrine increased blood pressure in both aortas, as well as the size of the RAo flow peak. The RAo blood pressure exceeded

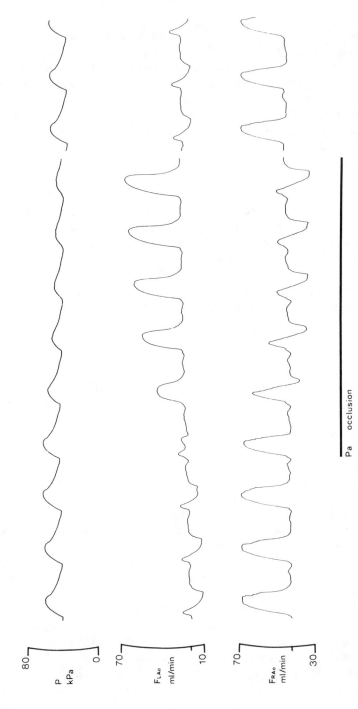

**Figure 3** Left and right aortic blood flow and right aortic blood pressure before and during occlusion of both pulmonary arteries in an anesthetized, openchest caiman. Note complete reversal of the flow patterns.

that in the LAo throughout the cardiac cycle. Acetylcholine eliminated the retrograde flow during mid- to late systole, and LAo blood pressure exceeded that in the RAo during part of the cardiac cycle. This suggests the operation of a right-to-left shunt, as described by Grigg and Johansen (1987). A similar LAo flow pattern was seen upon the injection of isoproterenol (isoprenaline), which reduced the systemic vascular resistance.

One interesting aspect of a partial pulmonary bypass of the type created by the acetylcholine injection is that the right ventricular output exceeds that of the left ventricle (since blood flow from the lungs into the left atrium and ventricle is reduced). Evidence for a partial pulmonary bypass has been presented (Grigg and Johansen, 1987; Axelsson et al., 1989; see foregoing), but there are no results indicating the development of a complete pulmonary bypass in vivo [although Grigg (see Chap. 18) hypothesized that this may occur].

A complete bypass was created in one experiment, in which one of the caimans, anesthetized and with the thorax opened, was subjected to a mechanical occlusion of both pulmonary arteries. As shown in Figure 3, the flow patterns in the two aortas were completely reversed within one or two beats, with a more or less maintained systemic blood pressure. This flow pattern was never seen, even after very high doses of acetylcholine, and may never occur in vivo. It does show, however, that the flow profile in that aorta that is not perfused by "its own" ventricle, is dependent upon the events in the other aorta (possible effects of transmural squeeze or flow through the foramen of Panizza), regardless of which of them is currently unperfused.

In conclusion, the findings discussed suggest that LAo blood normally derives from the RAo, and that LAo flow can be manipulated by injection of pharmacologically active substances: for instance a partial pulmonary bypass can be created by a constriction of the pulmonary vasculature caused by acetylcholine injection. Further work to elucidate the fascinating physiological significance of the anatomical peculiarities of the cardiovascular arrangement in crocodilians must, clearly, also include direct measurements of blood flow patterns in the major vessels.

### References

Axenborg, J. (1989). BIOLAB—A computerized on-line system for physiological measurements in experimental animals. *Comput. Methods Prog. Biomed.*, **28**:75–85.

Axelsson, M., Holm, S., and Nilsson, S. (1989). Flow dynamics of the crocodilian heart. *Am. J. Physiol.*, **256**:R875–R879.

Grigg, G. C. (1989). The heart and patterns of cardiac outflow in Crocodilia. *Proc. Aust. Physiol. Pharmacol. Soc.*, **20**:43–57.

Grigg, G. C., and Johansen, K. (1987). Cardiovascular dynamics in *Crocodylus porosus* breathing air and during voluntary aerobic dives. *J. Comp. Physiol.*, **157**:381–392.

Greenfield, L. J., and Morrow, A. G. (1961). The cardiovascular hemodynamics of Crocodilia. *J. Surg. Res.* **1**:97–103.

Panizza, B. (1833). Sulla struttura del cuore e sulla circolazione del sangue del *Crocodilus lucius*. *Biblioth. Ital.*, **70**:87–91.

Webb, G. J. W. (1979). Comparative cardiac morphology of the Reptilia. III. The heart of crocodilians and a hypothesis on the completion of the intraventricular septum of crocodilians and birds. *J. Morphol.*, **161**:221–240.

White, F. N. (1956). Circulation in the reptilian heart *(Caiman sclerops)*. *Anat. Rec.*, **125**:417–432.

White, F. N. (1969). Redistribution of cardiac output in the diving alligator. *Copeia* **1969**:567–570.

# 20

## Coronary Circulation in Seals

**ROBERT ELSNER**

Institute of Marine Science
University of Alaska
Fairbanks, Alaska

**ATTILIO MASERI**

Hammersmith Hospital
London, England

**FRANCIS C. WHITE**

University of California, San Diego
School of Medicine
La Jolla, California

**MICHAEL de BURGH DALY**

Royal Free Hospital
School of Medicine
London, England

**RONALD W. MILLARD**

University of Cincinnati
College of Medicine
Cincinnati, Ohio

## I. Introduction

The terrestrial mammalian heart is almost exclusively dependent upon aerobic energy sources. Induction of hypoxemia or anemia results in an increased coronary blood flow (CBF), and oxygen demand may eventually exceed supply. Maintained hypoxia or ischemia leads to a loss of contractile function, and tissue damage rapidly follows. A decreased oxygen supply produces several immediate effects on myocardial metabolism. Utilization of cardiac tissue glycogen is accelerated, and oxidation of fatty acids is inhibited. However, to what extent an essentially aerobic organ, such as the terrestrial mammalian heart, can utilize anaerobic glycolysis to maintain function or to salvage ischemic tissue has not been conclusively shown. It is likely to be quite low (Rovetto et al., 1973).

Marine mammals contrast with terrestrial mammals in several respects relevant to this topic. Dives of seals in their natural habitat are usually brief and undemanding. Nevertheless, the ability to resist the progressive asphyxia of long dives is a remarkable and important feature of the seal's physiological armor. Some, perhaps all, of these aquatic species that are adapted to a diving habit have superior tolerance to asphyxia through the integration of respiratory, cardiovascular, and metabolic responses protecting the brain and heart (reviewed by Elsner and Gooden, 1983; Daly, 1984; Spyer, 1984). Both of these organs, dependent upon oxidative metabolism in terrestrial mammals, can be partly supported in seals by anaerobic processes during severe diving asphyxia (Kerem and Elsner, 1973; Kjekshus et al., 1982).

A slowing of the seal's heart rate is precipitated by diving, cardiac output is reduced, and myocardial oxygen demand declines. Consequently, myocardial perfusion is reduced, as first demonstrated by Blix et al. (1976). Vasoconstriction of the peripheral circulation occurs; hence, oxygen delivery and utilization are lowered in all organs except the brain. The pronounced bradycardia of seals during dives is accompanied by little or no decline of diastolic arterial pressure. Coronary perfusion pressure is maintained in this condition by the combined peripheral vasoconstriction and the Windkessel action of the seal's distensible bulbous structure of the ascending aorta (Rhode et al., 1986). The reduced resistance of ventricular ejection into this structure may also lower afterload and, thereby, the left ventricle energy demand (Campbell et al., 1981).

These responses, highly developed in marine and freshwater species of aquatic animals, are also partially demonstrable in terrestrial animals, including humans, and they resemble the more general vertebrate reactions to asphyxia. Well-regulated neural integration is characteristic of the seal's diving response. Diving activates components of both sympathetic and parasympathetic divisions of the autonomic nervous system. In the heart, parasympathetic effects appear to be dominant; hence, the profound bradycardia. Some diving mammals have elevated oxygen storage capacity by virtue of both elevated blood volume and high hematocrit. In addition to the well-known cardiovascular adaptations to diving, seals also have remarkable tolerance to low blood oxygen concentrations. Arterial $Po_2$ values decline to about 8 or 10 mm Hg during their longest dives (Elsner et al., 1970; Kerem and Elsner, 1973). The seal heart has appreciable energetic reserves of myoglobin and glycogen, which can supplement blood oxygen storage during long dives (Blessing and Hartschen-Niemeyer, 1969; Kerem et al., 1973). It can operate periodically on anaerobic metabolism, producing lactate (Kjekshus et al., 1982) and has an advantage over the hearts of terrestrial mammals here.

We postulate that the conversion to partial dependence upon anaerobic metabolic resources, signaled by net myocardial lactate production, occurs as a consequence of an intermittent cessation of perfusion, and that the reduced CBF is implicated in the initiation of that anaerobiosis. The oscillating perfusion during the dive suggests a switching between oxidative and anaerobic processes that results in an effective means by which the available oxygen reserves of circulating blood and myocardial myoglobin may be extended (Elsner et al., 1985). Competing neural and metabolic influences are also suggested. In fact, the effectiveness of neurally mediated vasoconstriction is evidenced by the net lactate release. The intermittent restoration of flow would then flush out accumulated acid metabolic products and resupply oxygen.

## II. Cardiac Metabolism and Mechanics

There are important differences in myocardial metabolism between conditions of hypoxemia and ischemia (Liedtke and Nellis, 1980). Hypoxemia with maintained or elevated CBF in terrestrial mammals results in a modest episode of anaerobic glycolysis. If myocardial perfusion is adequate, lactate and hydrogen ions are removed. However, in the ischemic condition, they accumulate, and glycolysis is inhibited by the increasing acidity. The seal heart shows an extraordinary ability to recover from severe and long hypoxia, when compared with the similarly treated pig or dog heart (White et al., 1990). Our evidence indicates that this hypoxemic tolerance results from an exquisite balance between reduced cardiac energy requirements and metabolic reserves (oxygen supply and unusually copious anaerobic resources) and by a related intermittent metering of sufficient coronary perfusion to provide oxygen and the washout of potentially damaging metabolic products.

Our earlier research efforts concentrated upon understanding the cardiac adaptations of seals to asphyxia, such as might be encountered during prolonged diving. We based those studies on the supposition that seal cardiac muscle might be unusually resistant to hypoxia, and also to ischemia, because of its resistance to hypoxemia in long dives. That premise was tested in experiments providing for measurements of CBF and left ventricular muscle segment dimensions before, during, and after restrained laboratory dives in conscious animals recovered from surgical instrumentation. These were harbor and spotted seals, closely related species, the maximum diving time of which is about 20 min. The experimental dives were of variable durations from a few seconds to 15 min.

The cardiovascular responses may be summarized as the following: bradycardia amounting sometimes to as low as one-tenth of the nondiving heart rate and an average decline in myocardial blood flow of roughly similar magnitude; but showing highly variable oscillations and frequent periods of flow cessation; maintained or slightly decreased stroke volume; lowering of contractility (left ventricular $dP/dt_{max}$) as much as 43%; unchanged ventricular endo/epicardial perfusion ratio; no evidence of ischemia, such as dilation of the left ventricle or electrocardiographic alterations; and progressive myocardial lactate and hydrogen ion production, despite continued oxygen consumption at the reduced rate (Kjekshus et al., 1982; Elsner et al., 1985). Left ventricular segment dimensions, measured with implanted crystal sonomicrometers, were sometimes unchanged;

but more often, were decreased throughout systole and diastole during experimental dives, indicating that the ventricular volume was reduced, and the ventricular wall tension was lowered. As expected, the cardiac oxygen consumption declined during dives along with the lower heart rate. More surprising was the observation that the heart of the experimentally dived seal produced lactate, starting a few minutes after the beginning of a 10- to 15-min experimental dive, despite a substantial remaining oxygen content in arterial blood and a continued oxygen uptake.

The apparently paradoxical situation of simultaneous aerobic and anaerobic cardiac metabolism was clarified by an examination of myocardial blood flow in the conscious seal with the instantaneous, dynamic technique of implanted coronary flow transducers. These studies revealed that intermittent fluctuations in CBF occurred (Elsner et al., 1985). We suggest that the vagally induced decline in heart rate and the decreased inotropic state lead to a reduced CBF, mediated by lowered metabolic demand combined with reflex coronary vasoconstriction. Incidentally, dogs that were trained to voluntarily immerse their snouts in water responded with bradycardia, decreased CBF and myocardial oxygen consumption, and reduced contractility (Gooden et al., 1974). Coronary collateral morphology is not as well developed in seals as it is in dogs.

## III.  Regulation of Coronary Blood Flow

The major determinants of CBF are afterload (aortic pressure), myocardial compression, myocardial metabolism, and neural regulation (Feigl, 1983). Our results indicate that experimental dives in seals result in little or no change in afterload or myocardial extravascular compression and an overall decrease in myocardial metabolism. The prompt onset and the rapidly changing character of the CBF oscillations suggest the functioning of sequential, neurally mediated coronary vasoconstriction and subsequent vascular relaxation, associated with metabolite accumulation.

Cholinergic innervation is vasodilator in its effect on the coronary arteries of dogs (Feigl, 1983), but there are examples of vasoconstrictor activity in other species (see later). It is now well known that the vascular endothelium has an important role in the production of vasoactive substances (Furchgott, 1983; Vanhoutte et al. 1986; Bassenge and Busse, 1988). Both relaxing and constricting factors appear to be produced.

## IV.  The Seal

Several lines of evidence provide insight into the mechanisms governing CBF in seals during underwater submergence. We have used anesthetized seals in laboratory studies in an effort to clarify some of the related reactions. Although many kinds of anesthesia depress or eliminate the diving responses, they can be simulated in the urethane-anesthetized, openchest seal by appropriate stimulation of carotid chemoreceptor or of airway afferent inputs to the central nervous system (Daly et al., 1977). This approach requires activation of carotid body chemoreceptor signals by intracarotid injection of small quantities of cyanide (0.1–0.2 mg). Alternatively, an effective response can be produced by direct electrical stimulation of the superior laryngeal nerve (3–6 V, 1 ms, 15–20 Hz).

Applying these techniques during induced apnea to three young male open-chest spotted seals (*Phoca largha*), body weights 32–38 kg, a marked brady-cardia and reduction of CBF (electromagnetic flowmeter) were produced (Fig. 1). The reduced CBF persisted, despite maintenance of a high heart rate by electrical cardiac pacing at 130 beats/min (Fig. 2), evidence that the reduction in CBF was not determined exclusively by the slower heart rate. Resting CBF was reduced by intracoronary injection of the $\alpha_1$-adrenergic agonist, phenyle-pherine (Fig. 3) and that response was eliminated by the $\alpha$-receptor blocker, phentolamine. In contrast, the intense vasoconstriction in the coronary circulation produced by the previously described methods was not affected by intracoronary injection of phentolamine, indicating that the strong response originating from the experimental procedures was not mediated by an $\alpha$-adrenergic mechanism. Apparently two distinct mechanisms can result in reduced CBF. One of these, $\alpha_1$-adrenergic activation, may not function or is overridden during the simulated dive conditions. The mechanism for this limitation may be the suppression of norepinephrine release by cholinergic activation (Cohen et al., 1984). There appears to be a distinct species difference between seals and dogs in this respect, inasmuch as carotid body chemoreceptor stimulation produced reflex canine coronary vasodilation (Ito and Feigl, 1985).

In the absence of pharmacological intervention, determination of the value of arterial diastolic pressure at the level at which left anterior descending ar-tery flow ceased shows a "critical closure" of resistance vessels at about 50 mm Hg, an unusually high value of zero-flow pressure (Sherman et al., 1980) probably generated by intense activation of coronary vascular smooth-muscle tension.

Another approach to this problem is currently being applied in an attempt to elucidate the underlying mechanisms governing the coronary vasoconstrictor activity. Isolated coronary artery ring segments have been studied in a controlled-temperature Krebs solution bath, pH 7.4, arranged for the determination of isometric tension of the coronary vascular smooth muscle in response to various neurotransmitters and pharmacological agents. Segments excised from branches of the left anterior descending coronary artery responded to micromolar con-centrations of acetylcholine with a muscarinic (blocked by atropine), endothe-lium-dependent, constriction of prostanoid origin (blocked by indomethacin). Similar increased tension by acetylcholine has been demonstrated in isolated

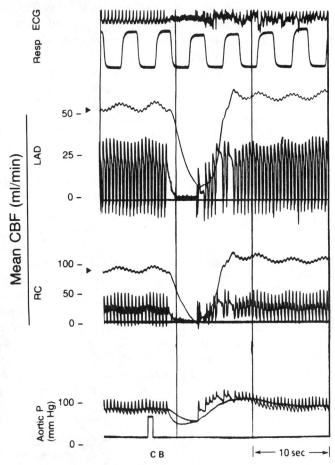

**Figure 1** (above and facing page) Reduction of mean and instantaneous coronary blood flow (CBF) in response to carotid body stimulation by intracarotid cyanide (CB) and by electrical stimulation of the superior laryngeal nerve (SLN). Records from above downward, ECG, electrocardiogram; Resp, respiratory excursions (inspiration upwards); LAD, left anterior descending artery mean and instantaneous flow; RC, right coronary artery mean and instantaneous flow; P, mean and instantaneous blood pressure. Mean CBF indicated by pointer at left of tracing. For clarity, calibrations of the instantaneous blood flow traces have been omitted.

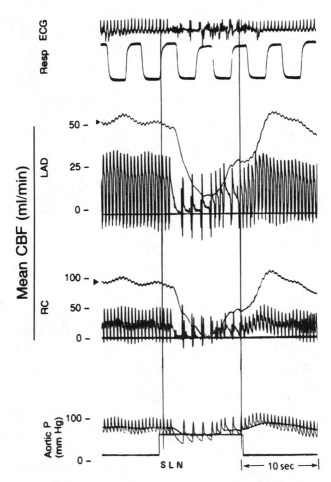

**Figure 1** Continued

coronary arterial segments of other species (rabbit: de la Lande et al., 1974; cattle: Kalsner, 1979; Garland and Keatinge, 1982; pig and human: Kalsner, 1985). Related effects have been described in perfused left ventricular slabs (cattle: Kalsner, 1979; and pig: R. Elsner, I. S. de la Lande, and E. Elsner, unpublished observations). However, responses of the large conduit portions of the left circumflex coronary artery to similar concentrations of acetylcholine produced relaxation of the preparation. This latter result is consistent with our angiographic observations (Fig. 4) that simulated dives in three conscious harbor seals did not result in visible constriction of the circumflex artery. This result

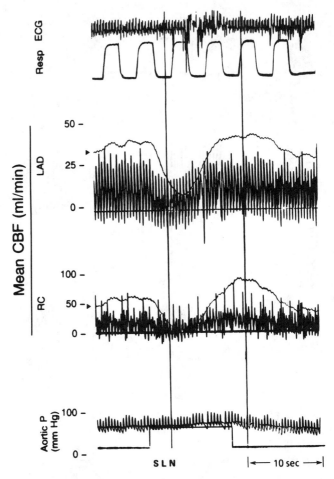

**Figure 2**   Decrease of coronary blood flow produced by superior laryngeal nerve stimulation during cardiac pacing at 130 beats/min (abbreviations as in Fig. 1).

contrasts with the marked constriction of renal and other arteries observed during dives (Elsner and Gooden, 1983). As seen in Figure 4, the flow of contrast medium through both left and right main coronary arteries was arrested during the dive, indicating an increased coronary vascular resistance downstream from the circumflex artery, presumably originating from small artery or from arteriolar constriction.

Our results give little support for an α-adrenergic mechanism for increasing tension in the coronary vascular smooth muscle. Relaxation of the coronary ring segments was the dominant response to norepinephrine, and it

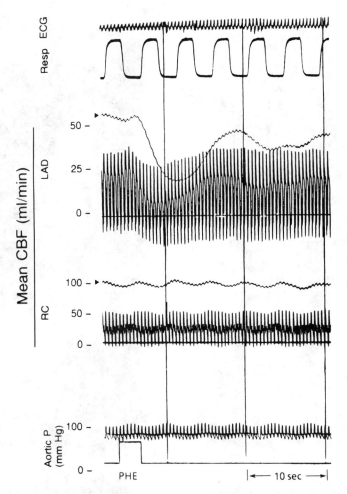

**Figure 3**  Phenylepherine (PHE, 10 μg) injected into the left anterior descending coronary artery and resulting in decreased LAD flow (abbreviations as in Fig. 1).

was reversed only upon administration of the β-blocker, propranolol. Some prostaglandins have been shown to elicit potent vasoconstriction in the arterial circulation, including that of the coronary bed (Kalsner, 1977; Needleman et al., 1977). Their local synthesis can be blocked by the cyclooxygenase inhibitor, indomethacin. Decreases in oxygen tension result in increased prostaglandin production and contraction of isolated coronary segments of beef cattle (Kalsner, 1977). The question of repeated restoration of CBF following the

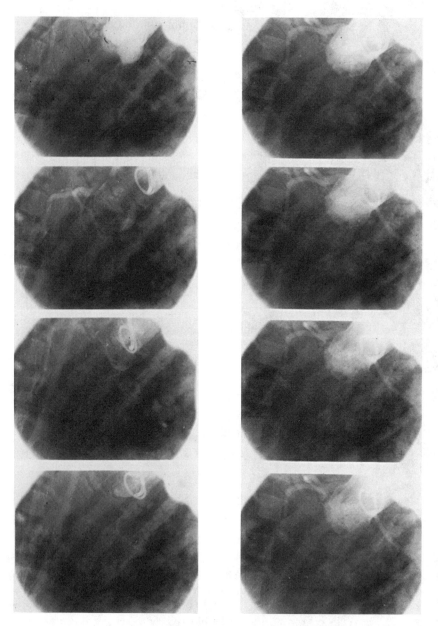

**Figure 4**  Angiography of aorta and main coronary arteries of conscious spotted seal during (left) quiet rest and (right) an experimental dive. Frames taken from cineradiographic film: 0.2 sec apart during rest, 1.5 sec apart during dive. It can be seen that the coronary flow of the contrast medium was arrested during the dive.

episodes of vasoconstriction may be related to the local effect of lowered oxygen tension within the vascular smooth muscle (Gooden and Elsner, 1985; Rubanyi and Paul, 1985).

Although other vasoconstrictor influences have not been eliminated, the blockade of acetylcholine-induced constriction of isolated coronary artery rings by indomethacin lend support to a prostaglandin action. Prostaglandin activation, operating through the mechanism of parasympathetic innervation of the seal's coronary vasculature, therefore, is an attractive hypothetical explanation of the results presented here. This postulated mechanism is, however, unsupported by positive morphological identification of cholinergic innervation of these vessels. Responses to acetylcholine in segments of the circumflex coronary artery stand in marked contrast with those of the smaller branches of the left anterior descending artery. Large conduit portions of the circumflex artery were used in these tests, and the relaxations produced were not altered by indomethacin. They were, however, abolished by removal of the endothelium (R. Elsner and I. S. de la Lande, unpublished results).

Despite the incomplete nature of our present knowledge, some speculation concerning regulation might be useful. Preliminary evidence suggests a sequence of events for describing the mechanisms leading to the intermittent nature of CBF in the experimentally dived seal. Combining the results of the various investigations described here, we may postulate that 1) in the diving response, involving both sympathetic and parasympathetic stimulation, parasympathetic dominates; 2) acetylcholine released in or near resistance vessels results in 3) prostanoid stimulation of vascular smooth muscle, leading to 4) critical closure of resistance vessels; 5) cholinergic-induced relaxation of large conduit coronary arteries; and 6) subsequent relaxation of resistance vessels owing to accumulation of vasoactive metabolic products. This formulation, although presently speculative, is consistent with what we now know. Variations in receptor type and density may exist along the arteries, providing likely candidates for differential regulation of vascular smooth-muscle activity.

## Acknowledgments

The research reported here has been supported in part by National Institutes of Health Grants HL-16020 and HL-23950; the American Heart Association, Alaska Affiliate; the National Science Foundation; the British Heart Foundation, and the University of Alaska. We wish to thank D. R. Bacon for expert technical assistance. Kjell Johansen showed much interest in diving physiology throughout his career, and he was an enthusiastic contributor to our discussions of the regulations involved.

## References

Bassenge, E., and Busse, R. (1988). Endothelial modulation of coronary tone. *Prog. Cardiovasc. Dis.*, **30**:349–380.

Blessing, M. H., and Hartschen-Niemeyer, E. (1969). Uber den Myoglobingehalt der Herz und Skelettmuskulatur insbesondere einiger mariner Säuger. *Z. Biol.*, **116**:302–313.

Blix, A. S., Kjekshus, J. K., Enge, I., and Bergan, A. (1976). Myocardial blood flow in the diving seal. *Acta Physiol. Scand.*, **96**:277–280.

Campbell, K. B., Rhode, E. A., Cox, R. H., Hunter, W. C., and Noordergraaf, A. (1981). Functional consequences of expanded aortic bulb: A model study. *Am. J. Physiol.*, **240**:R200–R210.

Cohen, R. A., Shepherd, J. T., and Vanhoutte, P. M. (1984). Neurogenic cholinergic prejunctional inhibition of sympathetic beta-adrenergic relaxation in the canine coronary artery. *J. Pharmacol. Exp. Ther.*, **229**:417–421.

Daly, M. de B. (1984). Breath-hold diving: Mechanisms of cardiovascular adjustments in the mammal. In *Recent Advances in Physiology*. Edited by P. F. Baker. London, Churchill–Livingstone, pp. 201–245.

Daly, M. de B., Elsner, R., and Angell-James, J. E. (1977). Cardiorespiratory control by the carotid body chemoreceptors during experimental dives in the seal. *Am. J. Physiol.*, **232**:H508–H516.

de la Lande, I. S., Harvey, J. A., and Holt, S. (1974). Response of the rabbit coronary arteries to autonomic agents. *Blood Vessels*, **11**:319–337.

Elsner, R., Shurley, J. T., Hammond, D. D., and Brooks, R. E. (1970). Cerebral tolerance to hypoxemia in asphyxiated Weddell seals. *Respir. Physiol.*, **9**:287–297.

Elsner, R., and Gooden, B. A. (1983). *Diving and Asphyxia, a Comparative Study of Animals and Man*. Monograph No. 40 of the Physiological Society. Cambridge, Cambridge University Press, pp. 168.

Elsner, R., Millard, R. W., Kjekshus, J. K., White, F. C., and Blix, A. S. (1985). Coronary blood flow and myocardial segment dimensions in diving seal. *Am. J. Physiol.*, **249**:H1119–H1126.

Feigl, E. O. (1983). Coronary physiology. *Physiol. Rev.*, **63**:1–205.

Furchgott, R. F. (1983). Role of endothelium in response of vascular smooth muscle. *Circ. Res.*, **53**:557–573.

Garland, C. J., and Keatinge, W. R. (1982). Constrictor actions of acetylcholine, 5-hydroxytryptamine and histamine in bovine coronary artery inner and outer muscle. *J. Physiol.*, **327**:363–376.

Gooden, B. A., and Elsner, R. (1985). What diving animals might tell us about blood flow regulation. *Perspect. Biol. Med.*, **28**:465–474.

Gooden, B. A., Stone, H. L., and Young, S. (1974). Cardiac responses to snout immersion in trained dogs. *J. Physiol.*, **242**:405–414.

Ito, B., and Feigl, E. O. (1985). Carotid chemoreceptor reflex parasympathetic coronary vasodilation in the dog. *Am. J. Physiol.*, **249**:H1167–H1175.

Kalsner, S. (1977). The effect of hypoxia on prostaglandin output and on tone in isolated coronary arteries. *Can. J. Physiol. Pharmacol.*, **55**:882–887.

Kalsner, S. (1979). The effects of periarterial nerve activation on coronary vessel tone in an isolated and perfused slab of beef ventricle. *Can. J. Physiol. Pharmacol.,* **57:**291–297.

Kalsner, S. (1985). Cholinergic mechanisms in human coronary artery preparations: Implications of species differences. *J. Physiol.,* **358:**509–526.

Kerem, D., and Elsner, R. (1973). Cerebral tolerance to asphyxial hypoxia in the harbor seal. *Respir. Physiol.,* **19:**188–200.

Kerem, D., Hammond, D. D., and Elsner, R. (1973). Tissue glycogen levels in the Weddell seal. *Comp. Biochem. Physiol.,* **45:**731–737.

Kjekshus, J., Blix, A. S., Elsner, R., Hol, R., and Amundsen, E. (1982). Myocardial blood flow and metabolism in the diving seal. *Am. J. Physiol.,* **242:**R97–R104.

Liedtke, A. J., and Nellis, S. H. (1980). Effects of coronary washout on cardiac function during brief periods of ischemia and hypoxia. *Am. J. Physiol.,* **239:**H371–H379.

Needleman, P., Kulkarin, P. S., and Raz, A. (1977). Coronary tone modulation: Formation and actions of prostaglandins, endoperoxides and thromboxanes. *Science,* **195:**409–412.

Rhode, E. A., Elsner, R., Petersen, T. M., Campbell, K. B., and Spangler, W. (1986). Pressure–volume characteristics of the aortae of harbor and Weddell seals. *Am. J. Physiol.,* **251:**R174–R180.

Rovetto, M. J., Lamberton, W. F., and Neely, J. R. (1973). Comparison of the effects of the anoxia and whole heart ischemia on carbohydrate utilization in isolated working rat hearts. *Circ. Res.,* **32:**699–711.

Rubanyi, G., and Paul, R. J. (1985). Two distinct effects of oxygen on vascular tone in isolated porcine coronary arteries. *Circ. Res.,* **56:**1–10.

Sherman, I. A., Grayson, J., and Bayliss, C. E. (1980). Critical closing and opening phenomena in the coronary vasculature of the dog. *Am. J. Physiol.,* **238:**H533–H538.

Spyer, K. M. (1984). Central control of the cardiovascular system. In *Recent Advances in Physiology.* Edited by P. F. Baker. London, Churchill–Livingstone, pp. 163–200.

Vanhoutte, P. M., Rubanyi, G. M., Miller, V. M., and Houston, D. S. (1986). Modulation of vascular smooth muscle contraction by the endothelium. *Annu. Rev. Physiol.,* **48:**307–320.

White, F. C., Elsner, R., Willford, D., Hill, E., and Merhoff, E. (1990). Responses of harbor seal and pig heart to progressive and acute hypoxia. *Am. J. Physiol.,* **259:**R849–R856.

# 21

## Autonomic Nerve Function and Cardiovascular Control in Lungfish

**STEFAN NILSSON and SUSANNE HOLMGREN**

University of Göteborg
Göteborg, Sweden

## I. Introduction

Cardiovascular events associated with various physiological situations have been relatively well described in a number of vertebrate species, including the lungfish. A comprehensive study of cardiovascular functions in *Protopterus* (Johansen et al., 1968) describes changes in pulmonary blood flow, arterial blood pressures, and heart rate in association with air breathing. However, as with most other cardiovascular events elegantly described in several studies of nonmammalian vertebrates, the control systems that regulate the heart and vasculature have received relatively little attention.

The aim of this chapter is to summarize the knowledge about the structure and function of the autonomic nervous system and the closely related chromaffin system. There is rapidly increasing evidence for the function of neuropeptides as neurotransmitters in the autonomic nervous system of all vertebrate groups. However, to our knowledge, there is as yet no information about the presence of neuropeptides in the autonomic nervous system of lungfish. We have, therefore, performed a study in *Protopterus annectens* and *Lepidosiren paradoxa,* using antisera and fluorescence histochemistry on stretch preparations and sections of the gut, as described for teleosts by, for example, Burkhardt-Holm and

Holmgren (1989). An attempt is also made to construct, from the utterly frag-
mentary information available, a hypothetical "working model" for how the heart
and vasculature are controlled in dipnoans (as exemplified by *Protopterus* and
*Lepidosiren*).

## II.  Organization of the Autonomic Nervous System

Langley (1898) proposed the term *autonomic nervous system* for "the sympathetic
system and the allied nervous system of the cranial and sacral nerves, and for
the local nervous system of the gut," and introduced a subdivision of the autonomic nervous system into three parts: the sympathetic, the parasympathetic,
and the enteric (Langley, 1921). This anatomical subdivision is still used for
mammals, and it is useful also for the nonmammalian vertebrates. However,
since the equivalents of sacral parasympathetic pathways are difficult to distinguish in nonmammalian vertebrates, particularly in fish, a modified terminology
has been suggested (Nilsson, 1983), in which the autonomic pathways leaving
the brain are referred to as *cranial autonomic pathways,* and those leaving the
spinal cord as *spinal autonomic pathways.* The term *enteric nervous system* is
used not only for the "true" autonomic (motor) neurons intrinsic to the gut, but
includes also the enteric sensory neurons that are usually difficult to distinguish
from each other.

It should be stressed that there is a very clear distinction between the
*anatomical* terminology (e.g., sympathetic, or cranial autonomic, or parasympathetic) and the *functional* terminology that relates to the nature of the transmitter substance released from the nerve terminals of a certain neuron [e.g.,
*adrenergic* for neurons releasing epinephrine (adrenaline) or noreprinephrine
(noradrenaline), or *cholinergic* for neurons releasing acetylcholine]. In spite of
this, literature describing mammalian systems often refers to adrenergic neurons
as sympathetic, although it is clear that sympathetic postganglionic neurons may
release one or more of several neurotransmitters.

In recent years, evidence is accumulating for the involvement of several
nonadrenergic, noncholinergic (NANC) neurotransmitters. Most of these are
neuropeptides, and the distribution and functions of these in all vertebrate groups,
and many invertebrates, have been the subject of much interest (recently reviewed
by Holmgren, 1989).

The arrangement of the cranial autonomic pathways is relatively similar
in all vertebrates (with the possible exception of the cyclostomes). Generally,
long preganglionic fibers run to ganglia in or near the target organs, synapsing
with short postganglionic neurons. The spinal autonomic ganglia (paravertebral
ganglia) form distinct sympathetic chains of the mammalian type in teleosts and
in amphibians, reptiles, birds, and mammals, whereas in elasmobranchs, there
are only scattered longitudinal neural connections.

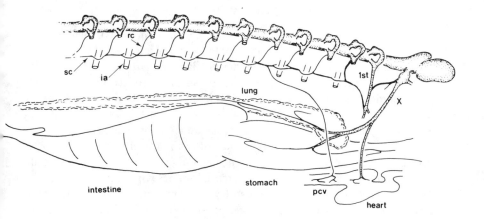

**Figure 1** A summary of the arrangement of the autonomic nervous system in a lungfish. The sympathetic chains (sc) are very delicate, and are connected to the spinal nerves by rami communicantes (rc). The chains run close to the dorsal aorta, and sometimes form loops (annuli) around the intercostal arteries (ia). The cranial autonomic (parasympathetic) outflow is restricted to the vagus nerves (X), which send branches to the heart, the gut, and the lung. Nerve fibers from the vagi and from the anterior part of the sympathetic chains join the first pair of spinal nerves (1st). Direct nerves from the sympathetic chains run to the posterior cardinal veins. Chromaffin tissue is present in the atrium of the heart, in the left posterior cardinal vein (pcv; "azygos vein"), and in the walls of the intercostal arteries. (After Jenkin, 1928.)

The presence of sympathetic chains in lungfish was overlooked by several investigators. In his major investigation of the anatomy of *P. annectens,* Parker (1892) concludes, "No traces of a sympathetic were found." The first description of sympathetic chains in a lungfish was made by Giacomini (1906), and later Jenkin (1928) provided a detailed description of the sympathetic chains in *L. paradoxa.* The following account and Figure 1 is a brief summary of the arrangement of the autonomic nervous system in lungfishes.

### A. Cranial Autonomic (Parasympathetic) Nervous System

In *Protopterus* and *Lepidosiren,* the cranial autonomic (parasympathetic) system is restricted to the vagus (X) nerve, whereas in *Neoceratodus* autonomic fibers may also be present in the oculomotor (III) nerve (Nicol, 1952). Vagal fibers run to the gut, the lung, and the heart; the right vagus innervates the left half of the lung and vice versa. Apart from the "normal" innervation of the heart, vagal fibers may innervate the chromaffin cells in the atrium (Scheuermann, 1979; see later).

## B. Spinal Autonomic (Sympathetic) Nervous System

The sympathetic chains in *Protopterus* and *Lepidosiren* are extremely delicate longitudinal nerve cords, which run close to the dorsal aorta, sometimes forming loops (annuli) around the intercostal arteries. Ganglion cells occur either in small ganglia that, at least in *Lepidosiren,* are too small to produce visible swellings on the cords, or scattered in groups of two to three along the length of the cords. Sometimes the chains will split off a fine "dorsal branch," which runs laterally and dorsally and enters the dorsal musculature along an intercostal artery (not shown in Fig. 1). The chains are connected to the spinal nerves by fine *rami communicantes,* and nerve fibers from the sympathetic chains innervate the chromaffin tissue in the walls of the intercostal arteries (Giacomini, 1906; Jenkin, 1928; Holmes, 1950). There are also nerves, which in *Lepidosiren* leave the sympathetic chain at the level between the fourth and the fifth spinal nerves, and run to the posterior cardinal veins, possibly innervating the chromaffin tissue that is present in the wall of at least the left cardinal vein (azygos vein) (see Fig. 1).

In most vertebrates, many postganglionic spinal autonomic (sympathetic) neurons are adrenergic (cf. Nilsson, 1983), but histochemical studies of *Protopterus* and *Lepidosiren* have failed to provide unequivocal evidence for the presence of adrenergic nerves in these species. This means that if, indeed, the adrenergic nerves are poorly developed or even absent, any adrenergic control of organ functions in dipnoans must rely on either release of catecholamines from endogenous chromaffin tissue (such as may be true in the heart, see later), or variations in the plasma levels of catecholamines released from chromaffin tissue in the walls of blood vessels.

## C. Enteric Nervous System

There are no anatomical descriptions of the dipnoan enteric nervous system, but recent immunohistochemical studies of regulatory peptides in enteric neurons have provided some information about the organization of the gut innervation in lungfishes (see Sect. III).

## D. Chromaffin System

By definition not a part of the autonomic nervous system, but sharing many features with the adrenergic neurons, are the chromaffin cells. These cells are so named because of their reaction with dichromate solution, which stains them brown owing to oxidation of the stored catecholamines (Coupland, 1972). With the introduction 25 years ago of the highly specific and sensitive Falck–Hillarp histochemical technique for monoamines (Falck and Owman, 1965), catechol-amines have been demonstrated in cells in which the "classical" chromaffin

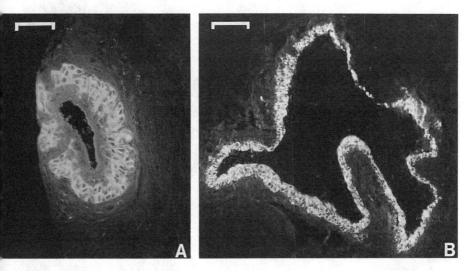

**Figure 2** Falck–Hillarp fluorescence histochemistry showing chromaffin cells (A) in the wall of an intercostal artery and (B) lining the anterior part of the left cardinal vein in *Protopterus aethiopicus*. Calibration bars = 100 μm (A) and 200 μm (B). (From Abrahamsson et al., 1979a.)

reaction may not have been tested. However, the term *chromaffin* is used here to describe catecholamine-storing nonneuronal cells.

In lungfish, at least in *Protopterus* and *Lepidosiren,* chromaffin cells are present in at least three locations: the walls of the intercostal arteries (Giacomini, 1906; Holmes, 1950), the anterior part of the left posterior cardinal vein (azygos vein) (Giacomini, 1906), and in the atrium of the heart (Fig. 2 and 3; Abrahamsson et al., 1979a; Scheuermann 1979; Axelsson et al., 1989). Among the vertebrates, the only other group possessing intracardiac catecholamine-storing cells (which contain appreciable amounts of epinephrine or norepinephrine), is the cyclostomes. This mode of adrenergic control of the heart may be a truly primitive condition (for discussion, see Nilsson, 1983).

Chemical analysis of the catecholamines stored in the chromaffin tissues of *Protopterus* revealed a dominance for epinephrine (compared with norepinephrine) in the intercostal arteries and the posterior cardinal vein, whereas the reverse was true for the heart (Table 1). A storage of dopamine in the atrial cells has been postulated (Scheuermann et al., 1981). Some of the enzymatic equipment necessary for endogenous synthesis of catecholamines has been demonstrated in the intercostal arteries and the atrium of *Protopterus* (Abrahamsson et al., 1979).

Although a word of caution is in order because of the very few observations

**Figure 3**   Falck–Hillarp fluorescence histochemistry showing chromaffin cells lining the atrial lumen of the heart of *Protopterus aethiopicus*. Calibration bar = 100 μm. (From Abrahamsson et al., 1979a.)

made, it appears that the catecholamine stores are substantial, and that humoral (circulating) catecholamines released from these stores may be of importance in the adrenergic control of various functions in lungfishes. "Stress," induced by chasing the animal by hand around its tank for 10–15 min, generated a substantial increase in the plasma concentrations of catecholamines, particularly epinephrine (see Table 1). The concentration reached is high enough to affect smooth muscle of the spleen and lung, and may also influence the function of the ventricle (Abrahamsson et al., 1979b).

## III.   Control of the Gut

The dipnoan gut is, essentially, a straight tube, with a thin-walled stomach and a more substantial intestine, with a spiral valve similar to that found in elasmobranchs. Lymphoid tissue, the spleen, and the pancreas, all are embedded in the gut wall. A *muscularis mucosae* is present, and the smooth muscle of the gut wall is arranged into circular and longitudinal elements (Parker, 1892).

**Table 1** Catecholamine Levels in Some Tissues (μg/g Tissue) and in Blood Plasma (μM) from *Protopterus aethiopicus* (mean values)

| Tissue | Epinephrine | Norepinephrine | Comment |
|---|---|---|---|
| Heart (whole) | 4.2 | 70.8 | Catecholamines are present in the atrium only |
| Proximal part intercostal arteries | 216 | 94 | Single observation |
| Left cardinal vein | 0.55 | 0.03 | Low figure owing to the presence of nonchromaffin tissue |
| Blood plasma (μM) | 0.13 | 0.14 | Control |
| Blood plasma (μM) | 0.35 | 1.72 | "Stressed" |

*Source:* Abrahamsson et al., 1979a.

There are no detailed descriptions of an enteric nervous system in dipnoans, but immunohistochemical studies have demonstrated a few serotonergic [5-hydroxytryptamine (5-HT)-containing] nerves, and several types of peptidergic nerves within the gut (Tables 2 and 3).

*5-Hydroxytryptamine.* A few single nerve fibers showing 5-HT-like immunoreactivity were present in the intestinal wall of *Lepidosiren,* and bundles of fibers form a moderately dense plexus in the muscle layer/myenteric plexus of the rectum (Fig. 4).

*Enkephalin.* Nerves showing enkephalinlike immunoreactivity occur both

**Table 2** The Presence of Neuropeptide- and 5-HT-like Immunoreactivity in the Gut and Lung of *L. paradoxa* (L) and the Stomach and Lung of *P. annectens* (P)

| Tissue | Enk | Gal | G/CCK | 5-HT | NT | NPY | SST | SP | VIP |
|---|---|---|---|---|---|---|---|---|---|
| Stomach | P | L | P | | L,P | | P | P | L,P |
| Intestine | L | L | | L | L | | | | L |
| Rectum | L | | L | L | L | L | L | | L |
| Lung | P | | | | | | | | L,P |

Enk, enkephalin; Gal, galanin; G/CCK, gastrin/cholecystokinin; 5-HT, 5-hydroxytryptamine; NT, neurotensin; NPY, neuropeptide Y; SST, somatostatin; SP, substance P; VIP, vasoactive intestinal polypeptide.

**Table 3**  The Distribution of Neuropeptides and 5-HT in Different Layers of the Gut in *L. paradoxa*[a]

| Tissue | Enk | Gal | G/CCK | 5-HT | NT | NPY | SST | VIP |
|---|---|---|---|---|---|---|---|---|
| Stomach | | | | | | | | |
| Mucosa | − | | − | − | + + | − | − | |
| SM | − | | − | − | | − | − | + + |
| CM | − | + | − | − | + + | − | − | + + |
| MEP | − | + | − | − | − | − | − | + + |
| Intestine | | | | | | | | |
| Mucosa | − | | − | − | | − | | |
| SM | | | | − | | − | | |
| CM | | + + | − | − | + + | − | | + + + |
| MEP | + | + + | − | + | + + | − | | + + + |
| Value | − | + | + | − | + + | − | + + | + + |
| Rectum | | | | | | | | |
| Mucosa | − | − | | − | | − | − | − |
| SM | − | − | | − | | − | − | + + + |
| CM | + + + | − | + + | + + + | + + | + | − | + + + |
| MEP | + + + | + | + + | + + + | + + | + | + + | + + + |

[a]CM, circular muscle; MEP, myenteric plexus; SM, submucosa. Other abbreviations as in Table 2.

in *Lepidosiren* and *Protopterus*. The immunoreaction is only partly quenched by met-enkephalin, which indicates that the immunoreactive material may be more similar to some other opioid peptide than met-enkephalin.

In *Lepidosiren*, only a few single immunoreactive fibers are present in the intestine, whereas a well-developed myenteric plexus of bundles, and smaller bundles running along the circular muscle are found in the rectum (see Fig. 4). In the stomach of *Protopterus*, fiber bundles are frequently observed in both the muscle and submucosa/mucosa.

*Galanin.*   Occasional single fibers showing galaininlike immunoreactivity were observed in *Lepidosiren* in the stomach muscle layer, in the intestinal valve, and in the myenteric plexus of the rectum, and small bundles were present in the muscle layer of the intestinal wall.

*Gastrin and Cholecystokinin (CCK).*   Fibers showing gastrin/CCK like immunoreactivity are restricted to a dense nerve net in the myenteric plexus of the rectum in *Lepidosiren*. This agrees with the distribution in *Squalus,* in which the innervation of the rectum is predominant (Holmgren and Nilsson, 1983). In *Protopterus* a moderate innervation is present in the stomach myenteric plexus.

*Neurotensin.*   A moderately dense innervation by bundles of neurotensin immunoreactive fibers forming a plexus was observed in the stomach and intestine of *Lepidosiren* (see Fig. 4), whereas the innervation was dense in the rectum.

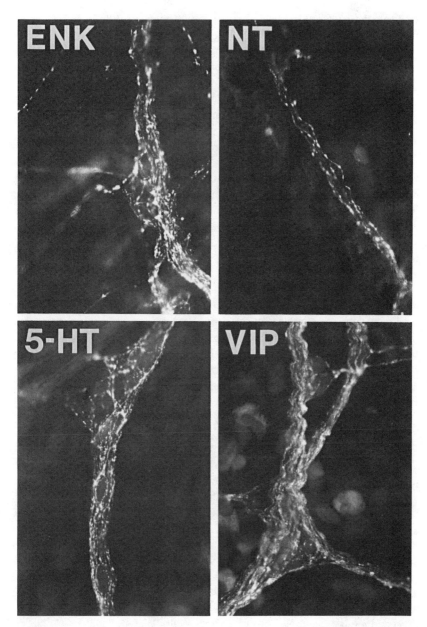

**Figure 4** Peptidergic nerves in the gut of *Lepidosiren paradoxa*: ENK, enkephalinlike immunoreactivity in the rectum; 5-HT, 5-HT-like immunoreactivity in the rectum; NT, neurotensinlike immunoreactivity in the intestinal valve; VIP, vasoactive intestinal polypeptidelike immunoreactivity in the intestine. (Original magnifications × 250).

In *Protopterus,* a moderate amount of nerve fibers were present both in the mucosa/submucosa and the muscle layers of the stomach.

*Neuropeptide Y.* Occasional single fibers showing neuropeptide (NPY)-like immunoreactivity were observed in the rectum of *Lepidosiren* only.

*Somatostatin.* Small bundles of apparently nonvaricose somatostatin immunoreactive fibers are present in moderate numbers in the intestinal valve and the rectum of *Lepidosiren.* In the stomach of *Protopterus,* numerous weakly immunoreactive fibers were observed.

*Vasoactive Intestinal Polypeptide (VIP).* In *Lepidosiren,* VIP immunoreactive fibers are present throughout the gut: in bundles of variable thickness forming a network plexus in the submucosa and myenteric plexus and in small bundles running parallel to the circular muscle fibers. The innervation is moderate in the stomach, more dense in the intestinal wall (see Fig. 4) and rectum. Bundles running in the intestinal valve contain a large proportion of apparently nonvaricose fibers. In the stomach of *Protopterus,* the innervation is very dense, both in muscle and submucosa/mucosa, and ganglion cells are observed in the submucosal plexus.

In conclusion, it appears that the most dense peptidergic innervation of the lungfish gut, is by nerves containing a VIP-like peptide. This is consistent with most other fish species studied (see Bjenning and Holmgren, 1988). Furthermore, neurotensinlike material is present in a well-developed nerve net in both species studied. In *Lepidosiren* it is obvious that the rectum is the most densely innervated part of the gut. In comparing the stomachs from *Lepidosiren* and *Protopterus,* it appears that the innervation of the *Protopterus* stomach is the more varied.

## IV. Control of the Lung

Cholinergic agonists (acetylcholine, carbachol) contract the smooth muscle of the lung of *Protopterus*; this effect can be abolished by the muscarinic cholinoceptor antagonist atropine. Catecholamines (epinephrine, norepinephrine, isoproterenol) show both excitatory and inhibitory effects (Johansen and Reite, 1967; Abrahamsson et al., 1979b). A cholinergic innervation of the *Protopterus* lung by fibers running in the vagus nerve has been demonstrated (Fig. 5). Ganglion cells are present within the vagus (Parker, 1892; Giacomini, 1906; Jenkin, 1928), and pharmacological evidence also supports the presence of ganglionic synapses in the vagal pathways to the lung (see Fig. 5; Abrahamsson et al. 1979b). There is, however, no evidence for an adrenergic innervation of the dipnoan lung (Abrahamsson et al., 1979a; Axelsson et al., 1989).

Recent immunohistochemical investigations of the lungs of *Protopterus* and *Lepidosiren* have demonstrated at least two neuropeptides in nerves within the lung wall (see Table 2). Nerves showing enkephalinlike immunoreactivity

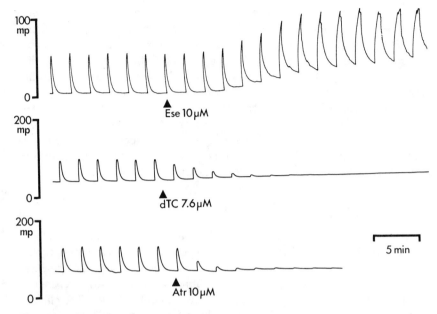

**Figure 5**  Effects of cholinergic drugs on contractions of the lung of *Protopterus ae-thiopicus* produced by electrical stimulation of the vagus nerve with 20-Hz, 1-ms pulse duration and 10 V for 20 sec every 2 min. Addition of eserine (Ese) produced an increase in contraction force and duration (upper trace), while *d*-tubucurarine (dTC) or atropine (Atr) abolished the response to nerve stimulation (middle and lower traces). (From Abrahamsson et al., 1979a.)

were observed in occasional fibers in the lung wall of *Protopterus*. In addition, VIP-like immunoreactivity was present in moderate numbers of nerve fibers in the lung wall of both *Protopterus* and *Lepidosiren*; some of these fibers run along small vessels. The physiological function of the peptidergic nerves is not known.

## V.  Control of the Cardiovascular System

A high degree of separation is maintained between the oxygenated blood from the pulmonary vein, and the deoxygenated venous blood from the systemic veins, despite the single ventricle of the dipnoan heart (e.g., Johansen and Hol, 1968; Johansen and Hanson, 1968; Johansen et al., 1968; Szidon et al., 1969; Johansen and Burggren, 1980; Burggren and Johansen, 1986). The oxygen-rich blood passing the heart is directed into the ventral channel of the bulbus cordis, which, in turn, is divided into the three anterior pairs of gill arteries. The second and third of these form a direct connection into the dorsal aorta, and the corresponding gill arches do not carry functional gill filaments. Venous blood from the systemic circulation passes the heart and is directed into the dorsal channel of the bulbus cordis, which continues as the fourth and fifth pairs of afferent branchial arteries. The corresponding gill arches carry functional gill filaments, allowing branchial respiration.

The arrangement of the circulatory system in lungfish allows a certain degree of circulatory adjustment between air and water breathing. The cardiovascular control systems are not, however, well understood, and the following account on possible physiological control mechanisms has been pieced together from those scattered fragments of information that are available.

### A. Heart

Cardiac control in lungfish resembles that in other vertebrates in that the heart receives an inhibitory, cholinergic vagal innervation. High doses of acetylcholine caused bradycardia in vivo, and the cholinoceptor agonist carbachol produced strong negative inotropic effects on atrial, but not ventricular, strip preparations in vitro (Johansen and Reite, 1968; Abrahamsson et al., 1979b). The cholinoceptor antagonist atropine did not alter the heart rate of *Protopterus* in vivo (Johansen and Reite, 1968), whereas an atropine-induced increase of heart rate and a blockade of the cyclic changes in heart rate associated with air breaths in *Lepidosiren* were demonstrated by Axelsson et al. (1989) (Figs. 6 and 7). Therefore, a tonic cholinergic vagal influence on the heart of *Lepidosiren* was concluded, and the variation in heart rate associated with air breaths appears to be due to a modulation of this inhibitory tonus.

An excitatory innervation of the heart by adrenergic nerves is found in all vertebrate classes, with the exception of cyclostomes, elasmobranchs, dipnoans, and some teleost groups (cf. Nilsson, 1983). In cyclostomes and dipnoans, there is a massive storage of catecholamines in chromaffin cells within the heart, but the exact role of these endogenous catecholamines is not clear. In cyclostomes, depletion of the catecholamine stores with reserpine impairs cardiac function, eventually causing cardiac arrest (e.g., Bloom et al., 1961).

Epinephrine produces positive chronotropic effects in *Protopterus* (Mohsen et al., 1974), but no inotropic effects of epinephrine on isolated strip preparations of *Protopterus* atrium in vitro could be demonstrated (Abrahamsson et al., 1979b).

In *Lepidosiren*, a decrease in heart rate was observed following injections of the β-adrenoceptor antagonist propranolol, and the presence of an adrenergic tonus on the heart was concluded (see Fig. 6). This tonus is probably due to release of catecholamines from endogenous chromaffin cells; whether or not this release is neurally controlled is unknown.

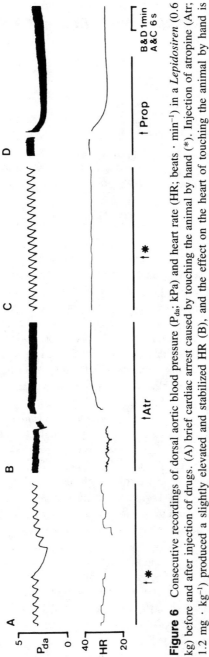

**Figure 6** Consecutive recordings of dorsal aortic blood pressure ($P_{da}$; kPa) and heart rate (HR; beats · min$^{-1}$) in a *Lepidosiren* (0.6 kg) before and after injection of drugs. (A) brief cardiac arrest caused by touching the animal by hand (*). Injection of atropine (Atr; 1.2 mg · kg$^{-1}$) produced a slightly elevated and stabilized HR (B), and the effect on the heart of touching the animal by hand is abolished (C). (D) additional injection of propranolol (Prop; 2.7 mg · kg$^{-1}$) produced decreased HR and $P_{da}$. Time marker in (B) and (D), 1 min; in (A) and (C), 6 sec. (From Axelsson et al., 1989.)

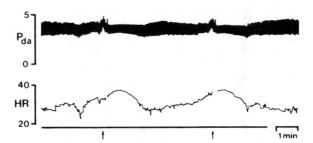

**Figure 7**   Recordings of dorsal aortic blood pressure ($P_{da}$; kPa) and heart rate (HR; beats $\cdot$ min$^{-1}$) during two consecutive breathing cycles in a *Lepidosiren* (0.6 kg). Note increase in HR that starts before each breath (arrows). (From Axelsson et al., 1989.)

## B.  Vasculature

Pulmonary and systemic vascular beds of *Protopterus* are constricted by acetylcholine and epinephrine, whereas the branchial vasculature is constricted by acetylcholine, but dilated by epinephrine (Johansen and Reite, 1968; Reite, 1969). Adrenergic vasomotor nerves appear to be absent in both *Protopterus* and *Lepidosiren* (Abrahamsson et al., 1979a,b; Axelsson et al. 1989) and, therefore, any *adrenergic* vascular control, must be due to circulating catecholamines.

A fourfold (*Protopterus*) or 1.5-fold (*Lepidosiren*) increase in pulmonary blood flow occurs in association with air breaths; this effect is, at least in part, due to a redistribution of the cardiac output into the pulmonary circuit (Johansen et al., 1968; Axelsson et al., 1989; Fig. 8). A hypothetical model for how such redistribution could take place has been offered by Fishman and co-workers (1985). Their model is based on the control of two sphincters: the ductus arteriosus and the pulmonary artery vascular segment (pavs), and on the control of a branchial bypass shunt in the fourth and fifth branchial arteries (Fig. 9). The validity of the model clearly needs further confirmation.

The ductus arteriosus is a short muscular anastomosis connecting the fused second and third branchial arteries with the fused fourth and fifth branchial arteries. It is well innervated by nerve terminals filled with small, clear vesicles, interpreted as cholinergic. However, the effect of acetylcholine (a dilatation of the ductus) was weak, whereas norepinephrine caused a clear constriction.

A segment of the pulmonary artery (pavs) was also identified as a possible site of vasomotor control: constriction of this segment would, just as in amphibians and reptiles, impair blood flow to the lung. The pavs receives a scarce innervation by "cholinergic-type" nerve terminals, and some constrictor effect of acetylcholine was demonstrated.

The gill shunts (Laurent et al., 1978) have been postulated as vessels that

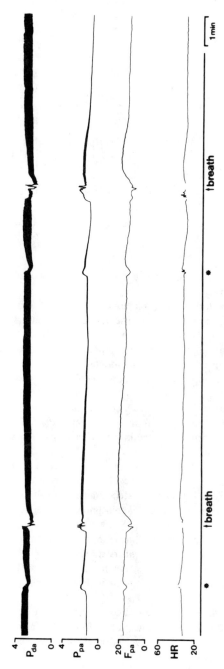

**Figure 8** Recordings of dorsal aortic blood pressure ($P_{da}$; kPa), pulmonary arterial blood pressure ($P_{pa}$; kPa), pulmonary arterial blood flow ($F_{pa}$; ml · min$^{-1}$) and heart rate (HR; beats · min$^{-1}$) during two consecutive breathing cycles in a *Lepidosiren* (1.7 kg). In many cases, there appears to be a release of air from the lung (*) 2–3 min before the animal surfaces to breathe. Note especially the increase in pulmonary blood flow ($F_{pa}$) associated with each breath. (From Axelsson et al., 1989.)

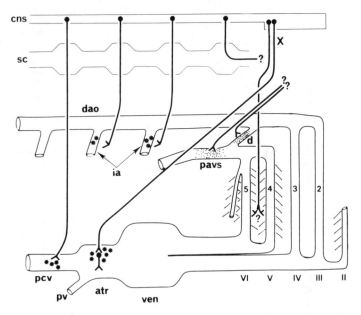

**Figure 9** Highly hypothetical diagrammatic summary ("working model") of possible cardiovascular control functions in a lungfish.

The *heart* receives inhibitory vagal cholinergic fibers, which produce negative chronotropic and inotropic effects on the heart. The variations in heart rate associated with air breaths appear to be controlled by such fibers. Chromaffin cells (*) in the wall of the atrium (atr), storing mainly norepinephrine, are probably the source of the observed adrenergic β-adrenoceptor-mediated cardioexcitatory tonus.

The *systemic vasculature* appears to lack an adrenergic innervation of the type found in most other vertebrates. Instead, there may be an adrenergic control by humoral catecholamines (mainly epinephrine) released from chromaffin tissue in the walls of the intercostal arteries (ia) near their branching off from the dorsal aorta (dao). Catecholamines may also be released from the chromaffin tissue in the left posterior cardinal vein (pcv; "azygos vein"), but the role of this release is not clear.

The *branchial vasculature,* notably the gill shunts in branchial arches V and VI may be operated by vagal fibers of unknown nature. However, it is unknown whether or not these shunts are at all innervated. Humoral catecholamines may also affect the branchial vasculature, but whether the plasma levels of epinephrine or norepinephrine in vivo are high enough to affect these vessels remains to be elucidated.

The *ductus arteriosus* (d) is innervated by nerve fibers, some of which come from the vagus (X). The nature and function of these fibers are unknown.

A *segment of the pulmonary artery* (pavs) is innervated by nerve terminals with small clear vesicles, characteristic of cholinergic neurons, but the origin and role of this innervation is not clear.

The *chromaffin tissue* in the walls of the intercostal arteries is innervated by fibers from the sympathetic chains (sc). There is a direct nerve from the sympathetic chain to the posterior cardinal vein, which could possibly control release of catecholamines from chromaffin tissue in the wall of this vein.

could let blood pass the respiratory parts of the branchial arches V and VI. Whether these vessels are innervated, or indeed under any control, is not known.

In the model by Fishman et al. (1985), water breathing (e.g., during prolonged submersion) is associated with closure of the gill shunts and the pavs, and opening of the ductus. This would force blood to the respiratory parts of branchial arches V and VI, and away from the lung into the dorsal aorta. There is a substantial right-to-left shunt in the heart. During air breathing, on the other hand, blood would bypass the respiratory parts of the branchial arches V and VI and enter the lung through an open pavs. The ductus would be closed, and intracardiac shunting small.

Very clearly, much further work on the physiological control of the dipnoan vasculature is needed to clarify the changes associated with various physiological events, for instance, redistribution of blood flow in association with air breathing. In addition to the classic cholinergic and adrenergic systems, such studies should include the role of neuropeptides in cardiovascular control.

## References

Abrahamsson, T., Holmgren, S., Nilsson, S., and Pettersson, K. (1979a). On the chromaffin system of the African lungfish, *Protopterus aethiopicus. Acta Physiol. Scand.,* **107**:135–139.

Abrahamsson, T., Holmgren, S., Nilsson, S., and Pettersson, K. (1979b). Adrenergic and cholinergic effects on the heart, the lung and the spleen of the African lungfish, *Protopterus aethiopicus. Acta Physiol. Scand.,* **107**:141–147.

Abrahamsson, T., Jönsson, A.-C., and Nilsson, S. (1979). Catecholamine synthesis in the chromaffin tissue of the African lungfish, *Protopterus aethiopicus. Acta Physiol. Scand.,* **107**:149–151.

Axelsson, M., Abe, A. S., Bicudo, J. E. P. W., and Nilsson, S. (1989). On the cardiac control in the South American lungfish, *Lepidosiren paradoxa. Comp. Biochem. Physiol.,* **93A**:561–565.

Bjenning, C., and Holmgren, S. (1988). Neuropeptides in the fish gut. A study of evolutionary trends. *Histochemistry,* **88**:155–163.

Bloom, G., Östlund, E., von Euler, U. S., Lishajko, F., Ritzen, M., and Adams-Ray, J. (1961). Studies on catecholamine-containing granules of specific cells in cyclostome hearts. *Acta Physiol. Scand. Suppl* **53**:1–34.

Ganglion cells within the sympathetic chains are few and scattered, and it is not known to what extent the pathways shown in this summary involve ganglionic synapses within the sympathetic chain ganglia, nor to what extent fibers from the sympathetic chains are involved in cardiovascular innervation.

*Other abbreviations*: cns, central nervous system; pv, pulmonary vein; II–VI, branchial arches; 2–5, efferent branchial arteries.

Burggren, W. W., and Johansen, K. (1986). Circulation and respiration in lungfishes (Dipnoi). *J. Morphol. Suppl.* **1**:217–236.

Burkhardt-Holm, P., and Holmgren, S. (1989). A comparative study of neuropeptides in the intestine of two stomachless teleosts (*Poecilia reticulata, Leuciscus idus melanotus*) under conditions of feeding and starvation. *Cell Tissue Res.,* **255**:245–254.

Coupland, R. E. (1972). The chromaffin system. In *Handbook of Experimental Pharmacology,* Vol. 33. Catecholamines. Edited by H. Blaschko and E. Muscholl. Berlin, Springer-Verlag.

Falck, B., and Owman, C. H. (1965). A detailed methodological description of the fluorescence method for the cellular demonstration of biogenic monoamines. *Acta Univ. Lund. Sect. 2,* **7**:1–23.

Fishman, A. P., DeLaney, R. G., and Laurent, P. (1985). Circulatory adaptation to bimodal respiration in the dipnoan lungfish. *J. Appl. Physiol,* **59**:285–294.

Giacomini, E. (1906). Sulle capsule surrenali e sul simpatico dei Dipoi ricerche in *Protopterus annectens. R. Acad. Lincei,* **15**:394–398.

Holmes, W. (1950). The adrenal homologues in the lungfish *Protopterus. Proc. R. Soc. Lond. Ser. B,* **137**:549–565.

Holmgren S. (1989). *The Comparative Physiology of Regulatory Peptides.* London, Chapman and Hall.

Holmgren, S., and Nilsson, S. (1983). Bombesin-, gastrin/CCK-, 5-hydroxytryptamine-, neurotensin-, somatostatin-, and VIP-like immunoreactivity and catecholamine fluorescence in the gut of the elasmobranch *Squalus acanthias. Cell Tissue Res.,* **234**:595–618.

Jenkin, P. M (1928). Note on the nervous system of *Lepidosiren paradoxa. Proc. R. Soc. Edinb.* **48**:55–69.

Johansen, K., and Burggren, W. W. (1980). Cardiovascular function in the lower vertebrates. In *Hearts and heart-like Organs,* Vol. 1, Edited by G. H. Bourne. London, Academic Press.

Iohansen, K., and Hanson, D. (1968). Functional anatomy of the hearts of lungfishes and amphibians. *Am. Zool.* **8**:191–210.

Johansen, K., and Hol, R., (1968). A radiological study of the central circulation in the lungfish, *Protopterus aethiopicus. J. Morphol.* **126**:333–348.

Johansen, K., and Reite, O. B. (1967). Effects of acetylcholine and biogenic amines on pulmonary smooth muscle in the African lungfish, *Protopterus aethiopicus. Acta Physiol. Scand.* **71**:248–252.

Johansen, K., and Reite, O. B. (1968). Influence of acetylcholine and biogenic amines on branchial, pulmonary and systemic vascular resistance in the African lungfish, *Protopterus aethiopicus. Acta Physiol. Scand.,* **74**:465–471.

Johansen, K., Lenfant, C., and Hanson, D. (1968). Cardiovascular dynamics in the lungfishes. *Z. Vergl. Physiol.,* **59**:157–186.

Langley, J. N. (1898). On the union of cranial autonomic (visceral) fibres with the nerve cells of the superior cervical ganglion. *J. Physiol. (Lond.,)* **23**:240–270.

Langley, J. N (1921). *The Autonomic Nervous System,* Part I. Cambridge, Heffer.

Laurent, P., DeLaney, R. G., and Fishman, A. P. (1978). The vasculature of the gills in the aquatic and aestivating lungfish (*Protopterus aethiopicus*). *J. Morphol.*, **156**:173–208.

Mohsen, T., Lattouf, H., and Jadoun, G. (1974). Variations des effects de l'adrénaline sur le coeur isolé de *Protopterus annectens* (Poisson Dipneuste) selon la dose et selon la phase du cycle biologique de l'animal. *C. R. Soc. Biol.*, **168**:915–919.

Nicol, J. A. C. (1952). Autonomic nervous systems in lower chordates. *Biol. Rev. Camb. Philos. Soc.* **27**:1–49.

Nilsson, S. (1983). *Autonomic Nerve Function in the Vertebrates*. Berlin, Springer-Verlag, pp. 1–253.

Parker, W. N. (1892). On the anatomy and physiology of *Protopterus annectens*. *Trans. R. Ir. Acad.*, **30**:109–230.

Reite, O. B. (1969). The evolution of vascular smooth muscle responses to histamine and 5-hydroxytryptamine. I. Occurrence of stimulatory actions in fish. *Acta Physiol. Scand*, **75**:221–239.

Scheuermann, D. W. (1979). Untersuchungen hinsichtlich der Innervation des Sinus venosus und des Aurikels von *Protopterus annectens*. *Acta Morphol. Neerl. Scand.* **17**:231–232.

Scheuermann, D. W., Stilman, C., Reinhold. C. H. and DeGroodt-Lasseel, M. H. A. (1981). Microspectrofluorometric study of monoamines in the auricle of the heart of *Protopterus aethiopicus*. *Cell Tissue Res.*, **217**:443–449.

Szidon, J. P., Lahiri, S., Lev, M., and Fishman, A. P. (1969). Heart and circulation of the African lungfish. *Circ. Res.*, **25**:23–38.

# AUTHOR INDEX

*Numbers in italics give the page on which the complete reference is listed.*

# SUBJECT INDEX

## A

Acclimation, 30
  definition, 31
  genetic basis, 31, 32
Acclimatization, 30
Acetylcholine
  amphibian heart, 248ff
  seal coronary circulation, 367
Acid–base balance in arachnids, 182,
    185ff
Acid–base receptors, 109
Acidosis, 49
Acute adaptation
  definition, 32
  genetic basis, 32
Adaptation, 21
  acute, 29
  definition, 29, 31
  hypoxia, 286
  long-term, 29
  physiological, 236, 251
  temperature, 289
  time and, 29
Air breathing, 71, 105
Airflow, unidirectional, 160
Airway receptors, 110
Allometry, 239
  metabolic rate, 239
Allosteric effectors, 272
Alphastat hypothesis, 111
Altitude, adaptations, 271
Alveolar gas, ideal, 86

Amphibians
  cutaneous gas exchange, 80
  heart ontogeny, 241
  heart function, 247
  skin, 81
Amphiuma, 108
Anatomic diffusing capacity, 159
Anatomy, cardiovascular, 339ff
Anemia, hypothermia, 301
Angiography, seal coronary circulation,
    369
Annelids, blood, 315ff
Aortic body, 122, 136
Apnea, 130
Arachnids, 169ff
  blood gases, 177
  exercise, 181
  fat stores, 180
  gas exchange, 178ff
  metabolic rate, 178ff
Arginine vasopressin
  hypoxia, 306
  thermoregulation and, 305
Arginine vasotocin, thermoregulation
    and, 305
Arousal state, 132
Arteries, hypertrophy, 222
Asphyxia in diving seals, 364
ATPase, 29
August Krogh principle, 22
Autonomic nervous system in lungfish,
    378ff
Avian lung, evolution of, 161ff